In the Name
of the Father

IN THE NAME
OF THE FATHER

———>•<———

Washington's Legacy, Slavery,
and the Making of a Nation

———>•<———

François Furstenberg

THE PENGUIN PRESS

NEW YORK

2006

THE PENGUIN PRESS
Published by the Penguin Group
Penguin Group (USA) Inc., 375 Hudson Street, New York, New York 10014, U.S.A. • Penguin Group
(Canada), 90 Eglinton Avenue East, Suite 700, Toronto, Ontario, Canada M4P 2Y3 (a division of
Pearson Penguin Canada Inc.) • Penguin Books Ltd, 80 Strand, London WC2R 0RL, England • Penguin
Ireland, 25 St. Stephen's Green, Dublin 2, Ireland (a division of Penguin Books Ltd) • Penguin Books
Australia Ltd, 250 Camberwell Road, Camberwell, Victoria 3124, Australia (a division of Pearson Australia
Group Pty Ltd) • Penguin Books India Pvt Ltd, 11 Community Centre, Panchsheel Park, New Delhi—110
017, India • Penguin Group (NZ), Cnr Airborne and Rosedale Roads, Albany, Auckland 1310,
New Zealand (a division of Pearson New Zealand Ltd) • Penguin Books (South Africa) (Pty) Ltd,
24 Sturdee Avenue, Rosebank, Johannesburg 2196, South Africa

Penguin Books Ltd, Registered Offices:
80 Strand, London WC2R 0RL, England

First published in 2006 by The Penguin Press, a member of Penguin Group (USA) Inc.
Copyright © François Furstenberg, 2006
All rights reserved

Illustration credits appear on page 337-338.

Library of Congress Cataloging-in-Publication Data
Furstenberg, François.
In the name of the father : Washington's legacy, slavery, and the making of a nation
/ François Furstenberg
p. cm.
Includes biobliographical references and index.
ISBN 1-59420-092-0
1. United States—Politics and government—1789-1815.   2. Washington, George, 1732-1799—
Influence.   3. Presidents—United States—Biography—History and criticism.   4. Slavery—Political
aspects—United States—History—18th century.   5. Slavery—Political aspects—United States—History—
19th century.   6. Textbooks—United States—History—18th century.   7. Textbooks—United States—
19th century.   8. Political culture—United States—History—18th century.   9. Political culture—United
States—History—19th century.   I. Title.

E310.F97 2006
973.4'1092–dc22   2006043481

Printed in the United States of America
1   3   5   7   9   10   8   6   4   2

Designed by AMANDA DEWEY

To my parents,
Gilberte and Mark

CONTENTS

—➤•◄—

In the Name of the Father

Prologue:

WHAT THE NATION WAS UP AGAINST

————→▸•◂←————

Here, perhaps, I ought to stop. But a solicitude for your welfare, which cannot end but with my life, and the apprehension of danger, natural to that solicitude, urge me, on an occasion like the present, to offer to your solemn contemplation, and to recommend to your frequent review, some sentiments which are the result of much reflection, of no inconsiderable observation, and which appear to me all-important to the permanency of your felicity as a people.

—Washington's Farewell Address, 1796[1]

The Farewell

Philadelphia—Thursday morning, September 15, 1796. David Claypoole, longtime Philadelphia printer and newspaper publisher, received an unusual visitor. Tobias Lear, President George Washington's personal secretary, had come to deliver a note summoning him to the executive residence. When Claypoole arrived at the president's house that afternoon, he found Washington sitting alone in his drawing room. It was here that Claypoole received startling news: Washington was planning to retire from the presidency. He wanted Claypoole to publish an address making the announcement.

It was only fitting that Washington select Claypoole, who had a long history publishing important patriotic documents. He and his former partner John

Dunlap had in 1776, when soldiers in the Continental army, printed the first broadside edition of the Declaration of Independence (figure 1), including George Washington's personal copy, which he ordered read to his troops, and which now sits in the Library of Congress. The pair had also printed draft copies of the U.S. Constitution for use by members of the Constitutional Convention in the summer of 1787; and had later published the new Constitution for the first time in

1. The "Dunlap Print" of the Declaration of Independence. This broadside was published by the order of the Continental Congress in 1776, and was the version Washington ordered read to his assembled troops in New York on July 9, 1776.

the *Pennsylvania Packet, and Daily Advertiser.* That newspaper had since been re-named *Claypoole's American Daily Advertiser,* and it would be the one to print Washington's Farewell Address.

In Washington's drawing room that afternoon, the two men discussed the mechanics of publishing the document, and agreed that the announcement would come out in Claypoole's Monday edition. No doubt flattered by the commission, and knowing the importance of the document that had been entrusted to him, Claypoole spent the weekend working on the printed version of the ad-

2. *The front page of* Claypoole's American Daily Advertiser, *the newspaper Washington selected to publish his Farewell Address in September 1796. The Address was never given as an oration: first published here, it would be circulated by the expanding network of printers around the country, republished in newspapers, pamphlets, broadsides, and books.*

dress, and sent a proof copy to Washington for corrections. Washington was "very minute" in his perusal, and after some last-minute editorial work a final draft was produced and returned to Claypoole. As Washington slipped out of the capital on Monday morning, Claypoole was putting the last touches on his afternoon edition (figure 2). *Claypoole's American Daily Advertiser* came out that day, looking as it always did, covered with advertisements on the front page (it was, after all, an advertiser). On the inside, however, readers found an unusually long article, without a title, merely carrying a heading: "To the PEOPLE of the UNITED STATES." Claypoole must have been thrilled. There was no bigger story than this, and in the fiercely competitive printing world of the early republic, it was a real coup.[2]

For Washington, the moment had been long in the planning. If his correspondence is to be credited, retirement was never far from his mind from the moment he assumed the presidency. Washington had made no secret of his desire to retire at the end of his first term in 1792. He had spent some time contemplating "the *mode* and *time*" for announcing his retirement, and asked James Madison to help him draft a farewell address to the nation. But he had been persuaded to stay in office. At a time when the great political figures of the age disagreed about most matters, all united in wanting Washington to remain president: Thomas Jefferson, Alexander Hamilton, James Madison, Gouverneur Morris, Edmund Randolph—all had urged him to stay in office. Now it was 1796. His second term had been unexpectedly divisive, and Washington, ever sensitive about his reputation, had been deeply stung by the political feuding that, more and more, slipped into personal attacks on the president. As if these were not reasons enough, Washington did not even think he would live long enough to see another term through. The precedent he would set, as a president who stayed in office until death, would not be auspicious for the new and still fragile republic. This time he would not be dissuaded from retiring.[3]

Despite his many accomplishments—at this point in his career, there was little doubt about his legacy—Washington was not retiring with a sense of complacent satisfaction. In fact, his outlook was anxious: he was fearful about the future of his nation and resentful of the attacks launched by his political opponents. "To the wearied traveller who sees a resting place, and is bending his body to lean thereon, I now compare myself," Washington wrote his friend and former secretary of war Henry Knox shortly before leaving office, and complained again—a constant theme in these last years of his presidency—about those who seek to "misrepresent my motives; to reprobate my politics; and to weaken the confidence which has been reposed in my administration."[4] Worried about his nation's future, Washington was determined to offer parting words of advice to his countrymen. He would address them directly, outline what he thought most threatened his nation, and urge them to act in ways he believed would best ensure the nation's existence.

Washington had a clear model at hand for this retirement: his own. In 1783, when he retired as commander in chief of the army, he had addressed the nation in the form of a letter sent to the thirteen state governors, asking them to "communicate these sentiments to your Legislature at their next meeting." Washington's long Circular to the States did more than declare his retirement; it offered detailed advice to Americans on establishing a nation. Americans, Washington wrote in 1783, were "from this period, to be considered as the Actors on a most conspicuous Theatre, which seems to be peculiarly designated by Providence for the display of human greatness and felicity," and he went on to offer some guiding principles he believed were "essential . . . to the existence of the United States as an Independent Power." "An indissoluble Union of the States under one Federal Head" was perhaps the most important, and would only succeed if Americans could "forget their local prejudices and policies."[5] This 1783 address was well received and widely read: it was reprinted in newspapers throughout the country, and in at least six pamphlet editions in 1783; Noah Webster and Caleb Bingham would both excerpt the address in their popular schoolbooks, ensuring that thousands and, eventually, millions of American children would read it aloud in school and at home. Pleased with its impact, Washington now planned another address upon this, his second retirement from public life.

If the 1783 address can be seen as the first draft of Washington's Farewell Address, he had since prepared a second draft. In 1792, near the end of his first term, Washington had begun composing a statement summarizing his political philosophy. In May of that year, he sent Madison a letter outlining the points he wished to make—largely the same he had made in his 1783 address—and asked for advice on its dissemination. Madison turned Washington's outline into a draft address, which he returned a month later, along with suggestions on its publication. Madison thought "a simple publication in the newspapers" would be the best approach. "A direct address to the people who are your only constituents," wrote Madison, "can be made I think most properly through the independent channel of the press."[6] Two aspects of this response are noteworthy. First, Madison urged Washington to direct the address directly to "the people," and not the states, as he had done in 1783, since they were now the national government's true constituents. Second, Madison believed "the press"—the newspapers, political pamphlets, and other printed works burgeoning during in the post-Revolutionary United States—would be the best way to reach "the people."

When Washington stayed on for a second term, he set this 1792 draft aside for later use. Four long years later, with the Federalists and Republicans now split into two antagonistic parties, Washington again began planning for his retirement, and this time it was to Hamilton that he turned for advice. In May 1796, Washington sent Hamilton a draft, which included extensive quotations from Madison's draft, but which, given the bitter experiences of the last four years, added more heated warnings against partisanship and foreign intrigue. This draft was in many respects a product of the criticism Washington had received in his second term. His remarks were largely defensive in tone, occasionally verging on self-pity. To the modern reader they have a distinctly Nixonian tone. Hamilton removed the most exaggerated pathos, and boiled the draft down to its most essential elements, using Washington's instructions to develop a new version, which he and John Jay "proceeded deliberately to discuss and consider . . . paragraph by paragraph, until the whole met with our mutual approbation."[7]

The text was perfected over the course of subsequent months, as Madison's revised draft passed back and forth between Washington in Philadelphia and Hamilton and Jay in New York. Presided over by Washington, jointly written by Madison and Hamilton, with important contributions from John Jay, the Farewell Address might well be seen as the last—and certainly the most influential—Federalist Paper.

THE SUM OF Washington's military and political experience, dressed up in the prose of Madison, Hamilton, and Jay, and backed with the considerable authority of Washington's personal prestige, the address was a sensation. Never given as an oration, it made its way to the public as Madison had first suggested: through the medium of "the press," disseminated by the elaborate network of printers doing so much to bind the young nation together.[8] Published by Claypool on the afternoon of September 19, three other newspapers, including John Fenno's Federalist *Gazette of the United States,* had already picked up the address and reprinted part of it in their evening editions of same day.[9] Within three days, it had been published by three more Philadelphia newspapers, including Benjamin Franklin Bache's fiercely anti-Washington *Aurora,* six New York papers, and two Baltimore papers. Readers in the District of Columbia, Wilmington, Delaware,

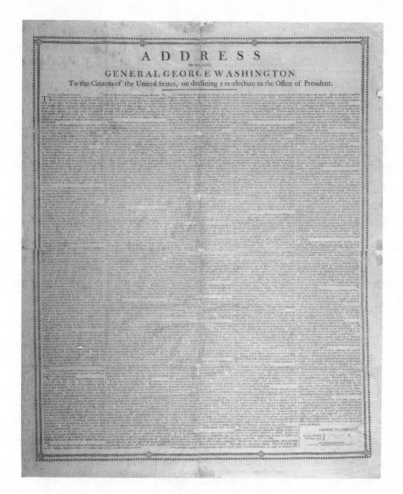

3. Broadside of Washington's Farewell Address published in 1796. Washington's Farewell Address would be published in numerous forms—including such broadsides, which could be posted in public places and read aloud—teaching Americans how to think about their nation.

and Norwich, Connecticut, could all read the full text in local newspapers. By October 1, readers as far north as Portland, Maine, and as far south as Charleston, South Carolina, had the text available to them. Eventually, nearly every newspaper in the nation and some abroad would publish it—readers in Kentucky, Ohio, and Tennessee reading the text shortly before it was published by the *Chronicle* and *Times* in England. At least forty pamphlet editions of the address would soon be run off the presses, along with broadside copies to be posted in public spaces, or preserved by patriotic readers. Official, governmental agents were also involved: the Commonwealth of Massachusetts, for instance, ordered the Farewell Address printed with that year's *Acts and Laws*. The dissemination of this text, in short, was as close to universal as was possible in this pre-mass-media age.[10]

Washington must have been gratified by the impact of his address. Emotional expressions of thanks began pouring in from across the country. James McHenry, Washington's secretary of war, reported from Philadelphia that the address was received "with the strongest expressions of sensibility. I am well assured," he added, "that many tears were shed on the occasion." "All seem to agree in the solid truths which the address contains," reported Bartholomew Dandridge a day later.[11] Washington had followed Madison's early advice, casting the address as an unmediated personal appeal from Washington directly to his countrymen. Indeed, it would be hard to exaggerate the importance of this aspect of the address, delivered with all the paternal authority of a man many considered their political father, and addressed in the most familiar terms to "you."

The Threats: Geographical, Political, International

Washington's Farewell Address did much more than announce his retirement. That matter was dispensed with in a few brief paragraphs, a mere 831 words of a 6,085-word address. All the rhetorical flourishes together—the retirement announcement, brief transition, and the final farewell—added up to just over one-fourth of the text. This was not some early version of a press release; it was, above all, a nationalist text. Just as with Washington's 1783 Circular to the States, its central message was the importance of Union. National unity, the address stressed from the very beginning, would preserve the nation's independence, peace, safety, and liberty. "The Unity of Government which constitutes you one people," it declared, "is a main Pillar in the Edifice of your real independence, the support of your tranquility at home; your peace abroad; of your safety; of your prosperity; of that very Liberty which you so highly prize." Without unity, liberty would inevitably collapse: "Your union ought to be considered as a main prop of your liberty, and that the love of the one ought to endear to you the preservation of the other." In one of its more elegant phrases, the address urged audiences "to think and speak" of the Union as "the Palladium of your political safety and prosperity." The ties binding the Union were more than political; they were "sacred ties," and the address's central message was clear: should the Union collapse, so would Americans' freedom, peace, safety, and prosperity.

What threatened this sacred Union? The largest part of the address, nearly one-half, elaborated at length on the three overlapping dangers that most threatened the nation's continued existence: (1) geographical division; (2) political faction; and (3) meddling by foreign powers. Because so much of the address focused on the dangers the nation faced at the end of the eighteenth century, no single document gives a better picture of what early American nationalism was up against.

At the top of the address's list of dangers was the specter of geographical division. "In contemplating the causes which may disturb our Union," read the address, "it occurs as matter of serious concern, that any ground should have been furnished for characterizing parties by *Geographical* discriminations—*Northern* and *Southern—Atlantic* and *Western.*" The essential problem here was the same as that addressed in Madison's famous Federalist No. 10: standard political theory of the age held that only small republics could survive, and that large republics inevitably collapsed. The address would have none of this: "Is there a doubt, whether a common government can embrace so large a sphere? Let experience solve it. To listen to mere speculation in such a case were criminal." The text urged its audience to consider the benefits of unity, and stressed that all sections, East and West, North and South, were bound in ties of affection as well as commerce, "directed by an indissoluble community of Interest as *one Nation.*"

Significantly, the danger of geographical separation was not limited to North versus South. The experience of Southern secession in 1861 has overshadowed the fact that during the first decades of the nation's existence, the greatest threats of geographical separation were not Southern. Far more threatening to the nation's existence during the 1790s was the possibility that the Appalachian and trans-Appalachian West might split off from the United States. Beginning with Shays's Rebellion in the late 1780s, and continuing throughout the 1790s—with the Whiskey Rebellion in western Pennsylvania; the establishment of the state of Franklin, in western North Carolina; and the continued dangers that Kentucky and Tennessee might break off from the Union and form separate alliances with Britain, Spain, or France—the greatest dangers to the nation's geographical integrity lay in the West.[12] Not until 1803, with the purchase of the vast Louisiana territory from France, would the problem of Western separatism finally be settled. At that point, the locus of disunion shifted to the Northeast. During the War of 1812, New England went as far as calling a convention in order to form a separate republic, perhaps in alliance with Great Britain. It was only in the 1830s that the South became the main sphere of geographical separation, and even then many in the North—including, most famously, William Lloyd Garrison—continued to advocate disunion. In short, the possibility that the nation might disaggregate geographically was never isolated to one region, and continued throughout the first decades of the nineteenth century: it was one of the most pressing and persistent dangers U.S. nationalism would confront.

The threat of geographical separation was not just a political problem, however. It was also a theoretical problem linked to one of the greatest ambiguities at the heart of U.S. nationalism. If government derived its just powers from the consent of the governed, it followed that the governed could withdraw that consent when they desired. Americans in 1776 had seceded from Britain, after all, and who was to say that Americans in 1796 or 1812 or 1861 no longer had the same right of secession? The Farewell Address confronted this ambiguity, and sought to reconcile the principle of consent with the political necessity of long-term national unity. It did so by reframing the idea of consent, turning it into a concept not of revolution, but of political obligation.

> This government, the offspring of our own choice . . . completely free in its principles . . . and containing within itself a provision for its own amendment, has a just claim to your confidence and your support. Respect for its authority, compliance with its Laws, acquiescence in its measures, are duties enjoined by the fundamental maxims of true Liberty. The basis of our political Systems is the right of the people to make and to alter their Constitutions of Government. But the Constitution which at any time exists, 'till changed by an explicit and authentic act of the whole People, is sacredly obligatory upon all. The very idea of the power and the right of the People to establish Government presupposes the duty of every Individual to obey the established Government.

The nation, deriving its legitimacy from the consent of the governed, imposed upon citizens a duty—"sacredly obligatory"—to respect, comply with, acquiesce to, and obey its law. Because the nation was republican, the address insisted, it "has a right to concentrate your affections." Here was a liberal defense of nationalism, grounded in the republican principle of consent. Even more, obedience would not simply result from Americans' rational consent to their government; it would also result from their "affections" for their nation. As to *how* that affection would be promoted—well, that is a question to which we shall soon turn.

The second national danger detailed in the Farewell Address was that of faction, or party spirit.[13] This was in some respects the threat Washington felt most passionately about, given the bitter and personal attacks he had endured during his final term in office. The matter was not merely personal, however, a question of his honor or reputation; it was fundamentally political and ideological. Many people worried that party spirit—or faction, as it was often called—would tear the Union apart. Such, after all, was the lesson taught by history, "in different ages & countries." The address was downright Shakespearean on the subject:

> It serves always to distract the Public Councils and enfeeble the Public Administration. It agitates the Community with ill founded Jealousies and false alarms, kindles the animosity of one part against another, foments occasionally riot & insurrection. It opens the door to foreign influence & corruption, which find a facilitated access to the government itself through the channels of party passions.

Hark, what discord would follow. Next would come anarchy, which would lead in turn to "a more formal and permanent despotism . . . and sooner or later . . . [to] the ruins of Public Liberty." Faction: a universal wolf, "of fatal tendency."[14] Thus, the Farewell Address warned "in the most solemn manner against the baneful effects of the Spirit of Party," and urged its readers to equate partisanship with disloyalty. Historians and political scientists commonly turn to Madison's great Federalist No. 10 when considering the problem of faction in the late-eighteenth-century United States. In the nineteenth century, however, Washington's Farewell Address was far more widely read than any Federalist essay, and far more influential in framing the problem of faction for American audiences. Reprinted in pamphlets and newspapers, read by children in school and adults on Washington's birthday, the Farewell Address would teach nineteenth-century Americans about the dangers faction posed to the nation's existence.

The third and longest section of the Farewell Address concerned itself with the threat of foreign affairs. Because this section takes up such a large portion of the address—22 percent of the text—most historians have read the Farewell Address as a foreign policy document. And indeed, it is in the realm of foreign policy that the Farewell Address (most often read as a "realist" tract) has, since the Civil War, been most influential. In the early republic, however, what is notable about the address is its insistence that foreign affairs could not be separated from domestic political considerations. Foreign relations were essentially a *domestic* problem, and they related to the dangers of geographical separation and party faction. During Washington's administration, both Spain and Britain—whose empires bordered U.S. territory—engaged in continued attempts to break portions of the West off from the United States, attempts that were warmly welcomed by some alienated residents of the region. Foreign relations also connected to the problem of faction, as foreign powers meddled with domestic political divisions to advance their own interests. "How many opportunities do they [foreign attachments] afford to tamper with domestic factions, to practice the arts of seduction, to mislead public opinion, to influence or awe the public Councils!" The reference here was to France, and to its connections with Democratic-Republican political clubs. The address thus concluded with an extended warning against the "insidious wiles of foreign influence" that exacerbated geographic divisions and factional dissension, threatening the very existence of the nation.

Washington's Farewell Address was above all a political text. It will never rank among the great works of political theory, alongside tracts by John Locke or Jean-Jacques Rousseau, nor will it make its way into classes on Western political thought. But for nineteenth-century Americans, this address—published in newspapers year after year, reprinted in pamphlets and excerpted in almanacs, diffused on a scale unknown to the great political theorists who shaped the minds of Madison, Jefferson, Hamilton, or Jay—taught Americans how to act politically. If it left words of parting advice, it also left words of caution, promoting a sense of the republic's fragility, outlining the greatest threats to the nation. Today, it continues to tell us a great deal about the greatest dangers early U.S. nationalism would confront.

But the challenges facing the new nation were not just political—related to geography, foreign affairs, or partisanship. They were also conceptual, stemming from the problem of forging a stable nation from a moment of revolutionary rupture. The colonies had legitimated their break from Great Britain on radical principles of liberty, equality, and government by consent of the governed. Could a nation be constructed on such a foundation? Before they could even answer such a question, Americans would have to understand the contours of the problem.

Introduction:

CONSENT, SLAVERY, AND THE PROBLEM OF U.S. NATIONALISM

——+>•◄+——

There is nothing more common, than to confound the terms of *the American revolution* with those of *the late American war* . . . The American war is over: but this is far from being the case with the American revolution. On the contrary, nothing but the first act of the great drama is closed. It remains yet to establish and perfect our new forms of government; and to prepare the principles, morals, and manners or our citizens, for these forms of government, after they are established and brought to perfection.

—BENJAMIN RUSH[1]

ON JULY 9, 1776, in New York City, George Washington ordered his troops to assemble to hear the Declaration of Independence proclaimed. The men and women, soldiers and citizens, who gathered at six o'clock that evening to hear "the declaration of Congress . . . read with an audible voice," already knew that Congress had "declare[d] the United Colonies of North America, free and independent States": Washington had stated as much in his order.[2] What they heard that night went beyond a mere declaration of *independence,* however: it was a statement on the legitimacy of political authority, an assertion of political principles that would serve as the building blocks for a new nation. Over subsequent decades the Declaration of Independence and other founding documents, along with the political principles they articulated, would become canonical. They would be promoted through other kinds of texts: by millions of pamphlets and broadsides, almanacs and newspapers, paintings, prints, and even by material objects flooding the new nation. They would be reprinted in schoolbooks, geographies, readers, and primers to be read aloud and memorized by children. They would be proclaimed on patriotic holidays and festivals. Reaching millions of Americans—men and women, young and old, rich and poor, even slave and free—those texts would do more than promote liberal and republican values. They would reshape individual identities and foster political loyalties. Over time, those texts would create a nation. How that process happened, and the darker implications that lurked just behind, is the subject of this book.

Today, most Americans can recall at least some of the truths the Declaration of Independence affirmed: that all men are created equal, and endowed with the right to life, liberty, and the pursuit of happiness. But these were not the only self-evident truths the Declaration posited. Short on the heels of that great sentence came another, no less important principle: that "Governments are instituted among Men, deriving their just powers from the consent of the governed." It was a profound and indeed radical statement about political authority, fully in line with the secular and religious current swirling through the late-eighteenth-century intellectual world: only government grounded in the consent of the governed could be considered legitimate. It was on that principle that the Declaration of Independence went on to affirm that "whenever any Form of Government becomes destructive of these ends, it is the Right of the People to alter or to abolish it, and to institute new Government."[3]

Was it those rousing words that inspired the crowd assembled to hear the Declaration read to descend, that same night, on Bowling Green at the southern tip of Manhattan? In one of the many acts of popular protest that marked the American Revolution, New Yorkers set on a massive, ornate statue of King George III that had towered over the neighborhood since its dedication a few years earlier. Raised to commemorate the repeal of the Stamp Act, the statue had served as a landmark symbolizing New Yorkers' gratitude toward the king. Even more, it had symbolized their pride in a shared British identity—membership in the greatest empire of the age, an empire of liberty defined by a heritage of constitutional liberties and traditional Protestantism defended by resistance to tyrannical authority.[4]

Subsequent events had led New Yorkers to view the statue differently, how-

4. A mix of soldiers and citizens tore down this statue of King George III
on Bowling Green, New York, after they heard the Declaration of Independence read
on July 9, 1776. William W. Walcutt, Bowling Green—Pulling Down
the Statue of George III.

ever, and the crowd that descended on Bowling Green tore down a statue that
now symbolized the despotism of the British King—indeed, the illegitimacy of
monarchy itself. This was more than a symbolic act—tearing down the monarchy, renouncing traditional forms of political authority. It was also a military act,
for the massive lead statue of King George would be melted down, turned into
bullets, and used to shoot British troops.

Few acts better embodied the radicalism of the American Revolution. No
longer would Americans be governed by a king, this royal figure sitting astride
his horse, scepter in hand, towering over the people. By tearing down the statue—
and monarchy itself—the people were declaring themselves sovereign. It was a
proclamation of emancipation from the dead hand of the past, from the inherited customs and privileges that had traditionally legitimated government. Con-
fronting such prejudice and irrationality, the new nation would inaugurate a
novus ordo seclorum, a new order of the ages, not just for the Americas but for the

world. "The birthday of a new world is at hand," Thomas Paine wrote in *Common Sense*, his wildly popular pamphlet published that same year, and few phrases better captured this essential mission of the new American republic.[5] Americans would henceforth look to the future rather than the past, their government's legitimacy derived not from tradition or history, but "from the consent of the governed," as the Declaration of Independence had stated.

These were noble principles. Powerful revolutionary slogans. Good for tearing statues down, perhaps, but less useful for building them up. The Declaration of Independence had affirmed that it was the peoples' right to abolish illegitimate regimes and to replace them with new forms of government. And while it waxed eloquent about what made government illegitimate, the Declaration—along with most of the rhetoric of the Revolution—gave few clues about what would come next. Stable governments had traditionally been grounded in ancient tradition, or in a prehistorical, mythologized past. But the Revolution had created a definitive rupture with the past, melting King George III and all he symbolized into Revolutionary bullets.[6] Could a new nation be created without recourse to the past? Could new traditions be forged on the basis of liberal, Revolutionary principles?

One thing was clear: the new nation would be founded on the most basic republican principle, the consent of the governed.[7] This did not make the U.S. case peculiar, of course: all nationalisms, indeed all political regimes depend to some extent on popular loyalty.[8] The problem confronted by U.S. nationalism—unique at the time, but it would become the problem shared by all liberal nationalism—was that by explicitly legitimating itself in the consent of the governed, it demanded the peoples' express consent. The formulation raised obvious questions: Who, exactly, was to consent? How? What, precisely, was the definition of consent? A people who had risen up, denounced their government, and thrown it off by force of arms could not be said to have consented to their form of government. That much was obvious. But what about others who—in the language of the Declaration—"suffer, while evils are sufferable, [rather] than . . . right themselves by abolishing the forms [of government] to which they are accustomed"? By suffering rather than resisting, did such a people tacitly consent to their government? What about still others who—unlike the privileged American gentry of European descent in Britain's North American colonies—lacked the *power* to throw off their tyrannical governments? By not risking their lives, honor, and fortunes (in the sense of futures) in a struggle to emancipate themselves from tyranny, did such people *consent* to their government, however tyrannical? These questions were largely unanswered during the Revolution—perhaps they were simply unanswerable. Even today these questions remain as pressing as they did at the end of the eighteenth century, the dawn of the age of nationalism.[9]

The peculiarity of the U.S. case during its formative years, however, is that, even as the nation legitimated itself in the principle of consent—even as it loftily denounced "tyranny" and "slavery" and created a nationalism to implement the principle of consent—it confronted a stubbornly entrenched institution that seemed to epitomize the very denial of consent, the very antithesis of liberal government: the widespread institution of African slavery. The problem of consent, after all, was not merely a matter of abstract political theory, fodder for the political debates and epistolary exchanges of the men like Jefferson, Washington, and Madison who declared independence, won it on the battlefield, and cemented it in new forms of government. Even as they articulated a vision of political association grounded in the consent of the governed, their daily lives led them to the very opposite extreme: to slavery.

THE CENSUS OF 1790, taken after the formation of a new government, would count a population of nearly 700,000 slaves in the United States or 17.8 percent of the national population, a proportion that ran to 39 percent in Virginia, where slaves labored on the plantations of Jefferson, Madison, and Washington, among others, and where slavery was woven into the fabric of every aspect of their lives. Having played a central role in the economic, social, and cultural development of Britain's North American colonies in the seventeenth and eighteenth centuries, slavery would become ever more firmly implanted into the life of the southern and southwestern states through the first six decades of the nineteenth century: by which time the enslaved population of the nation would grow to nearly 4 million. Not only did this vast population personify what the lack of consent could mean, it also raised the possibility that slaves might not retain their status forever; that they might rise up in a revolution of their own, just as white Americans had done and, even more terrifyingly, just as slaves in nearby Haiti had done in the 1790s, a revolution whose echoes continued to reverberate in the United States. The presence of slavery, in short, undermined both the meaning of consent in the republic, and the very unity post-Revolutionary nationalism sought to enact. [10]

Slavery was not just a social and economic institution, however; it was also a political concept. The language of slavery had a long history in Anglo-American political culture. It had been prevalent in seventeenth- and eighteenth-century British political discourse, when Britannia ruled the waves, and Britons vowed they "never will be slaves," and it became even more widespread during the Revolutionary period, when Americans began to believe that, as John Adams put it in 1765, "There seems to be a direct, and formal design on foot, to enslave all America." So common was this rhetoric of slavery, it appeared "in every statement of political principle," according to the historian Bernard Bailyn, "in every discussion of constitutionalism or legal rights, in every exhortation to resistance."[11]

In many respects, the "problem" of slavery was less what seems to twenty-first-century readers the obvious contradiction between slavery and freedom, but rather a more specific tension between slavery and *consent*: after all, citizens and noncitizens alike were all constrained by some power in some ways. The millions of slaves gave a vivid image to all Americans—not just the enslaved—of what it meant to be subjected to rule without consent. A young Alexander Hamilton expressed the point succinctly. The "only distinction between freedom and slavery consists in this," he wrote: "In the former state, a man is governed by the laws to which he has given consent."[12]

How could a young nation reconcile slavery with the principles of consent and self-government? The traditional answer has been to see slavery and republicanism as oppositional and antagonistic features of the early republic. This book joins with those who call this view into question, arguing that slavery did not stand in opposition to American republicanism. Rather, it argues, slavery actually shaped the nation's liberal and republican traditions by subtly refashioning the meaning of consent. Slavery also shaped U.S. nationalism by destabilizing a placid vision of the future: the conceptual terrain on which the nation was mapping itself.[13]

Long-term existence had been the central problem of all republics, and the U.S. case would be no different.[14] Unable to turn to the past for legitimacy, vexed in the present by the problem of slavery—a slumbering volcano, as many whites imagined it, ready to erupt at any moment in insurrection and destroy the nation—U.S. nationalism worked by turning Americans toward their nation's bright future.

No one among the Revolutionary generation rejected the past and welcomed the future more emphatically than Thomas Jefferson. In a famous letter to James Madison, Jefferson, writing from Paris in September 1789, as revolution was breaking out in France, wondered "whether one generation of men has a right to bind another?" "The question," he observed, is "of such consequences as not only to merit decision, but place also, among the fundamental principles of every government."[15] Can one generation bind another into a political order without betraying republican principles? Jefferson's generation might consent to a new nation, but what would happen in the future to those who did not grant their consent?

By way of answer, Jefferson set forth yet another truth he took to be "self evident": "*the earth belongs . . . to the living*," he insisted, "the dead have neither powers nor rights over it." Determining the exact length of a generation— "18. years 8. months, or say 19. years at the nearest integral number"—Jefferson moved to his larger statement of constitutional principle. Every debt, he triumphantly concluded, "every constitution, then and every law, naturally expires at the end of 19. years. If it be enforced longer, it is an act of force and not of right."[16] No one can accuse Jefferson of inconsistency here: he carried his political principle to its logical, even its extreme, conclusion. Future generations could not be bound into an already existing political order. Each generation would have to write its own constitution anew, for only thus could the governed truly consent to their form of government. That, according to Jefferson, is how a truly liberal polity would function.

James Madison was always of a more practical mind.[17] Unlike Jefferson, he had not spent the previous years living in a heady Paris verging on revolution, cavorting in the salons of the great and the good of the French Enlightenment. He had spent a recent summer stuck in steamy Philadelphia, sequestered away with dozens of sweaty men working to forge a constitution that might satisfy a variety of competing interests, followed by a fall spent persuading a skeptical population to approve that constitution. Imagining his nation repeating this process every nineteen years must have horrified poor Madison. If so, his tact did not fail him. "The idea," Madison diplomatically began, "is a great one, and suggests many interesting reflections." However, he added, ever so politely, "My first thoughts though coinciding with many of yours, lead me to view the doctrine as not in *all* respects compatible with the course of human affairs." The practical problems were clear. Property would depreciate as the moment of renewal approached; a sense of obligation toward laws would weaken, leading to "licentiousness already too powerful." It would be absurd, Madison argued, to create a state in which "a *unanimous* repetition of every law would be necessary on the accession of new members." And so, he concluded, "I find no relief from these consequences, but in the received doctrine that a tacit assent may be given to established Constitutions and laws, and that this assent may be inferred, where no positive dissent appears."[18]

In their brief but tantalizing exchange, Madison and Jefferson touched on many of the questions that most vexed early U.S. nationalism, questions that will be central to this book. Most of all, they wrestled with the problem of consent: how to ensure that each person—in the present and in the future—truly consents to the government. In their exchange, Jefferson and Madison ran up against the limits of any purely voluntarist association. Madison's response suggested that, if there ever has been such a thing as a truly civic polity, grounded in the actual consent of the living, it was not to be in the post-Revolutionary United States.[19]

BUILDING ON RECENT STUDIES, this book focuses extensively on the ways that popular writing promoted American nationalism.[20] It argues that popular texts—pamphlets, biographies, schoolbooks, sermons, political orations, almanacs, newspaper reporting, broadsides, even material objects like ceramics and paintings—shaped ideas of nationalism and citizenship in ways that would have lasting consequences. Reaching out to vast American audiences in the present and the future, these texts provided the medium through which political ideologies were disseminated and nationalism forged.

These were not texts operating in a grand philosophical tradition; their context was not other theoretical texts written by a small group of important intellectuals. Rather, the context of these texts was a largely rural readership on the far shores of the Atlantic. These texts drew on more exalted works of political theory, translating ideas of European republican and Enlightenment writers for a popular audience, mediating between the experiences of the New World and the grand intellectual traditions of European thought. If they do not stand as great literary or political texts, they served a critically important political function, binding their readers to the nation. They were in this sense, *civic* texts, and it was largely from these sorts of texts that Americans of the early nineteenth century learned their political theory.

If Americans of the early republic absorbed the ideas of seventeenth-century English republicans—and they did—it is because the writings of radical republicans like Algernon Sidney and John Milton were excerpted in widely disseminated civic texts like almanacs and schoolbooks. If the meaning of citizenship in the early republic derived from Scottish Enlightenment principles—and it did— that is because David Hume's histories and Hugh Blair's sermons were reprinted in civic texts: geographies and almanacs produced by people like Jedediah Morse, readers and grammars compiled by people like Noah Webster and Lindley Murray. Insofar as Americans learned their politics from Jefferson or Hamilton, they did so as presented by civic texts, and mediated by printers and compilers of schoolbooks and writers of popular biographies. Unlike the rarefied works that have engaged so many scholars of early American history—books of high political theory bound in calfskin, folio editions published in limited numbers for wealthy eighteenth- and nineteenth-century readers—this book examines the texts that addressed and reached a broad readership in the farthest hinterlands of European culture: what Bernard Bailyn calls the marchlands of the West, where European thought met American social reality.[21]

My argument broadly stated is that civic texts helped to produce a nationalism that promoted consent to the constituted political authorities and a sense of mutual political obligation. These texts promoted political unity and loyalty by canonizing major documents—most important, the Declaration of Independence, the Constitution, and Washington's Farewell Address—and by creating a powerful mythology of the Founding Fathers centered around George Washington as the "Father of the Nation." By turning Washington into the national patriarch, these texts bound Americans into members of a single nation: Americans would unite as siblings under a common father. But as we will see, his was an ambiguous and complex fatherhood. Washington was both father to the nation and father to his slaves, and so the Washington mythology opened a space for the incorporation of slaves into this national family, with slaves, like white Americans, united in bonds of affection and gratitude to Washington. The paternalist ideology of nationalism blended into and eventually authorized a paternalist ideology of slaveholding as these texts promoted both nationalism *and* slavery in the name of the father.

Civic texts promoted nationalism not through formal political channels, but through affective, emotive, and even patriarchal appeals. It was by reading and listening to civic texts that Americans learned the meaning of citizenship, and future generations learned to subscribe to the values of their fathers. By learning to read with Washington's Farewell Address, by hearing the Declaration of Independence read at home and in public festivals year after year, by rereading Washington's words in almanacs and newspapers or by hanging a portrait of him on their walls—in short, by learning to venerate Washington as a common father—

Americans would continually recur to the moment of founding, and *choose* to grant their consent, if only tacitly, to the nation.

Operating in a broadly Protestant political culture, these texts appealed to a largely devout population by infusing nationalism with religious associations. The promotion and dissemination of civic texts was in many respects an evangelical movement, drawing on religious reading practices, religious forms of association, and appeals to the heart and to the emotions articulated in a distinctly evangelical Protestant key. Drawing on a long-standing Protestant emphasis on the Word, these texts infused major national symbols—George Washington, the Constitution, Washington's Farewell Address—with religious connotations. They paralleled religious practices in their methods of inculcating or internalizing nationalist principles among a broad population. In their attempt to reach into the interior lives of individuals, these texts operated not just on a public and political level, but on a more subtle, interior level. They fostered new ways for people to think about themselves and their place in society, promoting a typically modern idea of humans as active agents capable of making and remaking the world. This conception of the morally autonomous individual—the kind of person capable of granting his or her consent—would eventually serve as the building block for a liberal political order.

Drawing on the rich scholarship on nationalism in general, and on U.S. nationalism in particular, this work treats nationalism not as a natural, teleological, or fixed idea.[22] As understood here, it was a political project driven by popular writings that worked on two levels: first on the individual level, by reimagining what it means to be a morally autonomous agent; and second, on the collective level, producing a political unity by imagining a collective past, present, and future. The result was a nationalism that produced citizenship through tacit consent.

The turn toward tacit consent, this book argues, resulted in large part from America's confrontation with slavery. American nationalism—this process by which Americans "consented" to their nation, if only tacitly—cast both citizenship and slavery as a choice. Civic texts posited a narrative of the American Revolution as a tale of white Americans choosing to risk their lives to fight for their liberty: thus had they *earned* their liberty. Slaves, in contrast, by implicitly refusing to risk their lives fighting for their own freedom, were cast as incapable of citizenship. Offered the choice between liberty or death, they had *chosen* to live in slavery—a formulation that neatly erased slaves' actual resistance. By holding individuals responsible for resisting their oppression, civic texts shifted the moral burden of slavery onto slaves. They reduced slavery to a simple choice—active resistance or passive acceptance—and promoted the belief that slavery, just like freedom, resulted from individual choice. Civic texts could thus promote an idea of slavery grounded in liberal principles, injecting a shallow, decontextualized understanding of consent and indeed moral responsibility at the very core of America's political traditions.

Through these texts, the United States—born in revolution, but dedicated to creating a lasting political order—managed, at least temporarily, to reconcile the tensions generated by the country's dual commitment to consent and slavery. These texts promoted an ongoing consent to political authority among its citizens, both in the present and into the future. Through these channels, nationalism penetrated the intellectual life of individuals, reshaping their individual identities, and creating a liberal, republican individual equipped to consent to the polity. It created a nation that might endure in the face of many challenges, including the most profound and divisive one posed by the continued existence of slavery. As we will see, however, by seeking to reconcile these many contradictions—between slavery and republicanism, the will of the living and the consent of the future— U.S. nationalism ultimately generated an impoverished understanding of liberty and consent whose legacies outlasted the institution of slavery itself, and which continues to haunt the nation to this day.

I.

THE APOTHEOSIS OF
GEORGE WASHINGTON

That Washington was the man, & the only man, & it would seem even designed by Providence, to be at the head of affairs, in war & in peace, to the end of his administration, I as much believe as do any of his idolizers . . . Yet I do not believe that he ever exhibited a trait of the great military leader . . . or that in politics, or government, he ever originated an important idea, or was the first or even among the first, in any new & important political movement, or devised any policy conducing greatly to the welfare of the people or the government. Yet his fame has been growing continually—& taken all together, now stands higher, & less questioned, than that of any man who lives, or has lived.

—EDMUND RUFFIN, 1858[1]

To trace all the steps by which he ascended these pinnacles of fame will be the voluminous task of the national historian.

—THE REVEREND SAMUEL TOMB, 1800[2]

Washington Dies

It was a time of mourning. When George Washington died on December 14, 1799, news of his passing traveled rapidly through the towns of the Atlantic coast and the villages dotting the rural hinterlands. The response was instant and overwhelming. Church bells rang out across the country, and business ceased. "We have this day suspended all business on the news of Gen. Washington's death," wrote an Annapolis resident on December 17. Americans expressed their shock, dismay, and grief as the news traveled up the east coast. "The Shops and Stores were shut and all amusements suppressed, in every place as the afflicting tidings spread through the country," reported a Bostonian on December 27. "This event has cast a gloom over the whole continent." George Ticknor, though only a child at the time, remembered the scene vividly: "There never was a more striking or spontaneous tribute paid to a man than here in Boston," he recalled, "when the news came of Washington's death. It was a little before noon; and I often heard persons say at the time that one could know how far the news had spread by the closing of the shops. Each man, when he heard that Washington was dead, shut his store as a matter of course, without consultation; and in two hours all business was stopped."[3]

Newspapers, framed in black, published special editions announcing Washington's death, informed readers of upcoming parades and memorials, transmitted expressions of mourning from local officials, and reprinted Washington's most famous speeches. Americans, wearing black crape armbands or black ribbons on their lapels, gathered in mass parades, and listened to sermons and speeches. Groups ranging from the Society of St. Tammany to the Masons to the American Philosophical Society met to express their sorrow and pass resolutions of regret. Towns organized funeral parades amid buildings draped in black; processions were held in settlements as far west as Lexington, Kentucky, and Detroit, then still part of the Northwest Territory. These were emotional events—"Tears flowed from every eye," a visitor in Georgetown recorded, "and lamentations burst from every lip"—and with business shut down, the turnout was huge. "G. Wash[n] death celebration of," a Massachusetts farmer wrote in his diary for February 22, 1800, "—no business done."[4]

Shops may have closed and farmers ceased work during the ceremonies, but merchants around the country—and around the world—geared up for the occasion. Advertisements for the sale of black crape, by the packet, piece, or yard appeared in newspapers by the end of December.[5] Manufacturers as far away as London, Paris, and even China recognized the magnitude of the event, producing commemorative objects like plates, pitchers, quilts, clocks, necklaces, and rings (figures 6 and 7). Drawing, perhaps, on their revolutionary heritage, when consumer goods had taken on important political resonance, Americans imbued these sorts of objects with political, and even nationalist, significance.[6] Such

5. This engraving by William Birch portrays the procession in commemoration of
Washington's death in Philadelphia. Note the figure weeping in the foreground, and
the mother holding her son's hand as they watch the parade: such emotional images
did not just represent the Washington mourning; they helped to foster it.
W. Birch & Son, High Street, From the Country Market-place
Philadelphia: With the Procession in Commemoration
of the Death of General George Washington,
December 26th, 1799.

objects—lockets worn by women, armbands worn by men, pillows sewn by girls,
and banners held aloft by mourning artisans—drew large and varied segments of
the American population into the civic rituals of mourning.

Unlike other civic events—elections, for instance—these rituals were not
limited to a small number of white, male, propertied citizens. As "one of those
great events which . . . unite[s] public calamity with private affliction," Washington's death blurred boundaries between public and private life. Citizens and
noncitizens alike participated in mourning rituals taking place not only in the

halls of Congress, but also in streets, churches, and parlors—indeed, wherever commemorative souvenirs were worn or displayed. Even fashion became a form of civic expression. "I shall not have occasion now for any thing but Black, untill Spring," wrote Abigail Adams shortly after Washington's death. "At Present the whole Family are in full mourning." Through their dress, the elite women of Philadelphia could participate in this civic community united in grief. Just as "Members of Congress are to wear mourning the remainder of the Session," one Philadelphia woman noted that "Mrs. Adams has requested of all the Ladies that attend her levee to wear mourning." Such forms of civic participation allowed for elaborate displays, as Adams soon realized. "The Ladies Grief did not deprive them of taste in ornamenting their white dresses," she dryly observed after one reception. Some wore military sashes, "Others wore black Epaulets of Black silk trimd with black plumes or black flowers. Black Gloves & fans." These acts of mourning expanded the contours of the body politic, even beyond the sphere of the nation itself: "The whole universe, perhaps, for the first time," declared a French eulogist, "will unite in offering a tribute of gratitude to the memory of a mortal!"[7]

6. Pendant containing the interwoven hair of George Washington and Martha Dandridge Custis.

Closer to home, printers turned out orations, prayers, songs, pamphlets, biographies, compilations of Washington's writings, and prints of his image. Of approximately 2,200 publications to emerge from the presses in 1800, more than 400 dealt with Washington in some way.[8] In modern parlance, it was a major media event. The eulogies and character sketches published in 1801 were incorporated into volumes of Washington's writings, commemorative editions of the eulogies, and even in popular almanacs.

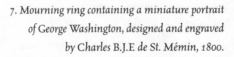

7. Mourning ring containing a miniature portrait
of George Washington, designed and engraved
by Charles B.J.F. de St. Mémin, 1800.

ORDER
OF THE
FUNERAL PROCESSION

The 31st of DECEMBER, 1799.

By direction of the Commitee of Arrangement.

Officer and

Eight Dragoons.

Sixth Regiment, in Platoons, by the left.

Eight pieces of Field Artillery.

Cavalry.

Rifle Company.

Militia Officers.

Officers of the Navy of the United States.

Officers of the Army of the United States.

Major Gen. Hamilton and Suite.

Citizens.

St. Stephen's Society.

Tammany Society.

Mechanic Society.

Masonic Lodges.

Grand Lodge.

Manhattan Company.

New-York Insurance Company.

United Insurance Company.

Branch Bank.

Bank of New-York.

Chamber of Commerce.

Marine Society.

Regents of the University.

Trustees of Columbia College.

President and Professors of ditto.

Physicians and Surgeons.

Gentlemen of the Bar.

Civil Officers of the City.

Civil Officers of the State.

Lieutenant Governor.

Civil Officers of the United States Government.

His Catholic Majesty's Consul and Gentlemen of that Nation.

His Britannic Majesty's Consul and Gentlemen of that Nation.

Music.

Anacreontic and Philharmonic Societies.

Clergy.

Twenty-four Girls, in White Robes.

Committee of Arrangement.

Bier.

The Horse in Mourning.

Cincinnati as Chief Mourners, and other Officers of the late war.

Corporation of the City.

Eight Dragoons.

Officer.

ALL the Procession to march four deep, except the Military.

General HUGHES is charged with the execution of the above order, subject to such further disposition as he shall judge expedient.

Jas. M. Hughes, Chairman,
Ebenezer Stevens,
Jacob Morton,
James Farlie,
John Stagg, junior,
⎱ Committee.

New-York, December 29, 1799.

8. Order of the Funeral Procession the 31st of December, 1799, which took place in New York City: one of dozens of funeral processions staged around the country after Washington's death.

And while some of these texts might have been ephemeral, few at the time believed they would soon be forgotten. They were intended to memorialize Washington not only for audiences in 1800, but also for future generations. "When men of common character are swept from the theatre of life," read one anonymous publication, "they die without the tribute of public notice or concern, as they have lived without claim to public esteem." But Washington was different:

> When personages of more exalted worth are summoned from the scenes of sublunary existence, their death calls forth a burst of general regret, and invigorates the flame of public gratitude. In obedience to the wishes, and to the voice of their country, the orator, the poet, and the historian, combine to do justice to the virtues of their character, while the labors of the painter, the sculptor, and the statuary, in perpetuating their likeness, do homage to their memory.[9]

Just as Washington had served his country in life, so would he continue to serve it in death. For the civic texts produced in the wake of Washington's death—the pamphlets, eulogies, almanacs, newspaper reporting, engravings, material objects, and biographies—were not merely recording Americans' sense of loss at Washington's death. They were producing bonds of unity among Americans. In a climate of real fear about the nation's instability, they posited a future of Americans recalling Washington's great deeds and forever worshipping his memory.

The Nation's Uncertain Future

Why did Americans respond so intensely to Washington's death? Part of the answer, of course, lies with the man himself. Washington remained, despite the partisan battles of the 1790s, the most beloved figure in the United States, and his death would have caused a public outpouring of grief no matter what the circumstances. Nevertheless, veneration for Washington does not explain the level of agitation that followed his death, which seemed excessive even to some admirers. In fact, a good deal of the response had more to do with the state of the nation than it did with Washington: it stemmed from pervasive fears about the nation's future inspired by the great transformations then under way throughout the Atlantic world.

As Washington's Farewell Address had testified, the last decade of the eighteenth century was a period of tumult in American politics that showed no obvious sign of ending. A series of bitterly divisive political disputes had split the nation sharply along ideological lines, and supporters of each political party believed that the other threatened the future of the nation, and its republican character. On the conservative wing of U.S. political life, Federalists feared that proliferating newspapers, novels, and political clubs were harbingers of an international Jacobin movement that would import what they saw as the chaotic excess of revolutionary France. Their opposition, meanwhile, the Democratic-Republicans, feared that the Federalists' crackdown on dissent, their increasingly authoritarian rule, and their growing alliance with Britain against republican France signaled an assault on their country's republican character, and a drive to reinstall monarchy in America. Both sides feared that the faction and party spirit would fatally undermine the nation's stability.[10] The last years of the eighteenth century would see continued secessionist plots in Kentucky and Tennessee and threatened nullification of federal law in Virginia and Kentucky, all casting the nation into a period of political dissension so serious that many believed, like Abigail Adams, that "we shall come to a civil war." Those fears would come to a head in 1800, as the bitterly contested presidential election deadlocked in the House of Representatives. Republicans accused Federalists of plotting Jefferson's assassination, or of seizing arms in federal arsenals in preparation for civil war. The Republican governor of Pennsylvania, in response, informed Jefferson that he could arm twenty thousand militia men, and was prepared to use force to retain power.[11] The nation, it seemed, faced an existential crisis.

The international context—in particular, the reverberations of the French revolution echoing throughout the Atlantic world—aggravated this situation. Europe was engulfed in a war that captured the Americans' attention, threatening to drag them down the same path. Closer to home, the Haitian revolution presaged still more trouble, as the refugees flooding into U.S. port cities from Saint Domingue arrived with tales of death and destruction, which threatened to spread from the Caribbean to mainland North America. Republicans, still largely centered in slaveholding states, saw a dreaded specter in the bloody scenes being enacted so nearby, while Federalists found added proof of the dangers resulting from excess liberty. The rebellion plotted by Virginia slave Gabriel in 1800 brought these fears home, seemingly portending a wave of domestic insurrections, and adding a powerful element to whites' fears of social and political chaos.[12] Nor did the fledgling nation successfully avoid foreign entanglements: it engaged in a quasi-war with France in the Caribbean; its shipping endured repeated assaults by various European powers; and its sailors were continually impressed by foreign armies, and sometimes sold into North African slavery. The U.S. government was able to muster little more than impotent protests at such outrages. "Verily," concluded one orator after Washington's death, summing up pervasive concerns about the nation's future, "the world is convulsed; and our own country, from various causes, is placed in a most hazardous situation."[13]

No one offered a better sense of this uncertainty than Henry Lee, Washington's fellow Revolutionary general, who delivered the official congressional eulogy in front of Philadelphia's assembled political class on December 26, 1799. Probably the most famous and widely circulated of all the eulogies—it coined the phrase "First in War, first in peace, first in the hearts of his countrymen"—Lee's oration would be published at least twenty times in pamphlet form, and reprinted in virtually every newspaper in the nation, and would open many of the collections of Washington eulogies that soon proliferated. Perhaps most significantly, it would later be excerpted in various schoolbooks during the first decades of the nineteenth century and would eventually be picked up by William Holmes McGuffey in his ubiquitous *Eclectic Reader* series, to be learned and memorized by generations of schoolchildren.[14] It was, in short, an exemplary civic text.

Like so many other Washington eulogies, Lee's began by describing his era as a time of frightening, unpredictable change: "when the civilized world shakes to its centre, when every moment gives birth to strange and momentous changes; when our peaceful quarter of the globe, exempt as it happily has been from any share in the slaughter of the human race, may yet be compelled to abandon her pacific policy, and to risk the doleful casualties of war." Now came Washington's death, a national calamity that exacerbated these worries about an unknown, uncertain future.[15] Washington had held the country together during its moments of greatest crisis, and had become the strongest symbol of its unity—"The love which was everywhere cherished for him," a nineteenth-century historian would later write, "in itself had become a bond of union." And now he was gone. "What limit is there to the extent of our loss?" asked Lee.[16]

Lee was hardly unique in expressing such sentiments. "But alas!" exclaimed the Reverend Josiah Dunham in Oxford, Massachusetts, "will not darkness now gather in our land? Though his departure was in renown, yet who knows but it is the LOUD HARBINGER of approaching calamity?" "Mourn, O *Columbia!*" a Baltimore newspaper proclaimed in the same vein, "thy FATHER and PROTECTOR is no more!" Washington's death had transformed a period of great uncertainty into one of acute crisis.

> *Ill-fated country—lo, of aid bereft*
> *Thy spear is broken and thy buckler cleft!*
> *What arm shall now a firm support bestow,*
> *And shield thee harmless from the threat'ning foe;*
> *Who, mid the storm, with fearless hand shall guide*
> *Thy course in safety o'er the troubled tide?*[17]

If such expressions smacked of pathos, the idea of Washington as a rock, holding the nation steady "mid the storm," was hardly unique to verse. A contemporary print, for instance, could have served as a visual representation of this poem (figure 9). In a terrible storm in the middle of the ocean, the print shows a rock standing firm amid lightning, wind, and crashing waves: a rock with Washington's name engraved on its side. Like a rock, Washington had remained steady, anchoring the nation amid buffeting political storms. Now, with the nation's father gone, who would ensure its survival, its stability? Would Americans, bereft of their rock, be able to preserve their nation?

The engraver of the below print suggested one possible response to this pressing question. As he intended it, his print represented not the danger that now

9. Broadside entitled General Washington, This Great and Good Man (1800), which graphically represents Washington as a rock standing firm amid the storms sweeping the Atlantic world.

faced the country in the wake of Washington's death; rather, it was meant "to imply the Duration of his [Washington's] Fame," even in times of "Adversity and
extreme Peril."[18] Civic texts like these—spoken, printed, and engraved—were deployed in the wake of Washington's death in order to address widespread fears of
the future by creating an image of Washington that could oppose change. Could
Washington, through his shared memory, continue to protect the nation? These
texts would help make it so.

Civic Texts: Creating a New Future

> The present, the future interests of the western world; and possibly, the in-
> terests of the whole universe, are connected, with the education; early
> modes of thinking; and consequent manly action, of the sons of Columbia.
> Your children, are a precious deposit; they are an invaluable loan . . . Incul-
> cate, on their infant minds, obedience to the laws of GOD and man; impress
> their gentle bosoms, with a serious love of order; learn them to reverence,
> the supreme authorities of the United States; teach them, to abhor a rest-
> less spirit of popular innovation, and to shun the fatal path, which leads to
> rapid change, and speedy ruin . . . bear ye in everlasting remembrance, this
> most solemn memento, that the voice of your departed, your beloved
> WASHINGTON, cries aloud from the tomb.
>
> —THE REVEREND GEORGE RICHARDS, 1800[19]

Civic texts would respond to fears about the nation's future by reaching out
to children. Consecrating a memory of Washington, they sought to create bonds
between present and future generations of Americans, to persuade audiences to
imitate Washington, venerate their fathers, and abide by the Constitution and the
nation's laws. Using Washington as a vehicle, these civic texts inculcated fraternal
bonds among Americans and forged a new national spirit, all in the name of the
father.

In the months following Washington's death, civic texts marshaled visions of
the future in order to assert stability in the present. With the nation's founding still
in living memory, rather than blurred by the warm haze of a mythologized past,
with its founders locked in bitter political conflict far removed from future generations' nostalgic image of a fraternal band of "brothers," it was not possible to op-

pose change by invoking time-honored traditions. Instead, civic texts projected the nation the other way: into an eternal future, giving an aura of permanence to a nation only a decade old.[20] Washington's memory did the trick admirably. "And his fame shall live," read one eulogy, "shall be transmitted from age to age, with growing lustre, till time shall be no more!" "The name of WASHINGTON," declared another eulogist, "will be revered until the fashion of this world has wholly passed away."[21] The implications were reassuring: if Washington's fame would endure until the end of time, surely Washington's nation would similarly endure.

And so Washington was rendered immortal. Though "born for the human race," Washington "still instructs, and inspires, by the words of Wisdom, falling from the lips of IMMORTALITY." "His memory will forever live," affirmed an Alexandria eulogy, "unhurt amidst the wreck of empire and the 'crush of worlds.'" Washington served as a counterweight to the chaos that surrounded the present and future, a "monument . . . which the remotest ages shall not be able to deface, nor the lapses of time itself be able to overthrow."[22] Even as they induced fears about the corrosive power of time—"time, which destroys every thing," "the wreck of empire and the 'crush of worlds,'" "lapses of time" that "overthrow"—these texts fought off the specter of change and collapse by invoking Washington's perdurable memory, thus offering reassurance that the nation would overcome the dangers of change and turmoil. His legacy, if remembered—his example, if followed—would provide safe harbor amid the stormy waters of the republic's future.

These texts did more than merely pass a message along: they were calls to action. Audiences were not to be passive recipients of the nationalist messages being transmitted; they were to respond with active remembrance and emulation. Declaring February 22, 1800, a day of official commemoration, the governor of Maryland asked citizens to "call to mind the virtues, public services and unshaken patriotism of the deceased." By remembering Washington, Americans would become active participants in the nation, and ensure its preservation for posterity. They would constitute a community: the nation. "Succeeding generations," predicted an Alexandria newspaper, "while they recount with pride, to their children, his toils and sufferings in the establishment of their freedom, will inspire them with emulations to imitate his exalted virtues."[23]

Ensuring the nation's stability involved more than just remembrance. It called for *emulation.* The call to emulation was built into the funeral processions themselves, as in Alexandria, where sixteen boys (one for each state)—each wearing a cap that proclaimed "*WASHINGTON our model*" in golden letters—marched under the inscription, "Let the sons of Columbia emulate the character of *WASH-*

INGTON." These appeals came from the highest authorities, both secular—"His example," wrote John Adams in a presidential message, "will teach wisdom and virtue to magistrates, citizens, and men, not only in the present age, but in future generations, as long as our history shall be read"—and sacred: "By imitating his unsullied virtues," promised the Reverend Joseph Story, echoing the language of Hebrews 11:4, "though dead, yet he shall live." This quasi-eternal emulation by Washington's future countrymen would allow him, "though dead," to bind and protect the nation: "his example shall live to instruct posterity—his virtues shall descend as a precious inheritance to future ages."[24]

By fostering active remembrance, by turning readers, listeners, and parade members into emulators, the process of appropriating these texts helped transform audiences into Americans. Collectively remembering Washington, emulating his virtues, and passing those virtues on to their children, it would fall to these newly constituted Americans to preserve the nation. Robert Liston, the British ambassador living in Philadelphia at the time of Washington's death, commented on the purpose—and on the effect, at least in his experience—of these kinds of texts:

> The leading men in the United States appear to be of the opinion that these ceremonies tend to elevate the spirit of the people, and contribute to the formation of a *national character,* which they consider as much wanting in this country . . . The hyperbolical amplifications, the Penegyricks in question have an evident effect especially among the younger part of the community, in fomenting the growth of that vanity, which to the feelings of a stranger had already arrived at a sufficient height.[25]

Whether it seemed distastefully excessive to British eyes or not, this veneration of Washington would mold young Americans' national character, fomenting their attachment to the nation. By urging the emulation of Washington, these sorts of texts were coaxing audiences into becoming not just better people, but better Americans. Cherishing Washington's memory, said a U.S. senator, "will make us better sons—better fathers—better husbands—and better citizens."[26]

Through the constant invocation of this familial rhetoric—Washington as father, Americans bound in fraternal bonds to one another—these texts sought to teach Americans to think of themselves as a national *family.* But this was not just any family; it was a family model grounded in late-eighteenth-century norms. The eighteenth century had witnessed the transformation of idealized notions of family, moving away from a hierarchical, patriarchal model of the family, in which fathers ruled over their subordinates, toward a model of family life grounded in bonds of sentiment, affection, and, above all, consent. This family model was itself being promoted through a wide range of popular texts—such as a widely circulated pamphlet by Mason Locke Weems, the popular author and bookseller, entitled *Hymen's Recruiting Sergeant,* which characterized marriage as "a match of *true love* . . . tender friendship . . . endearing attentions," and the parent-child relationship as one of "sentiments of tenderness and humanity."[27] Extending this model of the affective family to the nation could serve to unify Americans on grounds not of coercion, but of voluntary consent.

It also opened up a space for the participation of nonpolitical actors in the nation. If the above reference by a senator to sons/fathers/husbands suggested that certain forms of civic participation were relegated to males, the family model of the nation created by these texts injected daughters, mothers, and wives into the nation's civic life. In this sense, these were more than political texts. They were *civic* texts, expanding the boundaries of the polity beyond mere citizens to incorporate noncitizens—especially women and children, but also, as we shall see, in a more ambiguous way, slaves—into the political body. Such civic education could be performed by women as well as men—indeed, by women better than men, for it was they who would be charged with imparting nationalist virtues to their children, making them central actors in the dissemination of Washington's virtues, and thus in the nation's preservation.[28] This process of emulation was about more than political participation. It was about granting one's allegiance to the nation through channels traditionally deemed nonpolitical. These civic texts would teach children to strengthen the nation.

THE FOCUS of these texts was relentlessly on the future. The phrase "unborn millions" was ubiquitous. Residents of the nation's capital, listening to eulogies of Washington and recitations of his Farewell Address in Alexandria's Presbyterian church ("handsomely dressed in mourning") could look on the church's western gallery and see a portrait of Washington with the inscription: "Millions unborn shall venerate thy Name." An ode to Washington printed in a New York newspaper, and later reprinted in an 1810 schoolbook, predicted of Washington's grave: "No lapse of years shall soil the sacred spot, / No future age its memory shall blot; / Millions unborn shall mark its sacred fire, / And latest Time behold it, and admire."[29] For a people who could not look back toward a primordial shared past; for a people locked in bitter political combat; for a people whose territorial boundaries were unfixed and continually expanding—imagining a future of "millions unborn" substituted a future unity for present-day division and uncertainty. These mythic millions of unborn Americans still worshipping Washington—still consenting to the government of their own free will— affirmed the nation's perpetuity, and its republican character, at a time when both seemed perilously close to disintegration.

In a New York eulogy, the Presbyterian minister John M. Mason ("the great-est of American pulpit orators," according to the nineteenth-century chronicler Rufus Griswold) waxed poetic about "The historian of this period," long in the future, who would recount Washington's glory. A New York newspaper account imagined an anonymous unborn American, reading about Washington's deeds.

> *The world shall gaze with wonder and applause;*
> *While on fair hist'ry's page the patriot reads*
> *Thy matchless valor in thy country's cause . . .*
> *E'en unborn ages shall thy worth commend,*
> *And never fading laurels deck thy shrine.*[30]

Even more self-consciously, a Boston newspaper predicted: "We therefore carefully preserve all the details which reach us, that posterity, when tracing in the page of faithful History . . . may discern the full and strong proofs of the sensibility, affec-tion and gratitude of his Countrymen." This metaphor of history as a "page" car-ried the reassuring implication that history contained a larger order: planned, written, and endowed with higher meaning. Insofar as the future seemed uncer-tain to Americans, that was only because they could not discern what was written on the "page of history."[31] In a sense, these texts tried to freeze history. "*His mem-ory is embalmed* in the affections of his grateful countrymen," said Aaron Bancroft. "His name is written in the book of immortal fame: He shall be had in everlasting remembrance."[31] Washington's memory would remain immutable, teaching gen-erations of future Americans into eternity to follow the virtues of their fathers.

These texts were instructions on how to read Washington's writings—indeed, how to understand a whole nationalist canon. Many scholars have stressed that the meaning of any given text is not immanent or inherent to that text, but that it changes across space and time: as it is read, interpreted, or "appropriated" by readers. The appropriation of a text obviously differs depending on who is reading and when, on the social and cultural environment of readers, and it will more than likely vary from one generation to the next. "A history of reading and readers," as the historian of reading Roger Chartier puts it, "is thus an account of the historicity of the process of appropriation of texts."[32] Clearly, when it comes to texts as widely read and as broadly distributed as were these sermons, eulogies, pamphlets, broadsides—these civic texts—generalizing about how they were interpreted by audiences is difficult, perhaps even impossible. Their interpretive community was as large and diverse as the nation. On the other hand, these sermons, eulogies, and pamphlets offer some insight into how Washington's writings—as well as texts like the Declaration of Independence and the Constitution—were *intended* to be interpreted. For they contained very specific instructions on how Washington's writings should be appropriated. Indeed, it was largely through these texts that Washington's writings became veritable gospel, their perusal a rite of citizenship.

> Fellow-Citizens of the *United States!* Reperuse, with solemnized attentions, General WASHINGTON'S circular letter, to the Governors of the several States, at the conclusion of the late revolutionary war; review, President WASHINGTON'S admirable, incomparable, inaugural address, to the Representatives, and Senate of the Union; read again, and again, with that reverence, for superior wisdom, and virtue, which the moral, the religious page ought to inspire, his last national will, and testament, presented to every individual fellow-citizen, by the parental pen, of the benefactor, a father, and a friend.[33]

Such civic texts were creating and sacralizing a new gospel, providing an exegesis for their audiences. "By suddenly removing from us such a man as WASHINGTON, at a crisis like the present," affirmed one orator, "how forcibly does the Supreme Ruler teach as his own *sovereignty* and *independence,* and inculcate the duty of implicit and entire *submission* to his disposals!"[34] Both secular and religious authority was invoked to elevate Washington's writings into the nationalist canon, along with other great texts like the Constitution and the Declaration of Independence.

It was in the period following Washington's death that civic texts like these eulogies made the Farewell Address a statement of inviolable political principles. Although widely published in 1796, the address was republished only sporadically in the years following his retirement. Washington's death drove a resurgence in the popularity of the address, feeding a new wave of editions and launching the Farewell Address to the very peak of the nationalist civic canon, on par with the Declaration of Independence and the Constitution. After his death, printers around the country produced impressive pamphlet editions that, according to one authority, paid "unusual attention to standards of typography . . . printers

10. *It was in the period after Washington's death that his Farewell Address was made into a canonical text, reprinted and recirculated throughout the nineteenth century. Some prints, like this one, which probably dates from the mid-nineteenth century, were elaborately illustrated and designed. Washington's Farewell Address, n.d., n.p.*

stretched themselves to the utmost to make the appearance worthy of the content."[35] Such elegant editions served to exalt both Washington and his message. After Washington's death, the address was reprinted in virtually every American newspaper; included in schoolbooks and collections of Washington's writings; reprinted in biographies; and quoted in, even annexed to, published eulogies. The title of a Massachusetts eulogy was typical: *An Eulogy On The Illustrious Character Of The Late General George Washington . . . To Which Is Added General Washington's Parental And Affectionate Address To His Country, Declining Their Future Suffrages For The Presidency.*[36]

Along with this massive wave of dissemination came a clear commandment: "Teach your children to lisp his praise: Instill into their minds his spirit; and cherish in them the growth of his virtues." The call was heard throughout the American republic. "Teach it to your children," said David Ramsay to his Charleston, South Carolina, audience. "It is an invaluable legacy." The point was made over and over again: by following Washington's advice as presented in the Farewell Address, Americans could preserve their nation. Calling the Farewell Address "an oracle of political truth," Bostonian Timothy Bigelow believed it would serve as "a palladium, which, while carefully preserved, will perpetuate our Union and Independence; an amulet, which, if constantly improved, will render the body politic invulnerable, we might almost say immortal." Remembering Washington's words became a way of overcoming present-day turmoil. "Let Americans every," urged Isaac Story, "follow, with a conscientious observance, his *farewell advice. While that is our POLITICAL CREED—our strength will be preserved from captivity, and our glory from the hands of our enemies.*"[37]

Washington's Farewell Address became, in 1800, the national father's deathbed words—"the legacy, which, with parental tenderness, he has bequeathed to us"—sacred advice to be obeyed and internalized by all his children. Added to his authority as "father of the nation," the Farewell Address achieved the status of final, parting words never to be ignored. "Let every *American* transcribe the following few words [from Washington's Farewell Address], in letters of grateful sensibility," said one orator. "Ingrave them on the living tablet of the feeling heart, and treasure their precious contents in perpetual remembrance." "Let it be written in characters of gold, and hung up in every house," read the preface of a collection of Washington's writings published in 1800 that claimed to be sold "by all the booksellers in Virginia." "Let it be engraven upon tables of brass and marble, and, like the sacred Law of Moses, be placed in every Church, and Hall, and Senate Chamber of this spacious continent, for the instruction not only of the present, but of all future generations of *Americans*." Even the British Earl of Buchan, shortly after news of Washington's death made its way to England, agreed with such sentiments. "It seems to me," he wrote to Martha Washington, "that such maxims and advices ought to be engraved on every forum or place of common assembly among the people & read by Parents, teachers and Guardians to their children & pupils, so that true Religion & virtue its inseparable attendant may be imbibed by the rising generation to the remotes ages."[38]

If all Americans were metaphorical children under Washington the father, actual children were particular targets of his words. Sermon after sermon made the point. One eulogist even called for the words of Washington's Farewell Address to be fed to babies along with their breast milk. "Let that last Farewell awaken every tender emotion," he urged. "Let the infant cherub suck its honey with his earliest sustenance." Infants would be suckled on a diet of Washington's words, imbibing his virtue, and thus preserving the nation. At a later stage, children would use Washington's writings as textbooks. Even Washington's financial accounts offered valuable lessons for America's children. "A tin box, containing these accounts," said David Ramsay in South Carolina, perhaps overestimating the children's interest in account books, "is a monument of the disinterestedness of General WASHINGTON. Bring your children and your children's children to examine its contents. Show them the hand-writing of the father of their country; teach them thereon the lessons of economy, of order and method in expenses; teach them to love their country, and to serve it on liberal terms." Ramsay's hope would be realized some years later, as several schoolbooks reprinted Washington's accounts.[39]

By targeting children, these civic texts brought about the domestication of Washington's memory. Through such texts, Washington became both the public, political father and also the private, paternal father, forging nationalist bonds that transcended public and private spheres. By making Washington into the father of each family, these texts made the household a metaphorical incubator of national virtues. They modeled national bonds on family bonds, making public *virtù* an extension of private virtues. Civic texts would continue thus to domesticate Washington well into the nineteenth century. One 1845 book aimed at children, for instance, declared that "The first word of infancy should be mother, the second, father, the third, WASHINGTON."[40]

Exalted by such encomia, the Farewell Address would remain canonical throughout subsequent generations, as it became institutionalized in the educational and political infrastructure of American life. Thomas Jefferson, for instance, hoped it would be assigned as required reading at the University of Virginia, along with classic political theory by Locke and Sidney, and American productions like the Declaration of Independence, the Federalist Papers, and the Virginia Resolutions opposing the Alien and Sedition Acts. Some years later, John Quincy Adams, though from the opposite end of the American political spectrum, expressed similar veneration of the Farewell Address, hoping it would "serve as the foundation upon which the whole system of their [Americans'] future policy may rise, the admiration and example of future time." Already, by 1805, a Boston printer was producing a pamphlet that compiled the Massachusetts and U.S. constitutions, the Declaration of Independence, and Washington's Farewell Address, all of them, as the title stated, "*to be read as a School-Book in all the common schools.*"[41] Promoted in this way, the Farewell Address continued to be republished regularly throughout the first decades of the nineteenth century, and it is possible to map the number of new editions printed per year (figure 11).

Note the variations in editions of the Farewell Address over time. First published in 1796, the second great wave of editions occurred in 1800, in the wake of Washington's death. The Farewell Address was then published at a smaller rate until it rose again during the War of 1812, the next moment of national crisis, which involved not only the threat of the British army, but also the danger of New England secession. Indeed, it could be argued that the Farewell Address was

PUBLICATION HISTORY OF WASHINGTON'S
FAREWELL ADDRESS, 1796–1865

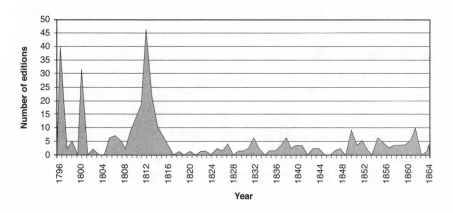

deployed principally during moments of national crisis, suggesting its role as a unifying text. Although this remains a speculative matter, the peaks in republication do seem to correlate to moments of concern about the nation's unity: after 1832, 1850, and then reaching another small peak during the Civil War. What is particularly intriguing about this trend is the high correlation with a graph of publications of the Declaration of Independence, another canonical text of early U.S. nationalism. (See appendix 2.)

This correlation is probably not coincidental for, like the Constitution, the Farewell Address would be deployed at moments of national crisis to help cement loyalty to the Union. During the crisis over New England secession amid the War of 1812, for instance, the Philadelphia printer Mathew Carey published a book entitled *The Olive Branch*, lambasting those who would seek to divide the Union. *The Olive Branch* quickly became a runaway bestseller, going through ten editions by 1818 and selling an estimated ten thousand copies. The book opened, on the front page facing the preface, with a long quotation from Washington's Farewell Address, under the caption: "The Voice of Washington." "The unity of government," the address was quoted, "which constitutes you one people, is dear to you. It is justly so." (Another quotation on this page previewed Lincoln's famous "house divided" speech by quoting from the New Testament: "Every Kingdom divided against itself, is brought to DESOLATION.") The book continued by quoting and celebrating Washington's Farewell Address throughout: "his last legacy, one of the noblest efforts of human wisdom, impressively urged his countrymen to frown indignantly upon any attempt to impair or dissolve the union."[42] Later editions extended the book through more than eighty-seven chapters and more than five hundred pages, adding warning after warning from Washington on the importance of safeguarding the Union. A generation later, ardent Unionists would invoke the same strategy in the face of the sectional crisis of the 1850s. Concluding a long speech on the importance of the Union, the lawyer and diplomat Richard Rush called on his audience to remember Washington's Farewell Address. "If all this and more be insufficient to rouse us in support of the Union, let Washington's parting advice do it. Let that bind all hearts together. He helped to form the Union; he took it, as the best and wisest step possible for us; he took it—he would have fought, he would have bled for it."[43] Looking back from the vantage point of the 1850s, it would become clear that these civic texts had succeeded in exalting the Farewell Address to the level of sacred text, turning it into a weapon in defense of the nation's integrity.

CIVIC TEXTS were largely didactic in purpose, providing a civic education for children, and a primer to parents on how to impart a sense of obedience to future generations. They emerged out of a Lockean pedagogical tradition dominant in Anglo-American eighteenth-century culture that sought to impart authority without overt coercion, couching calls to obedience in a rhetoric of voluntary consent.[44] The republication of Washington's writings, to be read privately, pronounced publicly, and eventually taught in schools, helped keep Americans mindful of threats to national unity, urging them to shun partisanship, avoid foreign entanglements, obey the country's laws, and most of all, to preserve the Constitution. "Let us rally round the Constitution," said one orator, shifting his sights from Washington to his nation, "let us support with our countenance the constituted authorities in its administration." "Above all," warned a Baltimore newspaper, echoing Washington's political philosophy:

> if contrasting their present happy situation with the condition of foreign countries, and if duly appreciating the superiority, her citizens are justly led to ascribe it principally to the mild and harmonious nature of their federal constitution, they should be peculiarly watchful to guard the provisions of that constitution from the violence of infringement and the evils of abuse.

Revolution would not be tolerated. "Should ye find serious cause to complain of any evil either in the Constitution, or Administration, of your government," warned another orator, "seek redress in a *constitutional* manner; for the Constitution itself provides for its own amendment, and for the punishment of misconduct in those who administer it."[45] These statements—delivered not only after Washington's death, but also on patriotic occasions like July 4, February 22, and during elections—spoke to the need to build national unity and to promote obedience to the Constitution. But it was a particular kind of unity and obedience: a republican one, grounded in *consent*.

We can see in these civic texts the emergence of a nationalist canon, centered on the Constitution and a set of "Founding Fathers," a canon that promoted a nationalism grounded on republican principles. Disseminated on a vast scale, these texts made it possible for Americans to reenact the founding moment of consent across space and time. If Americans in the present and future did not actually sign the Declaration of Independence, or vote on the Constitution, they would nevertheless consent to the nation by learning to read as children using these texts, memorizing them in school, reading them over and over again in biographies, histories, almanacs, and other civic texts, and continuing throughout adulthood to read them aloud and celebrate them at public and patriotic ceremonies. Civic texts made the act of reading itself—in public and private, in homes and schools, toasts and parades—into a moment of civic engagement, as audiences reaffirmed their consent to the nation, thus reaffirming its republican character.

There was, of course, something deeply paradoxical about this process, for civic texts ultimately succeeded in transforming the U.S. revolutionary tradition into a force to suppress change. They managed, in short, to reconcile two opposite impulses: a revolutionary impulse that made the nation independent on the one hand, with a conservative impulse to preserve the institutional order on the other. In his exchange with Madison cited earlier, Jefferson had suggested that in a republic, future generations had to be given an opportunity to consent to their government—a formulation that, while tempting for its intellectual consistency, was ultimately unrealizable. Madison rejected this proposal, but offered no alternative formulation other than that of tacit assent. Indeed, throughout his life Madison exhibited a powerful conservative strain relying heavily on tradition, stability, and custom—all of which stood in tension with the nation's revolutionary tradition.[46] The emergence of these civic texts in effect offered a middle ground between Madison's and Jefferson's positions. Ongoing acts of consent among future generations would be promoted through informal political channels: by teaching babies to "lisp" the name of Washington; raising children on an intellectual diet of patriotic texts and festivals; making children and adults, men and women, active participants in marches, parades, and other forms of quasi-political engagement. By reading Washington's Farewell Address, by attending a July Fourth ceremony, by solemnly commemorating Washington's death, Americans, citizens and noncitizens alike, could ratify the legitimacy of their republican nation.

Partisanship

Washington died, as we have seen, during a period of political warfare so intense that many people believed it threatened the nation, and so it is not surprising to see civic texts urging Americans to shun partisanship and unite as a single national family. To be sure, these calls to imitate Washington and cherish the Union might seem, at first glance, to have served specific partisan purposes. It is among the most familiar of political tactics, usually invoked during times of perceived national crisis: a partisan or regional agenda is couched in a rhetoric of national unity.[47] Indeed, many Federalists viewed Washington's death as an opportunity to bolster their flagging party and promote their agenda. "The orators upon this occasion (who are generally attached to the ruling system of politics)," wrote the British ambassador, confirming the Jeffersonians' worst fears, "have wisely seized the occasion to raise the publick esteem for the federal constitution, and to strengthen the hands of the administration of Mr. Adams, by dwelling upon the strong and unequivocal approbation which the late president gave to both."[48] Partisan as the intent may have been, however, the result was far short of what the Federalists might have hoped. If Washington had indeed become a "text," as some of these eulogies suggested, it is useful to distinguish between the intention of the text's authors and the meaning it was given by audiences. Much as they tried, the Federalists ultimately failed to turn Washington into a Federalist icon. After his death, Washington became a symbol largely emptied of particular partisan connotations. Understanding how this happened is of great importance for understanding the role of partisanship in an emerging U.S. nationalism.[49]

Upon reflection, what may be most surprising about the commemorations of Washington's death is the relative *absence* of partisanship—especially among the Washington administration's most vocal opponents. Despite the intense partisan bitterness characteristic of the period, few scornful words were printed about Washington. To be sure, attacking Washington had always been a toxic political move, and never more so than after his death.[50] But the Republicans' response to Washington's death was not simply respectful silence, a pause until the former political attacks could resume. Members of both political parties went to great lengths to commemorate his passing.[51] Republican governors in Pennsylvania and Virginia immediately declared days of mourning. The prominent jurist St. George Tucker sent a private note to James Monroe—Jefferson's ally, recently elected governor of Virginia, and fervent enemy of the Federalists since his recall as minister to France earlier in the decade—which, even as it revealed lingering partisan bitterness, attested to Republicans' determination to overcome partisan sentiments in order to venerate Washington. "Permit me likewise to felicitate you," wrote Tucker, "on the happy opportunity which presents itself of demonstrating by your first official act, that you have a soul capable of forgetting its own injuries, and of participating in the warm Emotions of public Gratitude, in spite of memory, and personal considerations."[52]

Even the most partisan Republican newspapers overcame their "personal considerations" to participate in these warm emotions. Accounts of Washington's death printed in Republican newspapers differed in few respects from those in Federalist newspapers. "The afflicting intelligence of the death of Gen. *WASHINGTON*," reported the Republican Hartford *Mercury*, "exhibiteth sorrow in every human breast; and the voice of mourning is heard from the South to the North." The *Mercury* even published Washington's Farewell Address along with a ringing endorsement. "We have this day published entire, the LEGACY, left by the great WASHINGTON, the '*Father of his Country*,' to his children. It ought to be read in every School and Family in the United States." The Boston *Patriot*, another Republican newspaper, told its readers: "Washington's farewell address, ought to be preserved in every family of the United States, in letters of gold—it cannot be printed or read too often." Endorsing the Farewell Address—with its warnings about the "the baneful effects of the Spirit of Party"—the Republican press joined with the Federalist press in paeans to national unity.[53]

But alongside this wariness of partisanship, another strain was emerging in the Federalist and Republican responses to Washington's death. The accounts of Washington's life disseminated by civic texts were, slowly and haltingly, creating a space for a partisanship compatible with nationalism. Americans of radically different political persuasions were uniting in veneration of Washington, even as they continued to fight about all matters political. But the fight would take place on the level of interpretation and appropriation, as both parties sought to imbue Washington with rival meanings. Federalists could not make Washington into a Federalist icon largely because Republicans worked to make him into a Republican icon. Indeed, the Federalists could only stand by fuming while the Republicans "usurped" Washington's memory for themselves: "He was publickly and pathetically lamented and extolled by the leaders of the [Republican] party," an irate Federalist later remembered. "Achilles himself was not more inconsolable for the loss of his Patroclus: and even in the sacrifices of twelve young Trojans to his manes, he was far outdone by [Jefferson,] this illustrious modern mourner, with the remarkable difference, however, that whereas the one made victims of his enemies, the other selected for immolation, the friends of the lamented dead."[54] No doubt, given Washington's oft-expressed hostility to partisanship, it would have been difficult for either party to turn Washington into a partisan figure. Nevertheless, by choosing to appropriate him rather than to spurn him, the Republican political machinery succeeded in blunting any partisan gain the Federalists could make of his death.

Republicans and Federalists thus fought their partisan battles on the level of interpretation: seeking to use Washington's legacy to their own advantage, and in the process endorsing his nationalizing principles. This form of political combat would prove of major significance in the creation of American nationalism. And as with Washington, so with the other iconic texts of U.S. nationalism, the Constitution and the Declaration of Independence: these works, too, rapidly became dissociated from any explicitly partisan meaning. Even as people of vastly differing ideologies, regions, and races contested the meaning of these national icons, they rarely questioned the legitimacy of the icons themselves. In this way, partisan and ideological division could be encompassed within a broader imagined unity. Throughout the 1790s, for instance, Democratic-Republican societies, like their Federalist counterparts, urged their members to read the canonical texts of American nationalism, to cherish the Union, and to preserve national unity. "Let me therefore crave your attention whilst I read this precious instrument," declared a Democratic speaker at a 1794 July Fourth celebration, preparing to read the Declaration of Independence. "May the truths which it contains sink deep in our hearts, and animate us all as with one soul, in the defence of our country."[55] Radically diverse groups—Federalists and Republicans, even, on occasion, masters and slaves—could disagree about virtually all matters, and nevertheless unite in invoking the same shared symbols. Meaning different things in different hands, the symbols themselves remained shared.[56]

After the election of 1800, Jefferson of all people, the founder of the United States' first political party, declared, "We are all Republicans, We are all Federalists." With Republicans in power, traditionally Federalist political rhetoric—invocations of unity, calls to cherish the Union and obey constituted authorities, condemnations of partisanship and faction—became staples of Republican discourse. Indeed, Jefferson would continue to promote allegiance to the nationalist canon of sacred texts, urging "reverence" for the Declaration of Independence and calling on Americans to a "pledge of adhesion to its principles and of a sacred determination to maintain and perpetuate them." And in his 1809 inaugural address, James Madison similarly called the Constitution "the cement of the Union." This quality in American politics—to encompass political division within a larger national unity—may indeed have been Washington's greatest legacy. As François Guizot, the French historian and politician, would later write, "he has had this true glory; of triumphing, so long as he governed; and of rendering the triumph of his adversaries possible, after him, without disturbance to the state."[57] Just as Protestants and Catholics could worship the same Bible, and yet disagree about its interpretation, so Federalists and Republicans continued to pledge themselves to the same canonical texts, and yet fight among themselves about their meaning, and about the meaning of the nation, without questioning its essential legitimacy. The nation, in other words, was beginning to take on religious connotations.

Nationalism and Religion

Civic texts sought above all to attach the affections of the people to the nation. But how to make an abstract entity like a nation into the object of affection? The question was particularly fraught, since this nation was grounded not on an ideology of divine right or ancient tradition, but rather on the consent of the living: Americans would have to be taught to give their allegiance *by their own choice*.

There was a close parallel here to religion—particularly to evangelical Protestantism—which also sought to establish sentimental, affective bonds among audiences, impart certain norms of behavior, and inculcate a voluntary attachment to abstract principles. Not surprisingly, then, religious sentiments would inform and join with nationalism in the early nineteenth century in powerful ways. Given the strength of religious sentiments throughout the colonies—which had promoted popular political mobilization during the Seven Years' War and then again during the Revolution—it is perhaps to be expected that religion would serve as a motor for promoting a popular new nationalism.[58] The connection between religion and nationalism was complex, however, and lay not merely at the level of analogy—their shared ability to impart certain norms of behavior and feeling. More fundamentally, the connection lay at the level of *belief*: the deeply held religious sentiments of a broadly devout population would be mobilized in order to further the nation-building project, rendering the nation into a quasi-religious construction. Civic texts were central players in this process, with Bible reading serving as the model for the reading of civic texts, and for the range of audiences they sought to reach.

To reconstruct the meaning a text had in a certain time and place, it is necessary to consider the social and cultural context in which it was read. This insight is useful to bear in mind when thinking about the religious nature of civic texts, for their most immediate context was religious. Civic texts would be disseminated to a largely Protestant readership, in part through the writings and endorsement of clergymen. They were to be read in much the same way religious texts were to be read: through a process of internalization. They would, over time, help transform national icons like Washington and the Constitution into sacred icons, much like the Bible or Jesus Christ himself.

According to Protestant theology, particularly its Calvinist and Puritan strains, a direct relationship with the Word was an essential component of spiritual life. Hence, the readership of the Bible was to be as close to universal as possible. The prologue to a 1540 edition of the Bible stated the range of its intended readership, which could serve as an ideal summary for the intended readership of civic texts:

> Here may all manner of persons, men, women, young, old, learned, unlearned, rich, poor, priests, laymen, lords, ladies, officers, tenants, and mean men, virgins, wives, widows, lawyers, merchants, artificers, husbandmen, and all manner of persons of what estate or condition soever they be, may in this book learn all things that they ought to believe, what they ought to do, and what they should not do.[59]

Civic texts replicated Bible reading not just in the universality of its readership, but also in the *practices* by which they should be read. Particularly in dissenting Protestant traditions, Bible reading was "invested with an extraordinary intensity," as the scholars Guglielmo Cavallo and Roger Chartier have observed. "Whether the Bible was read silently by individuals, read aloud to the assembled family in the privacy of the home, or read in church, Bible reading was present at every moment of existence."[60] The sermons, pamphlets, broadsides, almanacs, and other civic texts we have been examining drew both on the scope of the Bible's readership and on this model of "intensive reading," and mobilized it to nationalist ends. They would teach Americans—men and women, young and old, learned and unlearned, rich and poor—to read certain texts (like Washington's Farewell Address and the Constitution) with the same "extraordinary intensity" that they brought to their reading of the Bible.

The canonization of Washington and of his Farewell Address occurred not merely through the widespread dissemination of his image and his writings, then, but through the *way* audiences were told to read and interpret them: as sacred practice. Hymns and odes to Washington sung in churches; eulogies to Washington delivered by clergymen; his writings republished as catechisms or psalms; the Farewell Address recited in churches around the nation: all exalted Washington and his writings to the level of the sacred. Some clergymen even called for Washington's Farewell Address to be incorporated into the Bible itself. "Americans," urged one eulogist, concluding his exegesis of the Farewell Address, "bind it in your Bible next to the Sermon on the Mount that the lessons of your two Saviors may be read together." It is unclear if any of his listeners actually did bind Washington's Farewell Address in their Bible, but what is clear is that this method of joining texts was more than a mere metaphor. There was a long tradition in Anglo-American culture of binding certain religious texts—usually psalms—into family Bibles. In 1782, for instance, a Philadelphia publisher circulated proposals for what would be the first American Bible, concluding his proposal with an offer "to bind up [Nonconformist minister Isaac] Watts's Psalms with the above mentioned Bible." Clearly texts that were bound into a Bible were meant to foster certain kinds of religious practices like singing in church or reading at home. When this eulogist called for Washington's Farewell Address to be bound into his audiences' Bibles next to the Sermon on the Mount, thus making Washington into a "Savior" on par with Jesus, he was not just making a clear statement about the sacredness of a text like the Farewell Address, but was also urging his audiences to read the Farewell Address as they read the Bible. Converted into psalms, reprinted in almanacs, and bound into Bibles—the three most commonly owned books in early America—Washington's words would be disseminated on the scale of, and through the same means as, religion.[61]

If reading is, as the historian Roger Chartier argues, "the act by means of which a text takes on its meaning and acquires its efficacy," the meaning that was being created from Washington's writings was decidedly a sacred one, stamped with what one eulogist called "the sanction of divinity." Thanks to these kinds of civic texts—the eulogies, sermons, pamphlets, and more—the Farewell Address would be read with the same "extraordinary intensity" as the Bible. Certainly that is how religious authorities said it should be read. "There is nothing in profane history to which this sublime address to the states can be compared," the Reverend Thaddeus Harris told his Charlestown, Massachusetts, audience. "In our Sacred Scriptures we find a parallel in that recapitulation of the divine instructions and commands, which the legislator of the Jews made in the hearing of Israel, when they were about to pass the Jordan." Only a few weeks after Washington's death, a Boston newspaper ran an advertisement proposing to print a collection of Washington's writings, "to contain those invaluable Compositions of our late Chief and President, by which he communicated to his Country, and the World, a system of Political Morality, that can only be surpassed by the Scriptures of Divine Revelation." While it would be impossible to make generalizations about how texts as widely diffused as these were interpreted by their vast audiences, there is considerable evidence that at least some audiences did indeed imbue the Farewell Address with more than human authority. A report from Newark, New Jersey, for instance, recalled that when the Farewell Address was read at the close of a eulogy, "It was the voice of WASHINGTON, speaking from the tomb."[62]

THESE TEXTS endowed not just Washington's writings, but the symbol of Washington himself, with a strong measure of divinity. "Never, perhaps, were coincidences in character and fortune, between any two illustrious men who have lived, so numerous and striking, as between MOSES AND WASHINGTON," said Jedediah Morse in a widely reprinted eulogy. "Both were born for great and similar achievements; to deliver, under the guidance of Providence, each the tribes of their respective countrymen, from the yoke of oppression, and to establish them, with the best form of government, and the wisest code of laws, an independent and respectable nation." Some differences existed, to be sure. "It is true," admitted the Reverend James Kemp in a Maryland oration, "when Washington was called from his peaceful abode, no mountain smoked—no thunder roared—no voice was heard from heaven." Nevertheless, like Moses, Washington delivered his people, latter-day Israelites, to the Promised Land.[63] Other eulogies found Washington's likeness in the New Testament. "Favored beyond the leader of Israel, not only with the prospect, but with the fruition of the promised blessing," Washington "has retired," George Richards Minot announced in a eulogy that circulated so widely it would be excerpted in a later schoolbook, "like that prince of meekness, to the *Mount,* whence he is to ascend, unseen by a weeping people, to the reward of all his labors."[64]

12. *John James Barralet,* Apotheosis of Washington *(1802). This
popular image, which went through at least four printings
in the nineteenth century, infused the
Washington veneration with religious associations.*

The comparisons were obvious: was not Washington's mother also named
Mary? Some eulogists did not seem to mind verging on blasphemy. "Who can
behold such a character without an admiration, if it may be so expressed, *almost
to idolatry!*"[65] The religious analogy was promoted not only through written
texts, but also through images representing Washington as a saint ascending to
heaven after his death. The most widely disseminated of these was John James
Barralet's *Apotheosis of Washington,* begun in 1800, which portrayed Washington
ascending to heaven with various figures mourning below (figure 12). Depicted
as a saint, Barralet's Washington was being lifted from his tomb by a winged Father Time, and ascending to heaven. With the Indian below joining a female representation of liberty mourning Washington's death—both against a background

13. *Material objects like this pitcher—produced in England—diffused John James Barralet's* Apotheosis of Washington *in the most prosaic forms, integrating Washington veneration into Americans' daily lives.* "A Man / without example / A Patriot / without reproach." *Ceramic pitcher, Liverpool, England, 1800–1805.*

of forlorn women and children—the image invoked an ideology of universal and benevolent rule, casting Washington as a leader who unified public and private, secular and sacred realms. Truly did he rule in the hearts of all his people. Barralet's image was not merely disseminated through engraving and prints: it was also diffused through material objects, such as quilts or commemorative pitchers (figure 13). In another popular image, Washington soars on the clouds above Mount Vernon, as a winged cherub places a laurel wreath on his head (figure 14). These sorts of images, widely diffused as prints and material objects, performed the same kind of cultural work as the sermons and eulogies we have seen. In this sense, such images were civic texts, exalting and sacralizing symbols like Washington or the Constitution, nationalist icons that would bind the nation together.

The mourning commemorations themselves blurred the boundaries between secular and sacred rituals. On the one hand, they had an obvious secular element: the resolutions of Congress, the marches and parades in the streets, the toasts at various private meetings. On the other hand, the mourning in churches, the hymns and odes to Washington: all were clearly, as one eulogist commented, "of a religious nature." Nationalist rituals were rendered into religious rituals, nationalist practices into religious practices. A book originally published in 1800 (and then republished after the Civil War) entitled *Hymns and Odes on the Death of George Washington* announced on its title page that: "These are the united offerings of Piety, Patriotism and Genius, at the shrine of WASHINGTON." As Americans across the country worshipped at the shrine of Washington, commentators repeatedly drew explicit parallels between these mourning rituals and

14. *David Edwin after Rembrandt Peale,* Apotheosis of
Washington: *another image that helped to sacralize Washington.*

religious rituals. "And how suitable is it," exclaimed John Brooks, "that we *here* unite to mingle our griefs, and associate our solemn obsequies, with religious rites!" The very mourning rituals by which Americans remembered Washington became a way for audiences to think of the new nation in sacred rather than secular time, and to imbue the nation with religious significance. "In the history of mankind we shall often find remarkable similarity of events and circumstances, occurring in the most distant countries & periods of time," proclaimed a South Carolina eulogist. And so the comparisons between Washington and various religious figures carried, for him, a typological significance. "With this memorable mourning of the Jewish nation, for the loss of their eminently worthy and amiable Josiah," he added, "how striking is the resemblance that appears in the universal, unfeigned mourning, now exhibited by the American people, for the loss of their great, and excellent, and beloved WASHINGTON." Another eulogist found meaning in the biblical account of Moses's death, when "the whole Nation of Israel wept for Moses thirty days."[66] This moment of national mourning became the occasion for Americans to reenact sacred history.

IF IMAGES OF Washington as a saint carried a hint of Roman Catholic traditions, while the comparisons with Old Testament figures hearkened to Jewish traditions, the nationalist religion promoted by civic texts was articulated in a distinctly evangelical Protestant key. It drew on the most emotive aspects of Protestant theology to further the nationalist proselytizing. Terms like "feelings" and "heart" were ubiquitous. Washington's words were "to be engraved on every heart," his writings "engrave[d] . . . on the living tablet of the feeling heart," his Farewell Address bound "about our necks, and engrave[d] . . . on the tablet of our hearts." Washington would become "first in the hearts of his countrymen"; his Farewell Address, a text that would "bind all hearts together"; and the Declaration of Independence, a text whose truths would "sink deep in our hearts."[67] By thus internalizing Washington's words—by, so to speak, accepting him as their national savior—audiences would be born again as Americans.

Civic texts drew on old Protestant traditions to disseminate their nationalist religion. When they urged audiences to engrave Washington's Farewell Address onto their hearts, they were replicating the process by which the Bible was rendered into the primary source of religious authority: through the heart. The idea of inscribing certain important words on the heart descends from a passage in the Second Corinthians—in which the New Testament is said to be "written not with ink, but with the Spirit of the living God; not in tables of stone, but in fleshy tables of the heart"—and it would remain a prominent feature of Protestant pedagogy through several centuries.[68] Consider the great Protestant reading manual, the *New-England Primer,* estimated to have been published in somewhere between 3 and 8 million copies between the end of the seventeenth century and the middle of the nineteenth, a work that taught children both reading and religious mores at once. The little stanza that taught the letter "H" made the association between the heart and the Bible quite clear—"My Book and Heart/ Shall never part"—even adding a picture of a Bible inside a heart, a crude pictorial representation of how biblical verse is internalized (figure 15). To read the Bible properly, according to this Protestant understanding, was to "engrave" it into one's heart: to inculcate its message not through the rational workings of the mind, but through the affective workings of the heart.

This idea of engraving certain key words on the heart became a prominent feature of evangelical Protestantism, which emphasized internal, spiritual conversion over the more ritualized forms of high-church Protestantism. For evangelicals in particular, all reading was meant to replicate this model of Bible reading: it should touch the "heart" or the "affections," and further the process of internal conversion.[69] Evangelicals in the eighteenth century had relied considerably on publishing to promote their spiritual work—in 1740, at the peak of the First Great Awakening, 67 percent of publications treated religious topics—a phe-

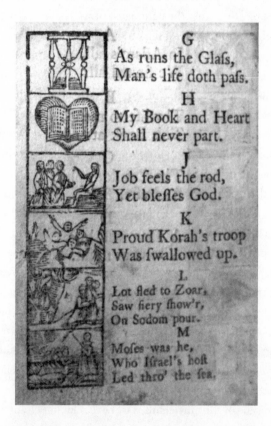

15. Page from The New-England Primer, improved . . . (New London: Printed by T. Green, 1785), offering a visual image of how the Bible is to be incorporated into one's heart. This understanding of how texts are internalized by readers would serve as a model for the reading of civic texts.

nomenon that would greatly increase in the nineteenth century, with the development of institutions (such as the American Tract Society) that printed millions upon millions of pamphlets and other religious literature: all meant to reform and convert sinners and touch the hearts of readers.[70]

This evangelical Protestant association between reading and spiritual life became a central strain in U.S. nationalism, and it shaped both the meaning of Washington as national icon—as "father of the nation"—and the process by which that symbol was disseminated and inculcated. Americans would be taught to "engrave" Washington's words on their hearts just as they had been taught to internalize passages from the Bible. They would be taught to take Washington into their hearts just as they took Jesus into their hearts. They would be taught to read the Constitution as they read the Ten Commandments. Few images made these associations among the nation, the Constitution, the Bible, and the founders clearer than the frontispiece to a 1792 Bible (the first to be printed in New York): The center of that image was an allegorical representation of America, a woman in a headdress, her elbow resting on a plinth with the names of Washington, Montgomery, Franklin, Warren, Adams, and other heroes of the American Revolution. In one hand she holds the U.S. Constitution, rolled into a scroll on her lap, while her other hand reaches forward to accept the Bible from a kneeling woman. Above the two stands a third woman holding a liberty pole with liberty cap held aloft.

Few images better portrayed the synthesis of nationalism, religion, and the Constitution. The association with Washington was made not just through his name inscribed on the plinth, but at the end of the Bible, which listed the names of subscribers. At the top of that list appeared: "GEORGE WASHINGTON ESQ. PRESIDENT OF THE UNITED STATES OF AMERICA."[71] Washington and the Constitution had been quite literally incorporated into this new American Bible. As Washington's words would be thus engraved on readers' hearts, his Farewell Address bound in family Bibles alongside Jesus' Sermon on the Mount, his words, and the sacred texts of American nationalism—the Declaration of Independence, the Constitution, the Farewell Address—would come to be read with the same mix of belief and obedience as the Bible.

Through the workings of civic texts like these eulogies and pamphlets, Washington's life itself became a "volume" to be read, studied, and even memorized by future generations, serving the same function the *New-England Primer* had served for generations of children in the past.

16. *Texts like the frontispiece to this 1792 Bible continually infused sacred elements into nationalist commemoration.* The Self-Interpreting Bible: Containing the Sacred Text of the Old and New Testaments (New York: Hodge and Campbell, 1792).

Providence has opened to our children a volume so pure and instructive, as *the life of* WASHINGTON! Ye American *parents,* and
teachers of youth! Study this volume; become masters of its important contents; transcribe them into your own hearts and lives; and
thus convey to them with happiest effect to your children and
pupils.[72]

Washington's life became, in effect, a sacred text. As they were disseminated
throughout the nation, civic texts helped inaugurate a veritable cult of Washington. They created nationalist traditions that could be replicated long into the
future by consenting Americans, perpetually bound together in everlasting remembrance of Washington: "It shall be the last national office of hoary dotage,"
read one such text, "to teach the infant that hangs on his trembling knee, to lisp
the name of *WASHINGTON.*"[73]

Contemporary observations suggest the success of this nationalist evangelization. A Russian traveler touring the United States in the early nineteenth century noted that the country was "glutted" with portraits of Washington. "Every
American," he wrote, "considers it his sacred duty to have a likeness of Washington in his home, just as we have images of God's saints." Such was the reverence
for Washington that his portrait was usually "the finest and sometimes the sole
decoration of American homes."[74] If many Protestant Americans would have
shuddered at this analogy between worshipping Washington and worshipping
saints, there was certainly nothing uncommon about imagining Washington as a
biblical character. For the same reason, Washington's home soon became a quasi-
religious site, as Americans from all regions began making pilgrimages to Mount
Vernon. Washington's tomb, in particular, was portrayed in numerous engravings, rendered into a familiar image for people who had never been anywhere
near the Potomac River (figure 17). Schoolbooks would later reinforce Mount
Vernon's religious associations, telling readers, in the words of one 1840 schoolbook: "Mount Vernon is sacred in the eyes of Americans; it is the spot to which
many a Pilgrim wends his way, anxious to drop a tear at the tomb of the Father
of his country."[75]

Civic texts, in short, were disseminated in much the same way—through the
same processes, located in the same psychic space—as religion. The parallels between the Washington mourning rituals and the rituals associated with the First
and Second Great Awakenings are marked. Mass gatherings by audiences in
towns and rural hinterlands; the use of newspapers to publicize these gatherings

17. *Washington's tomb was frequently represented in nineteenth-century*
engravings. Note the lone figure making his way, pilgrimlike, to the tomb.
Tomb of Washington, Mount Vernon, T. *Doughty, Del.*
from a drawing made on the spot by J. R. Smith.

and promote a sense of "event-ness"; sermons delivered by clergymen, later republished by printers; reports of the audiences' emotive responses—"Tears flowed from every eye . . . lamentations burst from every lip": all these characteristics of the Washington mourning rituals were also characteristics of mass religious revivals. Religion—and, more specifically, evangelical Protestantism—furthered the inculcation of U.S. nationalism, in the process fusing nationalism and evangelical Protestantism into a very potent mix. Indeed, it may not be an exaggeration to suggest that the dissemination of nationalism circa 1800 might itself be seen as a kind of Great Awakening—number 1.5, perhaps.

IN HIS INFLUENTIAL work on the origins of nationalism, Benedict Anderson equates nationalism not with an ideology like communism, liberalism, or fascism, but rather with a cultural system, like religion.[76] Tracing the process by which civic texts canonized nationalist icons like Washington offers persuasive evidence for Anderson's contention. Just as Christians had been taught to read and venerate biblical texts, and to follow their mandates, so were Americans taught to read a set of civic texts much as they read the Bible. Fusing nationalist symbols to sacred traditions, civic texts promoted what has properly been called a *civil religion*.[77] These civic texts thus help clarify something that has long remained unexplained in studies of American civil religion: how it was inculcated.

Certain aspects of all of this are worth noting, as they will be developed in subsequent chapters. First, the creation of a liberal U.S. nationalism entailed not simply the promotion of the most basic of its political exigencies, such as the creation of fraternal bonds among Americans and a sacred attachment to the political order. It also entailed the formation of the autonomous individual of liberal political theory, the individual endowed with moral agency who would be willing and able to give his or her consent to the political order; and in this project, religion was a central player. The idea that runs through all of Christianity, but which was particularly powerful in evangelical Protestantism—that grace is located within each individual—helped lay the foundations for a conception of individual autonomy which would eventually serve as the basis for liberal citizenship.[78] Versions of Protestantism that flourished in British North America had long emphasized a particular conception of individual moral autonomy, elevating human agency or autonomy as a central feature of religious life. But it was in large measure the evangelical Protestantism that flourished in the eighteenth and nineteenth century—with its emphasis on inner conversion and its rhetoric of the "heart"—that elevated a certain conception of individual moral autonomy. In distinction from many other forms of evangelical culture, as the religious historian Mark Noll argues, American evangelism particularly "stressed the need for moral choice": that redemption ultimately stems from the morally autonomous individual. This evangelical Protestant emphasis on the individual was particularly influential in the "religious populism" that swept through the nation after the American Revolution.[79] The emphasis on personalized readings of the Bible and inner conversion, and the insistence with which individuals were urged to engage in social action—all turned the focus of Protestant evangelicalism inward, toward the individual as locus of moral responsibility. In short, the language of evangelical Protestantism that civic texts spoke so fluently helped promote an idea of the individual as moral agent, which, as we will see, would become a central feature of U.S. nationalism and would powerfully inflect the meaning of freedom and slavery that would emerge out of it.

But if this conception of individual autonomy lay at the heart of an emerging liberal political practice, the religious traditions in which this conception developed contradicted other aspects of a nationalism based on consent, and raised troubling questions about the extent of its republican character. It will be obvious that giving the Constitution a divine authority—rendering it "our Ark of Covenant"—detracted from its republican nature. References to "the constitution God has given us," for instance, flagrantly contradicted the principle that the Constitution was founded on the consent of the governed.[80] Even conservatives committed to stability and respect for the government expressed some qualms. "That he ought to live in our Memories, and be transmitted to posterity as a Character truly worthy of Imitation is Right," Abigail Adams observed to her sister in late January 1800. But, she insisted, "To no one Man in America, belongs the Epithet of *Saviour* of his Country." One month later, Adams was even more bemused. "Two months have chiefly been appropriated to funeral honours to the memory of Gen'll. Washington," she wrote. "I know not that in any modern Times, either Kings or Princes have received equal honors."[81] Adams may have been motivated in some measure by jealousy on behalf of her husband, but the basic point was valid: such excessive veneration—verging on deification—carried dangerously antirepublican implications. Legitimating the nation on the authority of dead fathers or, even worse, on the basis of a single "savior," stood in violation of the most basic republican principles.

Resignation, Gratitude, and Consent

"A king is a king," the philosopher Slavoj Žižek has written, "because his subjects treat him like one and not the reverse."[82] Even in a monarchy, legitimacy must be cultivated. People must be persuaded to treat a king like a king—and thus imbue him with the political legitimacy necessary for the government to function. Where monarchies could appeal to tradition or to ancient, mythologized memories, however, the American republic—stripped of an ancient past on which to found its legitimacy, openly proclaiming that it was grounded on the consent of the governed—somehow had to bind Americans together on ahistorical, republican principles. One response was to turn veneration for Washington into a bond of union itself. But this response threatened to undermine the republican character of the nation—to turn Washington into a republican king.

Civic texts resolved this dilemma in two ways. First, the eulogies celebrated Washington not for his military or political achievements, but rather for his willingness to give up power. Second, they focused not only on Washington, but also on peoples' gratitude to Washington, freely given, which, according to the eulogies, was the true source of his greatness. Examining this aspect of the eulogies offers some instructive lessons about how civic texts more broadly worked to promote the often conflicting goals of nationalism and republicanism.

ONE SURPRISING ASPECT of the Washington commemorations was their general lack of interest in Washington as general or president. They skipped quickly over everything that made Washington a great military and political figure, to dwell at length on his willingness to give up power. "His only ambition"—so ran a common refrain—"is to enjoy the pleasing retrospect of a well spent life, far from the acclamations of the gratitude of his countrymen." This was, to be sure, the image of himself that Washington chose to project; but the alacrity with which it was taken up suggests there was something important happening here. Washington's "honest ambition," as it was frequently called, made him a modern-day hero, and distinguished him from tyrannical figures of antiquity like Alexander the Great or Julius Caesar. "Former heroes were stimulated to deeds of civil enterprise or exploits of martial achievement by ambitious designs of personal aggrandizement or the lawless lust of power," said Thaddeus Harris in a Charlestown, Massachusetts, eulogy. "But he accepted command with reluctance; exercised it with moderation; voluntarily resigned it . . . How matchless this conduct! How unrivaled does WASHINGTON appear."[83]

For his contemporaries, Washington's resignations—first as commander in chief of the army and again as president of the United States—stood as the most thrilling acts of his life. "Truly affecting and important was the scene, when he resigned his commission!" exclaimed Uzal Ogden in a widely reprinted eulogy delivered in New Jersey. "So august was the spectacle! So moving were the acts! To see the beloved and unconquerable Hero surrender the insignia of his trust in subordination to the civil power, and literally convert the sword into a ploughshare, was an instance of moderation and greatness, noble as rare." In-

18. John Trumbull, George Washington Resigning His Commission,
which hangs in the rotunda of the U.S. Capitol, exalted Washington's act of
resignation as commander in chief of the army in 1783.

deed, it would be difficult to exaggerate the impact of his resignation, not only for Americans, but throughout the Atlantic world. King George III, when told by an interlocutor that George Washington planned to return to his farm if successful in the war, is said to have replied, "If he does that . . . he will be the greatest man in the world."[84] Although the story may be apocryphal, it nevertheless suggests the power of Washington's iconic act among the Enlightenment intelligentsia of the Atlantic world, a wonder shared by many in the United States. "August Spectacle! Glorious Example!" said the Reverend Jonathan Mitchell Sewall. "For my own part, I never contemplate it, but each fibre vibrates with rapture, and the vital current trembles through every artery of my frame!"[85]

This sense of wonder and rapture was disseminated to Americans by civic texts like the eulogies and newspapers that commemorated Washington, and also in more vivid form by paintings and monuments. John Trumbull, a former officer on Washington's staff who was commissioned by Congress to paint a series of nationalist portraits to hang in the U.S. Capitol, chose to portray Washington's res-

19. The Washington Monument in Baltimore, Maryland.

ignation as commander in chief at the close of the Revolution as one of the central acts of the nation's founding. In fact, he made the resignation the very center
of one painting's action. With every eye in the painting turned to Washington's
outstretched hand—the glory of the act highlighted by the light that seems to
emanate from Washington himself—Washington resigns his commission (figure
18). Few images better portray the scene: Washington humbling himself by standing before a seated Congress, giving up the military power entrusted to him.[86]

The same moment was depicted in Baltimore, in the nation's first major
monument to Washington, constructed between 1815 and 1829 (figure 19). Standing 168 feet above the street, Washington holds his arm out, a rolled-up piece of
paper in his outstretched hand. One might assume, at first glance, that the paper
is the Constitution, or perhaps the Declaration of Independence. But instead it is
Washington's commission, being tendered in resignation. For nineteenth-century

audiences, this was the iconic moment of Washington's life, the moment that established his goodness as well as his greatness, the moment to be remembered in
monuments and memorials, in sermons, speeches, biographies—and in schoolbooks. "Who has not felt," read one sentence for practice and correction in an
1843 schoolbook, "the moral *Granjeur* of Washington?"[87]

This intense focus on Washington's act of resignation had an important ideological effect: it helped balance the antirepublican implications of the civic
texts' filio-piety. To celebrate Washington was not merely to celebrate a man; it
was to celebrate political principles of virtue and popular sovereignty. James
Monroe, still governor of Virginia in 1802, made this distinction clear. "It is
believed that it is the practice of all governments to dedicate certain days to publick festivity," he observed. "In the European monarchies it is the practice of
the people to celebrate the birthday of their King. Thus they degrade themselves
by an unbecoming personal idolatry. With us it is the practice to celebrate the
birthday of principle." Drawing—indeed, exaggerating—the contrast between
monarchical and republican forms of celebration, Monroe's conceit suggests
how U.S. civic texts worked to balance republicanism and nationalism. Thanks
to these and so many other civic texts, Washington would be remembered less for
his *use* of power than for his *abdication* of it. "It was for him to set as great examples in the relinquishment, as in the acceptance, of power," said the Presbyterian minister John M. Mason, in a New York eulogy. "No mortified ambition;
no haughty disgusts; no expectation of higher office, prompted his retreat."
Washington's resignations became the paradigmatic republican acts. By handing
power back to the people, his resignations, first as general, later as president, affirmed the political principle of *consent* at the heart of the United States' republican nationalism. Thus it was that for many Americans, as the Reverend Samuel
Stanhope Smith put it, Washington "appeared more great and worthy of esteem
in resigning, than he had done in gloriously using, his power."[88]

By emphasizing the extent to which Washington's true greatness had
stemmed from his abdication of power, rather than from its use, these texts
helped to resolve, or at least mute, the contradiction between liberty and authority they themselves had manifested. Again, few expressed this idea more clearly
than Henry Lee, in his famous eulogy. "To the horrid din of battle sweet peace
succeeded," said Lee, "and our virtuous Chief, mindful only of the common
good, in a moment tempting personal aggrandizement, hushed the discontents
of growing sedition, and, surrendering his power into the hands from which he
had received it, converted his sword into a ploughshare." This Old Testament

millennialism invoked ("They will beat their swords into plowshares"), Lee concluded with another line, soon to become among the most celebrated in American lore. Washington, he concluded, taught "an admiring world, that to be truly great you must be good."[89] Would celebration of Washington subvert the nation's commitment to republicanism? No, because it was not Washington, but Washington's goodness, his virtue—it was, in short, a political principle—that was being celebrated.

THE WASHINGTON EULOGIES mitigated the antirepublican overtones of the Washington cult in another way: by focusing on the public's sincere and universal demonstrations of *gratitude,* freely given. According to the commemorations, Americans' gratitude toward Washington testified to their republican character.[90] It offered a powerful rebuttal to skeptics of republicanism around the world who believed that republics were inherently ungrateful—that their commitment to the polity could not be sustained—and thus inevitably collapsed into anarchy or tyranny. Americans' gratitude toward Washington offered reassurance that the United States, in contrast to other republics throughout time, would remain steadfast in its republican virtue.

Focusing on the people's gratitude emphasized the element of consent involved in celebrating Washington. According to the eulogies, the celebrations were not a simple reflection of Washington's greatness. Instead, they turned this formulation on its head: Washington was great because of the peoples' freely given gratitude.[91] "How sublime, and how singular the glory!" exulted Samuel Stanhope Smith, "thus to receive the voluntary homage of a free, and a great people—the homage of equals paid, not to pre-eminence of rank, but of virtue—not extorted by the command of power, but the unconstrained effusion of the heart!" Focusing on the people rather than the person—on the worshippers, rather than the worshipped—amounted to a republican form of hero worship. "The Glory of our Country is promoted by the ceremonies which evince our sorrow for the death of WASHINGTON," reported the Boston *Mercury.* "We therefore carefully preserve all the details which reach us, that posterity, when tracing in the page of faithful History, the virtues and services of this illustrious American, may discern the full and strong proofs of the sensibility, affection and gratitude of his Countrymen." Public displays of gratitude were thus cause for great pride, offering "proof, singular and pleasing" of Americans' virtue. "This day we wipe away the reproach of republics, that they know not how to be grateful," declared an exultant John M. Mason. "Let not future inconsistency charge this day with hypocrisy."[92]

Far from reducing Americans to passive subjects guided by the beneficent hand of Washington, the displays of gratitude offered in the national mourning located Americans' *consent* at the heart of a new nationalism. "In defiance of a doctrine which DESPOTS have taught their *Slaves,*" said Joseph Allen in a Massachusetts eulogy, "that INGRATITUDE is the vice of a REPUBLIC, WE are assembled my FELLOW CITIZENS at the recommendation of our GOVERNMENT, to commemorate the virtues and deplore the loss of the BENEFACTOR of OUR COUNTRY." It was thus the very act of venerating Washington that distinguished the American republic from a monarchy. "Nations, it is true, have often assumed the garb of sorrow, and pompously displayed the emblems of grief for the death of Emperors or Kings," admitted Timothy Bigelow in a Boston eulogy. "But, on our happy shores, we fear no tyrant frown; we need nothing extraneous to prompt our sighs; our sorrows are the spontaneous effusions of grateful hearts; they demonstrate our respect to be sincere; and are scarce less honourable to the nation, than to the memory of him whose death they deplore."[93]

Through these sorts of civic rituals—both in public celebrations and in private reading—civic texts would expand the bounds of the nation beyond its political boundaries of citizens and soldiers to encompass the larger "population," a notion just then emerging as a political category, thus helping lay the groundwork for a new, modern form of politics.[94] By building monuments to Washington, by continuing to read and memorize his words, by raising their children on Washington's political virtues and values, Americans could enact the political order imagined by liberal political theory, engaging in daily acts of consent to the U.S. nation, acts that could be replicated long into the future among generations of unborn Americans.

Still, such vague formulations left out some difficult questions: who, precisely, was to engage in these acts of consent? The idea of the nation promoted by civic texts posited a nation of potentially limitless reach, both spatially and temporally. The nation was to extend until the end of time itself. Unfixed to any territorial boundaries, it contained within itself a world-historical mission to remake the world in its image. Nevertheless, if not well developed, it was clear that the universality of U.S. nationalism had its limits. As to where exactly those limits lay—well, that explosive matter was left for the millions of unborn Americans to work out.

2.

WASHINGTON'S FAMILY: SLAVERY AND THE NATION

—◦►◦◄◦—

The slaveholder, in cases not a few, sustains to his slaves the double relation of master and father.

—FREDERICK DOUGLASS[1]

George's Death and Martha's Predicament

"Washington's life," the historian Philip Morgan has noted, "was inextricably entwined with slavery."[2] His death was no exception. Washington had spent the day of December 12, 1799, touring his plantations and surveying his slaves' labor, even as the weather turned icy with freezing rain blowing through the Virginia countryside. It was a fateful decision. Upon his return, he sat directly down to dinner, still dressed in his wet clothes. He came down with a cold the next day that by the early morning of December 14 had become a severe throat infection. Ministered by his slaves over the course of a long and agonizing day, Washington's windpipe gradually closed, making it difficult for him to swallow and eventually to breathe. He knew his end rapidly approached as he lay on his bed, slowly suffocating. Summoned by his slaves, several anxious doctors bled him repeatedly—too much, though they could not know it—blistered his skin, and induced fits of coughing and vomiting in their dying patient.

Slavery was evidently on Washington's mind as he lay dying. Of the people in the room as Washington died, four blacks (two maids, a seamstress, and his butler, Christopher Sheels) outnumbered three whites (his doctor, his secretary, and Martha). But that was not the only thing that suggested Washington, on his deathbed, was wrestling with demons of his own making. At about 4:30 in the afternoon, probably quite scared and certainly in severe pain, though stoic as usual, Washington asked Martha to bring him two wills from his desk. Confirming their contents and, perhaps, casting a glance at Sheels, who refused to leave his bedside all day, Washington performed his last act. He had one will burned in the fireplace. A few hours later he was dead.

When the unburned will was made public, one provision stood out among all others: Washington had emancipated his slaves.[3]

IF WASHINGTON'S DEATH was a national tragedy for most Americans, for Martha Washington it was a personal one. Her life had already been full of personal trials: she had lost her first husband, Daniel Parke Custis, when she was twenty-six; she was the last survivor of eight siblings; she had seen all four of her children pass away; and now, suddenly, her companion of nearly forty-one years had died. Washington now faced the legal limbo that adhered to wealthy widows: vast property holdings, but owned in trust only. If some widows saw this situation as liberating—including, possibly, the twenty-six-year-old Martha Dandridge Custis, who had vigorously taken charge of her first husband's estate when he died in 1757—the sixty-eigtht-year-old Martha Dandridge Custis Washington could not have seen her new responsibilities as anything other than a burden. The complex task of managing her husband's estate, consisting of Mount Vernon and four other plantations, run by a labor force of 317 slaves, fell abruptly to her.

Nor could she mourn her own way, in private. Very little of the Washingtons' personal life since the Revolution had been private, and George's death was no exception. The remarkable public response to his death—and the claims made on his legacy by his mourning countrymen—added yet another burden, as Martha faced the unique duties incumbent upon her to continue managing her husband's legacy. As letters of condolence began flooding in from all over the country and even around the world, many of them enclosing copies of eulogies for her to read, others asking for locks of hair or other relics of her dead husband, the epistolary demands became so great that Congress extended her franking privileges. Even more distressingly, Washington reluctantly acceded to the request of Congress that her husband's body be removed from Mount Vernon, where she had hoped to keep it, and eventually to lie alongside it, and relocated to a national mausoleum to be built in the U.S. Capitol (a move that would never come to pass).

If all that were not enough, Martha also found herself obliged to fulfill the terms of her husband's final will: the emancipation of his slaves. George had spent many years thinking the matter of emancipation through, and the instructions he left in his will were careful and explicit. Legally, he could free just 124 of the 317 slaves working on his plantations at the time of his death—40 slaves were leased from a neighbor, and another 153 slaves were his only in trust.[4] Known as the dower slaves, they (or their mothers) had once been owned by Daniel Parke Custis, Martha Washington's first husband, and would pass to his heirs upon her death. Under the property laws of the age, Washington had controlled the use of—and benefited from the profit produced by—those slaves, but he never had the legal authority to free them.

Thus, Washington's will freed fewer than half the slaves working on his plantations—and, with the single exception of his wartime valet, William Lee, a public figure in his own right, freed none immediately. For the 123 slaves concerned, although their emancipation was proclaimed, their freedom would only come upon Martha's death. "To emancipate them during her life," Washington wrote in the will, "would, tho' earnestly wished by me, be attended with such insuperable difficulties on account of their intermixture by Marriages with the Dower Negroes, as to excite the most painful sensations, if not disagreeable consequences from the latter, while both descriptions are in the occupancy of the same Proprietor."[5] Washington saw no need to precipitate the breakup of the families formed among his and his wife's slaves, causing his wife painful sensations or "disagreeable consequences"—unwelcome appeals by desperate slaves, perhaps, or even the absconding of whole families. As for the slaves who were too young to be freed, they were to be provided for by their masters or mistresses, taught to read and write, trained into some useful profession, and freed at the age of twenty-five. Old slaves were to be provided for out of his estate.

All in all, Martha's various burdens—her obligations toward the national "family" mourning the father of the nation, and to her more immediate "family" of slaves—must have seemed overwhelming. It may not be surprising, then, that when Abigail Adams came to visit Martha some months after George's death, she observed Martha suffering under these many strains. "Mrs. Washington with all her fortune finds it difficult to support her family," wrote Adams, "which consists of three hundred slaves." According to Adams, the aspect that imposed the greatest pressure on Martha's second widowhood stemmed from the problems created by her husband's will. If George had intended the delay in abolition to spare Martha various "disagreeable consequences," his hopes were not borne out. In fact, George's will entailed consequences more burdensome and terrifying for Martha than anything he had anticipated.

Martha ultimately took it upon herself to free her husband's slaves early: some two years before her own death. But it was not humanitarian reasons that drove this early emancipation—the existing evidence suggests she disapproved of freeing slaves—nor was it from the expense or difficulty involved in "support-ing" the slaves.[6] It was out of fear. "It was found necessary," reported Martha's grandson, to free the slaves "for *prudential* reasons."[7] Hidden in this circumlocu-tion was the fact that George's deathbed emancipation had put Martha's life in jeopardy. As she and the slaves all recognized, the longer she lived, the longer their bondage extended. "In the state in which they were left by the General," wrote Adams, "she did not feel as tho her Life was safe in their Hands, many of [the slaves] would be told that it was [in] their interest to get rid of her—She therefore was advised to set them all free at the close of the year."[8]

Martha Washington, first First Lady, wife of the "father of the nation," lived her last days among hundreds of enslaved people she called family, people she believed would try to kill her.

Slavery and the National Family

After Washington's death, civic texts—eulogies, pamphlets, political orations, and more—helped create and consolidate the nation by casting it as a national family: Americans united as children under George Washington, the father. If this family metaphor served to unite nations in other national contexts, in the United States the metaphor could not bear the weight with which it was bur-dened. Even as it was being deployed to unify the nation after his death, Wash-ington's family—his private, posthumous family—was threatened by rebellion and murder. By more closely examining the nature of Washington's family, we see that Martha's dilemma carries important lessons on the nature of slavery within the national family.[9]

Civic texts domesticated Washington's image by making this public figure into the father of each private family. "Our country mourns her father": so stated the United States Senate in its resolutions republished in newspapers throughout the county.[10] The idea of Washington as father was articulated in nearly every eulogy, pamphlet, schoolbook, and image of Washington. "The American Family," declared Massachusetts clergyman David Tappan "is mourning its deceased Father." A eulogy delivered in Salem, Massachusetts, carried the metaphor further, casting Washington as both a father and even as a sort of mother. Washington, it announced, was inextricably tied with the American nation: "at whose birth he presided, whose infancy he nourished, over whose childhood he watched with a parent's care and solicitude, and which he never left till it had attained the strength of manhood." The idea of Washington as father was universal: "It was WASHINGTON," said Josiah Dunham, "who reared our infant country from a state of childhood and weakness, to that of manhood and strength." The widespread image of Washington as father offered a powerful means to assert common bonds of nationality, and to unite Americans as one single family.[11]

This was not a casual analogy; the metaphor of Washington as father of the nation was taken very literally. Perhaps no one pursued it further than the New York politician and diplomat Gouverneur Morris, in his widely reprinted eulogy. "Assembled to pay the last dues of filial piety to him who was the father of his country," began Morris's eulogy; he went on to push the metaphor to its outer limits, finding divine meaning in Washington's lack of birth children. Though Martha adored Washington, Morris stated, "no fruit was granted their union."

> Who shall arraign, Oh GOD! thy high decree? Was it in displeasure, that to the father of his country thou hadst denied a son? Was it in mercy, lest the paternal virtues should have triumphed (during some frail moment) in the patriot bosom? AMERICANS! he had no child—BUT YOU—and HE WAS ALL YOUR OWN.[12]

A reviewer of Morris's eulogy singled out this excerpt for quotation and criticism, even as it repeated the idea of Washington as father. "Heaven has surely done enough in making him the *father of a nation,*" the critic responded in equal earnestness. "Having bestowed so splendid a gift, it could not reasonably be censured for *withholding a son.*"[13]

Because Washington's fatherhood was understood so literally—and because it served as such a powerful means of uniting Americans—the eulogies dwelled on the details of his private life to learn about the precise nature of his paternity. "First in war, first in peace, and first in the hearts of his countrymen," the Virginia general Henry Lee famously declared in his eulogy of Washington. The oft-forgotten words that followed were just as important: "he was second to none in the humble and endearing scenes of private life."[14] To fully understand Washington's greatness, Americans would have to focus their attention on his private life. "It is not then in the glare of *public*," wrote Mason Locke Weems in his wildly popular biography of Washington, "but in the shade of *private life,* that we are to look for the man. . . . It is the private virtues that lay the foundation of all human excellence."[15] By focusing intensely on Washington's private life, such texts made Washington's family a matter of great political significance.

Here lay the problem, for Washington was not the father of a Northern, white, free-labor household, but of a Southern plantation. His "family" consisted not just of whites, but of hundreds of enslaved blacks. And the texts that celebrated Washington's paternity as "father of the nation," the texts that took his fatherhood so literally, were forced to take this aspect of his private life into account. They could not, and they did not, ignore Washington's ambiguous status as father to the nation *and* as father to his slaves; and in the process, they continually reminded audiences of the presence of slavery within the national family, and of the threat slavery posed to the nation's unity and stability.

No text better exemplified the ambiguous nature of Washington's paternity than Edward Savage's famous painting *The Washington Family* (figure 20). Painted in fits and starts between 1789 and 1796, Savage's painting was particularly influential in domesticating Washington's image; it would become one of the most famous and widely diffused images in nineteenth-century America. Though it was on public display virtually from the moment it was finished, its real fame was established through its widespread reproduction. Savage began reproducing the painting before he had even completed the original—at one point bragging somewhat tactlessly to Washington that sales of the prints would earn him at least $10,000 in a single year. Washington does not seem to have minded; he liked the painting so much he ordered four prints from the artist. Savage's efforts were responsible for only a tiny fraction of its mass circulation, however: the image would be reproduced in mezzotint, woodcut, lithograph, and even (by schoolgirls') embroidery. A half century later the painter Rembrandt Peale would comment that it was "Known all over the United States—No engraving having a more extensive sale."[16] Savage's painting helped introduce the Washington family into thousands of American homes, fusing individual and national families, persuading audiences to think of themselves as part of the Washington family.

Like so many of the texts that celebrated Washington, Savage's painting posited a glorious future for the nation. At a time when its very existence was still

20. *Edward Savage,* The Washington Family, *1789–96.*

precarious, the country split by bitter partisan quarrels, international turbu-
lence, and sectional division, such projections of Washington's image into a
serene future worked to unify the nation and calm the political storms afflicting
the young country. "In the General appears the serene commanding aspect of a
venerable man," a reviewer of the painting commented in 1802, "whose presence
alone calms the tempests." Indeed, this peaceful national future may well be the
subject of the painting. As one scholar has noticed, Washington is not the center
of the painting, nor is his family. The real center is the vista behind: the Potomac River stretching out to the west, the vast panorama of space that would ensure the nation's millennial progress through time.[17] Even the floor, which looks
something like a chessboard, recalls the western territories divided into perfectly
geometric patterns, ready for future settlement: from nation to township to family. The title of the painting—*The Washington Family*—is intentionally ambiguous, referring not just to Washington's immediate family, but also to the legions
of countrymen in the present as well as the future who would hang his picture on

their parlor walls, who would settle the western territories depicted in the painting, and who would continue to think of Washington as their own father. By locating Washington at the head of the national family, this painting tempers anxieties about the nation's future.

But hidden away in the shadows of Washington's family portrait is a figure who disrupts any simple account of the nature of this national family and its future: a black slave. Is he William Lee, Washington's valet during the war, who was freed by Washington's will? Or is he Christopher Sheels, the man who stood by Washington's bedside all day, refusing to leave his post as Washington died—a dower slave who could not be freed by Washington (and who had unsuccessfully tried, a few years earlier, to run away to freedom)? The man's identity is not clear, for the largely featureless face renders this figure, alone in the painting, anonymous.[18] If the spectral slave is in Washington's family portrait, he is not of Washington's family, standing to the side, off the chessboard that composes the floor of the room. His clothing only adds to his marginality, the doublet blending into Martha's chair, the same color as the curtains. While everyone else looks forward, he looks off to the side, averting his eyes from the new slaveholding capital, and indeed from the family itself. He is a shadowy figure who complicates the meaning of Washington's paternity.[19] Was he, one wonders, among the slaves who threatened Martha Washington's life? His presence serves as a reminder of the presence of slavery within the national family. Would American slaves threaten the future of the national family as the Washington slaves had endangered Martha's future?

THE INSTITUTION OF SLAVERY in North America had always brought with it fears of insurrection. Whites during the colonial period both feared and expected that slaves would resist their bondage in violent ways. "The one reaction to slave conspiracies most notably lacking" during the colonial period, the historian Winthrop Jordan has noted, "was *surprise*."[20] This fear of slave insurrection would hardly end with the Revolution: to the contrary, the specter of whites fighting to free themselves from what many called British slavery suggested that blacks might do the same with regard to American slavery.

Fear of slave insurrection would persist as an undercurrent in many popular texts of the post-Revolutionary period. "Throughout the [late-eighteenth-century] literature," the historian David Brion Davis remarks, "slavery appears, with metaphorical regularity, as the architectural flaw, the noxious weed in a garden, the hidden disease in an otherwise sound and growing body."[21] Surely the most famous instance appeared in Jefferson's *Notes on the State of Virginia*, the only book Jefferson ever wrote, a text that was widely read and discussed in the nineteenth century. (So canonical had it become by the late 1820s, the abolitionist David Walker would take aim at its arguments on race in his 1829 pamphlet denouncing slavery, *Appeal to the Coloured Citizens of the World.*) "Can the liberties of a nation be thought secure?" asked Jefferson, who (notwithstanding his deism) famously predicted divine retribution for the sin of slavery. "Indeed I tremble for my country when I reflect that God is just: that his justice cannot sleep for ever: that considering numbers, nature and natural means only, a revolution of the wheel of fortune, an exchange of situation, is among possible events: that it may become probable by supernatural interference! The Almighty has no attribute which can take side with us in such a contest." With one half of Virginia's population transformed by slavery into "despots," and the other half into "enemies," Jefferson gloomily predicted that slavery "will probably never end but in the extermination of one or the other race." Jefferson would continue through the rest of his life to express similar fears. "If something is not done, and soon done," he wrote to the Virginia jurist St. George Tucker in 1797, "we shall be the murderers of our own children . . . [for] the revolutionary storm now sweeping the globe will be upon us."[22]

Jefferson's "revolutionary storm" referred not just to the revolutions sweeping across Europe—these inspired euphoria rather than terror in Jefferson—but to the storm taking place just off the North American coast, in the former French colony of Saint Domingue, or Haiti as it would be called after it achieved its independence. Nothing during the early republican period fanned the fears of slave insurrection—and an apocalyptic war between the races—more than the Haitian revolution, the volcano that sent refugees pouring into American cities, filling newspapers with lurid tales of violence, and slave owners' imaginations with even more terrifying images.[23] "When the Negro grasped desperately at freedom too, he confirmed America's great expectations as well as one of America's greatest fears," observes Winthrop Jordan. "St. Domingo suggested an awful progression in racial slavery: white rule, insurrection, black usurpation." The fears inspired by the Haitian revolution were widespread, noted by foreign travelers and Americans alike. In 1793, for instance, the French minister Edmond Charles Genet commented on the "terror among all the owners of blacks" inspired by the revolution in Saint Domingue. The thousands of desperate refugees pouring into U.S. seaboard cities carrying tales of death and destruction personified the fate that might well await Americans. "The scenes which are acted in St. Domingo," James Monroe anxiously predicted, "must produce an effect on all the people of colour in this and the States south of us." Numerous were the predictions of apocalyptic doom if slavery continued its present course. "Will not our posterity curse the days of their nativity with all the anguish of Job?" asked St. George Tucker, inverting the familiar trope of jeremiad to castigate his present by invoking future generations of tormented Americans. "Will they not execrate the memory of those ancestors, who, having it in their power to avert evil, have, like their first parents, entailed a curse upon all future generations?" The specter of Saint Domingue loomed even larger with Jefferson, who expressed terror at the idea of these "Cannibals of the terrible republic" pulling into American ports, sending "black crews, supercargoes & missionaries thence into the Southern states," fomenting insurrection throughout the Americas.[24]

These fears of slave insurrection exacerbated uncertainty about the nation's stability that George Washington had expressed in his Farewell Address. In 1800, in the year following Washington's death, they struck American shores when a conspiracy of slaves introduced the specter of Saint Domingue to Virginia. Gabriel's Rebellion, coming in the midst of heated political battles between Federalists and Republicans leading up to the election of 1800, linked partisan feuding with the threat of slave insurrection in the minds of many.[25] Fears of slave insurrection and the threat it posed the nation would only grow during the first decades of the nineteenth century. "The danger of a more or less distant but inevitable conflict between the white and the black inhabitants of the Southern states of the Union," wrote Alexis de Tocqueville when he toured the United States in the 1830s, "perpetually haunts the imagination of the Americans, like a painful dream." To his surprise, Tocqueville found this fear common in the North: "The inhabitants of the North discuss these perils daily, although directly they have nothing to fear from them." But it was in the South, not surprisingly, that Tocqueville found these fears most pervasive, attested to by the very silence he encountered: "In the Southern states everyone is quiet; no one speaks of the future to strangers; they avoid explaining it to friends; everyone hides it, so to speak, from themselves. There is something more terrifying about the silence of the South than the clamorous fears of the North."[26] Nor was Tocqueville the only foreign traveler to notice this pervasive terror among Southerners. "I know that the southern men are apt to deny the fact that they do live under an habitual sense of danger," wrote Frances Kemble, a British diarist who lived in Georgia for several years in the late 1830s. But, she added, "a slave population, coerced into obedience, though unarmed and half fed, *is* a threatening source of constant insecurity, and every southern *woman* to whom I have spoken on the subject, has admitted to me that they live in terror of their slaves."[27]

These fears culminated in 1831, with the revolt by Nat Turner in which dozens of whites were slaughtered, many in their sleep. Turner's insurrection, in the words of Thomas Gray, the man who recorded and published Turner's *Confessions*, "could not fail to leave a deep impression, not only upon the minds of the community where this fearful tragedy was wrought, but throughout every portion of our country, in which this population is to be found."[28] Gray's prediction seems to have been borne out. The insurrection, wrote Jane Randolph to her husband Thomas Jefferson Randolph, grandson of the former president Thomas Jefferson, has "aroused all my fears . . . and indeed . . . increased them to the most agonizing degree . . . My most torturing imagination had never conjured up anything so terrifick as this unpitying and horrible slaughter, and the very excitement and appalling precautions which it is thought necessary to take up even here . . . keep up my fears." If her fears were calmed during the day, "by night my fears return in full force, and there is no scene of horror that my imagination does not conjure up." Like Martha Washington, Jefferson's grandchild-in-law lived in fear that her black "family" would murder her.[29]

Paranoia about slave insurrections would continue as long as the institution of slavery endured. The most dramatic episode occurred in Mississippi in 1835, when "the insolent behavior" of several Mississippi slaves led to a local panic among white residents. In Madison and Hinds counties, women and children were collected in a central place and guarded by armed militia, while squads of men roamed the country seeking out "the imagined insurrectionists." Several whites and more than a dozen blacks were hung. Similar panics recurred throughout the antebellum period. The historian Clement Eaton concluded "that the Southern people suffered at time and in certain sections from a pathological fear of their slaves."[30] It is precisely this fear that made John Brown's raid on Harpers Ferry in 1859 so spectacular. The aim of Brown's raid was not a military takeover of the South; it was to inspire slaves to rise up in revolution. For white Southerners, there could be no more terrifying specter. Within individual families and within the national family, so long as American slavery endured, the possibility that slaves might rise up and destroy the nation would continue to haunt Americans.

THE THREAT SLAVERY posed to the nation's future was a theme in the eulogies that followed Washington's death. George Richards, a former schoolmaster and pastor of the Universalist church in Portsmouth, New Hampshire, dwelled at length on Washington's slaveholding in his popular eulogy, imagining the fate that would have awaited the nation had Washington (and, presumably, others) emancipated slaves too soon. "Could the patriot, the lover of his country, have justified the action, to his better feelings, if a dangerous precedent, originally established, by so august a character, had loosed the universal bonds of servitude, throughout the southern provinces?" he asked. "In truth, insurrection, rebellion, plantations destroyed, and cities ascending in flame, might have been the unhappy effects of premature benevolence." For Richards, the consequences of such "premature benevolence" were nearly apocalyptic: "The convulsions which would, inevitably, have followed in the south, must have shaken the different States to their centres; burst the last, feeble legaments [sic] of a dissolving confederacy; and laid waste a consuming continent in the blaze of servile, or civil war."[31] Such expressions linked the fear of slave insurrection to the nation's very existence. This linkage was clear in a funeral eulogy delivered by Samuel Stanhope Smith, president of Princeton College. Defending Washington's controversial policy of neutrality toward France during the 1790s, Smith urged his listeners to look around at their happy circumstances. Had Washington given in to the partisan fighting that exploded around his policy of neutrality, Smith argued, the nation's future would be grim indeed. "We might have been the prey of civil discord—we might, like the wretched inhabitants of Saint-Domingo, have been the dreadful victims of domestic treason."[32] Reaching for examples of political faction and civil discord, Smith, living in New Jersey, invoked the specter of the Haitian revolution.

Fears about partisan quarreling continually slipped into fears about slave insurrection, stoking doubts about the nation's stability—even for non-slaveowners like Smith, not to speak of slave owners throughout the South.[33] The continued presence of slavery made whites throughout the country—in New Hampshire and New Jersey as well as in Virginia and South Carolina—ever more anxious about the dangers of disunity, and about the nation's potential to explode into servile or civil war. The *Monthly Magazine and American Review,* in the same issue it reviewed various Washington eulogies, concluded an article on slavery with these gloomy words: "It would extend this paper too much to investigate the grounds of that terror which prevails among us respecting negro in-surrections."[34] Hopes about the nation's future were repeatedly marred by these apocalyptic fears of slave insurrection: "a consuming continent in the blaze of servile, or civil war."

Civic texts addressed these anxieties about the national family and its poten-tial to collapse into insurrection and anarchy by promoting two distinct narra-tives of Washington and slavery. The first, which might be called an abolitionist interpretation, dwelled on Washington's decision to free' his slaves, linking his status as emancipator of his slaves to his experience as Revolutionary general leading the emancipation of his nation from Britain. This narrative reconciled troubling contradictions between the Revolution's rhetoric and the continued presence of slavery. It also muted the threat of slave insurrection—and threats to national unity—through a teleological account of inevitable future emancipa-tion: if slavery was an unfortunate legacy inherited from the pre-British past, it was also an institution the American Revolution had inexorably set on the path of extinction. The second narrative deployed a myth of plantation benevolence that appeased dreaded fears of slave insurrection. Though it posited no moment of eventual abolition, it portrayed slavery as a benign institution grounded on values of paternal affection, and it even created a space in which slavery could be reconciled with the principle of consent. Both narratives promoted a paternalist ideology of early American nationalism, casting it in very different ways. And both located slavery squarely at the center of Washington's life.

Washington as Abolitionist

Washington's life was marked by ambiguity and silence on the question of slav-ery. During his early life, Washington displayed a callousness toward slavery typ-ical of most eighteenth-century planters. Over the course of his long career, however, he seems to have become persuaded of the immorality—or at least the impracticability—of slavery in the new republican nation. Nevertheless, al-though he was occasionally importuned, Washington never spoke out publicly against the institution. In his private correspondence, Washington sporadically expressed a desire to free his slaves, and stated on a few occasions that he was contemplating schemes to do so. He never did act against slavery during his life, however; it was only after his death that he finally expressed his will, in a very public gesture against slavery. Given his silence and ambivalence during his life, it was possible for his posthumous mythmakers to mold him in whatever image they wished to promote.

Washington's slaveholding was a troubling matter for some people. "It must be owned that he was a slaveholder," declared his early biographer John Corry, "and his exemplary kindness to his dependants cannot reconcile us to that inconsistency in a man who was so strenuous and successful an assertor of liberty."[35] One way of resolving this "inconsistency" was to cast Washington as a proto-abolitionist. The awkward fact that Washington remained a slaveholder throughout his life could be downplayed, and his posthumous emancipation highlighted. In this narrative of Washington's life, his will became a canonical text: a final farewell address to the nation, to be read and remembered along with his other major writings. Unveiled soon after his death, the will was widely republished and quickly became a celebrated document. In 1800 alone, Washington's will was published as a pamphlet in thirteen separate editions, included in

21. Father Tammany's Almanac, for the Year 1801 (Philadelphia: Printed for William Young, 1800), with a reprint of Washington's will. Note the clause at the bottom of the right-hand page, in which Washington wills freedom to his slaves.

the compilations of Washington's writings published after his death, added as an appendix to innumerable printed eulogies and proliferating biographies, published in newspapers throughout the country, and reprinted in many collections of Washington's writings.[36] It was even included in some almanacs, to be read alongside the time of the sunrise and sunset and various other practical information (figure 21). This breadth of circulation added Washington's will to the emerging canon of nationalist texts. Americans were urged to read his will along with his other great works, and to observe its words of wisdom. "When the lore of independence thunders on the tongue, and shouting millions gladden at the sound," said George Richards in his New Hampshire eulogy, imagining future celebrations of Washington and the nation, "the will, the testament of WASHINGTON, should always close the public service of the joyous day."[37]

Just as he had when he resigned his commission as commander in chief of the army in 1783, as he had when retiring from the presidency in 1796, Washington had again left the nation some parting words of paternal advice upon this, his final retirement. And the message he gave his countrymen, according to this reading of Washington's life, was decidedly in condemnation of slavery. "What sweet emotions of philanthropy moved in his breast," asked a Baltimore eulogist, "while he penned that *heaven-inspired* sentence; ALL MY NEGROES ARE TO BE FREE?"[38] More overt statements were expressed farther north. "How amiable, how consistent is the character of this illustrious man!" exclaimed Timothy Bigelow, lawyer, Freemason, and Massachusetts Federalist. "Himself the champion of political freedom, he disdained to hold his fellow-creatures in abject domestic servitude. An advocate for mild and equal laws, he disclaimed the right of unlimited control over the actions of others." Although Washington had held slaves his entire adult life—only freeing them in his will, in an ambiguous gesture that dumped the whole problem into his wife's lap—Washington was here rendered into someone who "disdained to hold his fellow-creatures" in slavery. Inconsistency, ambivalence: all complexity was elided. And so Washington's posthumous emancipation could be cast as an act to be emulated by his mourning countrymen. "Highly honourable would it be to our fellow-citizens in the South, if this magnanimous example should have its proper effect," Bigelow continued. "If, in their treatment of the wretches subjected to their power, they would emulate the benevolence of Washington; if, obedient like him to the voice of humanity, justice and religion, they would abandon the savage claim of holding human beings in slavery, and repeal every statute in their code which countenances a principle so derogatory to the laws of Freemen."[39]

This narrative of Washington as proto-abolitionist provided a happy resolution to the problem of Washington's slaveholding. By freeing his slaves, Washington proved himself true to his republican principles, resolving the troubling inconsistency that had plagued his life and continued to plague the nation's. "In the *public* legacy of the Father of our country, we have the means to support and perpetuate the fair fabric of national independence and happiness, which his hand erected," declared Aaron Bancroft, who would become a biographer of Washington. "His *private* Will testifies that the love of liberty in him was a living principle. He has undone the heavy burden and let the oppressed go free." The will, in this reading, served as a capstone, cementing Washington's greatness. "The character of WASHINGTON is complete," concluded a New York newspaper in reference to the will. "Nothing human could add to it—nothing detract from it." Washington's deathbed emancipation thus became the culmination of a lifetime commitment to freedom for all people. "The last authenticated act of his life was worthy of himself," declared Thomas Thacher in a Massachusetts eulogy. "Thus *uniform* in all his conduct, was this FRIEND of the *Rights of Mankind*— thus consistent, were his *Republican Principles.*"[40] The problem of Washington's slaveholding—here taken to be antagonistic to republican values—was resolved into a coherent narrative. Becoming the emancipator of *all* his people, white as well as black, Washington stood firmly on the side of antislavery, antislavery on the side of republicanism. Making Washington into a proto-abolitionist would thus serve the cause of antislavery and even—in some hands—of racial equality.

No eulogy made this case better than one delivered by Richard Allen, cofounder of the African Methodist Episcopal Church, in Philadelphia, and reprinted in newspapers in Baltimore and Philadelphia, and perhaps elsewhere.[41] "Our father and friend is taken from us," Allen's address began—his "our," the very first word of his eulogy, projecting his audience of African Americans into the American family. "We, my friends, have peculiar cause to bemoan our loss. To us he has been the sympathizing friend and tender father." Washington was here cast as "father" not just to whites, but also to black Americans. Like other eulogists, Allen argued that Washington's greatness stemmed not from his role as general, but from his status as *emancipator*: it was Washington's resignation, his refusal to enslave his people, that made Washington the *true* father of his people. Allen's eulogy went further than others in connecting Washington's status as emancipator during the Revolution to his status as emancipator of his slaves. "If he who broke the yoke of British burdens 'from off the neck of the people of this land,' and was hailed his country's deliverer, by what name shall we call him who se-

cretly and almost unknown emancipated his 'bondwomen and bondmen'—
became to them a father, and gave them an inheritance!"[42] Washington was here
cast as an emancipator of a different kind. By making manumission the act that
turned Washington into "our friend and father," Allen inverted the language of
patriarchy so often used to legitimate slavery. He made blacks, both slave and
free, the *true* sons, who were *truly* delivered, by Washington, now "father of all
our people." Likening black slaves freed in Washington's will with white Americans who had once been enslaved by George III, Allen's eulogy sought to create
familial bonds between Washington's black and white "children." As father to
both, Washington played the role of Moses, delivering "his people," white and
black, from bondage.

What gave this eulogy its power was its link to a conception of the Revolution
as a struggle against slavery: the moment when Americans freed themselves from
the "slavery" of the British. As we shall see, this understanding of the Revolution
was a powerful one, and played an important role in shaping later U.S. national-

22. *Rendering of the proposed seal for the United States, which depicted*
Americans as Israelites freed from slavery.

ism. It promoted an understanding of the United States as a new Israel, its people delivered from bondage into freedom. Perhaps no text made this association more clearly than Benjamin Franklin's proposed seal for the United States depicting a scene not from the American Revolution, but rather from the Old Testament (figure 22). In a typological reading of U.S. history, this proposed seal for the United States depicted the Egyptian Pharaoh (standing in for the British) and his army being destroyed by the closing waters of the Red Sea, as the Israelites, led by Moses (standing in for Americans and Washington), watch the cataclysm from the sea's far shore. In short, it was Americans—white Americans—who, like the ancient Israelites, had been led out of slavery into the promised land of freedom.

The language of slavery and emancipation powerfully shaped this account of the Revolution and of U.S. history. By disdaining to make himself tyrant after the war, Washington had, according to a New York eulogy, gone "to his humble retirement, pursued by the tears, the prayers, the affections of an emancipated, a grateful people." Washington was thus recast as a latter-day Moses. "Did the leader of the hosts of Israel deliver that nation from Egyptian bondage?" asked Jonathan Mitchell Sewall. "So did WASHINGTON ours from the galling yoke of British tyranny . . . After rescuing a nation from slavery, did the former lead them to the very borders of the promised land? WASHINGTON did more—He put us into the full possession of the heritage of our Fathers." Washington was in every sense an emancipator: "He himself retired to private life," averred John Foster in a Boston eulogy, "and rejected every other compensation but the heartfelt pleasure of having emancipated millions from the yoke of bondage, and laid a foundation for the freedom and prosperity of millions more, yet to be born!"[43] White Americans, in this account, defined themselves not so much in opposition to slavery, but as a people freed "from the yoke of bondage."

This narrative of American history as a progression from slavery to freedom suggested that all slavery—of whites to the British, as of blacks in chattel slavery—would eventually end with emancipation. In this regard, it responded to fears about the chaos chattel slavery threatened to wreak upon the nation. Would slavery explode—as it had in Saint Domingue—in an eruption of violence, destroying the nation from within? This narrative provided a reassuring answer: the Revolution had set slavery inexorably on the path to emancipation. Just as Washington had ended his life as emancipator, so would the nation live out its republican credo and, in the course of time, abolish slavery. In the meantime, of course, this storyline had little to say about the continued existence of slavery within the nation.

SOON AFTER INDEPENDENCE, a history of slavery was developed to explain its presence in a republic whose guiding principle—government by consent of the governed—had suddenly made the institution problematic. Slavery, according to this history, was yet another barbarous legacy inherited from the past, much like feudalism, entail, and associated evils of unjust societies. "Our forefathers sow[ed] the seeds of an evil, which, like a leprosy, hath descended upon their posterity with accumulated rancour, visiting the sins of the fathers upon succeeding generations," wrote the Virginia jurist St. George Tucker. Imposed by the past's dead hand, responsibility for the institution did not fall on the living. "It is ... unjust to censure the present generation for the existence of slavery," Tucker insisted. The Revolution—understood as a struggle in which enslaved Americans had freed themselves from British bondage—was the conceptual glue holding this narrative together. White Americans, just like enslaved Africans, were victims; the true oppressors had been the British. "This infernal trafic originated in the avarice of British Merchants," said George Mason in the Constitutional Convention. What was more: "The British Govt. constantly checked the attempts of Virginia to put a stop to it." Many others agreed. "I am not the man who enslaved them," wrote Henry Laurens, the wealthy South Carolina planter who served as president of the Continental Congress; "they are indebted to Englishmen for that favor." Charles Fenton Mercer of Virginia, one of the guiding lights behind the colonization movement, similarly held that slavery was "fastened upon" Americans by England.[44]

The most famous instance of this view of slavery stands in Thomas Jefferson's first draft of the Declaration of Independence, where he assailed the British monarch for allowing the slave trade to the Americas, calling it a "cruel war against human nature itself." The Continental Congress had enough sense to delete this passage, but it could only have been written by someone who believed that living Americans could not be held responsible for the crimes of past generations of Britons. And this view would persist for many years. In the 1850s, commenting on the history of slavery, Richard Rush, eminent lawyer and diplomat, and son of Benjamin Rush, signer of the Declaration of Independence, placed the blame for slavery squarely on England's shoulders. "England forced upon us the importation of slaves from Africa," Rush insisted. "We strove to prevent it while colonies, but could not."[45] This invented past conveniently absolved the living of any responsibility for the institution. Slavery was a legacy of a barbarous past; it was the dead, not the living, who were to blame.

This understanding of slavery as a legacy inherited from the past allowed many to believe that the republican revolution had placed it on the path toward extinction, a belief that defused any need to act against it. Consider one of the most famous spokesmen for American liberty, Patrick Henry, who assailed slavery as "a principle as repugnant to humanity as it is inconsistent with the Bible and destructive to liberty." Henry perceived the evils of slavery as clearly as anyone: "I will not, I can not justify it." And yet his solution was to put faith in a benign republican future, imagining that "time" would eventually free his slaves. "I believe a time will come when an opportunity will be offered to abolish this lamentable evil." Jefferson held out the same hope for the magical workings of "time." In 1814, though frustrated by "the general silence which prevails on this subject as indicating an apathy unfavorable to every hope," Jefferson continued to insist, "Yet the hour of emancipation is advancing, in the march of time." Jefferson's last word on the subject, a mere six weeks before his death—still counseling inaction, still looking to beneficent time—was almost poignant in its Enlightened blindness: "A good cause is often injured more by ill-timed efforts of its friends than by the arguments of its enemies. Persuasion, perseverance, and patience are the best advocates on questions depending on the will of others. The Revolution in public opinion which this cause requires, is not to be expected in a day, or perhaps in an age; but time, which outlives all things, will outlive this evil also."[46] Madison, the last of the Founding Fathers, also never stopped believing, as he wrote in 1831, "that the time will come when the dreadful calamity" would end. Washington, first of the founders, held the same belief in the power of time to resolve the problem of slavery. When asked to speak out against slavery, he refused, stating that he expected "to see some plan adopted, by the legislature by which slavery in this Country may be abolished by slow, sure, & imperceptable degrees." He looked to a benign futurity, to "time alone," as he once put it.[47]

This view that slavery would disappear through the workings of time was spread not just through the founders' words, but also pictorially, through popular prints and images of Washington. Among the most startling of these are later reproductions of Savage's portrait, which provided a stark account of slavery disappearing from the national family. Updating the Washington family for the rising middle class of the mid and late nineteenth century, these reproductions preserve the Washington family, the core of Savage's painting, but alter the sur-

23. E. B. *and* E. C. *Kellogg*, The Washington Family (*c. 1845*), *lithograph.*

roundings in important ways. The neoclassical columns and chessboard floor—tokens of an Enlightenment sensibility—have been replaced by a Victorian parlor, that spatial manifestation of middle-class family norms. The wilderness in the background, the Potomac River stretching out to the western Appalachians, has been tamed, converted into wallpaper in one portrait (figure 23), viewed on the side through a window in the other (figure 24). But most important of all, the slave in the Washington portrait has disappeared: erased in one portrait, replaced by a white butler in the other.[48] One might say that these paintings offer a pictorial representation of the founders' belief that slavery would simply disappear in the course of time. Slavery has been erased from the national family. The uncertain future—and, in particular, the threat that slavery posed to the nation's continued existence—has been overcome in this reassuring account. If slaves were present as a legacy inherited from the past, they were destined—as a result of the principles proclaimed by the Revolution and implemented by the Founding Fathers and the founding documents—to disappear.

Of course this was not how Washington had experienced slavery. His decision to emancipate had been a halting one, long reflected upon but only acted upon

24. *William Sartrain after Christian Schuessele*, The Washington Family (1865).

at the very last minute, in the throes of painful suffocation and bloodletting, the result of indecision and procrastination that continued until the very end. The very ambiguity of his act and his words ensured that, if this abolitionist interpretation of his life would later become dominant, in the early nineteenth century it was not the only way to imagine Washington's relationship to slavery.

Washington and Paternalism

If some popular texts promoted an image of Washington as proto-abolitionist in order to oppose slavery and to appease anxieties about the future, other texts posited a very different account of Washington's relationship to slavery. Numerous descriptions of Washington as "father" of his slaves promoted a paternalist view of slavery that emphasized the affective bonds between master and slave, bonds that paralleled those among white citizens. They used Washington's national paternity to promote an emerging myth of plantation benevolence. This narrative of Washington and slavery did not try to erase the presence of slavery from Washington's life. It integrated it into his daily life from childhood to death.

Just as Washington's image had been domesticated by civic texts—the public figure rendered private "father" to each American family—so this narrative would offer a domesticated image of slavery, transforming the image of the labor regime slowly but surely into what many nineteenth-century Americans would call it: the "Domestic Institution."[49] A response to fears of insurrection and national instability, the image of Washington as benevolent patriarch also erased the coercion involved in slavery, planting seeds that would later flower into a proslavery nationalism.

Popular accounts of Washington's death promoted the view that sentimental bonds had united Washington's family, both white and black. Audiences expressed keen interest in Washington's last moments, and were rewarded with detailed descriptions of Washington's heroic bleedings, his composure in the face of death, and his last words. The classic deathbed scene in Western literature had long involved the dying patriarch surrounded by his family, and Washington's death was no exception.[50] Many accounts of Washington's death specifically mention the presence of his slaves in the room at the time of his death, and pic-

25. *Anonymous, Death of Washington Dec. 14 AD 1799. In truth, blacks in the room as Washington died outnumbered the whites. Note the stoicism of the whites in this fictionalized portrait, which contrasts with the weeping slaves.*

torial representations based on these accounts proliferated. Figure 25, for instance, dating from the middle of the nineteenth century, invited antebellum audiences into Washington's private life, making them spectators of Washington's last moments. The print depicts Martha with a steeled look, sitting near her two grandchildren, two doctors, and two slaves. One of the slaves at the foot of the bed is on his knees, weeping. Interestingly, the slaves are the figures who express the most emotion in the painting. Perhaps because he had no children of his own, Washington's relations to his slaves here seem to offer evidence of his benevolent fatherhood. Like grieving children, they weep and kneel—unlike the white adults in the painting, who retain a certain emotional self-control.

We saw in the last chapter that Washington's fatherhood, the affection his white countrymen expressed for him, was understood to be freely given, rather than coerced. The paternalist account of Washington's fatherhood made much the same claim: Washington's fatherhood of his slaves was understood to rest on affection, rather than coercion. "His mansion was the seat of hospitality," said eulogist Jonathan Mitchel Sewall; Washington "was idolized by his domestics." A correspondent who attended the funeral at Mount Vernon attested: "I had the best opportunity of observing the countenances of all. Every one was affected, but none so much as his domestics of all ages." Washington's private goodness bore on his public greatness, and it was important for such images to show that Washington was benevolent in every respect. "That he was compassionate and humane," Timothy Bigelow said in his Boston eulogy, "is honourably told by the tears of his disconsolate domestics." Such images of Washington, the benevolent patriarch, tied to his slaves by bonds of sentiment and affection, offered further evidence of his virtue—in the process reorienting the place of slaves within the national family. This strategy of integrating slaves into the community of mourning was not isolated to one region. In the middle of January 1800, the *Gazette* of South Carolina gave its readers an account of the memorial procession that had taken place in New York two weeks earlier. A bier was born by members of the Society of Cincinnatus, it reported. "Immediately followed, The General's Horse, in Mourning, Led by two black Servants in complete mourning, with white Turbans, Cincinnati as Chief Mourners, and other officers of the late war."[51]

In the late eighteenth and early nineteenth centuries, slaves were repeatedly portrayed as part of Washington's family circle. One of the most famous anecdotes of Washington's childhood originates from a sketch in Jedediah Morse's *Geography* (1789), which, much as Mason Locke Weems's biography later would, emphasized Washington's filial obedience. As a boy, according to this account,

26. *Anonymous*, Washington's Interview with His Mother.

George signed up to serve as cabin boy aboard a ship. When his mother heard the news, she broke down into tears, and urged George to abandon the project. Ever conscious of his filial duty, George promptly complied.[52] The story was picked up from Morse's widely disseminated *Geography,* its sentimental connotations enhanced, and reprinted in other accounts, including the eulogies that followed Washington's death. It was even represented in pictorial form later in the century (figure 26). Breaking the news to his evidently stricken mother, this painting portrays a young Washington in the parlor of a middle-class home, complete with cat and dog. Just outside the inner family circle—holding the youngest child—stands a slave. Mother, sibling, and slave: all rendered as part of the Washington family.

If it is tempting to see this narrative as convenient window dressing masking the brutal realities of exploitation and oppression, that explanation is true, but also a bit too easy. The paternalist understanding of slavery served a more urgent purpose: it responded to anxieties about slavery's place within the national family, and the potential of slavery to subvert national unity. Thomas Thacher, in a Boston eulogy, made this aspect clear. Alongside his celebration of Washington's posthumous emancipation, Thacher added a paean to his lifetime of benevolent mastery. "As a master," Thacher averred, "he united dignity and authority with such mildness of temper, as procured prompt obedience and warm attachment." Thacher went on to make a particularly telling observation. "And it is worthy of remark," he added, "that in all the important scenes he hath passed through, and the high trusts he was obliged to repose on the fidelity of his attendants, that there never hath appeared an instance of treachery in any member of his family. While this demonstrates his penetration and insight of human nature—it evidences the excellency of his heart and manners, in thus commanding the good affections and esteem of all degrees of men."[53] By casting slaves as part of the Washington family—happy children united in bonds of affection to Washington the father—this narrative of Washington and slavery helped appease dreaded fears of slave insurrection, or "treachery," as Thacher put it. The irony, of course, was that Washington's benevolence had not spared Martha from terror about *her* safety at the hands of slaves.

Other eulogists made similar observations. The clergyman and former schoolteacher George Richards also focused his attention on Washington's benevolent slaveholding, and even invoked scriptural authority to endorse his benevolence:

> As a master, WASHINGTON "gave to his servants, those things that were just and equal." His paternal care of the aged and infirm; his tender solicitude for the maintenance of infancy, and childhood; his superior attentions, to the adornings of youth and riper years, with the social jewels of industry, temperance, honesty, and the moral virtues, furnish incontestable evidence, that he was governed by noble principles of the *Chaldean* sage, who feelingly acknowledged, his man servant, his maid servant, as "bone of the bone," of human nature, and "flesh of the flesh" of fellow man.[54]

This description of Washington's benevolent and paternal mastery rested on scriptural authority. In this regard, it previewed the arguments of later proslavery theorists, who often invoked examples of biblical slaveholding to exalt slavery as a righteous institution. This paternalist account of slavery—of Washington's benevolent fatherhood—bears startling resemblances to the account of Washington as father to *white* Americans promoted in his eulogies. Aaron Bancroft, in an 1807 biography of Washington's life, drew on this paternalist under-standing of slavery to exalt Washington's benevolent mastery. "In domestick and private life, he blended the authority of the master with the care and kindness of the guardian and friend," Bancroft began, injecting a nineteenth-century under-standing of the father as both guardian and friend. "Solicitous for the welfare of his slaves," Bancroft wrote, "while at Mount Vernon, he every morning rode round his estates to examine their condition; for the sick, physicians were pro-vided, and to the weak and infirm every necessary comfort was administered."[55]

All of this is not to say that these Northerners were proslavery. But whether opposed to or supportive of slavery, their texts used the figure of Washington as father to extend the sentimental image of parent-child relationships to the rela-tionship between master and slave. By depicting Washington's slaveholding as grounded in affection and gratitude, these accounts fit slavery, without any con-tradiction at all, into the nationalist narrative of Washington as "father of the nation." Indeed, this emerging paternalist narrative of slavery—slaves bound in affection and gratitude to Washington the father—paralleled the paternalist ac-count of nationalism that civic texts had been promoting: Americans unified in bonds of affection and gratitude to Washington the father. The fantasy of the grateful slave, which would become one of the driving tropes of later proslavery theory, comes to seem, in retrospect, not so distant from the republican account that posited white Americans bound together in gratitude toward Washington. The mourning rituals of 1800 had balanced the antirepublican implications of hero worship with the notion of consent: Americans freely expressing their *grat-itude* to Washington, in contrast to monarchical subjects coerced into obedience to a tyrant. By much the same logic, the paternalist image of slavery injected an element of consent into the institution.

SLAVEHOLDERS in the United States, the historian William Freehling has noted, to a much greater extent than slaveholders elsewhere in the New World, "con-stantly demanded proof that blacks *consented* to be ruled from above . . . The U.S. slaveholder insisted peculiarly often, with peculiar vehemence, that his was a paternalistic institution and that his dependents consented to his benevolent rule."[56] The reasons for this insistence are not hard to discern. It served two pur-poses: first, it responded to dreaded fears of slave insurrection by positing a soci-ety of happy slaves tied to their masters through bonds of affection. Second, it resolved the troubling place of slavery in a nation committed to the principle of government by consent of the governed.

The affection that linked Washington to his slaves would become particularly prominent in mid-nineteenth-century pictorial representations. Many images and anecdotes of Washington at home with his slaves were disseminated through the nineteenth century, as a more fully developed paternalist ideology of slavery matured.[57] Consider Junius Brutus Stearns's 1851 painting of Washington "as a farmer at Mount Vernon" (figure 27), which built on accounts of Washington as benevolent slaveholder to portray slave and free, black and white, coexisting in harmony under the benign supervision of father George Washington. At one side of the painting, Washington's two stepgrandchildren play, while in the middle, Washington's slaves take a break from their Arcadian labors. Washington comments on the scene from the side, perhaps suggesting some new agricultural innovation to his companion. Such depictions preserved an eighteenth-century image of Washington only in the manner of his dress; they were clear products of the nineteenth century in their portrayal of Washington as benevolent father, attached to his slaves by sentimental bonds: an image that would powerfully rein-

27. *Claude Regnier after Junius Brutus Stearns,* Life of George Washington: The Farmer, *lithograph, 1853.*

28. *Nathaniel Currier,* Washington at Mount Vernon, *1787, lithograph (1852).*

force the century's paternalist ideology of slaveholding. The great nineteenth-century printing firm of Currier and Ives, which diffused cheap prints on a massive scale, would draw on Stearns's painting to reproduce a portrait of Washington with his slaves on Mount Vernon (figure 28). These portrayals did not shy away from slavery, nor did they cast it as an unfortunate legacy of the past thankfully on the path to extinction. In these accounts, it was a benevolent institution.

By the 1850s, the paternal had become the political. With nationalists seeking to hold the American family together in the midst of bitter sectional quarrels, Washington would continue to serve as both symbol and model of the unified American family. Washington, wrote the lawyer Richard Rush, was "the head of a well-ordered family, himself the regulator of it all, under maxims that best conduce to order because not too rigid." The connection here to politics was obvious. "We see his attention to the comfort of his servants, slaves, and others. His government of them, upper and subordinate, appears to have been perfect, by his union of discipline with liberality."[58] If only Americans could continue to emulate this model of fatherhood—well-ordered discipline tempered with liberality—they could hope to emerge from the crisis of the Union. But of course this was not the path taken. Washington as father would remain a contested symbol, the paternalist account continuing to rival the abolitionist.

29. *The Great Seal of the Confederacy.*

Perhaps, then, it is not surprising to learn that Washington, father to his happy slaves, would be appropriated by The Confederate States of America upon its founding. In 1861, Washington became the father of not one but two nations. Even as the North in the Civil War invoked Washington to sustain the cause of national unity—often by reprinting or repeating the Farewell Address—the South invoked Washington to sustain the cause of secession and the defense of slavery. Jefferson Davis would be inaugurated as president of the Confederate States of America on Washington's birthday: February 22, 1862. And the new nation placed Washington on its seal (figure 29) and its currency (figure 30).[59] Even the most prosaic items, such as envelopes, bore Washington's image, insisting on his status as Founding Father

30. *Confederate currency with portraits of George Washington.*

31. "One of the Rebels. Geo. Washington."
Confederate envelope design.

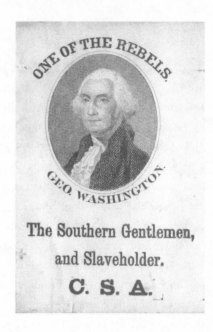

of the Confederate States of America: as Southerner and slaveholder (figure 31). Just as the United States had done two generations earlier, the Confederate States of America made George Washington the father of its nation: a nation now dedicated to the preservation of slavery. Meanwhile, Northerners continued to insist that Washington was the father of *their* country, attaching his image—and selections from his Farewell Address—on *their* envelopes (figure 32).

Lincoln famously said that, though locked in terrible combat, North and the South "both pray to the same God."[60] True enough: and his name was Washington.

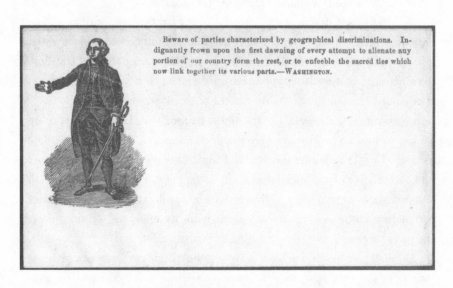

32. Union envelope design bearing an image of Washington with a quotation
from his Farewell Address on the importance of Union.

Toward a Consenting Republic?

Few Americans are unfamiliar with the story that is often told about the history of the abolitionist movement. Drawing on the liberal ideology of the Revolution and on the documents produced by the nation's founders, committed opponents of slavery battled to end the institution by deploying the nation's ideals of liberty and equality. In this account, the nation's progress from slavery to abolitionism can be seen as the history of America itself. "The story of antislavery," in this understanding, "begins with the principles of the Revolution."[61] This narrative has in large measure become dominant, in part because it rests on well-demonstrated facts. The abolitionists did indeed draw on the Revolution's rhetoric of freedom, and on the memory of the Founding Fathers, in order to combat slavery. As they learned, using the Founding Fathers—and especially Washington—to attack the institution of slavery was a potent weapon in their ideological arsenal.[62] Many people thus draw the conclusion that abolitionism was the necessary outcome of the nation's founding principles. American nationalism, for these people, is essentially a *civic* nationalism: grounded in rights and principles, rather than on descent or race.

As the historian David Brion Davis has pointed out, however, "there are hazards in imaging antislavery as a telic force, flowing irresistibly toward its moment of destiny." These hazards are several. First, this account fails to explain why the institution of slavery, far from withering away, grew during the first decades of the nineteenth century. If slavery was banned in the new states of the Northwest, it expanded massively into the new states of the Southwest, the population of slaves growing exponentially along with the nation.[63] In addition, this teleological account forces historians to see the development of the antebellum South through the eyes of abolitionists: as a deviant outgrowth of American society, unrepresentative of the liberal democracy sweeping through the North. Finally, and perhaps most important, it fails to account for the complexity of American nationalism in the early nineteenth century: for its ability to tolerate and even encourage the growth of slavery during its formative decades.

Although an abolitionist narrative of the Founding Fathers did indeed emerge in the early nineteenth century, another narrative emerged alongside. Along with the civic elements of U.S. nationalism—the rhetoric of liberty and equality—emerged a patriarchal rhetoric that would provide the seeds for a powerful language of exclusion and oppression. The civic texts that cast Washington as father of the nation authorized a paternalist account of slavery just as easily as they did an abolitionist account. Indeed, the threat slavery posed to the nation—the threat of insurrection, servile war, quarrels among brothers—may well have strengthened the patriarchal elements of early U.S. nationalism, pushing it more toward a nationalism of descent than would otherwise have been the case.

The particular challenge of U.S. nationalism was to reconcile consent with stability and continuity: to find a way for future generations voluntarily to give their consent. Did these paternalist strains betray this essential principle? Washington's fatherhood always existed in tension with the principle of government founded in the consent of the governed. Civic texts offered one resolution, providing a mechanism by which future generations could freely give their consent to the nation. They made the act of reading itself into a moment of civic engagement, as audiences continually reaffirmed their consent to the fathers—and to the nation—in the face of threats of political faction and geographical divisions. In much the same way, civic texts helped to resolve, at least temporarily, the "problem" of slavery. They promoted a paternalist vision of slavery grounded in bonds of affection. Slaves might not, admittedly, have given their formal consent to their status. But the obvious bonds of affection linking them to their masters—the tears they shed upon Washington's death, for instance—seemed to signal a *tacit* assent to their enslavement. The paternalist image of slavery responded to a whole set of vexing dilemmas: not only did it appease fears of slave insurrection and national instability, it allowed for a reconciliation between slavery and a U.S. nationalism itself increasingly tilting toward the doctrine of tacit consent.

All nations are torn between tacit and explicit consent.[64] None allows its citizens to vote on a new social contract every generation. The continued presence of slavery within a polity committed to liberal principles put U.S. nationalism under even greater strains than most, however, pushing it farther in the direction of tacit consent, and farther away from explicit consent. Insofar as the paternalist image of slavery helped mask the brutal coercion involved in its enforcement, then, perhaps it merely highlighted the lesser forms of coercion involved in persuading free Americans to "consent" to their nation. Slavery was, more and more, strengthening a passive understanding of citizenship intertwined with an ideology of paternalism as a core feature of U.S. nationalism.[65]

3.

MASON LOCKE WEEMS: SPREADING THE AMERICAN GOSPEL

—⊳•◁—

Alas! How is the last free Government on earth to be preserved—that Almost Divine Governm[t] for which Washington fought, for which Henry plead; and for whose Birth, for whose Eventful Birth as one of the Goddesses of old, All Europe and America were wrapt in flames of war? Why, it is to be preserved, as you of all men best know, only by the VIRTUES and these cannot grow unless those noxious weeds the VICES be rooted out. But what can so vegetate the Seeds of the Virtues in the bosoms of the American Youth as the warm fostering sunbeams of WASHINGTON'S GODLIKE EXAMPLE, & HIS GRAND COMPEERS FRANKLIN & MARION? And what can so kill the seeds of the VICES as the caustic solutions prepared by the Guardian care of the Serio-Comic Muse?

—MASON LOCKE WEEMS[1]

DECEMBER 1799, somewhere near Dumfries, Virginia: Mason Locke Weems—doctor, minister, author, and book peddler—was traveling the backcountry selling books and pamphlets, as he had done throughout the Middle Atlantic and Southern states for most of the past decade. Almanacs and spelling books were selling particularly well that month.[2] Earlier in the decade, Weems had earned and then lost a small fortune selling large, multivolume works of European origin like Oliver Goldsmith's *Animated Nature* and William Guthrie's *Modern Geography*.[3] Toward the end of the decade, however, he began selling smaller, cheaper books, many by domestic authors. He realized he could earn more money by selling a larger volume of cheap books than a small number of expensive ones. And besides, the more books he distributed, the more he could, as he liked to put it, "do good in Society."[4] So Weems had begun selling schoolbooks and almanacs and other such ephemera. He had even begun experimenting a bit with some of his own "scribblings," as he called them. After all, who better than a bookseller to judge the tastes of the reading public?

It was probably sometime in late December, on his way home to his wife and children in Dumfries, a Virginia town not far from Mount Vernon, that Weems heard about Washington's death, as the news made its way along the dilapidated dirt roads of the Virginia backcountry. Fortuitously, Weems had begun composing a brief didactic tract about Washington several months earlier—a cross between a sermon and a biography, drawing out Washington's virtues for the benefit of readers. Ever the salesman, Weems knew a golden opportunity when he saw one. "I've got something to whisper in your lug," he wrote in early January to Mathew Carey, the Philadelphia publisher and Weems's partner in the Southern book trade. "Washington, you know is gone! Millions are gaping to read something about him. I am very nearly prim[d] & cock[d] for 'em."[5] Here was an opportunity to do good and to make money—two activities Weems most loved.

Traveling the country from New York to Georgia, Mason Locke Weems spent more than thirty years distributing a vast array of books—popular biographies, geographies, novels, plays, scientific books, religious books, political tracts, schoolbooks, spelling books, and almanacs—and through them, connecting audiences throughout the towns and hinterlands of the Middle Atlantic and Southern regions of the United States to intellectual currents in the larger Atlantic world. But if Weems's life epitomizes a certain kind of cosmopolitanism, it was one he translated into a distinctly American register. Promoting personal traits he and many others believed would create good republican citizens, forging bonds of fraternal attachment among Americans, the texts Weems composed and sold served to create consenting Americans. Throughout his career, Weems engaged in a complex dialogue between producers and audiences that was integral not only to the *dissemination,* but also to the *formation* of civic texts. Operating within a larger Atlantic world involving the circulation of ideas, goods, and people, Weems's life and texts help explain how the Enlightenment currents of the eighteenth-century Atlantic world fed into the evangelical, republican nationalism of the nineteenth-century United States.

Weems produced one of the best-selling and most important texts of the early republic, and it is from his biography of George Washington, first published in 1800 and subsequently revised over the next nine years, that many of the most famous stories and images of Washington stemmed—Washington and the cherry tree, Washington who cannot tell a lie, Washington of deep and overt piety. The Washington who became the icon of nineteenth-century nationalism was in no small part a Weems creation. But, as we shall see, this Washington did not emerge fully formed from Weems's head. It resulted from a complex back-and-forth between Weems and his reading public.

Clergyman to Evangelical Bookseller: "True Philanthropist and Prudent Speculator"

Mason Locke Weems was born October 11, 1759, in Anne Arundel County, Maryland. Descended from the ancient Wemyss family of Scotland, Mason Loch or Locke was the youngest of nineteen siblings. Weems was well educated for his day. Sent away at age ten, he graduated from the Kent County Free School, which later became Washington College in Chestertown, Maryland. In the mid-1770s Weems left America to study medicine in Edinburgh. Little is known about the years he spent in the cultural and intellectual ferment at the height of the Scottish Enlightenment. Whether he studied with some of the great thinkers of the era is a matter for speculation. His later devotion to many tenets of the Scottish Enlightenment—the spread of knowledge, the progress of society through greater education and civilization, the importance of virtue and the dangers of vice—suggests that his Edinburgh education left a lasting impression on Weems, while the references in his later books to such ancients as Plato and Lycurgus, as well as a full cohort of such eighteenth-century thinkers as Montesquieu, Paine, and Voltaire, suggest the extent of his reading.[6] But Weems was not just a product of the great secular Enlightenment thinkers of the era; his intellectual outlook was profoundly marked by a deep religious faith, which began within the Anglican Church and moved gradually toward Methodist evangelism. Indeed, it might be said that Weems personified the marriage of evangelical piety, republicanism, and commonsense moral philosophy that would become so central to nineteenth-century American intellectual life.[7]

33. *Anonymous,* Parson Mason Locke Weems
(c. 1810), oil on canvas.

Weems's life in Europe remains hidden behind a fog of unprovable speculation. Some reports claim that he served as a surgeon aboard a British ship, others
that he returned to Maryland during the war, though no solid evidence connects
him to either the patriot or loyalist forces.[8] By the early 1780s Weems was in England, studying to become an Anglican minister. This was itself a curious career
choice for a future patriot, given the connection between Anglicanism and loyal-
ism during this period. But whatever his political leanings, they seem to have
been overshadowed by a proto-evangelical religiosity. One oft-repeated story
about Weems's life in London has it that a group of his friends, concerned about
frequent disappearances and fearing he might be up to no good, once followed
him through the back alleys of London, down into a wretched cellar. "But their
suspicions were soon changed on following him into his subterranean apart-
ment," writes John Davis, a Briton who encountered Weems on his travels
through the United States, and who recorded this story.

They found him exhorting to repentance a poor wretch, who was once the gayest of the gay, and flattered by the multitude, but now languishing on a death bed, and deserted by the world. He was reproving him tenderly, privately, and with all due humility; but holding out to him the consolation of the sacred text.[9]

It would be wise to treat this account with some skepticism, since it strikingly parallels other stories about Weems's early years, but at the very least it suggests how Weems later chose to present his early life: engaged in acts of piety with strong evangelical overtones and, one might call it, moral reform.[10] Weems's studies in London ended with his ordination into the Church of England. One of the first American clergymen to be ordained after the Revolution, thanks in large part to the intervention of John Adams and Benjamin Franklin—a story that provides an interesting footnote to Anglican Church history—Weems returned to the newly independent nation in 1784 to become rector of All Hallows' Parish in Anne Arundel County, Maryland.[11]

Weems threw himself into his religious work with gusto, and was considered a rising star in a Maryland church searching for a new Episcopalian identity.[12] His activities were not limited to ministerial duties during this period, but combined religious profession with charity, education, and other kinds of reform activities. Weems helped found a "Corporation for the Relief of the Widows and Children of the Clergy of the Protestant Episcopal Church in Maryland"; superintended a neighborhood school for girls; and regularly preached to local African Americans.[13] But even as Weems pursued his pastoral duties, he was moving away from Episcopalian orthodoxy toward a broadly ecumenical posture.[14] His sympathy toward Methodism particularly troubled some of his superiors. One of these, the Reverend Thomas John Claggett, wrote a colleague about his "uneasiness" caused by "Our friend M^r. Mason Weems ... [who] has adopted a Line of Conduct that I fear will be greatly prejudicial to ye Church; he has I understand introduced ye Methodist Hymns & Tunes in ye publick Service." Ignoring Claggett's warnings, Weems had even preached in a Methodist meetinghouse. "His conduct (I verily believe) has materially affected ye Interest of our Church in this Quarter & I do suppose that should his example be followed by one or two more of our Ministers; that very speedily two or three Parishes will be entirely lopped off from our Church." Despite these reservations, Claggett confessed an admiration for Weems's "Zeal & Attention to ye Duties of his sacred Office."[15]

Weems's zeal evidently knew few bounds, and in the late 1780s, he found a new avenue to disseminate the Church's teaching: prayer books. In November 1788, he purchased two dozen, presumably to give away or sell. In 1789, Weems cooperated on the sale of the *Proceedings* of the Maryland Episcopal convention.[16] It was around 1791 that, according to a friend's diary, Weems's lifestyle became increasingly peripatetic. Although Weems may not have known it at the time, he was moving toward a peddling way of life.[17] He was also moving away from the Church, perhaps due to the disapproval of his fellow clergymen, or perhaps due to the chronically low pay. As his bookselling grew, even his friend the Reverend William Duke fretted over Weems's circulation of *Onania, or the Heinous Sin of Self Pollution, and All Its Frightful Consequences in Both Sexes, Considered.* "I see Weems' publication on *Onania* is in a good many hands," wrote Duke, surely intending no pun. "I am afraid," he added, that the book is read more "as a matter of diversion than serious consideration."[18]

Sometime in late 1791 or early 1792, Weems gave up his rectorship. In 1791, he undertook the publication of a book of sermons by Robert Russel.[19] It must have met with some success, since in 1792 Weems took on an ambitious printing of Hugh Blair's *Sermons* on his own account. Believing it was "a Work . . . most *happily* calculated to enlarge the Reign of Piety and Virtue," Weems sought Washington's endorsement for the publication. But to no avail: it turned out to be a disappointing venture that left him with surplus copies for years to come.[20] By 1794, Weems had left the Church and moved definitively into bookselling. He struck up a relationship with Mathew Carey, an Irish immigrant and printer then establishing himself in Philadelphia, and began traveling the Middle Atlantic region selling books full-time.[21]

In 1795 Weems married Frances Ewell, daughter of a prominent Virginia family, and relocated to Dumfries, Virginia. He had already met Washington in the late 1780s through the intermediary of Washington's friend Dr. Craik (the same doctor who would bleed Washington so profusely on his deathbed), and no doubt thanks to Ewell family connections, Weems occasionally came into contact with Washington during the next few years. In 1795 Weems again sought Washington's endorsement for Blair's *Sermons,* hoping to unload the copies still in his possession.[22] His request stands as one of his earliest statements of his career goals, and of the fusion of republicanism and religion that Weems always personified: "I have taken upon me to circulate moral and Religious books among the People," wrote Weems, adding that with such a mission, "I know that your Excellence, as Father of the People, is not displeased." After his relocation, Weems occasionally ministered at the local Episcopal parish, Pohick Church—which, as the church closest to Mount Vernon, gave him some grounds for his later self-appellation as "Rector of Mount-Vernon Parish."[23]

THIS SEAMLESS SHIFT from clergyman to bookseller was a change of means rather than ends. The "zeal" that previously characterized Weems's ministerial activities would now drive his bookselling. "I live but to urge on the Great Work of Co-operating with the Author of all good in diffusing Light Love and Bliss among his Rational Family on earth," wrote Weems in 1800. "But for this I w^d instantly wholesale my books & quit the business forever."[24] Financial motivations were ever-present, sometimes expressed with startling rapacity, but they did not contradict Weems's zeal to sell books; they complemented it. The promotion of public virtue and morality was never dissociated from the quest for personal profit. Beyond earning him money—and it is not clear how much money it actually brought him—Weems's bookselling was a religious, political, didactic, and moral activity.[25] It made him an evangelist of nationalism. Weems would diffuse Anglican "Rational" light with Methodist evangelical fervor—"glow[ing] with a book vending enthusiasm"—and unite both with a proto-capitalist ethic stressing diligence and self-control.

When it came to the inculcation of a work ethic, Weems never wavered. He viewed the accumulation of wealth not with distaste, but with the same proto-capitalist enthusiasm as Franklin, going so far as to publish Franklin's essay "The Way to Wealth" in a collection of moral tracts and in his popular almanacs.[26] Weems's writings consistently portrayed thrift, self-control, and industry as virtuous, and condemned gambling as a subversion of all.[27] The first edition of his Washington biography affirmed the dignity of labor, arguing against the idea that "labour is a low-lived thing, fit for none but Negro-slaves!" His pamphlet against adultery similarly cast an opposition between inherited wealth—"of the hereditary and effeminating sort"—and wealth created by dint of the active individual: "the brave and healthy offspring of his own virtues. The credit which his HONESTY commended, was doubled by his INDUSTRY, and trebled by his prudence." Indeed, one might say that Weems's worldview constituted "not simply a means of making one's way in the world," as Max Weber famously wrote of Ben Franklin, "but a peculiar ethic."[28]

To see this enterprise—this attempt to reshape individuals and the larger culture through reading—as purely secular would be a serious mistake, however.

Weems united his religious calling with his nationalizing and moralizing missions, and with the market imperatives of his bookselling. His lifelong conviction that reading could touch the deepest emotions—that it could, as it were, enact an inner, spiritual conversion—closely connected to his evangelical faith. As evangelical Protestantism began its second great resurgence in the early nineteenth century, the fires of revival spreading across the trans-Appalachian upper South, eventually to burn their way through the coves and hollows into the eastern seaboard, Weems would come to look like a pioneer not just of nationalism, but of a particular brand of Protestant evangelical nationalism.[29] And evangelical he leaned. His pamphlet against drunkenness, for instance, recounted a story of John Wesley preaching to hard-drinking English coal miners and persuading them to abandon drink. "Could millions of *wrangling* sermons on INFANT BAPTISM, or ADULT BAPTISM, on FREEWILL or ELECTION, have produced the good of this one, on 'Repentance and *Faith working by Love?*'"[30] The waves of evangelical religion that have repeatedly washed across America's cultural landscape have generally shunned the formal, theoretical aspects of religion—debates about infant baptism, free will, and election—to focus on the individual, and on inner spirituality. Weems would use his texts to touch the inner spirit, to enact individual and national conversions, and bring a new birth to the nation.

Weems's combination of publishing, bookselling, and itinerant ministry marks him as a pioneer of the tactics used later in the nineteenth century by Methodists who flooded the nation with evangelical texts.[31] He was in this sense a transitional figure, for Weems's bookselling strategies also drew on those developed by itinerant preachers during the First Great Awakening. Like the clergymen who traveled the American colonies two generations earlier, Weems roamed through the United States drawing crowds to mass events. While selling his books, he would occasionally pause to minister to a parish, preside over marriages and funerals, or deliver impromptu sermons, often later reprinted in his pamphlets. Whether knowingly or not, Weems followed in the footsteps of the great eighteenth-century evangelist George Whitefield. Like Whitefield, Weems possessed "the evangelist's ability to persuade them [his audiences] to purchase books." Like Whitefield, Weems used newspapers to publicize his upcoming arrival in a town, to promote his books, and to disseminate his message. Like Whitefield, Weems held little reverence for established ecclesiastic authorities— where Whitefield had once dismissed what he called "Doctors of Divinity," Weems dismissed local "Bishops and Lords Spiritual," and mocked the mores of a "Bench of Bishops." Like Whitefield, Weems had a very low regard for slavery.

And like Whitefield, Weems appears to have been a memorable preacher. "He preached in every pulpit to which he could gain access, and where he could recommend his books," recalled a bishop of the Virginia Episcopal Church.[32] His itinerant preaching and selling made Weems something of a folkloric character. "He always preached, when invited, during his travels," wrote the nineteenth-century literary compiler Benson Lossing, "and haranged people at public gatherings at courts and fairs, where he offered his Bibles, and other good books, for sale. His fund of anecdote was inexhaustible; and after giving a promiscuous audience the highest entertainment of fun, he found them in good mood to purchase his books."[33] Preaching to whites and blacks alike, peddling his message and his books to crowds in churches, courthouses, and state houses across Middle Atlantic and Southern states, Weems reached audiences only dreamed of by most authors of the period.

WEEMS JOINED FORCES with Mathew Carey in 1794 (as Whitefield and Benjamin Franklin had joined forces earlier in the century), neither guessing the association would change both their lives. Carey was another cosmopolitan figure of the period. An Irish Catholic immigrant from Dublin who landed in Philadelphia in 1784, Carey arrived as a political refugee fleeing governmental reprisals over his outspoken pro-Irish views. Like Weems, Carey began his career with the support, if not the patronage, of some of the most prominent figures of the era. Thanks to a loan from LaFayette, whom he had met while working for Benjamin Franklin in Paris, Carey was able to establish himself in Philadelphia's burgeoning publishing industry.[34] After a brief spell editing a newspaper—which led to a duel with a rival newspaper editor—Carey started *The American Museum,* a monthly magazine that reprinted an eclectic mix of "transient" works, mostly by American authors. Perhaps the anti-English feeling bred during his years as an Irish radical led him to sympathize with the new politico-literary project promoting U.S. literature. His efforts to encourage a national literature through *The American Museum* earned him praise from such eminent figures as Benjamin Rush, John Dickinson, Francis Hopkinson, and George Washington. "For my part," Washington wrote Carey, "I entertain an high idea of the utility of periodical publications; insomuch that I could heartily desire copies of the Museum and Magazines, as well as common Gazettes, might be spread through every city, town, and village in America. I consider such easy vehicles of knowledge, more happily calculated than any other, to preserve the liberty, stimulate the industry, and meliorate the morals of an enlightened and free people."[35] But praise was not income, and the magazine folded in 1792.

Turning his attention to the books, Carey began looking for ways to make inroads into the Southern book market, then still closely tied to the London printing industry. Weems was a natural choice: a like-minded nationalist whom Carey considered a salesman of rare abilities. ("Your book no longer sells," Carey once wrote one of his authors, "I have accordingly given it into the hands of Mr. Weems, who will clear it off if anyone can.") The Protestant clergyman with evangelical leanings joined forces with the Irish Catholic publisher, and the two became business associates and then friends in a thirty-year-long relationship that has rightly been characterized as "a comic marriage of endless wrangling."[36] Over the years, they quarreled, attacked each other bitterly, and repeatedly split up. But time and again they renewed their association and their friendship.

Ultimately, it seems clear that they remained partners not only because it made good business sense for both of them, but also because both believed in the importance—perhaps even the moral and political necessity—of their work: for enlightenment, for society, and most especially for the nation both were trying to strengthen. Both believed in the power of texts to bind a nation together. "The Press is the grand engine to silence the dogs of war & to bring back the golden age of Light, Liberty and Love," Weems wrote Carey in 1801, who, having committed his life to printing, could only have agreed. "Need I tell you the glory that awaits him who stands by & gallantly plays off a piece of Celestial Artillery?" It was a conviction Weems retained throughout his life. "He who does the most good in this world will be the most glorious in the next," Weems wrote Carey after more than fifteen years of bookselling. "Twas this expression that first set me on vending books. I feel the same passion now to multiply the Copies of Good books, especially those that tend to display the charm & happiness of Pure Religion & Politics."[37] The martial metaphors that pervade Weems's correspondence hint at the way he viewed his life's work: as a war to promote religion and morality and to defend the republic from all enemies. And he would have no more effective weapons in this crusade than the pamphlets he wrote and sold.

Weems and Antipartisanship

In the middle of 1799, his wife undergoing a difficult pregnancy and his broken wagon making travel impossible, Weems spent an uncharacteristically long period at home in Dumfries, Virginia. No doubt exasperated with this sedentary life, his quill appears to have provided an outlet for his energy. It was a singularly productive period. In addition to finishing the first draft of his Washington biography and revising a book of sacred dramas, Weems composed a fascinating political pamphlet condemning partisan faction. A second and similar pamphlet followed three years later. None of Weems's texts more clearly express his nationalist mission than these; they help situate Weems's famous biography of Washington in its proper context. In these pamphlets—as in his biography—Weems followed Washington's Farewell Address in identifying partisanship and section-

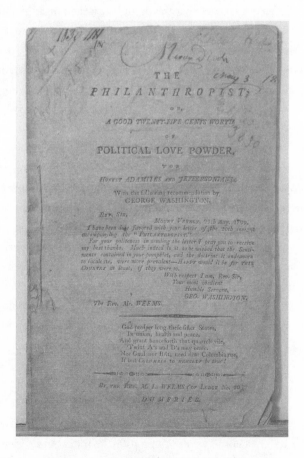

34. Title page of Mason Locke Weems, The Philanthropist, with an endorsement from Washington.

alism as the two greatest threats to the nation's survival. As in his biography, his pamphlets sought to overcome these threats by carving out a middle ground between Federalist and Republican extremes.

Weems's first pamphlet, *The Philanthropist; or, A Good Twenty-Five Cents Worth of Political Love Powder, for Honest Adamites and Jeffersonians,* appeared in 1799, shortly before the election of 1800, at a time when many feared that conflicts between Democratic-Republicans and Federalists might well explode into civil war. The pamphlet was a hit. It was published in at least four editions in 1799 alone, including two in Virginia and one in Charleston.[38] Condemning party divisions, and urging Americans to replace partisanship with Christian charity, the pamphlet was based on an essay by the Scottish moral philosopher William Laurence Brown that had won a prize from the Teylerian Society of Haarlem, in the Netherlands. What the pamphlet lacked in originality, it made up for with strategic acumen. Weems drew shamelessly on Washington's stature to promote his message, and his sales. The pamphlet opened with a dedication to the former president stressing the importance of both religion and national unity, praying that Americans would learn "that reverence for the Eternal Being; that veneration for the laws; that infinite concern for the *National Union*; that unextinguishable love for our country . . . which have raised you to Immortality, and which alone can exalt us to be a great and happy republic."[39]

Weems sent Washington a copy of his work, and Washington responded with an invaluable endorsement, which Weems immediately had printed on the pamphlet's cover (figure 34). Sales were brisk, thanks in part to the low price. "In 3 days I sold 350 at a dollar per dozen," reported Weems.[40] Newspapers around the country printed excerpts, and Weems reproduced selected portions of the pamphlet in his widely disseminated almanacs: a remarkable diffusion for ideas first penned in a dense tract of Scottish moral philosophy.

The Philanthropist sought to erect a framework for patriotic loyalty grounded in both secular and religious values, and based in mutual obligation and equality— equality not of size, wealth, or talent, but "equality of *mutual dependence,* of *civil obligation,* of *social affection,* of *dutiful obedience* to the *laws.*" Echoing Washington's Farewell Address, Weems argued that the nation's republican character imposed "*particular obligations*" on Americans, "*native* or *adopted* sons of Columbia . . . to love their country." "Our land is signally favor'd of heaven," Weems insisted, "our government has every thing to make it dear to us." For Weems as for Washington, it was the very principle of consent that produced the particular obligations of obedience. To this principle of consent, Weems added the obligation imposed by the nation's Revolutionary heritage: the blessings of the republic "bought by the dearest blood of our Fathers." Imperiling the nation, however, was the "furious party spirit" that threatened to rend asunder the "one *great political body.*" In response, Weems appealed to fraternal affection. "O then let us live together as brothers," the pamphlet urged. "And O, if our own happiness is dear to us, let us forever remember that in *exact* proportion as we lessen our mutual love we lessen our own happiness, we dissolve the golden bands of union, we become weak, contemptible, and an easy prey to any cruel and watchful enemy."[41] If this text appears to be an almost perfect restatement of the themes of Washington's Farewell Address—the warning against partisanship, the association of partisanship with division and weakness against foreign enemies—that was no coincidence. As he spread the tenets of Scottish Enlightenment thought through the American countryside, Weems's text was carrying forward Washington's political message, using Washington's prestige to advance the cause of national unity—and to sell pamphlets.

"YOU HAVE NO doubt seen how my little Son of the goosequill has sped," Weems wrote in 1801, "how on the wings of the Newspapers he has travell'd from Augusta to the Province of Maine? I mean . . . my political Placebo, my aristocratico-Democratico political Anodyne, '*The Philanthropist.*'" The pamphlet's success inspired Weems to envision another, similar work. "Were I able to print, I shou'd in 8 weeks have ready for the press a piece that w^d set on edge the cursed teeth of Tyranny, but sooth & comfort the nerves of all honest Republicans":

> Tis written, "On the Excellencies of a Republican Government." A view is exhibited of the *Nature* of a Republic, in order . . . To attach to it, the affections of the People, its peerless beauties are display^d, and to heighten those Beauties, they are contrasted with the Deformities & Horrors of Monarchy. The Gratitude due for such a Gov^t. such a Cœlo-descended Governm^t, and the fine Virtues which we shou'd cultivate in order to give it Sempeternal duration.[42]

Weems believed his pamphlets, if engaging enough, if disseminated broadly enough, could "attach . . . the affections of the People" to the nation. He believed that popular texts like his could promote virtues among readers that would give the nation "Sempeternal duration."

Weems published this pamphlet in 1802, its title summarizing his aims: *The True Patriot; or An Oration on the Beauties and Beatitudes of a Republic; and the Abominations and Desolations of Despotism. With an Affectionate Persuasive to the American People to Fear God, and to Honor Their Rulers; To Love One Another; and to Beware of Discord.* Once again uniting religious imperatives with the spread of nationalism, the pamphlet originated as an oration Weems delivered in the New Jersey State House in December 1801. As Weems recounted it, his sermon was a resounding success: "Scarcely had I quitted the Rostrum," he reported, "before I was surrounded by the Members, the Govr a leur tête. The Govr press^d my fist—thank^d me for my performance—insisted I sh^d print it; his Excellency's proposition was seconded, thirded &^{c}. &^{c}. by the Hon'ble the House. Quid multis?" Ever the salesman, Weems had barely finished his political sermon before he began to sell a pamphlet not yet in print. "The Govr without my knowledge got out a Subscription paper, & presented it to the Council who desir^d 50 Copies . . . I believe I cou'd easily have gotten 500 Copies engag^d."[43] Weems's account strains credulity: it is easier to imagine Weems running the state without the governor's knowledge than the governor passing out a subscription paper without Weems's knowledge.

This pamphlet was based on the *Discourses* by the great seventeenth-century republican Algernon Sidney, a text Weems had long admired.[44] It extended the *Philanthropist*'s argument, calling on Americans to venerate their nation. In language that would be echoed by Abraham Lincoln, Weems affirmed that his mission was to ensure that "the *last, best,* trial of free government . . . [shall not] fai[l] upon the earth." Like Weems's other writings, this one urged obedience to the nation's laws. "Nothing of all this lower world, neither gold nor silver, nor father nor mother, nor wife nor children, are half so dear as the laws."[45] To this end, the largest part of the text enumerated the advantages of republican government, contrasting the glories of republican government to the misery of monarchy. The pamphlet ended by condemning faction on the authority of both Washington and Divine law, casting national unity as the last barrier to chaos and civil war.

> Shall *we,* whom GOD has thus raised up as an *ensign* of *hope* to the nations, that here the oppressed of other lands might find a place of rest—Shall *we* reject this *counsel* of GOD against ourselves, and against mankind; and by a *discord* worse than *devilish,* plunge into such horrors of civil war, as shall blast the goodliest design that

GOD ever formed for a nation's weal, and convert our Eden into a
wild of blood and murder?? Father of mercies—GOD of Washington, forbid!!

Thus linking the nation to God's will, the pamphlet closed by connecting both to
the authority of George Washington. "May we duly reflect," Weems wrote, para-
phrasing Washington's Farewell Address, "on the INFINITE IMPORTANCE OF NA-
TIONAL UNION to our COLLECTIVE and INDIVIDUAL WELFARE!"[46]

This promotion of the antipartisan message of Washington's Farewell Address met with success. "Thank God," Weems wrote Carey in 1802, "the True Patriot goes off manfully—Feds or no Feds they all seem to approve it." But direct
sales represented only a small fraction of the ultimate dissemination of the pamphlet's message. As with his previous pamphlet, Weems recycled this essay in
numerous forms, including excerpts in his broadly disseminated almanacs. Almanacs were, for Weems, the ideal vehicle to disseminate his nationalist gospel,
since "its *cheapness* puts it in the power of the poorest citizen to possess one."
For this reason, he often inserted some form of moral instruction. "Considering
what a *favorite* an Almanac is in every family, whether Christian, Jew, or Gentile,"
Weems wrote, "needs must an Almanack should be made of good stuff." In 1804,
trolling for subscriptions in South Carolina and Georgia, Weems began selling
Weems's Washington Almanac, containing an abridged version of his *True Patriot.*
Reprinting his views on the excellencies of the republic, Weems believed the almanac was "Admirably calculated (by making us sensible of our *great political
advantages*) to inspire *gratitude to heaven, union among ourselves,* and that cheerful obedience to the laws, which alone can render our peace and prosperity *everlasting.*"[47] As with the *Philanthropist,* this pamphlet popularized the ideas of a
"high" European work of political theory—in this case, Algernon Sidney's discourses—transmitting its arguments to readers of pamphlets and almanacs
throughout rural and small-town America.

As with all Weems's writings, this almanac urged readers to overcome political divisions. "How can generous Americans mention that glading word '*Republic,*'" it asked, "without awakening the sweetly mournful memory of their
beloved Washington, '*that first and greatest Revolutionary Character,*' as Mr. Jefferson well observes." Having Jefferson endorse Washington—this, in 1804, an
election year full of bitter partisan quarrels—was a clever tactic indeed. Weems
was here doing something Washington himself had largely failed to do during

his political career: promote a nationalist message while stripping it of any partisan veneer. Even advertisements for the almanac promoted these antipartisan views.

> *God prosper long Columbia dear,*
> *In Plenty, Love and Peace,*
> *And grant henceforth that quarrels vile*
> *'Mongst Fed's and Dem's may cease!!!*

Weems sought through his texts to create unity in the face of bitter political divisions by appealing to common fathers, common symbols, and even common politics. "I have no doubt," Weems bragged, "but I shall be able to sell among the *Good Republicans* of the South, at least 10,000 Almanacs for this coming year— *My Alm^c* I mean, entitled Weems's Washington Almanac."[48]

Through these experiences selling his political pamphlets and almanacs, Weems learned how to promote a certain image of Washington to appeal to deeply divided Americans. In Weems's hands, a depoliticized Washington could be a fantastically effective vehicle for promoting national unity, and for overcoming social and political conflict.

Weems's writings collapsed the boundaries between what scholars often consider "high" and "low" political thought. Intellectual historians often have trouble explaining how it is that the disembodied intellectual traditions they study actually influenced the society in which they were articulated: were they reflecting trends already in existence, or shaping new developments in the political culture? The relative influence of liberal versus classical republican ideas on American politics, for instance, is generally examined through the writings of a few major political figures.[49] Or Scottish Enlightenment thought is shown to exert an influence on American political culture, but precisely *how* that influence occurred on a popular level is left assumed, rather than demonstrated. What the pamphlets Weems wrote and sold demonstrate—and what civic texts more broadly demonstrate—is that these grand intellectual traditions permeated deep into the American hinterland, and they offer one explanation as to how transatlantic intellectual traditions were embodied in American political practice. Weems's career ultimately makes it difficult to separate high intellectual thought from popular political life. Does Weems belong to the Enlightenment world of Hume and Smith, Sidney and Harrington, or does he belong to the agrarian world of rural farmers and small-town tradesmen? The answer, of course, is that he belongs to both, and as we shall see, the civic texts he wrote and sold resulted in good measure from both these worlds.

WEEMS'S TWO political pamphlets help clarify his aims for the Washington biography. First composed just before Washington's death in 1799 (the same year he published the *Philanthropist*) and subsequently revised over the next few years (as he published and sold the *True Patriot*), the biography would have precisely the same purpose as those pamphlets: to mute partisan faction by deploying a depoliticized Washington. "And O!," read the biography's first edition, "should it [the biography] be so favored as to suggest to the *children,* now that their father is dead, the great duty of burying their quarrels and uniting to *love* and to promote each others good—It will be master of great joy to one who can sincerely subscribe himself the lover of all who fear God, honor the *President* (be he Adams, be he Jefferson) revere the laws, and are not given to change." Weems's private correspondence attested to these aims: "Adams and Jefferson both will approve of our little piece," he wrote Carey.[50] This suprapartisan rhetoric anticipated Jefferson's inaugural address the year after Weems's biography was published, with its declaration that "We are all Republicans, We are all Federalists." (Indeed, one could call Jefferson's address downright Weemsian.)

Just as his two pamphlets had done, just as his almanacs and even his newspaper advertisements had done, Weems's *Life of Washington* would promote Washington's antipartisan views. The text called on its audience to "join in this divine prayer of our WASHINGTON 'that our union and brotherly love may be perpetual,'" and reminded readers of "the horrors which may result from writing and talking so as to create parties and factions among us." Where Washington's Farewell Address had imagined the dangers of faction ("It agitates the Community with ill founded Jealousies and false alarms, kindles the animosity of one part against another, foments occasionally riot & insurrection"), Weems's biography went even further, representing the horrors of faction in his inimitable style:

> With horrid imprecations, with faces black with rage, and eye balls flashing fury, they [partisans] fly at each other like tygers. They plunge their knives, swords and daggers into each others hearts. Pale and staggering, with mutual curses in death, they sink to the ground. The streets are floated with blood. The dead bodies lie in

> heaps on heaps, while women and children, with wringing hands
> and heart-piercing cries, demand their husbands, their fathers, and
> their brothers . . . These *O accused Faction and Party!* These are
> your bloody fruits!

Exaggerated and entertaining as it was, this opposition between political union
and social chaos was entirely Washingtonian, and it persisted in the biography's
final edition. Reminding readers of the *"evil"* that "Washington most dreaded,"
Weems warned that sectional faction could result in "a SEPARATION OF THE STATES,
and consequently, civil war." In no small part it would be from texts like Weems's
that a generation of Americans learned to associate the perpetuation of the
Union with the perpetuation of civil order itself, to think of secession, as Abraham Lincoln later would, as "the essence of anarchy."[51]

The condemnation of partisanship—and the view that it would lead inevitably to anarchy—ran through the entire biography and across its many editions. The 1800 edition continually invoked Washington, and quoted from his
Farewell Address, to reinforce its message. It closed by summoning Washington
to overcome an imagined civil war, calling on audiences to forget class and political divisions, and to rededicate themselves to the nation's founding principles.

> O my countrymen! If we would partake, with our WASHINGTON,
> of those eternal delights which are prepared for the Children of
> Peace; let us, with him make a covenant with our souls to fly from
> party spirit, as from the bane and damnation of all Republics . . .
> Let us all (whether Peasant or President, whether for Adams or Jef-
> ferson) as dear *children* of God, and *brothers* of WASHINGTON, *shun,*
> as we would *hell-fire,* every word and act that may needlessly pro-
> voke each other to *wrath* and *strife.*[52]

To this argument Weems added the force of Christian obligation he had evoked
in his previous pamphlets: "it was eternal LOVE that called *Light* out of *Darkness,*
and smiling Eden out of wild confusion . . . it is love alone that can relax the iron
brow of obstinacy, unloose the hard grip of prejudice, and constrain passion herself, with a sweet ingenuous blush, to own that she may have been in the wrong."[53]
As in his other writings, Weems merged Christian benevolence and republican
antipartisanship into a nationalist rhetoric of "love"—love among siblings of a
common father—in order to unite Americans.

Weems's Washington: A Primer

Broad as the dissemination of his political pamphlets was, Weems's biography of Washington targeted a much larger audience. Much like the eulogies that followed Washington's death, the final version of Weems's *Life of Washington* (it was completed in 1809, and remained unchanged in the dozens of editions that followed) focused on children. Weems once called his *Life* "a moralizing School book"; intending the biography for the "Young Reader," Weems dwelled at length on Washington's childhood. He depicted young George bursting with generosity, honesty, and piety, all virtues to be emulated by his readers. Though "born to be a soldier," young George was gentle, and endowed with a deep sense of fraternal feeling. Not a child born into the privileged plantation gentry and driven upward by intense ambition, Weems's Washington was a charming young rural lad: "his little naked toes scratch[ing] the soft ground." "Happily for America," Weems observed, "George Washington was not born with '*a silver spoon in his mouth.*'" Educated in an "*old field school,*" he learned habits of industry by working "in the back-woods" and "pursuing the laborious life of a woodsman." The book was evidently designed for young, yeoman-class, rural readers, and to encourage them to identify with Washington.[54]

Weems larded the biography with anecdotes displaying George's virtue. The cherry tree story demonstrated Washington's honesty.[55] Another anecdote, of Washington praying at Valley Forge, illustrated his piety. Almost certainly sprung from Weems's imagination, this portrayal of Washington's religiosity would be disseminated not only textually but also pictorially, teaching children of Washington's supposedly overt piety, and urging them to emulate his example (figure 35). Weems's story of Washington praying at Valley Forge would later be excerpted in various schoolbooks, including William Holmes McGuffey's wildly popular *Eclectic Reader* series. Through McGuffey, this anecdote displaying Washington's piety would be read aloud by millions of children throughout the nineteenth century: part and parcel of the wide-scale evangelization of the public sphere.[56] Indeed, the image of Washington as a not-so-closet evangelical continues to resonate in debates today about the religious leanings of the Founding Fathers, a subject on which Weems was something of a pioneer.

Weems also dwelled on the "parental and filial love" between George and his father—a theme that echoed and promoted new configurations of parent-child

35. The Prayer at Valley Forge, *painted by* H. Brueckner;
engraved by John C. McRae.

relations emerging in the nineteenth century.[57] He peppered the biography with paeans to virtue and condemnations of vice that corresponded in both message and style to his morality pamphlets. As in Weems's 1810 pamphlet *God's Revenge Against Gambling,* readers learned that Washington filled his time with "innocent and manly exercises," unlike the wastrels who engaged in "raking and gambling. Weems also included a sensationalist anecdote about a "wretched man!" undone by gambling who ends his life in desperation: "he seizes the pistol; drives the scorching bullets through his brain; and flies a shrieking ghost to join the mournful throng." Anticipating his later morality pamphlets *God's Revenge Against Duelling* and *The Drunkard's Looking Glass,* Weems used Washington to condemn both activities. The biography even promoted marriage and procreation, the theme of Weems's contemporaneous pamphlet *Hymen's Recruiting Sergeant.* Condemning bachelors as "depopulators of your country," Weems made marriage and childbearing into patriotic acts—though, perhaps not surprisingly, he remained silent about Washington's own lack of children. Washington, wrote Weems, "was the *second* son, by a *second* marriage":

a circumstance which it is hoped will effectually stop the mouths of those enemies to American population, who are eternally bawling against *second* marriages. And it is likewise hoped, that it will comfort the nerves of those *chicken-hearted* bachelors, who are afraid to wed—afraid to wander in the Elysian fields of *matrimony* . . . Timid Mortals! Depopulators of your country! Take courage and be *happy!*[58]

This passage was enough to stop the Virginia jurist St. George Tucker in his tracks. "I never got further than half the first paragraph," he wrote the Virginia lawyer and biographer William Wirt. "I shut the book as soon as I had read it, and have no desire to see any more about it."[59] But the opinion of Tucker—professor of law at William and Mary College—hardly mattered to Weems's target audience, and certainly did nothing to dampen the book's popularity.

Above all, Weems would use Washington to teach virtue to America's youth.[60] "To promote the love of virtue among our fellow citizens," read the first page of the first edition, "is, unquestionably, the most important service we can ever hope to render them." Weems would accomplish this noble task by "setting before them the bright example of persons eminent for their virtues." This goal endured throughout future revisions. The preface to an 1801 edition restated it: "YOUTHS of AMERICA, IMITATE YOUR WASHINGTON." The fourth edition incorporated this purpose into the title: *An history (4th edition greatly improved) of the Life and Death of Gen. George Washington . . . Exhibiting his very extraordinary Character . . . well worthy the perusal of every Young Man.* Washington's virtues, as listed in the title page, included "early prudence—admirable fortitude—rigid temperance—unwearied industry—honor unblemished, and uncorrupted patriotism." The text itself reinforced this message.

When our children and our childrens [*sic*] children, hearing the great name of WASHINGTON re-echoed from every lip with such veneration and delight, shall ask their fathers "what was it that raised WASHINGTON to this godlike height of glory?" Let them be told, that, "it was his *virtues*, his *great virtues*, those precious plants of life, the native shoots of a soul like his early watered with the rich dews of heaven-born religion."[61]

The biography was as much an instructional book as a history: a how-to manual on raising virtuous Americans. As early as August 1800, Weems had determined it would be "sold as a School book." Long after he sold Carey the copyright, Weems continued to suggest new revisions, "so great [is] the interest I take in setting Washington before the youth of our Country."[62]

Didactic as was the book's purpose, the narrative was hardly pedantic. Evert and George Duyckinck, the great nineteenth-century literary compilers, called Weems "a Livy of the common people. He first gave the fact and then the moral, and neither of them was dull."[63] The description is apt. Weems's biography was an entertaining history of the Revolution and early national period, tracing Washington's career as general and president. Creating memories that might unify Americans as one family, Weems's biography "forgot" the most partisan elements of Washington's public life. It presented a history of the Revolution without loyalists; a history of the constitutional period without anti-Federalists; and a history of the 1790s without partisan battles between Federalists and Republicans. And it was a history of the nation without slavery. By focusing on Washington's Revolutionary activities, Weems remained on firm nationalist ground to create a mythologized past of national unity. Keeping the focus on Washington's private life, Weems removed Washington from the partisan political sphere, erasing the bitter quarrels that divided the young nation in order to create an apolitical father all Americans could love.

Why did Weems's stories of Washington become so well known? In large part it was from the remarkable popularity of the book, of course. But their fame also resulted from the republication of Weems's tales by *other* civic texts reprinted and circulated to even broader audiences. Weems's anecdotes were reprinted in publications of the American Tract Society, an evangelical organization that published millions of tracts in the nineteenth century. His cherry tree story would be featured in prints and cartoons through the nineteenth century. Many schoolbooks also picked up Weems's anecdotes—particularly the cherry tree story. One scholar of early American schoolbooks found variations on Weems's cherry tree story in more than twenty-five schoolbooks of the nineteenth century, including the most popular of all, William Holmes McGuffey's readers.[64] Thanks in large part to these media, it would be Weems's Washington that millions of Americans would know from their earliest childhood.

Weems's Washington would be a huge hit. Grant Wood's *Parson Weems'* *Fable* (figure 36), painted years after Weems had passed away, testifies to the en-

36. Grant Wood, Parson Weems' Fable, 1939, oil on canvas.

during fame of Weems's stories, and to his success in this nationalist project. With Weems pulling back the curtain on Washington confessing to his father (with ax in hand), Wood's painting assumed a familiarity with the cherry tree story, and poked fun at the mythmaking process by depicting Washington's iconic head—the Gilbert Stuart portrait of him as an older man—sitting atop a child's body. Directing the viewer's eye with an orthogonal line toward the back left of the painting, nearly hidden by the curtain, Wood also highlighted the erasure involved in these nationalist memories: off in the distance, slaves harvest fruit from the same kind of tree young George just killed with his ax.[65]

Wood was hardly the first person to draw attention to the role of slavery in the Washington mythology. Although Weems had sought to erase slavery from Washington's life, other versions of Weems's story, carried by other popular texts, cast the institution in a more paternalistic light. William Makepeace Thayer's *The Farmer Boy, and How He Became Commander in Chief,* published in 1864, is a case in point. Thayer was a popular author of biographies and children's books whose numerous biographies together sold more than 1 million copies. Covering much the same ground Weems had—Washington's homespun roots, his generosity, his honest ambition, and so forth—Thayer's biography aimed, like Weems's, "to magnify the patriot virtues, and the priceless worth of the government under which we live . . . [and to] inspire the hearts of American youth by the noblest examples of patriotism and virtue." Much like the texts that poured out in the wake of Washington's death, much like Weems's biography itself, Thayer hoped his book would "awaken" in his readers "a desire to imitate the example and emulate the virtues of this greatest and wisest of Americans." And apparently Thayer could find no more effective vehicle to awaken virtue in his audience than Weems's cherry tree story. "I will tell you the story of his little hatchet," says the book's narrator, "as it may serve you good stead in the day when you may be tempted to wander astray from the path of truth and virtue."[66]

One Christmas Day—so the story begins—George was given "a little Indian tomahawk," which made him "as happy as happy could be." Armed with his new toy, George roamed through his father's plantation, hacking away: "chopping away at the hard-seasoned beech and maple logs, as if it lay with him, for that day at least, to keep the whole family, white and black, from freezing." George's whole family—black and white—took little note of his activities, however, and young George's enthusiasm soon grew excessive. Among his targets he set on a fine young English cherry tree—his father's favorite. The next morning his father saw the tree "and was sorely displeased." So far the story has followed Weems's almost identically—though without Weems's characteristic exuberance. In Weems's account, young George is confronted by his father, guilty hatchet in hand, and after some reflection—for it was a *hard* question—he confesses to his guilt. *The Farmer Boy,* however, adds a twist.

George's father does not at first suspect young George; he is "quite sure that it was the work of some of the black children." And so Augustine "went straightaway down to the negro quarter, bent on finding out, and bringing the unlucky culprit to severe account." Augustine's is no mean plantation of one or two slaves, but a large-scale operation with slave quarters and gangs of slaves. Augustine proceeds to interrogate more than a dozen of his "black children," each of whom denies responsibility, before coming to Jerry: an "audacious, mischief-making, neck-or-nothing black brat." Upon being confronted, Jerry, too, denies responsibility. But his reputation undoes him: Augustine refuses to believe Jerry's denial. "Ah! Jerry," says he, "if you always told the truth, I should know when to believe you; but, as you do not, you must take the consequences of your evil ways." And so Augustine descends on Jerry to beat him.[67]

At just this moment—"in the very nick of time"—young George walks by, "hatchet in hand," and, "without a moment's hesitation," runs up to his father just as he prepares to whip Jerry.

> "O papa, papa!" cried he, "don't whip poor Jerry: if somebody must be whipped, let it be me; for it was I, and not Jerry, that cut the cherry-tree. I didn't know how much harm I was doing; I didn't indeed." And the child began crying piteously.
>
> With a look of glad surprise, his father, dropping the switch, caught his brave little boy in his arms, and folded him tenderly, lovingly, to his bosom. "Now, thanks be to God," cried he, "thanks be to God, that I have a son whose love of truth is greater than his fear of punishment! Look on him, my black children, look on him, and be as near like him as you can, if you would have the love of your master and the good-will of all around you."[68]

Weems's story is here modified in fascinating ways. George becomes not just a model of honesty and filial obedience, but a model of virtue and fraternal loyalty—toward slaves, also described as Augustine's "children." Even more, the story makes Washington into a Christ-like figure: not, as his eulogists had it, because of his successful leadership; but rather because he willingly sacrifices himself for a fellow sinner, ready to submit to whipping that another might be spared. But this is not just any fellow traveler: this is a black slave. Naturalizing the relationship between Washington and his slaves, emphasizing Washington's goodness toward his black "family," it is not hard to see how Weems's story, thus altered, could nurture a mid-nineteenth-century paternalist view of slavery.

The virtues that Washington displays here—the honesty, the courage—are models not just for white children reading the tale, but for slaves in the story, who would, presumably, become better slaves by loving truth more than fearing punishment. As we shall see in the next chapter, the attempt to foster virtue not just among whites, but among slaves too, would be a preoccupation of certain civic texts with powerful and unanticipated implications.

An "Ad Captandum" Book

Weems may have had a clear nationalist agenda, but he was also keenly responsive to his readership, and a knowledge of his audience is essential to understanding how his book emerged.[69] Although Weems was, of course, the "author" of *The Life of Washington,* his reading public in the Middle Atlantic and Southern states might be considered unacknowledged "coauthors." Tracing the evolution of the text during the years Weems wrote and rewrote his book, from 1800 to 1809, Weems emerges as something of a *mediator* between the text (as embodied in the book's initial form) and its audience. There was nothing unique in this: the civic texts of the early republic were not merely the concoction of a few printers and booksellers whose message was hegemonically imposed on a broad American public; they were the result of a complex interaction between authors, printers, and audiences.

A later commentator observed that Weems's book is "as American as apple pie, or spoon bread, or baked beans."[70] Like these culinary artifacts, it, too, was a product of the American backcountry, with a slightly Southern flavor. Weems began working on his biography in early 1799, just before Washington's death. The timing could hardly have been more fortuitous: "6 months ago I set myself to collect anecdotes of him," Weems reported shortly after Washington's death. By February 1800, Weems had completed the first edition, and rushed it into print on February 22, Washington's birthday—making it, one might say, the first President's Day sale. Weems confidently predicted success. "I coud sell thousands of them," he wrote Carey, in what turned out to be a huge underestimate. Weems nearly ran through two editions by July, and was already planning "a capital edition" for the fall. Robust sales continued all summer, and by August Weems was considering an obvious market: it could be "sold as a School book." Later that year, drawing on a martial metaphor he often used to describe bookselling, Weems said the booklet was among "the best ammunition I ever had in my cartouch box yet."[71] He would be proven right. His knowledge of his public's tastes combined with his remarkable salesman's abilities to enable Weems to turn the book into one of the greatest sellers of the nineteenth century.

"The truth is," Weems wrote Carey in 1809, the year he published the final revision, "Washington will . . . do more for you than any *one* book of the *same size,* you ever had anything to do with." He was not exaggerating: by 1825, the book was in its fortieth edition.[72]

ALSO—An HISTORY (4th edition *greatly improved*) of
THE LIFE AND DEATH OF
Gen. George Waſhington:

Carefully collected, in the neighbourhood of Mount Vernon, from the most authentic Documents: Exhibiting his very extraordinary Character, not on- ly as a Soldier and a Statesman, but as a Man; and a man of that early prudence—admirable fortitude—rigid temperance—unwearied industry----- honor unblemish'd, and uncorrupted patriotism, which rendered *him* the glory of human nature and admiration of the world, and *this his History* well worthy the perusal of every Young Man who wishes, like Washington, to *live*, greatly useful and happy; and to *die*, universlly lamented and beloved. With an elegant copperplate likeness of him. *Price* 37 1-2 cents.
━━━━━━━━━━━━━━━━━━━━━━━━━━[R. COCHRAN, Printer.]━━

37. Advertisement for Mason Locke Weems's Life of Washington (*c. 1803*).

Weems brought a vast knowledge of Americans' reading tastes to his biogra- phy, having spent most of the prior decade selling books from New York to Geor- gia. "A one-man market research enterprise," Daniel Boorstin called Weems. "Never was a cult devised for an audience better pre-tested, nor a national hero more calculatedly concocted to satisfy the demand."[73] Fortunately, Weems left copious traces of his market research in his lengthy correspondence with Carey, which provides invaluable insight into popular reading tastes of his age. Weems's letters are littered with advice on how "to *strike* the Popular Curiosity" of his Southern and Middle Atlantic public, and he did not mince words. " 'Tis in your power thr'o the divine blessing to do great things in this country," he told Carey in 1797, "if you will but follow my prescriptions."[74]

What did Weems prescribe? First, and perhaps most important, a text had to be accessible to be popular. By 1800, after six years of selling books full-time, Weems had developed a strategy for pricing books to reach the broadest possible audience. Price had been a source of some tension between Weems and Carey. Their first collaboration involved high-priced European books: Oliver Gold- smith's *Animated Nature* and William Guthrie's *Modern Geography*. Impressive salesmanship by Weems brought in an estimated $60,000, but the profit margin on the enterprise was so slim that Weems's expenses ate up all Carey's profit and left Weems in debt.[75] This venture, however, stands largely as atypical of Weems's career. With a few notable exceptions, Weems spent most of his life selling high volumes of low-priced books: almanacs, schoolbooks, spellers, pamphlets, and so forth.

His perennial best sellers included "A *full assortm^t of school books*, little Histories interesting & curious, Voyages, travels, fine Novels, &^c. &^c. &^c." Weems developed his strategy early and never abandoned it: "small, i.e. quarter of dollar books, on subjects calculated to *strike* the Popular Curiosity, printed in very large numbers and properly *distributed*." Low prices ensured high sales and a steady market. "I w^d circulate millions" of books, Weems insisted. But: "This cannot be effected without the character of *cheapness*. Let but the public point to me and say, '*there goes the little Parson that brings us so many clever books and so cheap*,' and I ask no more." Weems continually reiterated his desire to sell books that were "*cheap*—mighty cheap—monstrous cheap," and chided Carey when he forgot this most important lesson. "Our Country," he insisted, "is made up of that small fry . . . It is but rare that I want to see an Author that stands higher than a dollar." The same applied to the Good Book itself: "As to the Bible, Mr. Carey, if you wish to make this, as it *may be made* a Source of *profit for life*, you must make the whole Republic your Purchasers. But you can hardly count on Plebian Pence, while you have put your Book at Patrician Price."[76] Focusing on this "Plebian" market had numerous advantages, not only financial but political. (According to Weems, competition for the Bible was stiff. "Your Bible proposition has knock'd up just such a dust here among the Printers," wrote Weems in New York, "as woud a stone if thrown smack into the centre of a Hornet's nest. The whole swarm is out. You hear of nothing here now but printing the Bible. Collins is going to print a bible—Swords is going to print a bible—Hopkins is for a bible—and Durell for a Folio! Everything that can raise a type is going to work upon the Bible. You'd take New York to be the very town of Man-soul, and its printers the veriest saints on earth. The town is prodigious healthy!! You remember what the five righteous w^d have done for Sodom. Tis well Tom Paine doesn't hear of all this. He'd [*get drunk?*] an hour sooner than common.")[77]

Equally as important in determining a book's popularity was its genre. History sold well, though Weems lamented the absence of popular histories and personal memoirs of the Revolution. "I do firmly believe," wrote Weems in 1799, "that if I had but some specimens of a well approv^d history of the American War & Revolution . . . fill^d with some chapter selected from the most interesting & affecting part of the history, well *printed* and adorn[d] with one or two Cuts best fitted ad captandum &c. I have no doubt but I coud make you a great deal of money."[78] Weems repeatedly urged Carey to send him more histories. During the 1790s, he asked for books like John Smith's *Generall Historie of Virginia* ("I coud sell you many a thousand of that curious work"); Charles Rollin's *Ancient History* ("No book w[d] succeed better!"); Thomas Hutchinson's *The History of Massachusetts*; and David Ramsay's *History of American Revolution*.[79] Most popular of all were accounts of well-known Revolutionary leaders. "If you coud get the life of Gen[l]. Wayne, Putnam, Green &c.," wrote Weems in 1797, "Men whose courage and Abilities, whose patriotism and Exploits have won the love and admiration of the American people, printed in small volumes and with very interesting frontispieces, you w[d], without doubt, sell an immense number of them."[80]

History was not the only popular genre. Weems also sold geographies, novels, plays, scientific books, religious books, political tracts, schoolbooks, spelling books, and almanacs.[81] One important draw was sentimentality. "I cou'd vend an infinite number of *fine sentimental moral Novels*," wrote Weems, adding, "my heart w[d] concur in the work." Weems frequently asked for "fine Sentimental Novels, entertaining histories &[c]. &[c].," again adding, "I could vend a vast many." Another popular feature was "curious" tales. Weems often called for "little Histories, interesting & curious" or "curiosity stirring voyages & travels." Curiosity drove the demand for Aeneas Anderson, *Narrative of the British Embassy to China* ("a curious work," wrote Weems), and also, no doubt, for Fenelon's *The Adventures of Telemachus, the Son of Ulyssses / Les Aventures de Telemaque fils d'Ulysse* (sold in both English and in French); *Letters Written by A Turkish Spy*; and William Alexander's *The History Of Women, From The Earliest Antiquity To The Present Time: Giving An Account Of Almost Every Interesting Particular Concerning That Sex, Among All Nations.* So important was it that works be "curious," Weems even urged Carey to enliven his Bible. "To have it said that Carey's bible contains more Curious things than were ever seen in any other bible, wou'd be a great Matter." This demand for "curious anecdotes" explains why Weems entitled his biography: *A History of the Life . . . of General George Washington . . . containing many curious and valuable ANECDOTES.* It also explains the memorable stories that Weems added over the years—including the anecdote "too valuable to be lost, too true to be doubted," of young George and the cherry tree.[82]

By the late 1790s, then, Weems had established himself selling particular kinds of books: "fine Novels, entertaining histories, curiosity stirring voyages & travels . . . scarcely anything but Sable colour[d] Divinity." When it came to religion, the good parson's instructions were clear. "Let the Moral & Religious be as highly dulcified as possible. Divinity, for this climate, sh^d be very rational and liberal, adorn^d with the graces of stile, and cloth^d in splendid binding." Late-eighteenth-century Virginia lacked the stricter religious mores of New England, and had not yet been infused with the evangelical fervor of the Second Great Awakening, and so Weems had no luck selling what he called "Puritanically religious books." Instead, he requested books like Philip Doddridge's *The Rise and Progress of Religion in the Soul,* Robert Russel's *Sermons,* George Whitefield's *Sermons,* or more entertaining works like Madame de Genlis's *Sacred Dramas* and Henry Hunter's *Sacred Biography.* When Carey misjudged, Weems responded sharply. As to "Puritanical" books, he wrote in one of his favorite expressions, "you might as well send Fiddles to a Methodist conventicle."[83]

Religious tolerance in Virginia had limits, however, and called for careful salesmanship. The Episcopalian bishop William Meade, for instance, recorded his dismay at finding Weems selling Thomas Paine's *Age of Reason.* Meade confronted Weems, "and asked if it was possible that he could sell such a book. He immediately took out the Bishop of Llandaff's answer, and said, 'Behold the antidote. The bane and antidote are both before you.'" Meade here confused Llandaff with Richard Watson, but his description of the event certainly captures Weems's clever salesmanship. Demand for Paine's controversial tract was high, and Weems had learned how to sell it despite the disapproval of powerful clerical authorities. He removed certain sections of Paine's work, and only sold it alongside Watson's reply to Paine, *An Apology for the Bible.* Evidently he needed Watson to pull this off. Once Weems complained of having on hand "13 or 12 Cop[ies]. Of Paine," But lacking the "defense of Christianity (by Watson) The Bishops & Lords spiritual here w^d tear me to pieces if I sold them."[84]

Weems's experience thus taught him what made a book popular. Armed with this knowledge, Weems began drafting his biography of Washington in mid 1799. Its original title was "THE TRUE PATRIOT, OR BEAUTIES OF WASHINGTON: Abundantly Biographical & Anecdotal Curious & Marvellous" (anticipating the title of his 1802 pamphlet, *The True Patriot; or An Oration on the Beauties and Beatitudes of a Republic*). "'Tis artfully drawn up," Weems commented when he finished the first draft in 1799, "enliven^d with anecdotes, and in my humble opinion, marvelously fitted, 'ad captandum—gustum populi Americani!!!![']"[85] As Weems revised the biography, he continued to add more of the "curious" stories that proved so popular. The 1806 edition, still only eighty pages, contained two new anecdotes, including the cherry tree story.[86] The 1808 edition grew to more than two hundred pages, with still more stories, including Mary Washington's dream and George Washington praying at Valley Forge. Weems made only minor changes before selling the copyright to Carey later that year, after which Carey set the book to stereotyped plates, churning out the text year after year.

Although didactic in its conception, Weems never sacrificed drama to instruction. The book was "gay and sprightly."[87] And it was highly sentimental. His Washington was not the distant, reserved man his contemporaries knew, but a maudlin figure more suited to the emerging sentimentality of nineteenth-century culture. Seeing his father on his deathbed, for instance, young George "fell upon his father's neck . . . he kissed him a thousand and a thousand times, and bathed his clay-cold face with scalding tears." Speaking to George's father, Weems imagined the touching scene:

> He now gives thee his little strong embraces, with artless sighs and tears; faithful to thee still his feet will follow thee to thy grave: and when thy beloved cor[p]se is let down to the stones of the pit, with streaming eyes he will rush to the brink, take *one more* look, while his bursting heart will give thee its last trembling cry . . . *O my father! my father!*

These sentimental bonds made George "worthiest to be the founder of a JUST and EQUAL GOVERNMENT," and these same bonds would tie George as father to his American children.[88] Thus did Weems create not a distant patriarch, but a benevolent father, "feeling towards his countrymen the solicitude of a father for his children." Weems, perhaps more than any other person, accomplished the domestication (and the evangelization) of Washington, bringing "The father of his country . . . in the presence of his children," where he would remain.[89]

Weems had written a masterpiece, a work masterfully tuned to the "gustum populi Americani"—the popular tastes of Americans. The book was sentimental—sappy, later generations would say—but for the age, it suited perfectly. It was certainly moral. Its religion was a dulcified, almost mawkish brand of Christianity. The book was entertaining, instructive, gay, sprightly, and brief. And it was cheap. Weems wrote a text he knew would suit his audience perfectly. Indeed, one might even reverse the formulation and say that in certain respects the audience had created the text.

Discriminating the "Populi"

Since the very early days of mass printing, both radicals and conservatives have seen the widespread dissemination of print as a force that, almost of its own accord, undermines hierarchies. This was the case for early Protestants—"How many printing presses there be in the world," wrote the sixteenth-century Protestant John Foxe, author of the *Book of Martyrs*, "so many blockhouses there be against the high castle of St. Angelo, so that either the pope must abolish knowledge and printing or printing at length will root him out"—as it was for the elites of the late-eighteenth- and early-nineteenth-century United States, who complained about novel reading and its potential to subvert traditional social mores.[90] This association of print with democratization is one that historians have often accepted, seeing the expansion of reading as a process that continually undermined the cultural and political authority of elites. But in the early republican United States, reading did not necessarily undermine hierarchy and authority. Creating a republican nationalism, it was widely understood, involved the spread of reading and education. Reading would have to be, not abolished—the hope of seventeenth-century conservatives—but *controlled* so as to promote new forms of republican authority.

True, Weems edited and republished subsequent versions of the work in response to comments he received on his travels. But not every part of his audience was equal. The histories, novels, almanacs, biographies, and religious tracts Weems circulated rarely undermined the political and cultural authority of local elites. Throughout his bookselling career, Weems relied heavily on elite figures to assist him with the selection and circulation of his books and pamphlets. These local elites disproportionately influenced the circulation and the content of the texts he sold throughout the South. Consistent with his message to obey the Constitution and worship Washington, Weems's method of selling books ultimately reinforced existing cultural and social hierarchies.

There was, to be sure, a "democratic" aspect to Weems's bookselling, as his travels put him in contact with an extensive reading (and nonreading) public. In 1800, for instance, as he trolled New Jersey and New York for subscribers to Carey's Bible, Weems reported "toil[ing] from door to door throughout Philad[a] & the towns of Jersey," pushing Carey's Bible and his own Washington biography to "Journeymen[,] Hatters & Blacksmiths." Later that summer, he wrote about his sales strategy: "from breakfast till tea constantly engag^d in *walking, talking, pleading & preaching* to the Multitudes." This contact only increased as he devised new tactics to reach his audience, like preaching sermons "to get the People together." Weems often traveled "around with the Judges & Lawyers from court to Court," selling his wares at court dates, races, festivals, and other events printed in his almanacs.[91] So ubiquitous was Weems in these travels, he became a figure of folk mythology, remembered by people throughout the South on his wagon, with a fiddle at his side.[92] Weems's familiarity with the "Multitudes" did not, however, liberate him from the social and cultural hierarchies of the age.

Throughout his career, Weems cultivated the patronage of elite figures. At a young age, Weems enlisted John Adams and Benjamin Franklin to help facilitate his ordination as an Episcopal clergyman in England during the chaotic post-Revolutionary period. As a bookseller, Weems developed this sort of patronage into an art: four of the first five American presidents endorsed his books.[93] For his first publishing venture, a two-volume edition of Hugh Blair's *Sermons* published in 1792 and 1793, as we have seen, Weems solicited an endorsement from none other than George Washington. "It was suggested to me," he wrote, "that were your *excellency* & Some Other Leading Characters in Philadelphia to show a good will to this Work it might greatly Augment & accelerate its progress."[94] And we have seen how Washington endorsed Weems's first political pamphlet.

Perhaps more important than these endorsements, Weems developed a national network of local "adjutants," as he called them, to popularize his books. Weems once described his very successful method for selling Carey's Bible: "I wou'd dash thro' all the States with letters of introductory & Commendatory *from* the Greatest & *to* the Greatest men of our Country—I w^d. thus in every section enlist the Coadjutancy of the most Influential Characters to a book whose popularity cou'd not fail to insure a prodigious patronage & whose high amount w^d yield a noble Revenue for *several years.*" Throughout his career, Weems appealed to prominent local figures, "putting papers into the hands of Gentlemen of the first Wealth & Character in the Nation." He drew on local networks of hierarchy and authority, soliciting help from "your driving Major & Colonels, your sturdy Knights of wealth so rare and daughters fair that they can do what they please in their neighbourhoods." Weems understood how to get just the right endorsement for the intended market. In 1813, Weems wrote to Dolly Madison requesting her endorsement for Henry Hunter's *Sacred Biography,* certain that "A recommendation of it . . . from your pen w^d insure it a wide Circulation among your Fair Country women." "Hundreds of the clergy are ready to give me their recommendations," he added, "but as it is chiefly on the Ladies that I count for the Circulation of it, I had rather have a few lines from M^rs. Madison than from a whole Bench of Bishops."[95]

Through these sales practices, Weems prioritized the views of what would today be called "opinion makers" when composing his works. In 1800, for instance, while composing the first edition of his *Life of Washington*, Weems tested his material on local elites. "I have read it to several Gentlemen whom I thought judges," wrote Weems, "such as Presbyterian Clergymen, Classical Scholars &^c. &^c. and they all commend it much . . . I read a part of it to one of my Parishioners," he added, "a first rate lady, and she wish^d I w^d print it, promising to take one for each of her children (a bakers dozen)." Weems's ambitious plan to open bookstores throughout the South similarly depended on a nationwide network of elite patrons. In a characteristic burst of enthusiasm, Weems explained how his bookstore project could succeed. It would need "a man of Intelligence, activity and popular manners: One who can dash around with his books to the Courts; preach with the Preachers[,] reason with the Lawyers & Doctors, and render himself dear to the Leading Characters of Society, themselves purchasing his books and recommending them to all their Friends & Neighbours."[96] In other words, someone just like Weems.

Weems relied on his network of elite patrons partly for financial reasons. The nature of his book-peddling life meant he was always on the move, entering a town, drumming up business, selling what he could, and moving on. But he usually left a stock of books with an "adjutant" who could continue to sell them for a commission. Weems looked for established figures, perhaps a local newspaper publisher if one existed, certainly someone unlikely to disappear suddenly. Early in his career, Weems lost a good deal of money by choosing his adjutants poorly, and ended deep in debt. He did not quickly forget the lesson, limiting his adjutants to people of means. In so doing, he made local elites central players in the dissemination of printed materials throughout the South. They mediated between producers and audiences of texts, reinforcing their own cultural authority in the process. One might say that Weems wanted to have his cake and eat it, too. He wanted his books to conform to "popular taste" (gustum populi), while at the same time currying the favor of local elites.

Selling Marshall's Biography:
Weems and Civic Texts

Parson Weems was not the only person to recognize Washington's market value in 1800. Among the many people cashing in on Washington's "old bones," Washington's nephew and future Supreme Court justice Bushrod Washington stands out. Upon George Washington's death, Bushrod inherited Mount Vernon and Washington's papers, and understood the value of both. In October 1800, Weems and Bushrod discussed "co-operating . . . in that Great work his Uncle's Memoirs." Unlike Weems's "scribblings," this "Great work" would benefit from unique access to Washington's private, unpublished correspondence—a veritable gold mine that Weems could only admire with awe. After several false starts, Bushrod recruited John Marshall, chief justice of the Supreme Court, fellow Federalist, and friend of George Washington, to write the first authorized biography.[97]

Marshall was a remarkably poor choice. He had little conception of the work involved in such a task, little sense of the reading public, and his ardently Federalist politics made him suspect in the eyes of many Americans. Marshall agreed to the project in the hope of earning enough money to relieve his chronic debt. He and Bushrod were boldly optimistic about their prospects. They expected to get thirty thousand subscribers for the five-volume set—by way of comparison, their contemporary, South Carolinian David Ramsay, sold fewer than 1,600 copies of his *History of the American Revolution* in ten years—and demanded $150,000 for the American copyright.[98] Fortunately for Washington and Marshall, they were not the only ones with high hopes. A bidding war among publishers ensued, with the Federalist publisher Caleb P. Wayne of Philadelphia winning the American rights, though for less than the hoped-for price. The project was hugely ambitious. Wayne enlisted every postmaster in the country to get subscribers, and hired two subscription agents for good measure. In part thanks to Judge Washington's intervention, Weems became the agent for the Southern district.

Alas, the project was a spectacular flop. The work proved too demanding for Marshall, who was in mediocre health and whose judicial duties on the Supreme Court as well as the Virginia and North Carolina circuit courts left him at most five to six months per year for research and writing. The books endured long delays, sold far fewer copies than expected, angered customers around the country, and nearly bankrupted poor Wayne.[99] The first volume was published some three years behind schedule. Delay followed delay. In the fall of 1803, expecting to receive the manuscript from Marshall any day, Wayne rented a house and hired several printers ready to set it to press the instant it arrived. He was still waiting—having already incurred more than $2,000 in costs—in January 1804. To make matters worse, when he finally received the volume, it was not the five hundred pages promised, but eight hundred pages. The expense associated with the excessive length alone cost him $1,500 for the first two volumes.[100] As if all that were not bad enough, readers were bitterly disappointed when they finally received the first volume, which, aside from being too long, mostly concerned itself with the discovery and settlement of the continent. Washington did not even appear in it! Subject to devastating criticism, Marshall wanted to revise the first volumes before he even finished the next. The rest of the work fared no better. Volumes 2 to 4 narrated the history of the Revolution, leaving only the final volume for Washington's presidency.

Weems had a front-row seat at this catastrophic spectacle. His letters to Wayne indicate that he received constant feedback from his customers about the book's shortcomings. As Weems gathered information about the failures of Marshall's biography, he also learned how to make Washington appeal to a mass market. Like everyone else involved, however, Weems began the project with high hopes. He began subscriptioneering in December 1802, believing he could sell twenty thousand copies. Weems understood something many printers of the day ignored (and what many historians since have overlooked): the importance of rural readers, and their role in shaping the nation's literary culture. As he had repeatedly reminded Carey and now began to tell Wayne, "The Mass of Riches of Population in America lie in the Country. There is the wealthy Yeomanry."[101] The book's success, Weems believed, would largely depend on its ability to penetrate the rural market.

Standing most prominently in the way of success were Marshall's political views. Jefferson, for one, believed the book was written "principally with a view to electioneering purposes"—in 1802, he even tried to persuade Joel Barlow to write a history to counter Marshall's—and the suspicion was echoed throughout the Middle Atlantic and Southern states. These doubts troubled Weems. "The People are very fearful that it will be prostituted to party purposes," he wrote to Wayne, urging that the book not turn into a Federalist tract. "For Heaven's sake drop now and then a cautionary hint to John Marshal Esqr. Your all is at stake with respect to this work. If it be done in a generally acceptable manner, you will make your fortune, otherwise," Weems added in his characteristically colorful prose, "the work will fall an Abortion from the press."[102]

With Jefferson controlling the patronage of the Post Office, Wayne soon realized that postmasters were unlikely to cooperate in marketing the book. "The postmasters being in general (I believe) Democrats," Bushrod Washington asked, probably prompted by Weems, "are you sure they will feel a disposition to advance the work?" Weems's rural constituency became more important than ever. "If the Fed^s. sh^d be disappointed, and the Demo^s disgusted with Genl Marshal's performance," Weems wrote, reminding the publisher of his important services, "will it not be vastly convenient to have 4 or 5000 good Rustic Blades to lighten your shelves & to shovel in the Dol^s.?" In regions where Federalists dominated, Weems reversed his usual strategy, using partisan loyalties to help him sell the book, "interesting some of the most wealthy & Influential Federalists in your cause." Publisher and salesman alike knew, however, that the book's partisan slant would ultimately hurt sales. "Don't indulge a fear—let no sigh of thine arise," Weems consoled his anxious publisher. "Give Old Washington fair play and all will be well. I mean Let but the interior of the Work be *Liberal* & the *Exterior Elegant.*"[103]

If Marshall was a poor choice to pen a biography of Washington, Weems was an excellent choice to sell it. Wayne and Bushrod both recognized Weems's talents. "Such a man as Weems will get 5 subscribers where I should obtain 1," wrote Wayne. As a good Jeffersonian, Weems would not raise suspicions trolling through the Middle Atlantic and Southern states. At the same time, his ecumenical politics did not condemn Federalists a priori. In this regard his business interests allied with his political views. He welcomed any and all into his tent. Not just welcome: he would rush up and drag them in. Weems did not flinch while gathering subscriptions in western Pennsylvania, a hotbed of Republican partisanship. "The place [that] had been represented to me as a Nest of Anti Washingtonian Hornets who w^d draw their stings at mention of his name . . . However," he boasted, "I dash^d in among them, and, *thank God* have obtain^d already 17 good names, with hopes of more."[104]

There was only so much Weems or anyone could do, however. Plagued by logistical and conceptual defects, the book was destined to be one of the great failures of early American publishing. Weems eventually began selling his own biography and his almanacs to supplement his income, and then set about repairing his fractured relationship with Carey. By 1807, Weems had tired of the project. Wayne had published Marshall's fifth and most partisan volume, and Weems resolved to refocus his energies on other kinds of works. "I am not in my element," he wrote to Carey, "tis chiefly the best Religious Work Moral & Political (i.e. Republican) Books that I wish to circulate." Here lay the other flaw of Marshall's biography. Not only was it too partisan; it was insufficiently moral. "Ergo," Weems confessed to Carey, "in this History of Washington I *feel* no great interest. It is not half so moralizing & Republican as my own of which by the by I publish[d] here this winter and have nearly sold off the whole impression 1500 copies (of a 5th edition improv[d]. without frontispiece) at half a do[llr]." When, two years later, Weems solicited an endorsement from Jefferson for "this private Life of Washington," he stressed its political orientation and its didactic value: "I have not, like *some* of his Eulogists, set him up as a Common Hero for military ambition to idolize & imitate—Nor an Aristocrat, like *others,* to mislead & enslave the nation, but a pure Republican whom all our youth should know, that they may love & imitate his Virtues, and thereby immortalize 'the *last Republic now on earth*.'" On these grounds, Weems felt the book was appropriate to "heartily thank you for a line or two in favor of it—as a school book."[105]

"O THAT I HAD A GOOD CRIB of Historical, Biographical, curious & valuable Anecdotes &c," Weems once lamented.[106] Whatever Marshall's merits as a historian, he clearly was not going to produce a work filled with curiosities and anecdotes. Instead of waiting for somebody else to do the job, Weems simply filled the crib. His biography was hardly accurate. But that did not matter. It was a moral tract, just like his pamphlets against drinking, adultery, and gambling. Its purpose was to unite Americans—to "immortalize 'the *last Republic now on earth*.'" Weems thus recommitted himself to selling only the "the best Religious Work Moral & Political," to instruct America's youth. Admitting that he and Carey had endured some difficult times (mostly quarrels over money and bookselling strategies), Weems reached out to renew their bond.

> With education & capacity perhaps, equal to the generality of money making Lawyers I embark[d] 16 years ago in the laborious business of vending books—I acted on principle. I have never made much—owing to want of knowledge of Men & business. I am getting knowledge & therefore money. I am sure—very sure—

morally & *positively* sure that I have it in my power (from my universal acquaintance, Industry & Health) to make you the most Thriving Book-seller in America. I can secure to you almost *exclusively* the whole of the business in the middle & western parts of all these Southern states from Maryland to Georgia inclusive. I can push your books not only into many of the Colleges, & most of the smaller seminaries of learning, but also into almost every Congregation of Christians, whether Baptist, Presbyterian, Episcopalian, as also in the private libraries of Doct^rs. Lawyers & Divines.[107]

So Weems revived his fruitful, if not always profitable, association with Carey. In 1808, he again revised his Washington biography. Hoping to clear his debts, he sold Carey the copyright for $1,000, which he almost immediately regretted. Despite periodic entreaties, Weems never regained the copyright, and so further revisions of the biography were forestalled. But he had done enough. The biography would continue to sell throughout Weems's career and long after.

The difference between Marshall's failure and Weems's success offers an important lesson about civic texts. Marshall had tried to promote his own Washington, the Washington he'd known, and the Washington who emerged from the great correspondence sitting in chests in Mount Vernon. Weems, on the other hand, created the audience's Washington: a Washington who grew up like them, who lived the same experiences as them, experienced the same emotions as them—a boy with whom they could identify. Marshall sought to make Washington in the image of a distant hero, while Weems made him in the image of his audience. Not surprisingly, the audience let Marshall's biography founder, while Weems's met with unimaginable success.

Indeed, one might even say that it was *through* Weems that Washington was transformed into an icon suitable for American audiences. Through his efforts, Washington went from being an eighteenth-century member of the planter elite to being a backwoods, up-by-his-bootstraps, evangelical figure who could appeal to a mass audience. These qualities may explain why later intellectuals found so much to dislike in Weems's portrayal ("an impossible and intolerable prig," is how Albert Beveridge described Weems's Washington).[108] Thanks to Weems, Washington became, in effect, a reflection of his audience. One would not want to push this argument too far: Weems, as we have seen, could not and did not accomplish this icon-creation alone. Washington had been a hero to begin with, and Weems did not in a literal sense "create" Washington. But he did create the

Washington nineteenth-century Americans would come to know. As John Marshall had learned to his consternation, not any George Washington could be imposed on audiences. Weems had succeeded where Marshall failed because he let Washington percolate up from the reading public.

There is an important lesson here with respect to the transmission of political ideologies in the early republic. The intellectual and political traditions that historians and political theorists have found present in the early republic—Scottish Enlightenment moral theory, ancient Greek and Renaissance civic humanism, the liberalism of Locke and others—were not injected into American political life in a direct form. Rather, they came in a mediated form. The civic texts inspired by great republican and Enlightenment thinkers were composed and disseminated by men like Weems and Carey, Jedediah Morse and Noah Webster, people who translated the great debates of European political life and articulated them for a broad American public. But in the final account they were chosen, selected, and read by that American public, a public not just of voters or propertied men, but a public of readers who learned, through these texts, how to think about their loyalties to each other and to the nation. What examining civic texts helps to explain, in short, is *how* the great traditions of Western political thought penetrated the American periphery, and how they took on their peculiarly American forms.

WEEMS HAD BEGUN his career as a clergyman, and had continued his calling by other means. Through more than thirty years of exhausting labor, Weems lived almost every one of his days engaged in what he considered "this most important of all human pursuits, I mean the dissemination of books." Weems never lost his faith in the power of reading to promote virtue and unify the nation. "It is our lot to live in a time uncommonly important to Posterity," he wrote in 1821, after decades trudging through the back roads of rural America, "a time when the sacred fire of Liberty is confin[d] to one torch, and that burning in our own country. Vice is the Azote, and Virtue the Grand vital element of that fire, and my belief is that the day will surely come when to minds enlighted[d] like ours, nothing but what we have done to maintain that holy fire will afford us any pleasure."[109] This fusion of religion and nationalism remained embedded in the civic texts he wrote, and would persist in the civic texts that came after him. Finally, in 1825, in a small South Carolina town, Weems's health gave out, as he long predicted it would. He never made it back to Dumfries.

Weems's texts had helped to bind a nation together, and they succeeded for a time. But only for a time. A generation later the national unity Weems had helped forge at last collapsed, and the political faction that Weems long predicted might lead to civil war did in fact do just that. The "sacred fire of Liberty" that Weems had struggled so hard to maintain and to nurture through the dissemination of texts would burn for a time, but eventually explode. In 1862, while marching through the tidewater region of Virginia with the Union Army, John Adams's great-grandson Charles Francis Adams, Jr., would record his impressions of the region Weems had made his home. Traveling "in sight of Mt. Vernon," he saw a country that was "a picture of desolation—the inhabitants few, primitive and ignorant, houses deserted and going to ruin, fences down, plantations overgrown, and everything indicating a decaying country finally ruined by war." The next day Adams passed through Dumfries:

> once a flourishing town and port of entry, now the most God-forsaken village I ever saw. There were large houses with tumbled down stairways, public buildings completely in ruins, more than half the houses deserted and tumbling to pieces, not one in repair and even the inhabitants, as dirty, lazy and rough as they stared at us with a sort of apathetic hate, seemed relapsing into barbarism.[110]

One can only guess what Weems would have made of this picture of his beloved nation.

4.

CIVIC TEXTS FOR SLAVE AND FREE: INVENTING THE AUTONOMOUS AMERICAN

———◆▸•◂◆———

IN HIS 1845 autobiographical *Narrative*, Frederick Douglass, the escaped slave who became one of the most important and eloquent abolitionist activists of the antebellum United States, recalled a turning point in his life. He was still a boy, then living in Baltimore, and his master's wife had decided to teach him how to read. Douglass was just beginning to catch on when his master discovered these efforts. He burst out in fury. Douglass remembered the scene vividly. "'Now,' said he [the master], 'if you teach that nigger (speaking of myself) how to read, there would be no keeping him. It would forever unfit him to be a slave.'"[1] Immediately Douglass's education was forbidden.

Surely, in the long sweep of American history, there has been no more ill-advised warning than this one. The outburst was a major turning point in Douglass's life, redolent with both secular and sacred connotations. It redoubled his determination to read, setting him on a course of action that would permanently change his life.

> These words sank deep into my heart, stirred up sentiments in me
> that lay slumbering, and called into existence an entirely new train

of thought. It was a new and special revelation, explaining dark and mysterious things, with which my youthful understanding had struggled, but struggled in vain. I now understood what had been to me a most perplexing difficulty—to wit, the white man's power to enslave the black man.[2]

It is striking that Douglass, who had experienced the brutal violence of slavery firsthand, believed that *illiteracy* (as opposed to, say, brute force) explained "the white man's power to enslave the black man." The realization was more than intellectual; it was a "revelation" in all its religious sense. Joining the community of readers would be a new birth, converting Douglass from social death into new life.[3] Suddenly Douglass understood the essential connection between literacy and liberty, ignorance and the "fitness" to be a slave.

And so Douglass learned to read. Secretly, he made the local white boys into his teachers. Carrying a copy of Noah Webster's spelling book in his pocket, he would persuade the children to give him a few lessons. As his reading skills grew, Douglass saved up fifty cents to buy himself a copy of the *Columbian Orator,* a popular textbook of the era. "This volume was, indeed, a rich treasure," Douglass later wrote. "Every opportunity I got, I used to read this book. Among much other interesting matter," Douglass remembered several selections in particular. One was a dialogue between a master and a slave, in which the slave, who has just been captured after running away, boldly defends his attempted flight against his master's reproach. "I could not help feeling," Douglass said, "that the day might come, when the well-directed answers made by the slave to the master, in this instance, would find their counterpart in myself." Douglass also recalled a speech promoting Catholic emancipation in Ireland and several orations on the American Revolution, supporting the colonial rebellion.

> These were all choice documents to me, and I read them, over and over again, with an interest that was ever increasing, because it was ever gaining in intelligence; for the more I read them, the better I understood them. The reading of these speeches added much to my limited stock of language, and enabled me to give tongue to many interesting thoughts, which had frequently flashed through my soul, and died away for want of utterance . . . With a book of this kind in my hand, my own human nature, and the facts of my

experience, to help me, I was equal to a contest with the religious advocates of slavery.[4]

In the long history of reading it is hard to find a better statement of how texts shape a reader's sense of self, touching both the mind and the innermost essence of personhood, the "soul." Reading opened up new vistas for Douglass. It gave him the ability to articulate his opposition to slavery in ways he had never before possessed. And it led him to hate slavery more than ever. "The more I read, the more I was led to abhor and detest my enslavers." His master's prediction had been borne out: "As I read and contemplated the subject, behold! that very discontentment which Master Hugh had predicted would follow my learning to read had already come." Reading would now "torment and sting my soul to unutterable anguish. As I writhed under it, I would at times feel that learning to read had been a curse rather than a blessing . . . I envied my fellow-slaves for their stupidity."[5] By reading, Douglass had been made unfit to be a slave.

Douglass's account speaks to the power of texts like Noah Webster's *Speller* and the *Columbian Orator* to foster new ways of thinking about oneself. Douglass, when he finally succeeded in accessing these texts, underwent precisely the transformation civic texts were designed to enact: his reading set in motion the process that drove him toward rational argument, independence, and moral autonomy. Douglass's experience highlights a central feature of civic texts—and of early American nationalism more generally. For these texts did more than bind Americans together as a nation; that was only part of their work. They also sought to remake individuals into morally autonomous subjects.

THE HISTORIAN James Kloppenberg has argued that "we ought to think of autonomy rather than freedom as the aim of the American Revolution, autonomy not only for the nation, but for individuals as well." Individual autonomy is a prerequisite for a government grounded on the consent of the governed. "The concept of autonomy," Kloppenberg observes, "is inseparable from the concept of self-government, and inseparable from . . . nuances of restraint, law, and moral responsibility."[6] Autonomy as understood in this sense is defined by several interrelated features. First and perhaps most important is a view of the individual as a particular self defined by a sense of "inwardness": a self whose identity is located in the interior realm. Second is an idea of the individual as a morally self-governed agent endowed with the ability to act (or not to act) in certain ways. Last is a notion of human agency: the idea that worldly events are produced by human action rather than providential guidance, chance, or fortune. This conception of the individual—what Friedrich Nietzsche called "the sovereign individual . . . autonomous . . . in short, the man who has his own, independent, protracted will, and *the right to make promises*"—is anything but natural; it was the result of a centuries-long process of social and economic transformations and development in moral thought central to the evolution of Western culture.[7]

The autonomous individual is the basic building block for a political system, like that of the United States, founded on the consent of the governed. Only morally autonomous agents are endowed with the capacity freely to give their consent and obedience to the nation. Only in a society composed of autonomous individuals would it be possible—or even thinkable—to enact the political principle of George Washington's Farewell Address: "The very idea of the power and the right of the People to establish Government presupposes the duty of every Individual to obey the established Government." To realize this principle, it was necessary that Americans in the new nation think of themselves as morally autonomous. But if this understanding of the individual was the necessary foundation for a government based on consent, it was also something of a double-edged sword. For it raised a deeply vexing question: how could social order be maintained in a society composed of autonomous individuals unbound by coercive forms of restraint?

If this dilemma was difficult enough in any context, in the United States it was made all the more complex by the millions of slaves who inhabited the nation. "Slavery," as the historian David Brion Davis has written, "is the perfect antithesis of individual autonomy or self-sovereignty." In the United States the creation of an autonomous subject would become inextricably fused with debates about slavery. As we will see, it was largely in opposition to the idea of "the slave" that the autonomous American would be constructed. Where the free citizen was to be industrious, virtuous, thrifty, and religious, the slave was imagined as lazy, immoral, dissolute, and heathen. "Slavery," Davis notes, "stood as the central metaphor for all the forces that debased the human spirit."[8] If the slave were somehow to be educated into virtues of industry and intelligence, he would, as Frederick Douglass's master understood, cease to be a slave. Even more dangerously, slaves might rebel and unleash the specter of servile or civil war that so terrified Southerners.

There was a basic contradiction here: the morally autonomous subject was the foundation of a nation legitimated by consent, but to extend that autonomy to slaves would be to undermine the institution of slavery, and perhaps destroy the nation itself. Civic texts responded to this dilemma in a variety of ways. Some began to denounce slavery while promoting a market-oriented, capitalist culture, casting slavery as opposed to the nation's fundamental values.[9] These "free labor" accounts highlighted the contradictions between slavery and a republican nationalism based on the autonomous individual. Other texts, however— pedagogical texts for slaves, sermons for white slave owners, conduct manuals for reform-minded planters—would seek to reshape the meaning of slavery itself so as to reconcile it with an increasingly modernizing, liberal nationalism. In the process, they would reconfigure the meaning of both slavery and autonomy in subtle but important ways.

Schoolbooks as Civic Texts: The Hidden Bestsellers of Early American Literature

Few texts better served the purpose of reaching a reader's inner subjectivity than schoolbooks. Weems, for one, had always believed schoolbooks peculiarly well-suited to shape individual morality. "If you cou'd but view this business we are about to engage in, with my optics & impressions, you w^d never lose sight of School books," Weems wrote Carey in 1809, "you w^d dig for them as for hidden treasures & pile them up like Pyramids. War or no war People will have, but they *must have* school books. And by & by we may get most of our school books, like our national ballads & gazettes, to contain just what Ethics & Politics we please." Schoolbooks were, for Weems, the greatest tools for shaping individuals—so much so, he imagined his other writings as similarly didactic. When Weems had solicited an endorsement from Jefferson for his *Life of Washington,* as we saw, he asked "for a line or two in favor of it—as a school book."[10]

In his conviction that schoolbooks were a powerful weapon to forge "Ethics & Politics," Weems followed in a very long Anglo-American tradition. Schoolbooks— or primers or readers, as they were often called—had circulated very widely in the colonial period, and they would grow even more popular in the post-Revolutionary era. "Apart from the Bible," remarks a historian of schoolbooks, "the books most widely read in nineteenth-century America were not those written by intellectuals, but schoolbooks written by printers, journalists, teachers, ministers, and future lawyers earning their way through college."[11] These texts were not the productions of major political figures like Washington or Jefferson or Benjamin Rush, though they did sometimes include their words, and they certainly followed their ambition to promote education in the new republic. They were the work of less exalted figures like Weems, Jedediah Morse, or Noah Webster: teachers, clergymen, lawyers manqués, who sought through texts to promote nationalism and, even more, to reach individuals' inner realms so as to shape their behavior and their very understanding of themselves as moral agents.

THE HISTORY OF American schoolbooks begins with the great *New-England Primer*. Published in at least 205 editions before 1800, it is estimated to have sold somewhere from 3 to 8 million copies by 1830.[12] Based on a book called the *Protestant Tutor* first printed in England by the Nonconformist Benjamin Harris in 1679 (and in Boston in 1685), the first known edition of the *New-England Primer* dates from 1727, although earlier editions were almost certainly circulating in the late seventeenth century, shortly after Harris arrived in Boston and set up a "Coffee, Tee and Chucaletto" shop. Despite its name, the *Primer*'s influence extended well beyond New England—Benjamin Franklin, for instance, printed more than thirty-seven thousand copies of it in Philadelphia between 1749 and 1766—and it would continue to be reprinted in many states during the nineteenth century.[13] Emphasizing dissenting Protestant religious values above all, the book fused its religious message with a crude proto-nationalism, embodied in the frontispiece depicting the British king during the colonial period, and patriot figures like John Hancock and George Washington thereafter.

In its religion, the *New-England Primer* promoted an orthodox Calvinist faith, emphasizing man's depravity and constantly reminding readers of the death that awaited sinners and saints alike. "Be never Proud by any means, / build not thy house too high," read one selection, "But always have before your eyes, / that you are born to die."[14] (One can understand a great deal about the Puritan worldview by imagining children reading such selections in school and at home, thinking about them, perhaps, as they fell asleep.) The book's spelling lessons reinforced the Calvinist doctrine of original sin, teaching the letter A, for instance, not with a sunny quip about apples, as children's works would do in a more secular age, but with the couplet: "A: In *Adam's* Fall / We Sinned All."

Nonetheless, moral choice remained open, and crucial to the individual facing damnation. One of the *New-England Primer*'s longer stories, for instance, recounted a dialogue among a youth, Christ, and the Devil. As the Devil tempts the youth with earthly pleasures, Christ warns the boy of the Hell that awaits sinners. The youth hesitates, but decides that he can act as he pleases now, for there is always time to repent later. He is wrong, however: Christ is angered. The boy dies and is told he will go to Hell. Even as the young boy pleads for another chance, Christ refuses and Death comes to whisk him away to burn in eternal damnation. As the tale suggests, Calvinism pressed individuals to exert their moral will, even as the choice of salvation remained with God. "No mass or prayer, no priest or pastor," the great bibliographer Paul Leicester Ford observes of the *New-England Primer*, "stood between man and his Creator, each soul being morally responsible for its own salvation; and this tenet forced every man to think, to read, to reason."[15]

The *New-England Primer* thus promoted—or at least opened the possibility for—a conception of the individual as morally autonomous. Calvinism has been read by some scholars as "an ideology of transition," responding to the disorder of early modern society by promoting a turn inward, toward the individual.[16] The *New-England Primer* certainly fits this interpretation, highlighting the element of Calvinism that, with its emphasis on each person's inner depravity and its insistence on inner spiritual conversion, emphasized the inner sources of morality. For this reason, many scholars—perhaps none more influential than the philosopher Charles Taylor—have seen dissenting Protestantism as one of the major sources of the modern conception of the "self," and hence the basis for forms of political association based on contract and consent. Drawing on the Augustinian idea of grace as located within each person, Calvinism promoted a conception of "inwardness" and paved the way for an understanding of the individual as autonomous moral agent. Although strict Calvinism shunned the idea that one's actions could in themselves lead to salvation, by exalting the individual as moral agent it led to the idea that made it seem "obvious," according to Taylor, "that the only thing which could create authority was the consent of the individual."[17]

The evangelical Protestantism that flourished in the British colonies and, later, in the United States, further emphasized individual autonomy. Focusing on the importance of inner light, of feelings, and of the heart, evangelical Protestantism moved divine power to the background, highlighting individual moral choice and creating a whole vocabulary to imagine an autonomous individual whose moral sources lie within him- or herself. Post-Revolutionary evangelical Protestantism, with its insistent assault on hierarchy and its exaltation of popular forms of worship, was particularly important in fostering what the historian Nathan Hatch has called the "individualization of conscience." These individualizing implications were most evident during the eighteenth- and nineteenth-century revivals, which "demonstrated the possibilities of persuasion" in the advancement of religious aims. The proliferating of denominations—all lacking the coercive power of the state enjoyed by established churches, and thus forced to persuade audiences to *choose* one over the other—highlighted the increasing centrality of voluntarism to the American religious experience. Even strands of New England Calvinism—most obviously in the figure of Lyman Beecher—were recast in the nineteenth century along the idea that God exercised only persuasive power over individuals, and that it fell to voluntary individuals to grant their consent, whether it be to an association, to their God—or to the nation.[18]

Persuading individuals freely to grant their obedience would become the primary aim of educational texts in the post-Revolutionary period, a project prefig-

38. *Image of John Rogers being burned at the stake, from* The New-England Primer, Improved . . . (*New London: T. Green, 1785*).

ured in the Calvinist *New-England Primer*. One of its most remarkable selections told the story of the Protestant martyr John Rogers, a sixteenth-century clergyman who had published one of the earliest English Bibles. Rogers had been dramatically executed in 1555 in front of a large crowd, which included his wife and eleven children, after having refused the opportunity to recant his faith and save himself. The *New-England Primer* recounted the story and included a graphic picture of Rogers being burned at the stake (figure 38). The picture encouraged readers to imagine themselves as Rogers's children, learning from his example the virtue and steadfastness necessary to retain loyalty to one's faith—one's church, one's nation—in the face of great adversity. Alongside this image, the primer reprinted a letter Rogers had left for his children shortly before his death:

> *I leave you here a little Book,*
>   *for you to look upon:*
> *That you may see your Fathers face,*
>   *when he is dead and gone.*[19]

The idea that by picking up a book children would continue to look upon their father's dead face, and thus subscribe to his values, was a powerful means of transmitting moral virtues—of fostering within children the imperative to perpetuate the values of their fathers—and it recurs as a trope in many later civic texts as a means of transmitting the values and principles of the Founding Fathers after they, too, were dead and gone.

The less forgiving elements of the *New-England Primer*'s Calvinism declined in revised editions over the course of the eighteenth century—the sentence associated with the letter A, for instance, "In *Adam's* Fall / We sinned all," was changed to "Adam and Eve / Their God did grieve."[20] The *Primer*'s declining religiosity reflected the larger turn toward more secular schoolbooks as the eighteenth century drew to a close. Where an average of 92 percent of their content during the colonial era was related to religion, according to a study of some 1,370 early American readers, religious selections declined to 22 percent of readers' total content during the period from 1775 to 1825. In the fifty years after, the religious content would fall to a mere 5 percent.[21] Although the *New-England Primer* continued through many more editions, its influence had already waned by the end of the eighteenth century, with the appearance of newer schoolbooks grounded in more recent pedagogical theory and offering very different reading selections. The inculcation of moral autonomy remained a central feature of these newer texts, but it would now be promoted in a more recognizably liberal language, though one still resonating with evangelical chords.

From the Columbian Orator to the English Reader: The Making of the Autonomous Individual

Frederick Douglass was hardly the only person whose sense of himself was shaped by the *Columbian Orator*. First published in 1797 in Boston, the *Columbian Orator* was a popular schoolbook, reprinted no less than thirty-four times by 1840, selling by one estimate 200,000 copies, and perhaps many more. (A rough estimate of the number of editions printed in the forty years following its initial publication, as well as of the location of publication of various editions, is noted in appendix 3.) It was an unusually influential schoolbook: its readers included not just Douglass but Abraham Lincoln, Ralph Waldo Emerson, and Harriett Beecher Stowe.[22] Although the book does not appear to have been printed in any state south of Maryland—perhaps not surprisingly, given its overt antislavery sentiments—it was certainly circulating in parts of the deep South. Mason Locke Weems, for example, sold the *Columbian Orator* throughout the South during his career.

The differences between the *New-England Primer* and the *Columbian Orator* offer a crude standard by which to gauge the transformation of values in early American schoolbooks. The text was organized as a compilation of eighty-one selections totaling roughly three hundred pages (a few were added as editions were revised, though none seems to have been removed nor was the order of the selections changed). Each selection, designed to be read aloud, was meant to "inspire the pupil with the *ardour of eloquence,* and the *love of virtue.*"[23] Most of the selections were speeches, though the book contained a number of dialogues as well. Although a few selections were biblical, the majority dated from the eighteenth century. Of those that touched on ancient subjects—mostly relating to classical republican virtues—only five were actually penned by ancient authors; the rest were by modern authors reflecting on the virtues of ancient figures. The *Columbian Orator* had a broadly nationalist thrust, with strong leanings toward the Jeffersonian politics of Caleb Bingham, the schoolteacher and bookseller who compiled the work. It excerpted speeches by Washington and Franklin, and reprinted a section of Washington's Farewell Address on the importance of

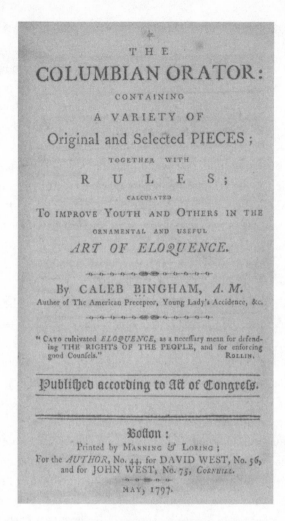

THE

COLUMBIAN ORATOR:

CONTAINING

A VARIETY OF

Original and Selected PIECES ;

TOGETHER WITH

R U L E S ;

CALCULATED

To IMPROVE YOUTH AND OTHERS IN THE

ORNAMENTAL AND USEFUL

ART OF ELOQUENCE.

By CALEB BINGHAM, *A. M.*

Author of The American Preceptor, Young Lady's Accidence, &c.

" CATO cultivated *ELOQUENCE*, as a neceſſary mean for defending THE RIGHTS OF THE PEOPLE, and for enforcing
good Counſels." ROLLIN.

Publiſhed according to Act of Congreſs.

Boſton :
Printed by MANNING & LORING ;
For the *AUTHOR*, No. 44, for DAVID WEST, No. 56,
and for JOHN WEST, No. 75, CORNHILL.

MAY, 1797.

39. Title page from the first edition of Caleb Bingham's
The Columbian Orator (1797).

Union. But the majority of the selections were political on a more subtle level: in the conception of the morally autonomous individual they promoted.

Like many schoolbooks of the period, the *Columbian Orator* drew on early modern pedagogical theory in connecting education to the formation of individual virtue. The debt to early modern thought was clear on the title page, which featured an epigraph by Charles Rollin, the seventeenth-century French educational theorist: "CATO cultivated ELOQUENCE as a necessary means for defending the RIGHTS OF THE PEOPLE, and for enforcing good Counsels." Rollin was one of the guiding lights of late-eighteenth- and nineteenth-century educational thought—his work had been particularly influential at Dartmouth College, where Bingham was educated—and he was often quoted in essays or orations on early American education. (His writings were considered important enough by the Philadelphia physician, reformer, and education advocate Benjamin Rush that he gave the book to his son Richard.) Rollin had argued that children should be taught to read with phrases that would "inculcate virtue." The purpose of education, he believed, was to train children into virtue: to "form in young men the honest man, the upright man, the good citizen, the good magistrate." Rollin's pedagogy stressed the use of example over precept; he believed moral education was best promoted through the model of exemplary figures: "Knowledge of the character and virtues of great men," he wrote, "leads to imitation." Teaching children to avoid vice, he stressed—in a passage that could have been penned by Weems or by almost any schoolbook author of the early republican period— "ought to be the chief End of Education; otherwise Learning, so far from being the Instrument of Virtue, serves only to promote and foment its contrary."[24] It might be a measure of Rollin's influence—and it is certainly a sign of a shared outlook on education—that an English edition of his *New Thoughts Concerning Education* was bound together with John Locke's *Some Thoughts Concerning Education* in at least one eighteenth-century edition.

Locke's *Thoughts Concerning Education* was surely the most important work of pedagogical theory for early Americans, a volume "whose influence on eighteenth-century English culture and especially eighteenth-century English literature," the scholar Jay Fliegelman has written, "can hardly be overemphasized."[25] Locke's theory of education rested on two basic principles. First, Locke believed that education was so essential to "the Welfare and Prosperity of the Nation . . . that I wou'd have every one lay it seriously to Heart." Locke's work on education should be seen as a companion to his more famous work on political theory. The two went hand in hand: Locke believed the purpose of education was to mold children into individuals capable of acting as the kind of rational subjects on which his political theory depended. "In a new political world in which government was to exist for the governed," Fliegelman notes, "the educational paradigm would provide a new model for the exercising of political authority."[26] Self-government in the political sense required self-government in the individual sense, and Locke's writings on education worked to promote the latter, just as his political writings promoted the former. Locke's second pedagogical principle regarded the malleability of children. "I imagine the Minds of Children as easily turn'd this or that way," he famously wrote, "as Water it self."[27] Locke believed the best way to mold children was by inculcating moral habits through repetition: intellectual, moral, and even physical. So important was the inculcation of habits, and so much did the physical connect to the moral, that Locke spent several pages discussing proper bowel movements.[28]

Locke's pedagogy, which would be taken up by eighteenth- and nineteenth-century educational texts, sought to foster the most essential trait for the autonomous individual: self-control. "The great Principle and Foundation of all Virtue and Worth, is plac'd in this," Locke wrote, "That a Man is able to *deny himself* his own Desires[,] cross his own Inclinations, and purely follow what Reason directs as best, tho' the Appetite lean the other Way." "It seems plain to me," Locke concluded, "that the Principle of all Virtue and Excellency lies in a Power of denying our selves the Satisfaction of our own Desires, where Reason does not authorize them. This Power is to be got and improv'd by Custom, made easy and familiar by an *early* Practice." The purpose of education, in this understanding, was to internalize forms of self-control. To that end, Locke condemned the use of physical punishment as counterproductive: "Such a Sort of *slavish Discipline* makes a *slavish Temper*," Locke argued, setting the figure of the slave in opposition to the self-controlled individual he hoped to develop. "The Child submits, and dissembles Obedience, whilst the Fear of the Rod hangs over him, but when that is remov'd, and by being out of Sight, he can promise himself Impunity, he gives the greater Scope to his natural Inclination; which, by this Way, is not at all alter'd, but on the contrary, heighten'd and increas'd in him; and after such Restraint, breaks out usually with the more Violence."[29] (Here was, in effect, the pedagogical underpinning of so many Southerners' fear of slave insurrection.) The best way to create social order, Locke believed, was not through external forms of discipline but through *internal* forms. "I cannot think any Correction useful to a Child," wrote Locke, "where the Shame of suffering, for having done amiss, does not work more upon him, than the Pain." Drawing on this pedagogical theory, eighteenth- and nineteenth-century educational texts would work to internalize habits of self-control guided not by force but by an inner compulsion: to create, in short, the autonomous, self-controlled individual.[30]

Locke's discussion of physical punishment leading to even greater violence touches on a major preoccupation of liberal political theory: ensuring social order in governments founded on consent. "The very idea of the power and the right of the People to establish Government," Washington's Farewell Address stated, "presupposes the duty of every Individual to obey the established Government." But how to persuade people to obey authority not founded in coercion? The answer was to turn inward: to harness the individual will by inculcating an ethic of *self-control*. The discipline of the new, modern order "was not to depend upon the authority of paternal kings and lords or upon the obedience of childlike and trustful subjects," the political theorist Michael Walzer has observed. It would be "voluntary, like the contract itself, the object of individual and collective willfulness."[31] The mission of these pedagogical texts was thus to foster a sense of internal discipline, a "collective willfulness" among Americans that would create order—or national allegiance—in a society grounded on nothing more than the consent of those individuals. No longer based on external force, obedience would result from interior compulsion: it would be voluntary. Hence, the importance of the tools of self-control Locke sought to inculcate. Shame, guilt, self-censure—all were different ways of constructing an inner voice, or conscience.

The *Columbian Orator* implemented this pedagogical theory by fostering an ethic of self-control within readers, and condemning habits that represented an absence of restraint.[32] One selection, for instance, imagined a dialogue between the ghosts of an English "duellist" and a "North-American Savage" mediated, rather fancifully, by the ghost of Mercury. The dialogue opens with the ghost of the Savage bragging that he died "very well satisfied . . . before I was shot, I had gloriously scalped seven men, and five women and children." The English duellist, meanwhile, comes across as equally lacking in the sort of virtue that maintains social order. "I was killed in a duel," he explains, his lack of self-control made clear from his behavior:

> A friend of mine had lent me a sum of money; and after two or three years, being in great want himself, he asked me to pay him. I thought his demand, which was somewhat peremptory, an affront to my honor, and sent him a challenge . . . The fellow could not fence: but I was absolutely the adroitest swordsman in England. So I gave him three or four wounds; but at last he ran upon me with such impetuosity, that he put me out of my play, and I could not prevent him from whipping me through the lungs . . . he will follow me soon . . . It is said that his wife is dead of grief, and that his family of seven children will be undone by his death. So I am well revenged, and that is a comfort.[33]

Each of these exaggerated figures represents the specter of uncontrolled wills. Both kill indiscriminately. Both murder women and children. Both lack a conscience and any sense of contrition for the action. Each in his own way represents the antithesis of the sort of virtuous, self-controlled individual these texts were seeking to create.

Such selections led readers relentlessly inward, toward an ethic of self-control. A "Dialogue on Cowardice and Knavery" featured various characters who were the stock in trade of these sorts of morality tales: a coward (who claims to be a soldier), a bankrupt (who claims to be a merchant), and a pawnbroker (who claims to be a banker). Teaching in a single dialogue the virtues of courage, honesty, and thrift, these figures and their doppelgangers personified the stark moral dichotomies—and the blunt moralizing—that ran through early American didactic literature. The hero of the dialogue, a character named "Trusty," summed up the lessons in a brief concluding soliloquy: "You have now learned the value of reputation and peace of mind, by the loss of them," he explains. "Let your future days be days of atonement. Let them be devoted, to honesty and fair dealing; and ever remember that integrity is the only road to desirable wealth, and that the path of virtue is alone the path of peace." The importance of thrift, honesty, and religiosity were repeatedly stressed in the *Columbian Orator*'s selections. "Whatever the licentious may say to the contrary," read a dialogue "On the Choice of Business for Life," "the happiness of society must rest on the principles of virtue and religion; and the pulpit must be the nursery, where they are cultivated."[34]

Reading was the key to inculcating a sense of moral autonomy. A dialogue on modern education pitted a foolish parent against a wise preceptor. The parent, hoping his son would learn the art of public speaking, asks, "What can be more useful for a child under such a government as ours, than to be able to speak before an audience with a graceful ease, and a manful dignity?" True, the preceptor responds, but "For that very reason I would educate him differently. I would lay the foundation of his future fame on the firm basis of the *solid sciences*; that he might be able in time to do something more than a mere parrot, or an ape, who are capable only of speaking the words, and mimicking the actions of others. He should first be taught to *read*."[35] In a sense, this selection encapsulated the aim of the book as a whole, and indeed of civic texts as a genre: to inculcate a sense of moral autonomy through reading. This faith in the power of reading to shape the individual was common to both evangelical and rationalist traditions. Reading cultivated a sense of inwardness—be it of the soul, or of the critical faculties—by touching the inner depths of the individual. Reading, uniquely, could produce the kind of discipline that was found wanting in physical punishment by "carr[ying] authority deep inside," creating the autonomous individual restrained purely through mechanisms of internal discipline.[36] The American individual who would result would be not "a mere parrot, or an ape," but an agent endowed with the moral autonomy to engage in acts of citizenship.

One of the most powerful tools for promoting self-control was the notion of a conscience, understood as the internalization of God's eye within each individual. "A sense of accountability to God will retard the eager pursuit of vice," read one selection in the *Columbian Orator*.[37] But increasingly the notion of conscience went further, locating accountability not just with God, but within one's *self*. The idea of conscience is an important feature of moral autonomy, implying, as the philosopher J. B. Schneewind has observed, "that we can be held responsible for ourselves . . . and suggest[ing] rewards and punishments dependent on our virtue or vice."[38] The rewards and punishments from obeying or betraying one's conscience carried penalties not just in the afterlife, but in the here and now: pleasure was to be gained by obeying, unhappiness by violating, the strictures of the conscience. These rewards could be material and immediate.

The point of these selections was to make such an ethic all but reflexive. A dialogue between a dissolute young man and his disapproving sister had the young man repent of his misguided ways. "Notwithstanding my gaiety; and my apparent contentment," the young man concluded, "I confess there is something within, which constantly admonishes me of my errors, and makes me feel unhappy."[39] It would be hard to give a better description of what the *Columbian Orator* aimed to do with such selections: to promote the idea that life is shaped by the choices of morally responsible individuals. Men should be estimated by their "deeds" and by their "hearts," the very embodiment of their interior selves.

ALTHOUGH CALEB BINGHAM'S *Orator* can be counted among the better-selling books of the late eighteenth and early nineteenth century, its sales were dwarfed by a schoolbook which surpassed it (and indeed every other), a book Abraham Lincoln would call "the best schoolbook ever put in the hands of an American Youth." Lindley Murray's *English Reader* was first published in 1799. Sales grew exponentially, and Murray soon became "the largest-selling author in the world in the first four decades of the nineteenth century." Where Bingham's *Orator* sold an impressive 200,000 copies, Murray's texts sold an estimated 12.5

million, a figure that does not include the 3 million books sold in Britain. The *English Reader* alone sold an estimated 5 million copies by 1850—astonishing numbers in any age. Lindley Murray's schoolbooks are said to have sold more copies in the English-speaking world than every other book save the Bible. From 1815 until the 1840s, when the McGuffey *Eclectic Reader* series overtook it in popularity, there can be no doubt that Murray's reader, as the historian Charles Monaghan puts it, "crushed all rivals."[40] (The number of editions of Murray's

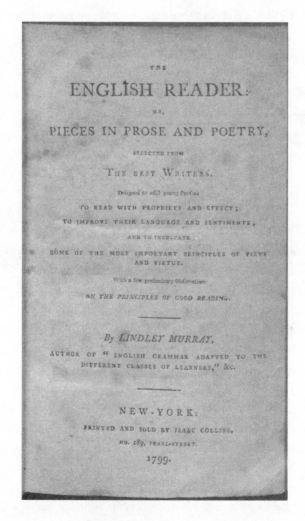

40. *Title page from the first U.S. edition of Lindley Murray's*
English Reader (1799).

English Reader is charted in appendix 4.) Murray followed up his *English Reader* with an *Introduction to the English Reader* in 1800, and then a *Sequel to the English Reader* in 1801. Put together, the three constituted a self-contained series to equip children with reading skills and virtues to shape them into morally responsible individuals.

Unlike the *Columbian Orator*'s dialogues, stories, and speeches largely set in the eighteenth century, Murray offered anecdotes mostly set in an ancient or biblical past. Like the *Columbian Orator*, Murray's *English Reader* sought above all to inculcate morality among its young readers. Murray called it "a work, which appeared to me likely to prove of peculiar advantage to the rising generation . . . at once calculated to promote correct reading; to give a taste for justness of thought, and elegance of composition; and to inculcate pious and virtuous sentiment." This aim was broadcast on the book's title page, which stated that selections had been chosen "to inculcate some of the most important principles of piety and virtue." The book's opening line reinforced this message: "Diligence, industry, and proper improvement of time, are material duties of the young." Murray's *Reader*, diffused in the millions of copies printed and incorporated into various school curricula, including the New York Free Schools, would seek to "inculcate" the building blocks of individual, moral autonomy among its readers.[41]

What virtues were to be inculcated? The first and perhaps most important was self-control: "He that is slow to anger, is better than the mighty; and he that ruleth his spirit, than he that taketh a city," read a typical selection. In order to inculcate an ethic of self-control, the *English Reader* sought to impart more prosaic habits like industry, punctuality, and subordination. "Diligence, industry, and proper improvement of time," read a sentence near the beginning of the work, "are material duties of the young." The importance of hard work was repeatedly stressed: "On whom does time hang so heavily, as on the slothful and lazy?" As with later moral reformers, Murray warned his readers away from drink: "Temperance, by fortifying the mind and body, leads to happiness: intemperance, by enervating them, ends generally in misery." Like many other didactic tracts of the period, Murray's *Reader* emphasized the importance of sentimental ties between parents and children, brothers and sisters: "What a smiling aspect does the love of parents and children, of brothers and sisters, of friends and relations, give to every surrounding object, and every returning day!"[42]

The book contained no end of pithy epigrams, valuable phrases, and didactic stories, all aimed to raise generations of individuals into habits of industry, thrift, temperance, and above all self-control. "What avails the show of external liberty," asked one selection, "to one who has lost the government of himself?" This "government of the self," it was understood, was intimately tied up with the logic of republican government. A report published by the New York Free School Society, which made Lindley Murray's texts required reading, averred that "a boy educated agreeably to this system, cannot fail to be made practically acquainted with the elementary principles of civil government, and thereby pre-eminently qualified to become a good citizen."[43]

Children were taught that their own fate depended less on external circumstance than on their own free choices. "The chief misfortunes that befall [us] in life, can be traced to some vices or follies which we have committed," read an epigram near the beginning of the work. This theme continued throughout: "Diseases, poverty, disappointment, and shame, are far from being, in every instance, the unavoidable doom of man," added another selection; "They are much more frequently the offspring of his own misguided choice." A later selection, drawn from Hugh Blair—a popular sermon that also appeared in other schoolbooks of the age—dwelled at length on this idea. Entitled "The misfortunes of men mostly chargeable on themselves," the selection emphasized the dangers of straying from a virtuous path. "Were we to survey the chambers of sickness and distress, we should often find them peopled with the victims of intemperance and sensuality, and with the children of vicious indolence and sloth." On the whole, Murray's text emphasized an exacting, severe morality that underlay the idea of the autonomous individual.

> But you, perhaps, complain of hardships of another kind; of the injustice of the world; of the poverty which you suffer, and the discouragement under which you labour . . . Before you give too much scope to your discontent, let me desire you to reflect impartially upon your past train of life. Have not sloth or pride, or ill temper or sinful passions, misled you often from the path of sound and wise conduct? . . . It is an old saying, that every man is the artificer of his own fortune in the world. It is certain, that the world seldom turns wholly against a man, unless through his own fault.[44]

Here, in a sense, was the counterpart to the code of moral autonomy. If humans were indeed self-governed, if they were indeed endowed with moral responsibility, and if they could indeed shape the world around them through their own actions, then who was to blame when things went badly? If at one extreme of fortune was Washington, and at the other a benighted slave, who was responsible for where each individual landed on the continuum?

THE *COLUMBIAN ORATOR* and the *English Reader* were particularly influential texts, but they were far from unique in exalting the individual as moral actor or in promoting the idea that the world is shaped by a series of individual choices. To read schoolbooks of the post-Revolutionary era is to enter a world where the virtuous but poor farmer is rewarded while the wealthy but corrupted ends in poverty, where the virtuous orphan receives a long-lost inheritance while the sinful one dies in his youth, and on and on and on. It was the great theme of children's literature of the era, as the historian Isaac Kramnick has observed: "success comes to the self-reliant, hardworking, independent individual."[45] Virtue always earns its reward in this morally just universe. Success results from virtue, failure from sin, and the success or failure we meet depends on the choices we make.

Noah Webster's *Grammatical Institute,* one of the bestselling schoolbooks of the post-Revolutionary period, featured a number of stories carrying this message. One notable tale recounted the story of Perrin, orphaned at a young age and educated at a charity school until the age of fifteen, when he was hired to be a shepherd. Orphans were a stock figure in children's literature of the period for, as Kramnick has noted, they personify the assumption "that the individual is on his or her own, free from the weight of the past, from tradition, from family." The figure of the orphan, he adds, "intensifies and dramatizes individuals' responsibility for their own fate by dint of their own hard work, self-reliance, merit, and talent."[46] Perrin certainly fits this bill. Falling in love with Lucetta, the daughter of a nearby shepherd, Perrin asks the father for permission to marry. Alas, the father refuses to consent to the marriage because of the young man's poverty. Soon after this rejection, Perrin finds a bag of gold, and his problems appear to be solved. But Perrin's conscience gets the better of him, and he announces the find in the newspapers—someone, he realizes, must have lost this great fortune. No one claims the gold, however, and so Perrin is able to marry Lucetta. He buys a farm. They have children. Years later Perrin happens to meet the man who lost the bag of gold lo those many years earlier. Perrin tells this stranger that his farm, his house, indeed all his property rightfully belongs to this man. Perrin asks only to stay on as tenant, promising to work hard. His honesty and industry move this stranger, who announces that he long ago forgot about the money, and so the hero keeps his farm.[47]

Caleb Alexander's *The Young Gentlemen and Ladies Instructor* makes the same point. One selection in this schoolbook tells of a wealthy woman who adopts a poor orphan and raises her, before experiencing a series of misfortunes. Her husband dies. She places her jewels with a man who goes bankrupt. Eventually she finds herself destitute. Just as she is to go into the poorhouse, her adopted daughter, now grown, takes in the widowed mother just as the mother had once adopted the orphan. The woman eventually dies, but the daughter unexpectedly inherits a fortune from a wealthy but unknown relative.[48]

Schoolbooks of the nineteenth century, the historian Ruth Elson remarks, "bombard the child with the idea, elaborately and richly illustrated, that virtue is rewarded and vice punished in an immediate material sense." By exalting this brand of morality, schoolbooks promoted the idea that each individual is ultimately responsible for success or failure alike. "Our good or bad fortune depends greatly on the choice we make," read a typical selection. External circumstances are mastered by the active, rational, moral individual: in these schoolbooks, "accidents happen only to those who deserve them." "The happiness of every man depends more upon the state of his own mind," read another selection, summing up this philosophy, "than upon any one external circumstance; nay, more than upon all external things put together."[49] In these texts, we can discern the contours of the autonomous American being invented.

The success of this project would become clear in the Jacksonian period, with its celebration of traits like "character," "will," and "the individual." "From beginning to end," as the historian John William Ward has remarked, "the period from 1815 to 1845 is dominated by the belief that the cause of man's success lies within himself." This was as true of Whig political culture as it was of the Democrats' celebration of Jackson, which came straight out of the moral tales of schoolbooks: a Jackson who grew up as an orphan, "bereft of the guardianship of father or mother," and who was in every sense "the architect of his own fortune." If schoolbooks taught Americans that virtue led to success, the very success of men like Jackson proved that they were indeed virtuous. Ward explains the logic: "Because they did not doubt that virtue does receive its own reward, believers in the myth of the self-made man were not arguing from cause to effect, they were arguing from effect back to cause: if Jackson succeeded he *had* to deserve success."[50] But if this ethic of the self-made man was common to all sides of partisan discourse of the era, it was also more than just political. Virtue, by the middle decades of the nineteenth century, was no longer understood in purely political terms—the abnegation of self-interest necessary to make a republic function—it now had larger and deeper connotations.

The project of shaping virtuous, self-controlled individuals would lead in a variety of directions, spilling over into the public realm, and driving reform activities from temperance to sabbatarianism, nativism, and antislavery. It lay behind the drive for refinement and self-improvement that was part and parcel of the bourgeois middle class emerging in the nineteenth century. And it would lead in economic directions: for the norms being inculcated through these texts were not just political or cultural. In addition to creating the preconditions of liberal citizenship, these works fashioned the traits necessary for rising generations to engage in the market economy continuing its long march across the continent.[51] They made private virtues not only civic but economic, fostering the self-reliance demanded of private enterprise. The self-controlled citizen would become the trustworthy merchant and the driven worker. The autonomous agency promoted by civic texts thus set the foundations not just for political forms of association based on consent, but for economic forms of association based on contract.[52] In this regard, these civic texts would perform the work Max Weber argued was so essential to the creation of a capitalist order: to persuade people that "Labour must . . . be performed as if it were an absolute end in itself, a calling." Such an attitude, he observed, "is by no means a product of nature. It cannot be evoked by low wages or high ones alone, but can only be the product of a long and arduous process of education."[53]

Slavery and Reading: The Specter of Uncontrolled Slaves

If the autonomous individual, shaped into habits of self-control through texts like the *Columbian Orator* and the *English Reader,* offered a solution to the problem of social order among free whites, the preservation of social order among slaves was something else entirely. Frederick Douglass personified the problem. An educated slave would be reborn into the kind of individual repelled by slavery. In the best of circumstances he would run away; in the worst: well, it was the stuff of slaveholder nightmares. The conspiracies and insurrections of Gabriel, Denmark Vesey, and Nat Turner—all widely publicized and perhaps widely exaggerated, all led by religious and literate blacks—had taught many whites across the South an important lesson, one that Douglass's master instinctively under-stood when he tried to prevent Douglass from learning to read, and which the fiery writings of radical abolitionists like David Walker only reinforced: educated slaves endangered the institution of slavery, and the preservation of peace and order in the South. How could social order be preserved in a republican nation in which slaves were a widespread presence?

Several responses emerged to this dilemma, all of them roughly contempora-neous. The first, of course, was to abolish slavery. Driven by an alliance of African Americans and dedicated whites, largely evangelical in orientation, the emergent abolitionist movement made slavery into the premier political and moral question of the age. Though it stirred the consciences of many, the abolitionist movement never succeeded in persuading a majority of Americans to renounce the institu-tion of their own free will. To the contrary, it created a backlash among white Southerners increasingly unified in defense of the institution. This story is too well known to need telling here, but it does set the context for other lesser-known movements that sought to resolve the tension between slavery and social order.

One of these was to rely on the coercive apparatus of the state by enacting re-pressive legislation to ban slaves and even free blacks from reading. Although this crackdown might limit the threat of widespread social unrest, it could not elim-inate more localized outbreaks. Even more problematically, this solution worked against the founding principles of the nation. Alongside this movement a third response thus emerged. Promoted by pedagogical texts circulated by evangelical clergymen and social reformers who wished to defend the institution of slavery, the aim of this third movement was to reshape the potentially revolutionary slave into a self-controlled and obedient servant.

FACED WITH internal assaults on the institution by slaves, and with a growing offensive by abolitionists in the North and across the Atlantic, states across the South during the 1830s passed a wave of repressive legislation regulating the dis-semination of education and literacy among slaves and free blacks and banning the circulation of controversial texts. Georgia began the trend in 1829 when it passed a law providing fines, whipping, or imprisonment for anyone teaching slaves or free blacks to read or write. Louisiana followed in 1830, outlawing the instruction of reading or writing to slaves. Slave education was already illegal in Virginia, but the state went further after Turner's insurrection in 1831, extending the ban to free blacks and mulattoes. North Carolina made it illegal for blacks to preach, and for anyone to give books to slaves. In 1832, Alabama banned all forms of slave literacy, prohibiting the instruction of slaves in reading, writing, or spelling, and outlawed assemblies and preaching by blacks, while Florida prohibited the unsupervised worship of free blacks. South Carolina passed the most comprehensive antiliteracy law in 1834, making it illegal to teach slaves to read or write, making the penalty for whites a fine and a prison term, and the penalty for blacks a fine and up to fifty lashes.[54]

These laws were in many ways the traditional response of authoritarian regimes confronted with sudden threats to their rule. As far back as 1543, Henry VIII, confronted by what he perceived as threats to his authority by growing reading of the Bible, imposed severe restrictions on Bible reading, and even burned Protestants for the act. In 1671, the governor of Virginia, William Berkeley, followed in this tradition. "I thank God, *there are no free schools* nor *printing*, and I hope we shall not have these hundred years," he remarked. "For *learning* has brought disobedience, and heresy, and sects into the world, and *printing* has divulged them, and libels against the best government."[55] His gratitude was short-lived, however; he would be faced with a rebellion only five years later. Antebellum white Southerners operated in this long tradition. In a sense, these antebellum literacy laws might be seen as a vindication of the bedrock Enlightenment idea that education and reading naturally subvert autocratic regimes like slavery, and lead people to freedom. Whatever the interpretation, it was clear that "Education and slavery," as Frederick Douglass succinctly stated, "were incompatible with each other."[56]

When Whitemarsh Seabrook, governor of South Carolina, said that teachers of slaves were fit for "a room in the lunatic asylum" he was expressing a commonly held view. To educate slaves was to give them the will to be free. Even more frighteningly, it was to arm them with the weapons of insurrection to enact that freedom. "Is there any great moral reason," asked an article in the *Southern Presbyterian Review,* "why we should incur the tremendous risk of having our wives and children slaughtered in consequence for our slaves being taught to read incendiary publications?" The South Carolinian Edward R. Laurens connected fears of slave literacy to abolitionist pamphlets and their alleged role in unleashing Nat Turner's rebellion. Abolitionist texts, he argued:

> produce revolt and insurrection. Well may Virginia and the Carolinians be indignant at the fanaticism, or the darker motive which

prompts this mad interference in their internal concerns. The horrible massacre of Southampton is still fresh in recollection, and the scenes which followed, when the innocent black was sacrificed to appease the manes of the murdered!

"It seems as if we were afraid of our slaves," complained one Southerner who opposed these coercive laws.[57] He was right.

The problem states were having with these coercive laws, however, was not just the difficulty in enforcing them: it is estimated that between 5 and 10 percent of slaves could read.[58] Even more problematically, they were ultimately difficult to justify in a republic, and proved to be easy fodder for abolitionist attacks on slavery as an antirepublican institution. The nation, after all, defined itself as a polity that renounced the kind of state coercion common to tyrannical regimes, and so the use of state power to deny slaves access to reading contradicted the very ideology on which the nation was founded. "White Southerners in the late eighteenth and early nineteenth century were in a unique position," notes the historian Janet Cornelius. "They sought to prevent enslaved African-Americans from learning to read just as mass literacy was being vigorously promoted in England and in the Northern United States as a positive good, necessary for training the citizens of a republic."[59] These laws only reinforced the abolitionist argument, casting slavery as a contradiction to American Revolutionary principles.

These coercive laws were not the only Southern response to the problem of slavery in a republican nation, however. Alongside these forms of state coercion was another project, a subtler and in some ways more encompassing project that sought to impose *internal* forms of self-control in slaves themselves. Promoted through didactic and religious texts like sermons and catechisms, the aim was to shore up slavery and protect the Southern social order in a manner more consistent with U.S. nationalism. These texts, aimed for an audience of slaves, sought to elevate them from ignorance and give them religion, even as they sought to keep them in slavery.[60] These texts would introduce slaves to the Bible, albeit orally. They would teach habits of order, industry, and discipline. Insofar as they carried messages to slave owners, they sought to mitigate the cruelties of slavery, and turn it into the benevolent, patriarchal institution promised by the proslavery argument—the institution as presided over by George Washington, father to both the nation and his slaves. Grounded in a Christian defense of slavery authorized by the Bible, written and circulated largely by religious figures, these texts would make slavery into what its defenders argued it was: an educational institution that enlightened the ignorant, gave Christianity to pagans, and improved the spiritual and material well-being of Africans. Much as civic texts tried to produce orderly republican citizens, these texts worked to produce compliant slaves. And much like the schoolbooks and other civic texts circulating for free Americans, these educational texts for slaves sought to inculcate personal and economic virtues in order to maintain public order and national unity.

Civic Texts for Slaves, Self-Control, and the Inculcation of Slave Autonomy

Most slaves did not have access to the civic texts that have so far been examined—the kind Douglass got his hands on, the kind engaged in the production of citizens. They were introduced to other kinds of texts, equally didactic in nature: sermons, catechisms, and pamphlets that both paralleled and diverged from civic texts for whites. Produced mostly by a cohort of dedicated clergymen who operated throughout the South until the Civil War—through Baptist churches and Methodist, Presbyterian, and Episcopalian missions—as well as a number of more secular-oriented reformers hoping to mitigate the cruelties and thereby shore up the slave regime, these texts taught not freedom and citizenship, but subordination and slavery. As civic texts for whites sought to unify their audiences under a paternalist nationalism, so these texts promoted a paternalist ideology of slavery, seeking to unite slaves and whites under a benign regime. As civic texts sought to inculcate a moral code appropriate for a republican and increasingly market-oriented nation, so these texts sought to inculcate a moral code appropriate for a slave society. They taught norms of obedience and industry and promoted internal forms of surveillance in order to decrease the necessity of coercive, physical discipline. But in doing so, they changed the relationship between autonomy and slavery, rendering them increasingly compatible—a development that would have important implications for U.S. political culture.

A good place to begin examining these pedagogical texts for slaves is with the Reverend Charles Colcock Jones, a Presbyterian, and undoubtedly the most famous minister to slaves in the antebellum South.[61] Born in Georgia and educated in the North—at Phillip's Academy, Andover Theological Seminary, and Princeton Theological Seminary—Jones moved to Georgia in 1830, and in 1832 returned to his home in Liberty County to begin working as a missionary to slaves.

That same year he published a pamphlet entitled *The Religious Instruction of the Negroes* based on a sermon delivered to an association of Georgia planters. Published in Princeton, New Jersey, and given away in order to promote its circulation, this pamphlet would eventually be revised into a book, published in 1842. Jones began his 1832 sermon sketching out the vices to which he believed slaves were subject. "The description which the Apostle Paul, in his Epistle to the Romans, gives of the Heathen world, will apply, with very little abatement, to our Negroes. They lie, steal, blaspheme; are slothful, envious, malicious, inventors of evil things, deceivers, covenant breakers, implacable, unmerciful." Jones argued that religious instruction was the best means of turning slaves into honest, obedient workers. When "obedience is inculcated as a *Christian duty,* binding on the Servants," Jones averred, "the authority of Masters is supported by considera-

41. *The Reverend Dr. Charles Colcock Jones, famed Presbyterian minister to slaves in Georgia. Charles Colcock Jones Papers, Manuscript Collection 154, Manuscripts Department.*

tions drawn from eternity . . . We believe that their authority can be strengthened and supported *in this way only*; for the duty of obedience will never be felt and performed to the extent that we desire it, *unless we can bottom it on religious principle.*" By inculcating slaves' obligations to their masters through a notion of "Christian duty," the religious instruction of slaves would serve the masters' interests even as it grounded the institution "on religious principle." The benefits to masters would quickly become apparent: "a better understanding of the mutual relations of Master and Servant," and "greater subordination, and a decrease in crime amongst the Negroes."[62]

A proper education would make better slaves, according to this line of argument. Religious education resulted in more than the "improvement in the external morality of the people"; it encouraged more efficient work habits. The planter Charles Cotesworth Pinckney, son of the Revolutionary leader of the same name and later the lieutenant governor of South Carolina, argued along similar lines as he recruited Methodist preachers to evangelize slaves. "Were true religion propagated amongst this numerous and important class," he promised in a widely read 1829 speech, "a sense of duty would counteract their reluctance to labor, and diminish the cases of feigned sickness, so harressing [*sic*] to the planter." The financial rewards to be gained from slaves' religious education were hardly beside the point: "To bring up our slaves in the knowledge and fear of God," one sermon in an Episcopalian collection concluded, "must needs be of great advantage to our temporal affairs." Another sermon, addressed to masters and mistresses, made the point baldly. Since planters' financial success "often depend[s] upon their [slaves'] diligence and fidelity," slave owners had a pecuniary incentive to ensure their slaves' good behavior. "I do not mean that the introduction of the Gospel upon a plantation in and of itself puts new life and vigor into the laborers and the soil which they cultivate, and necessarily makes them more profitable to owners, than plantations where the Gospel is not introduced at all," admitted the Reverend Charles Colcock Jones. "But I mean, that religious instruction is no detriment, but rather a benefit: that, other things being equal, the plantation which enjoys religious instruction will do better for the interests of its owner, than it did before it enjoyed such instruction."[63]

The point here and elsewhere was to "induce the slave to assimilate with the master and his interest" by promoting obedience, discipline, subordination, and other virtues. In an article on his experiences running large plantations in Georgia, the famed plantation manager Roswell King, later founder of Roswell,

Georgia, recommended setting slaves to work at an early age in order to keep them out of mischief and encourage them to "acquire habits of perseverance and industry." Religious education would teach them these habits. A major convention of planters and clergymen from several denominations that met in Charleston in 1845 made the uses of religion very clear, praising "the effects of the religious instruction of Negroes, upon *labour,* and upon *discipline.*" The aim of this brand of religious education was to cultivate an internal moral code among slaves that would prove more reliable, in the long run, than external forms of discipline. "Putting religion out of the question," asked the Episcopalian Thomas Bacon in a sermon to masters, "what better security have you for their good behaviour than the dread of the lash, or a continual, uneasy watch kept over them? Both these may find a way to disappoint."[64]

A proper religious education would also respond to fears of slave insurrection by promoting order and harmony on the plantation, "render[ing] them more contented with their situation, and more anxious to promote their owner's welfare." Fears of insurrection would thus be allayed. "There are some who object to the religious instruction of their people, on the ground that it has been the cloak assumed to cover the nefarious design of insurrection. To this we reply," Pinckney stated, "that such instruction was the best antidote to this very disease." The point was made by clergymen throughout the South. "Sound religious instruction," Jones insisted, "will contribute to safety."[65] So Jones and other clergymen would publish numerous sermons on slaves' religious instruction, as well as catechisms, primers, and psalms to foster new norms of slave behavior.

JUST AS IN the Washington eulogies aimed at children, just as in Weems's Washington biography and in his many other texts, and just as in the schoolbooks like the *Columbian Orator* flooding the nation, these texts for slaves sought to foster virtue and discourage vice. Slave owners' "domestic policy," explained a Baptist clergyman from Georgia in 1851, should be "based upon the principle, that virtue must be encouraged and vice restrained." Much as the educational texts for free subjects had done, pedagogical texts for slaves promoted obedience to authority, proper moral habits, and especially self-control. Sabbath schools for slaves, argued Jones, "promote cleanliness, neatness, order and good behaviour. Sobriety, honesty, good feeling, and subordination in the relations of life."[66] Slave educators designed a pedagogy—insisting on "punctual attendance" and "decent moral behavior"—that paralleled the educational practices being implemented in schools for free whites throughout the North. Even as Northern schools began following the educational system of the influential British theorist Joseph Lancaster, which emphasized habits of order, cleanliness, and punctuality, so did Jones urge the same behavior of slaves attending Sabbath schools: "the children being required to come with clean faces and hands, their hair combed, and clothes in good order, and to behave quietly, and be attentive and obedient, soon relish the exercise and improve under it in disposition, manners, appearance, intelligence and morality." Even some of the assigned texts were identical: one popular catechism for slaves reprinted excerpts from the catechisms of Isaac Watts, the famous hymn writer and Nonconformist minister—a text recommended by Lancaster, which Weems had sold throughout the South, and which was widely read by Northern white children. Watts himself had written that his hymns and poems "for use of children" were "intended to deliver children from the temptation of learning idle, wanton, or profane songs": which may explain why Charles Colcock Jones recommended Watts's psalms, hymns, and catechisms. "One great advantage in teaching them good psalms and hymns," Jones observed, "is that they are thereby induced to lay aside the extravagant and nonsensical chants, and catches and hallelujah songs of their own composing; and when they sing, which is very often while about their business or of an evening in their houses, they will have something profitable to sing."[67]

Pedagogical texts for slaves focused largely on virtues like honesty, industry, and restraint—traits related to an ethic of self-control. One sermon for slaves directed them to wake up every morning and pray that God will not only "govern your temper and your tongue," but also "keep your 'hands from picking and stealing, and your tongues from evil speaking, lying, and slandering.'" The Mississippi Baptist Association urged slaves to be "industrious, honest[,] faithful, submissing [sic] and humble." A sermon for slaves by the eighteenth-century Episcopalian clergyman Thomas Bacon, republished by Bishop Meade in 1851 and probably used by Methodist clergymen during the early nineteenth century, similarly reminded its slave audiences: "God has told all men, bond or free, 'thou shalt not steal.' This was spoken in thunder from Mount Sinai, and Moses was told to write it on a tablet of stone."[68] Another sermon warned, "God says all servants must not 'purloin' or steal, but show all good fidelity in all things." These calls for honestly extended not just to acts but to spoken words. "God is a God of truth, and hates all liars," declared one sermon for slaves. Stressing "the duty of strict honesty," it warned that "all kinds of dishonesty, no matter who commits it . . . are forbidden by God, and will be punished by him either in this life or in the next." An ever-vigilant God watched for theft or dishonesty on plantations, and He would not forget. "If you persuade a fellow-creature to lie or swear for you; to help you to deceive your owners or others; to cheat, rob, or steal; to get drunk with you or take part with you in any kind of wickedness," read this same sermon, "you may be sure that God will punish you."[69] Charles Colcock Jones went further than anyone, perhaps, hoping to stamp out all forms of sinful and disorderly behavior:

> Cursing and swearing; breaking the Sabbath; quarreling and fight-
> ing; lying and stealing; the oppression of the weak by the strong;
> neglect of children on the part of parents, or of parents on the part
> of children, or the neglect of one head of the family towards the
> other; neglect of the aged and sick; cruel acts towards dumb beasts;
> adultery and fornication; yea, all sins and improprieties . . . should
> be observed and corrected.[70]

The faith in these texts' ability to stamp out such habits was remarkable. Weems could hardly have hoped for more from the morality pamphlets he wrote and sold.

This didactic literature for slaves stressed obedience, perhaps more than any other virtue. "Obey their Masters according to the flesh," urged the Mississippi Baptist Association. The injunction, drawn from Colossians 3:22, was a favorite of these sermons and catechisms. "Brethren under the dispensations of God you have been brought into a state of bondage, however dark, mysterious and un-pleasant those dispensations may appear to you we have no doubt that they are founded in wisdom and goodness," argued the Baptists. The lesson was taught not just in sermons, but also in catechisms, whose answers were to be memorized and repeated by slaves at the end of a sermon:

> *Question 85.* What does the Bible say of the duty of servants?
>
> > Servants, obey in all things your masters according to
> > the flesh, not with eye-service, as men-pleasers, but
> > in singleness of heart, fearing God. Col iii.22.

Question 86. Will the faithful servants be rewarded by the Lord?

> Whatsoever good things any man doeth, the same
> shall he receive of the Lord, whether he be bond or
> free. Eph. Vi.8.

Question 87. Will unfaithful servants be punished?

> He that doeth wrong shall receive for the wrong he
> hath done. Col iii.25.[71]

The path to virtue lay through obedience to constituted authority. "You must show your religion in your station as servants," urged one sermon for slaves. "You must try to be better, more obedient, more honest, gentle, kind, good-tempered, and watchful over your master's interest, than those servants who make no profession to religion."[72]

One selection in an Episcopalian collection of sermons for slaves stated the point particularly baldly in its very title: "Servants Should Obey Their Masters." "You should remember that God has placed you where you are," the sermon averred, urging audiences "to be contented in that state in which it hath pleased God to call you; to be kind and obedient towards all whom he has placed over you." A favorite biblical illustration was the story of Joseph, rewarded for his obedience as a slave. "Joseph was a servant, who in all things obeyed his masters, 'not with eye-service but with singleness of heart, fearing God.' Here then is the pattern of a holy life of one who was once a servant as you now are. Copy this pattern, and who shall say that God will not bless you too?" Just as in so much Northern didactic literature—which often twinned the example of a good boy rewarded with a bad boy punished, or a good apprentice made wealthy and successful with a bad apprentice drunk, diseased, and in debtor's prison—this sermon offered a biblical antihero: a disobedient and dishonest slave whom God cursed, along with all future descendents, with leprosy. "Here now is the example of an unfaithful and dishonest servant which you should carefully avoid. If you shall do as Gehazi did, who can say but that God may visit you with some heavy punishment in this world, and with ever-lasting misery in the world to come?"[73]

Unlike Northern children, slaves did not need the example of Washington to be taught honesty and obedience. Another, even greater figure filled that role. After all, was not Jesus himself a slave? "Yes, the servant of servants," a man who "always yielded to those in authority," announced the Episcopalian sermon:

> Here then you have the example of meekness and obedience of the greatest and best man the world ever saw; even the man Christ Jesus. You see him in his office as a servant, going about on foot, serving poor and sinful men like us. What a pattern of faithfulness, meekness, and love, is here for you. Try to follow his example and God will surely bless you.

A popular Methodist catechism instructed slaves that obedience to their masters was in fact obedience to Christ, urging slaves to memorize the biblical injunction from Ephesians 6:5–6: "Servants be obedient to them that are your masters according to the flesh, with fear and trembling, in singleness of your heart, as unto Christ; not with eye service, as men pleasers, but as servants of Christ, doing the will of God from the heart."[74]

The emphasis on conduct over piety in these texts—of works over grace—was not too different from that of the average white Methodist in theological terms, as the historian of Methodism Donald Mathews has observed.[75] Indeed, it was quite consistent with the general turn toward voluntarism in nineteenth-century Protestant culture. But this religious ethos led in a decidedly different direction in the South than it did in the context of Northern evangelicalism: toward quiescence rather than activism. Promises that obedience in this world would be rewarded in the next reflected the most conservative aspects of evangelical Christianity, those that muted rather than fostered social activism. Some sermons went so far as to suggest that misery produced its own spiritual rewards. "The poor labourer enjoys his dry crust more than . . . [a rich man] does his rich fare," read a sermon for slaves by the Episcopalian Charles A. Ambler. "This ought to teach the poor of this world to be contented, and if they are satisfied with their little, they are better off than the rich and great, who cannot be satisfied with their much." By emphasizing the spiritual rather than secular rewards for obedience and good behavior, these clergymen fell back on deeply conservative doctrine. "What is the personal liberty of the African which he may abuse," Francis Asbury, first bishop of the American Methodist Church, famously asked, "to the salvation of his soul, how may it be compared?"[76]

IF WHITE CLERGYMEN were pushing this morality on slaves, did slaves necessarily accept it? Clearly not. The meaning slaves made of these pedagogical texts often differed quite dramatically from that intended by their authors. "Most slaves, repelled by the brand of religion their masters taught," observes the historian John W. Blassingame, "formulated new ideas and practices in the [slave] quarters." The reception of the preachers' message could not, in the end, be controlled. Slaves met the religious doctrines of white clergymen with evident skepticism, not to say outright disgust. "The preacher," recalled one ex-slave, "came and preached to . . . [slaves] in their quarter. He'd just say, 'Serve your master. Don't steal your master's turkey. Don't steal your master's chickens. Don't steal your master's hawgs. Don't steal your master's meat. Do whatever your master tells you to do.' Same old thing all the time."[77]

Slaves took up the masters' Christianity, but modified it in significant ways to suit their own religious practices and doctrines. They developed spirituals to express their religious feelings, and highlighted selections from the Bible that spoke to their condition. Where the missions to slaves liked to quote Bible selections that grounded slaveholders' authority in scripture, slaves stressed other passages. Emphasizing selections from Revelation, Matthew, John, Genesis, Isaiah, and especially Exodus, with its narrative of freedom from slavery, their religion nurtured a belief in the justice of their quest for liberty, and a conviction that the promised day would one day come.[78] This was not just a religious impulse, however; it was also a nationalist one. By highlighting the story of Exodus, slaves connected themselves to widespread accounts of the American Revolution as a reenactment of the Israelites' liberation from Egyptian slavery.

In thus modifying the masters' Christianity to suit their own ends, slaves powerfully promoted a sense of their moral autonomy. As the historian Albert J. Raboteau has argued, "the disregard slaves held for the morality preached by slaveholding Christians amounted to antinomianism."[79] And in some sense it followed from the pedagogical texts white clergymen were circulating. After all, to inculcate norms of self-control that would lead slaves to work hard and not steal of their own accord was also to foster in slaves an ability to arrive at their own interpretations of what scripture, and indeed any text, even one delivered orally, could mean. If choice, persuasion, and voluntarism were features common to nineteenth-century U.S. evangelism, slaves' willingness to reinterpret scripture to suit their own moral experience pushed that tendency to an extreme.

Most historians of slavery have emphasized that slaves' rejection of the masters' brand of Christianity led toward the development of an autonomous culture, largely separate from and often in opposition to that of white slaveholders. The Church, it is argued, was a central site of economic, social, and even political activity, and it was a source for the collective African American identity that developed during and after slavery. Even more, historians of slavery have shown that slaves' Christianity could be put to uses entirely oppositional to those intended by the texts we have been examining, often nurturing flight from slavery and resistance to the will of slave owners.[80] The only point to add here is that, while the Christianity of the slave quarters reinforced forms of communal autonomy it also strengthened notions of *individual* autonomy. The centrality of the conversion experience, the intense emotionalism characteristic of slaves' worship—features common to all evangelical forms of Protestantism, but even more strongly emphasized in the slaves' Christianity—particularly exalted the individual sense of self. Indeed, by elevating the sanctity of the individual as a source of innate moral dignity, Christianity itself could be made into a force that opposed the degrading nature of slavery. "The conversion experience equipped the slave with a sense of individual value," Raboteau observes, "which contradicted the devaluing and dehumanizing forces of slavery." Ultimately, slaves' ability to draw on a shared culture to reinterpret Christianity helped them "preserve some personal autonomy."[81]

SLAVE OWNERS well understood the dangers that slaves might interpret Christianity to their own purposes, and they worked hard to limit such creative appropriation. The most important rule when it came to the religious instruction of slaves was that scripture be taught orally. Mediated by whites, the meaning and the dissemination of lessons could thus, at least in theory, be strictly controlled. In any event, oral instruction was required by the law, and book after book reminded teachers to "communicate instruction altogether *orally*."[82] Catechisms emphasized this method of instruction in their very titles: *A Manual of Religious Instruction, Specially Intended for the Oral Teaching of Colored Persons.* "No law forbids the religious instruction of the Negroes, *orally*, by proper instructors," insisted Charles Colcock Jones, "and any minister of the Gospel, or any owner, may undertake the good work, and prosecute it as largely and as long as he pleases."[83]

Oral instruction ensured that white authority figures remained the mediators of religious instruction. T. T. Castleman, an Episcopalian clergyman who collected a series of sermons for slaves, specified that his book was designed "to be read especially on Sabbath evenings, by the master, mistress, or other member of the same." That such oral instruction undermined one of the central tenets of Protestantism seemed to bother few clergymen. "God has so especially connected the salvation of sinners with the preaching of the gospel," read a sermon in Castleman's collection, "there is more hope from hearing it from the mouth of those appointed to preach it or teach it unto us, than from reading it ourselves." The point was made over and over again. "Now it is not necessary that you should know how to read in order to search the Scriptures," stated a sermon for slaves. A decidedly un-Protestant parable expanded on the point.

> Suppose that there were two men, the one could see, and could read the Bible, the other was stone blind, and of course could not read a word. You will see at once that the man who could see, could search the Scriptures. But you ask me, how could the blind man do this? Now, suppose that the poor blind man had a kind friend—say his master or mistress—who could read the whole Bible to him, word for word. Could not he search the Scriptures as they went along reading to him? Could not he take in every word, and treasure it up in his heart? Could not he search the Scriptures in this way, just as well as the man that could see? So you see that it is not necessary that you should know how to read, just as well as by reading them.

Slaves could even model themselves after the greatest figure of all. "You cannot read or preach, as some other people," admitted Castleman. "But you can all pray," he added. "To do this you need not be able to read a letter in a book. Your Saviour has set you the example of praying in this way. His whole life was a life of prayer."[84]

Clergymen also crafted their classes carefully in order to control, as much as possible, the meanings that slaves would create from the sermons and catechisms being read to them. "In conducting the worship of God upon plantations," wrote the Reverend Alexander Glennie, an Episcopalian rector of South Carolina low-country parishes, in a book of sermons for slaves, "my habit is, after concluding the service, to question the people assembled upon the Sermon which they have just heard, which enables me to dwell more at large upon matters briefly touched upon in the Sermon." Misinterpreted sermons could lead to disaster for planters and clergymen alike. "This practice," Glennie added for good measure, "and the frequent use of our Church Catechism, is, I need scarcely say, the most important part of the duty of those engaged in the instruction of the Negroes." A favored pedagogy began with a sermon, followed by catechisms in which slaves memorized the answers to doctrinal questions. "The negroes are often better acquainted with the doctrinal than with the practical part of religion," commented one planter, "and my own experience is, that *preaching alone* does not convey sufficiently definite ideas to the African mind. They require, *in addition, catechetical instruction* in the principles of Christ." If this questioning period was, in some hands, intended to ensure that slaves took the proper meaning from these texts, rather than imposing their own, it could also lead in other directions. When giving religious instruction to slaves, for instance, a Baptist minister from Georgia urged that "questions should be asked, which will lead them to *think*, and encourage them to remember what they hear." This call echoed, in an almost perfect way, the selection in the *Columbian Orator* insisting on educational methods that would turn children into "something more than a mere parrot, or an ape, who are capable only of speaking the words, and mimicking the actions of others."[85]

Encouraging slaves "to *think*," these texts drew wittingly or unwittingly on Lockean pedagogical theory, discouraging the use of physical punishment and advocating the cultivation of internal forms of discipline instead. "The master rules to great disadvantage to himself who depends solely or mainly upon the fear of punishment," wrote a Methodist minister from New Orleans. "There is a higher law of control . . . The inner man should be addressed. Shame and mortification are heavier lashes than any whip thong." Secular plantation reformers made the same case. "The lash is, unfortunately, too much used," complained Roswell King. "Every mode of punishment should be divised in preference to that, and when used, never to lacerate." These texts sought to internalize discipline in ways that would have been very familiar to moral reformers in the North. Alternative punishments were urged: "In lieu of *corporal chastisement*," Charles Colcock Jones proposed, "Confinement and deprivation of privileges may be substituted." King suggested others: "Digging stumps, or clearing away trash about the settlements, in their own time; but the most severe is, confinement at home six months to twelve months, or longer . . . Any one returning intoxicated, (a rare instance,) goes into stocks, and not allowed to leave home for twelve months."[86] Such punishments would presumably foster self-discipline by leaving slaves alone with their consciences: just as prison reformers hoped to do with criminals. In time, religious instruction would teach slaves to police themselves, a far more effective method of discipline than state coercion. "Our Patrol Laws are not efficiently executed now," Charles Colcock Jones said to a group of Georgia planters, "and this proposed operation [religious instruction] will, to some extent, supply their place."[87]

Much as the *Columbian Orator* and other educational texts had sought to promote in readers "a sense of accountability to God," so these pedagogical texts for slaves sought to instill in slaves a conviction that "the eyes of Almighty God are continually upon them." Civic texts aimed at free audiences had developed the idea of a "conscience" as the internalization of morality in order to impose order on a society composed of free individuals. These pedagogical texts for slaves worked in parallel directions, inculcating an ideal of self-discipline by fostering a conscience. "No man willingly & on purpose breaks the duties, of which I have been speaking," warned a sermon for slaves published two years before the *Columbian Orator*, "without offences against his own judgement, against his own reason, & without secretly reproaching himself for so doing. On the other hand, no man steadily observes & performs these duties; especially, when they seem to be against his present interest, pleasure, or desire; without enjoying the praise & applause of his own mind." It is hard to find a better description of a conscience than this account of self-reproach for bad actions and applause of one's own mind for good actions. "You must always remember that you have a master in heaven," warned the Episcopalian bishop William Meade in a sermon for slaves. And unlike their worldly master, this one was ever vigilant. "His back is never turned upon you. His eye is always over you. From him nothing can possibly be hid. He will be angry with you for all your unfaithfulness and deceit. But he will also reward you fully for every service you do for your masters and mistresses here, if you do it also to please him." Fusing the authority of God with that of the secular master, these texts sought to inculcate in their slave audiences the idea of an ever-watchful eye that sees all things. And so Methodists in South Carolina "pointed [slaves] from earliest infancy to a MASTER in heaven, whose eye sees in darkness as in light."[88]

This master was always vigilant. No action went unnoticed, no sin unpunished. "Wherever you are," according to a sermon for slaves entitled "God's Eye Always On Us," "or whatever you are thinking, or saying, or doing, you should not forget the language of Hagar, 'thou God seest me.'" This notion of "God's

Eye" was a powerful concept. Teaching slaves to internalize God's eye would form a conscience, fostering self-supervision and ensuring good behavior when the master's back was turned. Thus, Bishop Meade urged slave owners to:

> instill good principles into their minds, by setting before them much greater rewards than our poor services, or even the whole world can afford; and awakening their *consciences* by the dread of much greater punishments, and pains far more intolerable than they could suffer by perishing of hunger, or cold, dying upon a rack, being cut to pieces, or whipped to death for their faults. The strongest tie upon the human mind is plainly that of conscience.[89]

These pedagogical texts for slaves, in short, sought to reach into the inner depths of the individual in order to inculcate norms of self-control and indeed self-regulation. Perhaps this should not be surprising. As reformers across the Atlantic world were learning at this time, internal discipline was a far more effective form of control than physical punishment. What makes this particular project significant is that it extended these new forms of self-supervision and self-control—autonomy, in short—to slaves. If the purpose of these texts was to shore up the stability of the slave regime and to make more efficient slaves, by internalizing norms of rationality and moral responsibility they subtly modified the very essence of what it meant to be a slave. They made it possible to imagine an autonomous, morally responsible slave. A Baptist pastor and slaveholder in Twiggs County, Georgia, revealed the extent to which whites expected these norms of discipline and autonomy to govern slaves' behavior when he wrote an obituary for a local slave who, "with unusual fidelity served his master, with an ability, both physical and intellectual."[90]

At their essence, these were efforts to change slaves' behavior and instill an internal moral code—to "form, or reform *the moral being*," as the report of an interdenominational meeting stated. Clergymen continually appealed to slaves in their capacity as morally responsible individuals: insisting that slaves were "moral beings," as a Baptist clergyman from Alabama put it, that each of them was "an immortal and accountable being," in the words of a Baptist minister from Georgia. While these clergymen had no intention of making slaves into citizens—their aim, as we have seen, was just the opposite: to make them better slaves—they nevertheless insisted that slaves were in fact "moral beings." Even more, they cultivated this sense of moral responsibility, believing that the internally driven, self-controlled slave would prove more effective than the coerced slave. "Can human beings who have no restraints but the handcuff and the lock-up, no stimulus but the lash, be safe, trustworthy or profitable?" asked the Methodist minister Holland McTyeire. "What is the service of man worth, if it be not a *willing* service? . . . There is this peculiarity in human labor—it can direct itself." These men wanted not just service, but "*willing* service." They wanted not just obedience, but "*cheerful obedience.*"[91] It is unclear whether they understood the paradoxical nature of the undertaking: to endow slaves with a conscience was also to make them into individuals with moral will and responsibility. And as we will see, this exaltation of moral autonomy in both free and slave was to have powerful implications not just on the meaning of slavery and freedom, but on the very structure of the American political tradition long into the future.

5.

SLAVERY AND THE AMERICAN INDIVIDUAL

———✦✦✦———

Men make their own history, but they do not make it just as they please; they do not make it under circumstances chosen by themselves, but under circumstances directly found, given and transmitted from the past. The tradition of all the dead generations weighs like a nightmare on the brain of the living.

—KARL MARX, *THE EIGHTEENTH BRUMAIRE OF LOUIS BONAPARTE*[1]

AMONG MANY OTHER SELECTIONS in Caleb Bingham's *Columbian Orator* was a fictional dialogue between a master and a slave, which opens with the master announcing that his slave has been caught running away—for the second time—and accusing him of being "an ungrateful rascal." The two engage in an argument about the morality of slavery. When the master tells the slave he was purchased fairly, and therefore owes the master his labor, the slave asks: "Did I give my consent to the purchase?" The question needs no answer; it is already clear through the slave's repeated attempts to escape: no, he has not consented to his slavery.[2]

This runaway is the model for what might be called a virtuous slave. His virtue emerges not just through his bold willingness to argue with his master, and not merely in his repeated attempts to escape. Its ultimate manifestation is the slave's willingness to accept death rather than remain a slave. "Alas!" exclaims this slave, "is a life like mine, torn from a country, friends, and all I held dear . . .

worth thinking about for old age? No: the sooner it ends, the sooner I shall obtain that relief for which my soul pants." Like the American founders who pledged their lives, their fortunes, and their sacred honor in fighting for their freedom, this slave prefers death over slavery. And the master is moved. "Is it impossible," he asks, "to hold you by any ties but those of constraint and severity?" The answer, of course, is no; he can only be held by coercion. And so the master, impressed by the virtue of his worthy slave, decides to grant him freedom. "Be free," he says.[3]

This dialogue raises several puzzling questions. The slave shows through his actions, and says in his words, that he refuses to consent to slavery. Why? Does such a statement imply that other slaves—those who do not run away, for instance, or those who fail boldly to argue with their masters about the injustices of slavery—have somehow consented to their bondage? What exactly prevents all slaves from running away just as this heroic slave did? The risks are severe, of course: brutal punishment if recaptured; and if not, days and nights alone, wandering through the woods with no food, no assistance, and every possibility of meeting death rather than freedom. But if these risks are enough to dissuade most slaves, does that mean that—unlike this fictional slave—they are too cowardly to risk their lives by freeing themselves? Are they, in effect, choosing slavery over death?

If a dialogue raising such questions seems both wooden and fraught to modern sensibilities, it did not to a young Frederick Douglass. This dialogue in the *Columbian Orator,* Douglass recalled, "powerfully affected me."[4] Indeed, so powerful was its effect, it seems to have served as the model for the title character in Douglass's only work of fiction, a short story entitled "The Heroic Slave." The story opens with a slave bemoaning his fate in a speech that echoes the slave from the *Columbian Orator.* "What, then, is life to me?" asks this slave. "It is aimless and worthless, and worse than worthless . . . born a slave, an abject slave." But no master is listening here to grant this poor slave his freedom. Unlike the slave in the *Columbian Orator,* this one berates himself for his lack of courage: "I neither run nor fight, but do meanly stand, answering each heavy blow of a cruel master with doleful wails and piteous cries." This portrait of a slave who neither fights nor runs, but submits—a slave who consents?—is precisely the opposite of the worthy slave depicted in the *Columbian Orator.*

With this specter of the submissive slave still hanging in the air, the narrative begins. The hero of the story—whom we meet in his moment of despair—is a slave named Madison Washington. As the name suggests, he stands in the tradition of the Founding Fathers. He was, Douglass writes, "a man who loved liberty as well as did Patrick Henry—who deserved it as much as Thomas Jefferson—and who fought for it with a valor as high, and arms as strong, and against odds as great, as he who led the armies of the American colonies through the great war for freedom and independence." He who cannot be named: George Washington. Like his namesake, this Washington is no cowering slave. If we first meet him berating himself for his cowardice, he quickly determines no longer to submit to slavery. Washington's soliloquy depicts him in the moment of his mental transition from slavery to freedom, transforming him from a slave who neither runs nor fights into a bold, heroic slave, courageous and upright, willing to risk his life fighting for his freedom. "Liberty I will have," he vows, echoing Patrick Henry and the slave in the *Columbian Orator,* "or die in the attempt to gain it." This slave named Washington thus shows himself to be a true descendant of the Founding Fathers. This vow of liberty or death is itself enough to enact a transformation in Washington. "At that moment he was free, at least in spirit," the narrator (Douglass) informs his readers. "The future gleamed brightly before him, and his fetters lay broken at his feet."[5] The rest of the story tells of how Madison Washington gained his freedom—not once, but twice: first by running away, second, after his recapture, in a heroic act of violent resistance.

Both these tales—the brief one in the *Columbian Orator,* and the longer one from Douglass's pen—make complicated associations between consent, slavery, and the legacy of the Founding Fathers. Both create a vivid image of a heroic slave: one who refuses to consent to slavery by running away or fighting. But they also portray what it is to be a cowardly slave: one who submits to his fate without running or fighting. In this regard, Douglass's hero could not be better named (the name was not his invention, but drawn from the record of an actual slave insurrection). If Madison Washington's willingness to fight for his freedom echoes George Washington's struggle against the British, Madison Washington's earlier lament that he neither runs nor fights, but submits to his master's cruel blows echoes James Madison's argument—the one we first saw formulated in the exchange between Jefferson and Madison in 1789—that "assent may be inferred, where no positive dissent appears."[6]

These two stories, in short, highlight the complicated legacy of the Founding Fathers and their relationship to the problem of consent: a legacy that led to freedom . . . and to slavery.

"HINDSIGHT," the historian David Potter once observed, is both "the historian's chief asset and his main liability."[7] Hindsight allows us to see what actors of the early nineteenth century did not know: that slavery would be abolished in the middle of the nineteenth century. Knowing this, we gain insight about the abolitionist movement in ways the historical actors never could have. We can see the continuities between the Revolution and abolitionism, tracing the ideas of liberty and equality abolitionists drew from the Declaration of Independence and other texts to cast slavery in opposition to the nation's founding principles.

It was perhaps the most common abolitionist tactic. When David Walker, an antislavery firebrand, published his *Appeal to the Colored Citizens of the World* (1829), he excerpted a long section of the Declaration of Independence to highlight American hypocrisy. "See your Declaration Americans!!! Do you understand your own language?" Walker cried out. "Compare your own language above, extracted from your Declaration of Independence, with your cruelties and murders inflicted by your cruel and unmerciful fathers and yourselves on our fathers and on us—men who have never given your fathers or you the least provocation!!!!!!" William Lloyd Garrison used the same strategy. "Assenting to the 'self evident truth' maintained in the American Declaration of Independence, 'that all men are created equal, and endowed by their Creator with certain inalienable rights,'" Garrison launched the first number of his great antislavery newspaper, *The Liberator,* by invoking the legacy of the Revolution: "I shall strenuously contend for the immediate enfranchisement of our slave population."[8] Casting themselves as the *true* descendants of the Founding Fathers and of the nation's founding principles, deploying a vast array of popular texts—pamphlets, newspapers, novels, and more—abolitionists sought to cast slavery as an antirepublican, anti-American institution.

Which is where we run into the problem of hindsight. Too often, the abolitionists' very success is taken as proof that they were right when they argued that slavery and American nationalism were incompatible. That slavery was eventually abolished seems to indicate that slavery was *destined* to be abolished by the long arm of the American Revolution. By harnessing the nation's Revolutionary legacy to their ends, abolitionists helped craft what the historian Nathan Huggins would later call the "master narrative" of U.S. history: "a national history, teleologically bound to the Founders' ideals rather than their reality . . . American history from the Revolution [seen] as the inexorable development of free institutions and the expansion of political liberty to the broadest possible public."[9] And so the story remains, even in many of the most prominent works of U.S. history, which continue to see in this expansion of American democracy proof that U.S. nationalism has been, in the final account, an emancipating force, and that slavery, racism, and exclusion have represented a paradox, a problem, or a contradiction to America's liberal democratic tradition.[10]

This master narrative persuades because it contains many important truths. U.S. nationalism has always contained a potent liberal strand promoting the expansion of political liberty. This was the strand on which abolitionists drew and which they ultimately made dominant. It was a liberalism with connections to a variety of intellectual traditions, including dissenting Protestantism, civic humanism, and Scottish Enlightenment values, a liberalism that could advance causes for social justice, and make it possible to attack slavery and, indeed, many other inequalities in American life.[11] The very success of abolitionism, at least according to this master narrative, proves that American nationalism is a "civic" nationalism based on liberal principles of individual rights. Unlike some other nationalisms, American nationalism is not grounded in racial or ethnic particularism.[12]

If this account of America's liberal nationalism helps explain how slavery was abolished, however, it fails to explain how slavery and racism endured for so long after the American Revolution—and indeed grew through much of the nineteenth century.[13] Most scholars today admit that racism, nativism, and various other exclusionary practices have persisted as important features of American political life. They disagree, however, about the nature of the relationship between the liberal, progressive elements of American nationalism and its exclusionary, reactionary elements. How, if at all, did the two strands relate to each other? Were racism, slavery, and inequality persistent features of an older order gradually disappearing in the face of new values of liberty and equality, as the "master narrative" implies? Were exclusionary practices "logically inconsistent" with the nation's liberal tradition, as one recent political scientist has argued in a magisterial survey of American political traditions? Do they represent a "contradiction to liberal democratic dictates"?[14]

The most common answer is to project this perceived split between the liberal and exclusionary strains of American nationalism onto geography. Northern abolitionists are thus said to have inherited and reforged a complex but potent liberal tradition, while Southern proslavery theorists turned to a deviant, exclusionary strain. The portrait that results hearkens back to the vision the great political scientist Louis Hartz had of Southern intellectual life: "an alien child in a liberal family, tortured and confused."[15] The defense of slavery stands apart from the American Revolutionary tradition of the Founding Fathers. It is not a revolution but a "counterrevolution." Only when Americans "thought of slavery *outside* the perspective of Revolutionary ideology," writes one of the foremost historians of proslavery ideology, did "they ascribe[e] good to it."[16]

But was slavery so alien to the Revolutionary traditions of the Founding Fathers? Let us return to the problem of consent. Jefferson, we will recall, had suggested that every Constitution, law, and debt should expire at the end of each generation—nineteen years, according to his calculation; only thus, he believed, could the nation be grounded on the consent of the living. Madison, the more practical thinker, had rejected this idea, falling back on a notion of "tacit assent," signified by the absence of positive dissent. This book has shown how civic texts sought to reconcile the tension between active and tacit consent by *persuading* people voluntarily to grant their consent to the nation. Civic texts promoted a paternalist nationalism founded on veneration for the Founding Fathers in order to attach the affections of Americans to their nation. At the same time, these texts sought to turn audiences into the kind of morally autonomous individuals who would be capable of granting their consent. Indeed, some pedagogical texts even worked to instill a sense of moral autonomy in slaves themselves: not just to make them more obedient workers but also to render their obedience consensual rather than forced.

The result was a resurgence of Madison's doctrine of tacit assent as a powerful strain in U.S. nationalism. Exalting the idea of individual autonomy, many popular texts—schoolbooks, almanacs, biographies, toasts reprinted in newspapers, sermons, and more—promoted the idea of slavery as a choice. They posited a narrative of the American Revolution as a story of white Americans risking their lives to fight for their liberty. Thus had they *earned* their liberty. Slaves, by contrast, who refused to risk their lives fighting for their own freedom could be said to have tacitly assented to their slavery. Offered the choice between liberty or death, slaves had *chosen* to live in slavery. By holding individuals responsible for resisting their oppression, these civic texts shifted the moral burden of slavery onto slaves. They reduced slavery to a simple choice—active resistance or passive acceptance—and promoted the belief that slavery, just like freedom, resulted from individual choice. Alongside the argument that slavery was gross hypocrisy, a betrayal of the Revolutionary traditions, lay a different and more complex narrative. Only when we avoid the pitfalls of hindsight can we reimagine a world in which the slave-owning South was not "alien" to the nation's dominant ideology, but embodied nationalist principles and practices just as much as—and perhaps even more than—the abolitionist North.

Revolution, Resistance, and Autonomy

Since the Revolutionary period, the concept of slavery had been a central feature of U.S. political discourse. Drawing on much older Protestant and republican theories of resistance, Patriot leaders during the 1770s mobilized popular opposition to British imperial maneuvers by invoking the specter of slavery.[17] This was the case in Massachusetts, where a resident remembered that "the people were told weekly that the ministry had formed a plan to enslave them." The same held in Virginia, where Patrick Henry was said to have called the political feud "a question of freedom or slavery"; Rhode Island, where Governor Stephen Hopkins feared that British taxation would reduce Americans "to the most abject slavery"; and South Carolina, where the Reverend William Tennent worried that Americans might "be reduced to a State of the most abject Slavery." For many white Americans, the American Revolution was nothing less than a struggle between freedom and slavery. "The time is now near at hand which must probably determine, whether Americans are to be, Freemen, or Slaves," wrote George Washington in 1776. "Our cruel and unrelenting Enemy leaves us no choice but a brave resistance, or the most abject submission. . . We have therefore to resolve to conquer or die." Such views rested on a well-understood historical schema. Without the virtue to sustain freedom, liberty would collapse into tyranny and enslavement. Only by assertive action—in the ultimate account, by risking their lives—could Americans preserve their liberty. "When republican virtue fails," Thomas Paine succinctly stated, in his wildly popular pamphlet *Common Sense*, "slavery ensues."[18]

This fear of slavery was not merely metaphorical; its conceptual force lay in the parallel with the African slave. "The word *slavery* used to express fears of oppression in a country where slaves are constantly before one's eyes or at least are a living presence," remarks the political theorist Judith Shklar, "has a different meaning from its use as merely a figure of speech." White Americans continually illustrated the danger of tyranny by reference to African slaves. In 1760, Joseph Galloway warned that by submitting to odious British policies, "You will become slaves indeed, in no respect different from the sooty *Africans,* whose persons and properties are subject to the disposal of their tyrannical masters." In 1774, George Washington warned that to "Submit to every Imposition that can be heap'd upon us . . . will make us as tame, & abject Slaves, as the Blacks we Rule over with such arbitrary Sway." A Philadelphian drew the same parallel one year later: "What security have we, that they [the British] will not one day portion amongst themselves, our fair inheritances, and force us into their new claimed fields, like *Guinea slaves,* to till the soil?" This belief that the British government, if not resisted, would enslave *all* Americans helps explain why the mildly obnoxious acts of an inept British administration inspired such heated resistance. As the colonists' liberties seemed increasingly under attack during the late 1760s and 1770s, even the cautious Washington concluded that the British government wished to "fix the Shackles of Slavry upon us," and "reduc[e] us to the most abject state of Slavery that ever was designd for Mankind."[19] The owner of hundreds of slaves, Washington did not use this term lightly. He knew what slavery meant.

Such statements offered a particular definition of both slavery and freedom. If people proved their virtue by maintaining their freedom, they proved their lack of it by submitting to slavery. "They, who are willing to be made slaves and to lose their rights, as Issachar, without one struggle," wrote a Massachusetts author in 1761, stating the point baldly, "justly deserve the miseries and insults an imperious despot can put upon them. They richly deserve to be trampled on by the whole chain of wretches."[20] This idea of slavery reflected long-standing Calvinist doctrine associating sin with slavery.[21] But the Revolution added a new twist, drawing on these religious connotations to cast slavery and freedom into conceptual opposites freighted with moral connotations. The moral opposition persisted even in the adjectives: just as "freedom" opposed "slavery" and "resistance" opposed "submission," so did "virtuous" oppose "abject," a word frequently associated with slavery, as in "abject slavery." This moralized understanding of slavery helped promote the idea that a virtuous person would resist slavery, even at the cost of life itself. An abject person, by contrast, would submit and would "justly deserve" the slavery that ensued. "At this auspicious period, the United States came into existence as a Nation," declared George Washington in his Circular to the States of 1783, a text whose fame was only surpassed by his later Farewell Address, "and if their Citizens should not be completely free and happy, the fault will be intirely their own." If Americans fell into tyranny and enslavement, they would have only themselves to blame. They would *deserve* their fate.[22]

IF THIS UNDERSTANDING of freedom and slavery existed before and during the Revolution, it became much more common after. Indeed, it was the Revolution itself, as narrated by the eulogies, biographies, schoolbooks, political pamphlets, almanacs, and other texts promoted in vast numbers through the nineteenth century, that powerfully promoted this idea of slavery and resistance. Portraying the Revolution as an act of successful resistance by a people threatened with slavery, this narrative of the Revolution cast freedom as the fruit of virtuous revolutionary resistance. Enshrining individual action as the motor of history, it provided an insidious new legitimation of slavery grounded in a tacit or implied consent.

The Revolution, as recounted by civic texts, linked freedom with an obligation to resist. The most extreme form of this view held that a person must be willing to sacrifice life in order to defend freedom. "Is life so dear, or peace so sweet, as to be purchased at the price of chains, and slavery?" asked Patrick Henry. "I know not what course others may take," he famously continued, "but as for me, give me liberty or give me death!"[23] That cry of liberty or death became the greatest of all Revolutionary slogans: Henry's speech was printed in no fewer than thirty-five editions of William Wirt's 1817 biography of Henry and excerpted in innumerable schoolbooks and other popular texts—including McGuffey's *Eclectic Readers*, of which between 50 and 120 million copies were eventually sold.[24] People might be endowed with natural liberty, the ubiquitous slogan implied, but they must nevertheless act to preserve that freedom. Many other texts agreed.

Consider Weems's account in his *Life of Washington*. Recounting the political events of the 1770s, Weems wrote that "we were not to be treated as *brothers,* but as *slaves!*" How did Americans react? Just as would any *"brave people, who know their rights,"* and are committed *"not to be enslaved"*: they "determined, at the risk of every thing short of their *eternal salvation,* to defend and to transmit them entire to their innocent and beloved offspring." These virtuous Americans, set against a government determined to enslave them, would ultimately show that "LIBERTY, heaven-born goddess, was to be bought for blood." They "rose up as one man . . . resolved like true-born sons of Britons to live free and happy, or, not to live at all."[25] William Wirt knew of Weems's biography—his fellow Virginian St. George Tucker had written to him about it—and so one wonders whether he may have been influenced by this account of Washington's determination to live free or die when he reconstructed Patrick Henry's speech. Daniel Webster was certainly familiar with Patrick Henry's speech when he drafted his oration at the dedication of the Bunker Hill Monument in 1825, which would be excerpted in pamphlets and readers throughout the subsequent decades, eventually to be read by millions of American children. "The hour drew nigh," said Daniel Webster in his great speech, describing the coming of the Battle of Bunker Hill in all its suspense, "which was to put the professions to the proof, and to determine whether the authors of these mutual pledges were ready to seal them in blood . . . Death might come, in honor, on the field; it might come, in disgrace, on the scaffold. For either and for both they were prepared." When Webster quoted Joseph Warren, the hero of Bunker Hill, were the words his, or were they Patrick Henry's, Wirt's, or Weems's? It hardly matters: their language was the most common rhetorical currency. "Under God, we are determined, that wheresoever, whensoever, or howsoever we shall be called to make our exit," Warren vowed in Webster's oration, "we will die free men."[26]

This narrative of liberty or death dramatically simplified the Revolution, as all creation myths do. It erased all historical contingency, substituting a heroic act of resistance as the motor of the Revolution—indeed, of history. "When the moment arrived which was to degrade and humiliate the American people to a condition with the slaves of the East," declared James Monroe to the Virginia General Assembly in 1801, "they proved themselves equal to the crisis. They declared themselves an independent people, and by an heroick exertion made themselves so." Washington was the central figure in this narrative of the Revolution as self-liberation from slavery:

> He burst the fetters of the land,
> He taught us to be free;
> He rais'd the dignity of man.
> He bade a nation be.

Even the *New-England Primer* was edited to reflect this altered understanding of the role of individual action in shaping historical events. Whereas children had once been taught the letter "W" with the couplet:

> Whales in the sea
> God's voice obey.

42. The evolution of the famous New England Primer suggests how new ideas of
human agency were being diffused to American reading audiences. The page on the left
is from the first edition of the New England Primer, reprinted in Paul Leicester Ford,
The New-England Primer: A History of Its Origins and Development. The page
on the right is from The New England Primer, Improved . . . (Albany, 1822).

the revised lesson read:

> By Washington
> Great deeds were done.[27]

It is hard to imagine a better example of this Revolutionary understanding of human agency and individual autonomy: God's agency, once the mover of all
worldly deeds, even those of whales, was supplanted by human agency, epito-
mized by a Washington who did great deeds.

By promoting this view of the Revolution as a heroic act of resistance, these
texts connected liberty with a will to resist. Consider a 1795 toast proclaimed at
a New York Republican Society's July 4 celebration, dedicated to "The People of
the United States." "May they always possess the wisdom to discern their rights,
virtue to deserve and courage to maintain and defend them." For this speaker,

the preservation of republicanism rested not only on people's "rights," but on the "virtue" necessary for Americans to "deserve" them. People, in other words, proved themselves *worthy* of freedom by resisting tyranny. Repeated in public occasions and reprinted in pamphlets and newspapers, this meaning of liberty rapidly spread throughout the nation's political discourse. The call to resist tyranny—for only thus would freedom be truly deserved—would infuse nearly every political battle of the early nineteenth century: party factions, trade disputes, and, of course, sectional conflict. A song from that same July 4 celebration merged British tyranny seamlessly into the tyranny of the Federalist Party. "Swear firmly to stand / 'Till oppression is driven quite out of the land," sang the group, concluding with the rousing vow that they would "DIE, OR BE FREE."[28]

People of vastly different social classes and political orientations used the same language. Railing against the War of 1812, for instance, the ardent Federalist Josiah Quincy warned that the people of Massachusetts would become "slaves" if they did not resist odious trade policies: "If the people of the commonwealth of Massachusetts shall ever become slaves," argued Quincy, "it will be from choice and not from nature; it will be, not because they have not the power to maintain their freedom, but *because they are unworthy of it.*" If people had to make themselves worthy of freedom, what did that say about people who found themselves in slavery? It was an awkward corollary Quincy fearlessly broached. If the people of Massachusetts sink into slavery, he warned, "we deserve what we endure. We deserve to be, what we are,—of no more weight than slaves."[29] If Quincy here saw a distinction between people with the power to maintain their freedom and others who lacked that power, he did not stipulate it, nor did many others: in most contexts, issues of power, circumstance, and contingency were erased. By viewing people—*including slaves*—as autonomous, self-willed individuals, these civic texts elided the vast difference between whites threatened with political slavery and blacks enduring chattel slavery. Instead, they drew the distinction between people who "deserved" freedom and people who did not, between those who had "chosen" resistance and those who had "chosen" slavery. By endowing slaves with autonomy, these texts made it possible to shift the moral burden of slavery from the slaveholder to the slave.

The belief that a failure to resist tyranny made people "tame" and "abject," suiting them for slavery, was repeatedly emphasized in popular texts. Consider a schoolbook edited by Weems's partner Mathew Carey, and endorsed by none other than Thomas Jefferson, which offered the following lesson:

Who lives, and is not weary of a life
Expos'd to manacles, deserves them well.

Another selection made the same point:

When liberty is lost,
Let abject cowards live; but in the brave
It were a treachery to themselves, enough
To merit chains.[30]

Such lessons provided a clear account of the origins of slavery. Slavery did not re-sult from conquest or misfortune. It resulted from a *choice* to live in slavery rather than die with virtue: a logic that neatly resolved problems about slavery's origins that had vexed seventeenth-century theorists. Even someone born into slavery had the capacity to resist or die trying. Understood this way, slavery could only be the well-deserved state of abject cowards.

Promoting a conception of the heroic individual agent grounded in the new theories of moral autonomy peddled by civic texts, this account of the Revolu-tion defined freedom and slavery as a personal choice. This idea made it possible to hold free whites and African slaves alike responsible for maintaining their freedom or submitting to slavery: each state depended on the inner spiritual worth of the individual human agent. White Americans could look back on the Revolution for confirmation that they were worthy. After all, they had resisted tyranny and gained freedom. By the same logic, the persistence of millions in chattel slavery suggested that, lacking the virtue to free themselves—having made the choice to submit to fortune rather than to resist or die—slaves *deserved* their obnoxious condition.[31]

IN A SET of penetrating essays, the historian Thomas Haskell argued that the century between 1750 and 1850 saw a radical transformation in how Euro-Americans understood their ability to shape individual and collective futures. This period saw the emergence of a new "cognitive style" based upon "changing concepts of personal agency and moral responsibility," and it resulted in an un-derstanding of individuals as "conscience-ridden." This new conception of the individual opened up novel ways of thinking about moral autonomy and human agency—"man" now understood "as a causal agent," with the "power to intervene in the course of events." Haskell argues that these breathtaking intellectual transformations led to a wave of humanitarian movements, of which antislavery was only the most famous. Haskell is surely right to note the shift in ways of thinking about the morally autonomous individual during this period; we have followed some of those transformations in this book. And it may indeed be something to celebrate, for these intellectual transformations made the great revolutions of the eighteenth and nineteenth centuries possible, inaugurating an era of political systems based on what Haskell calls a "society of self-governing individuals."[32] Haskell is also right to highlight the connection between this understanding of the morally autonomous individual and the reform movements of the period: opposition to corporal punishment, prison reform, the promotion of universal education, temperance, women's rights, and of course abolition.

If these new ways of thinking about the individual led to the American Revolution and later to abolitionism, however, they also led in other directions. By portraying the Revolution as an act of collective resistance to slavery, and positing the freedom that resulted as the fruits of humans' individual agency, this "exaggerated pride in man's role as a causal agent capable of shaping the future to his own will" provided the groundwork for an insidious new justification for slavery.[33] Ironically, this justification was grounded on precisely the same "concepts of personal agency and moral responsibility" that Haskell credits with antislavery. These notions of agency and moral responsibility, in other words, could lead in a variety of directions, some of them noble, others less so.

A broad range of texts disseminated this account of freedom, slavery, and individual agency and autonomy: to the politically inclined in speeches, pamphlets, and newspapers; to the religiously inclined through sermons and religious tracts; to a broad reading public through almanacs, magazines, novels, and histories; and perhaps most important of all, to the nation's children through schoolbooks and biographies. Consider, again, the *Columbian Orator*. "Heavn's!" exclaims a hero from Addison's *Cato*, a work excerpted here as in many other early American schoolbooks. "[C]an a Roman senate long debate / Which of the two to choose slav'ry or death!" Cato's answer was clear.

> *No, let us draw our term of freedom out . . .*
>   *in Cato's judgment,*
> *A day, an hour of virtuous liberty,*
> *Is worth a whole eternity of bondage.*[34]

The dichotomy was stark: slavery on one side; freedom (and possible death) on the other. Cato's "virtuous liberty" joined republican and Protestant currents to associate virtue with liberty and slavery with an absence of virtue—and eternal damnation. Such lessons taught that each individual had the capacity to *choose* liberty over bondage.

The point was repeated throughout the *Columbian Orator*—not just in the dialogue between master and slave that affected Douglass—as well as in dozens of other schoolbooks of the era. Consider a fictional dialogue between a white American and an Indian, in which the nobility of the Indian shines through in his last words, almost an echo of Cato's. "We had rather die in honorable war," the Indian tells his white interlocutor, "than live in dishonorable peace."[35] Adding a powerful dimension to the trope of the noble savage, this dialogue employed the same meaning of virtue as Cato and the American revolutionaries. Another selection from the *Columbian Orator* exported this idea to modern Europe, where French revolutionaries were praised for having "sworn that they will live FREE or DIE!"[36] In every instance, freedom resulted from a *choice* to resist tyranny, a willingness to sacrifice life for liberty, and a refusal to live in bondage. Those qualities made a person worthy of freedom.

But what about people who lacked those qualities—who had, as it were, made the wrong choice—were they fit only for slavery? That seems to have been the message in perhaps the most interesting and complex of the book's selections, a brief drama entitled *Slaves in Barbary,* written by David Everett, a Republican author and Dartmouth classmate of Bingham's. The drama tells of two Venetian brothers captured by Tunisian pirates and sold into slavery. Their refusal to submit to slavery brings them to the attention of the "Bashaw" of Tunis, who, moved by their virtue, sets them free.[37] The plotline emerges at the very beginning, where the first words of Amandar, an enslaved Venetian, establish his credentials as a worthy slave. "I ask the fatal blow," he tells his captor, "to put a period to my miseries." Amandar's willingness to die rather than live in slavery proves he is too virtuous to remain enslaved; his freedom becomes inevitable. The drama repeats the message that virtue results in freedom when a group of captured sailors are sold at a slave auction—all except one sailor, who refuses to submit. Teague, a fiery Irish prisoner, tells his captors that had he known the slavery that awaited him, "I would have fought ye till I died."[38] Instantly, the Bashaw takes an interest in the man, praises his "inborn virtues," and buys him in order to set him free. Virtue—understood as a willingness to resist enslavement, a willingness to sacrifice one's life—results in freedom.

These characters are contrasted to an African American slave who makes a brief appearance in the drama. Though he is given a fairly sympathetic role, the contrast between this slave and the worthy ones could not be more striking. At the auction where Teague refuses to be sold into slavery, this "honest Negro lad" is described by the auctioneer as an excellent purchase: "He is bred to his business." Unlike Teague and Amandar, who prove their virtue by rebelling, this young man is bought for a hefty sum because, as the buyer explains, "He is trained into his business." What makes this exchange particularly interesting is that the dialogue here dwells not on the man's race or religion, but on his inner character. Lest this subtlety be lost on the book's young readers, a witness to the auction makes the point explicit. "Courage is a very good recommendation for a sailor, or soldier; but for a slave, I would give as much for one of your faint-hearted cowards, that you find hid in the hold in time of action, as for a dozen, who will meet you with a pistol at your head."[39] Race is clearly a factor here—it is no coincidence that the cowardly slave is black—but race *alone* did not justify slavery. Just the contrary: the Barbary drama attacks the hypocrisy of a drunk white American who praises liberty even as he whips his black slave. Racial ideologies joined with this rhetoric of virtue and resistance to associate whiteness with virtue and blackness with degradation. This was not a contradiction to American's nationalist ideologies. Race *united with* nationalist ideologies to posit that black slaves were unworthy of freedom.

Another, dramatic anecdote made similar associations between virtue and resistance. The story about Quashi may be apocryphal, but its interest lies less in its accuracy than in the breadth of its circulation, which was wide indeed. Its earliest known publication dates from a 1793 issue of the *Massachusetts Magazine*. The story was later reprinted in several textbooks, including an 1802 Mathew Carey publication entitled *The Columbian Reading Book; or, Historical Preceptor*, an 1804 antislavery book that called it a "well-attested relation"; and a schoolbook entitled *Biographical Sketches and Interesting Anecdotes of Persons of Colour*, which was assigned in the New York African free schools, and which was widely used in other schools as well.[40] The story tells of a slave named Quashi who grows up as his master's "play-fellow" and whose noble virtues promote him to plantation overseer. Falsely accused of some act, Quashi cannot bear the prospect of being whipped—his smooth skin was unbroken by whip marks—and "dread[ing] this mortal wound to his honour," runs into hiding. His master chases him through the plantation and catches him. Down they fall. After a "severe struggle," Quashi emerges victorious and, seated on his master's breast, holds "him motionless." When Quashi produces "a sharp knife," the master lies "in dreadful expectations, helpless, and shrinking into himself." At this point, however, the story takes a sudden and unexpected turn.

> "Master [said Quashi], I was bred up with you from a child: I was your playmate when a boy: I have loved you as myself; your interest has been my study; I am innocent of the cause of your suspicion; had I been guilty, my attachment to you might have pleaded for me—yet you have condemned me to a punishment, of which I must ever have borne the disgraceful marks—thus only can I avoid them." With these words, he drew the knife with all his strength across his own throat, and fell down dead, without a groan, on his master, bathing him in blood.[41]

Quashi finds not emancipation, but a bloody, self-inflicted death. Freely chosen, enacted by his own hand, this suicide affirms the view that slavery results from individual choice. Quashi represents that contradiction in terms, a virtuous, honorable slave. His life could end only in death or freedom, never in slavery. So Quashi proves his virtue by refusing to continue submitting to slavery. The fictional slave in the *Columbian Orator,* just like Douglass's "Heroic Slave," found freedom by running; Quashi found death. By choosing to resist slavery rather than to submit—even at the cost of life itself—all proved themselves worthy.

Race reinforced the connections between freedom, virtue, and whiteness, on the one hand, and slavery, sin, and blackness on the other. But the correlations were not exact. Some Europeans had to prove their fitness to be citizens: a 1782 Georgia law, for instance, mandated the deportation of all Scotsmen except those "who have exerted themselves in behalf of the freedom and Independence of the United States."[42] Meanwhile, African American slaves such as Quashi or the runaway described in the *Columbian Orator* could prove their virtue: that is, their unfitness to remain slaves. Instances of virtuous African Americans appear to have been, if not common in early American popular literature, at least not unusual. An antislavery almanac from the late 1830s, for instance, graphically depicted the evils of slavery in its image of a virtuous slave who ran away and ultimately hanged himself—"that he might not again fall into the hands of his tormenter" (figure 43). Another widely reprinted book narrated the story of "several runaway Negroes"—their virtue already apparent in their attempted escape—captured and condemned to hang. The captors proved reluctant to execute the slaves, however, and offered a slave his life if he would execute his friends. But the slave "refused it: he would sooner die." "The master [then] fixed on another of his slaves to perform the office. 'Stay,' said this last, 'till I prepare myself.' He instantly retired to his hut, and cut off his wrist with an axe. Returning to his master, 'now,' said he, 'compel me, if you can, to hang my comrades.'" Perhaps the juxtaposition of such virtuous actions with the lowly condition of African American slaves explains why this gruesome story appeared in an early book of jests.[43] Such irreconcilable contradiction—virtuous slaves—resolved itself as a form of humor. The logic was deeply self-serving, of course, for it meant that the only incontrovertible proof of virtue in a slave was death. The humor was dark indeed.

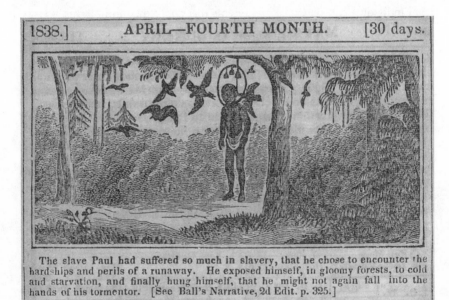

1838.]   APRIL—FOURTH MONTH.   [30 days.

The slave Paul had suffered so much in slavery, that he chose to encounter the hardships and perils of a runaway. He exposed himself, in gloomy forests, to cold and starvation, and finally hung himself, that he might not again fall into the hands of his tormentor. [See Ball's Narrative, 2d Edit. p. 325.]

43. *The illustration attached to the month of April in this antislavery almanac depicts a slave who hanged himself rather than return to slavery. From N. Southard, ed.,* The American Anti-Slavery Almanac for 1838 (*Boston, vol. 1, no. 3*).

THE HISTORIAN David Brion Davis has observed that the American Revolution "may have raised obstacles to 'unearned' emancipation. Since the Revolution tended to define liberty as the reward for righteous struggle, it was difficult to think of freedom as something that could be granted to supposedly passive slaves." If the connection between metaphorical and chattel slavery led some people—mostly slaves or free blacks and a few whites such as the political leader James Otis and the theologian Samuel Hopkins—toward abolitionism, that was by no means the only logical outcome. For many people the conclusion was quite different: just as white Americans acted to resist their enslavement, so it fell to chattel slaves to resist theirs.[44]

One of the principal aims of civic texts, as we saw in the last chapter, was to endow all humans, including slaves, with some basic level of moral autonomy. Having helped shape morally autonomous agents who could engage in the most basic act of citizenship—granting their consent—these texts held that people gained not just citizenship, but freedom or slavery through individual *choice:* through heroic and violent resistance. The choice to resist or submit fell to every person, including those born into slavery. Which choice had slaves apparently made? Their continued enslavement gave the answer: unlike white Americans, "they did not, as a group, emancipate themselves."[45] Slavery was increasingly coming to be seen as a condition brought about by a series of poor choices. Rather than being a person who resists violently, the slave was, in the words of Frederick Douglass's fictional slave, "a person who neither runs nor fights, but merely stands" in the face of tyranny. By tacitly consenting to slavery, slaves proved that they deserved their fate.

Of course this view of slavery was empirically unfounded, erasing important features of early American life. As generations of scholarship have shown, the diversity of social experience in early America—once the lives of women, free blacks, Indians, indentured servants, and others are considered—collapses any simple binary between slavery and freedom. Far from representing some truth about the early United States, this figure of the slave who chooses slavery, thus making himself unworthy of freedom, is closer to what Slavoj Žižek calls an "ideological myth": a myth that serves both to "explain" slavery and "to justify present exploitation."[46] The lack of empirical grounding is thus beside the point: this ideology existed to erase awkward facts and to overcome irreconcilable contradictions. To illustrate the point—to see the ideology erasing awkward facts—let us turn away from representations of slavery in popular media and toward some responses to actual slave resistance. Since the historiography on slavery has focused more on slave resistance than on responses to it, the conclusions will necessarily remain provisional. An initial glance, however, seems to confirm the currency of civic texts' account of freedom and slavery resulting from individual choice. It informed the two most common responses to resistance: outright denial on the one hand and the admission that resistance made slaves worthy of freedom on the other.

Fit to Be Free

Historians now recognize that slave resistance in the nineteenth century most commonly took nonviolent forms: theft, arson, lying, work slowdowns, and other forms of day-to-day rebelliousness. Few whites in the period, however, viewed such acts as forms of resistance. That should not be surprising. America's Revolutionary ideology privileged confrontation—preferably to the death. William Wirt's Patrick Henry had not urged Americans to resist nonviolently, after all: he urged them to *fight*. Racial prejudice further contributed to whites' refusal to see nonviolent resistance as true resistance, pushing them toward racist stereotypes of blacks as lazy, deceitful, and supine. America's Revolutionary ideology thus combined with racism to make it easy for whites to deny that most forms of slave resistance constituted *true* resistance.[47]

Denial of slave resistance was more difficult, of course, in instances of dramatic insurrection—often explicitly modeled on the American Revolution—and these forced whites to confront the problem of slave resistance more directly. But just as with more mundane forms of resistance, many white commentators refused to believe that escape and even rebellion constituted *true* resistance to slavery. If the specific strategies varied, all united in denying that slaves were agents of resistance. John Hope Franklin and Loren Schweninger have noted as much in their study of slave runaways, who were often described as kidnapped, lured away, or otherwise manipulated by outside forces. Similar strategies inevitably attributed slave insurrection to outside influences: French revolutionaries, Northern abolitionists, free blacks, providential retribution, anyone but slaves themselves. The denial of slaves' agency extended even to the most dramatic instance of slave resistance in the Atlantic world: the Haitian revolution of the

1790s. As the historian Ashli White has shown, "Accounts in American news-papers . . . generally denied that the slaves were the authors of revolution. Instead, contemporary commentators looked to other groups—French republicans, colonists, and anti-slavery activists among others—as a way to explain the upris-ing." Such accounts confirmed the fantasy that only outside manipulation pre-vented slaves from submitting to slavery, and they persisted until the very end of legalized slavery. "No attempt at insurrection in the South has ever originated from the domestic negro," insisted an anonymous Southern author in 1861, "but such nefarious designs have always been fomented from other sources—such as Vesey, of St. Domingo, and Northern incendiaries."[48]

Other explanations cast resistance in terms of social deviance. In 1851, a New Orleans physician believed he had discovered a new disease: "drapetomania, or the disease causing Negroes to run away." The same held for insurrection. The Haitian revolutionaries were not engaged in a manly struggle for freedom; they were "Cannibals," Thomas Jefferson wrote. They were "spurred on by the desire of plunder, carnage, and conflagration," insisted the Pennsylvania Gazette, "and not by the spirit of liberty, as some folks pretend." This same rhetoric reappeared years later in response to Nat Turner's 1831 revolt. Rebellious slaves were "de-luded wretches," "mad—infatuated—deceived by some artful knaves, or stimu-lated by their own miscalculating passions." Newspapers described them as a "set of banditti," driven by a lust for white women—almost anything save rebels risk-ing their lives in a fight for freedom. Instead of confirming rebellious slaves' manhood, proving that they, at least, deserved freedom, revolt revealed their de-pravity, even their monstrosity. "What strikes us as the most remarkable thing in this matter," opined the Richmond Enquirer after Turner's revolt, "is the horrible ferocity of these monsters. They remind one of a parcel of bloodthirsty wolves rushing down from the Alps." These self-serving accounts of slave insurrection were disseminated far more widely than counternarratives by slaves and others who portrayed insurrection as revolutionary resistance. The possibility that slaves might be capable of manly resistance, and therefore worthy of freedom, was rarely articulated in public. Public discourse insisted that American slaves did not fight for their freedom. When alternative explanations failed, even no ex-planation seemed more persuasive. "What the ulterior object was, is unknown," the Richmond Constitutional Whig commented after Turner's revolt. "The more intelligent opinion is that they had none."[49]

Still other responses to slave insurrection affirmed slaves' innate docility. Ac-cording to the historian Douglas Egerton, a myth arose after the execution of

Gabriel, famed leader of the Virginia slave conspiracy of 1800, that he "lost all firmness [and showed] nothing but abject fear" when he approached the scaffold.[50] Egerton finds no evidence for this story. But evidence is beside the point. By portraying Gabriel as an antirevolutionary, "abject" in fear, too cowardly to die for his freedom, this story distinguished Gabriel and his compatriots from leaders of the American Revolution; it proved they were ultimately unworthy of freedom. Similarly, when Nat Turner was finally captured, news reports insisted that "he displayed no sort of enterprise in the attempt to escape, nor any degree of courage in resisting the person who captured him." Even more improbably, another newspaper explained how Turner was caught. Spotted by a local white,

Discovery of Nat Turner.

44. *"Discovery of Nat Turner" reprinted from William Cullen Bryant and Sydney Howard Gay, A Popular History of the United States, From the First Discovery of the Western Hemisphere by the Northmen, to the End of the Civil War, vol. IV (New York, 1881).*

"Nat hailed him and offered to surrender . . . The prisoner, as his captor came up, submissively laid himself on the ground and was thus securely tied—not making the least resistance!" Even Turner's months-long escape after the rebellion proved his cowardice. During that time, one newspaper claimed, Turner had "wished to give himself up, but could never summon sufficient resolution!" The *Richmond Enquirer* ultimately concluded that Turner was "a wild fanatic or a gross imposter—but without possessing a single quality of a Hero or a General—without spirit—without courage, and without sagacity."[51] Later depictions would counter this view of Turner, portraying his capture in a heroic light. An 1870 print, for instance, showed Turner proudly approaching his captor, armed, his back firm and upright, prepared to meet his fate (figure 44). Both depictions of Turner's capture make rival claims about his virtue: one portrays Turner as a coward, while the other makes him out to be a rebel resisting slavery. Both accounts—the pro- and antislavery versions, we might call them—seem to assume that only through virtuous resistance could Turner genuinely deserve his freedom.

OF COURSE NOT EVERYONE denied the existence of slave resistance. Consider one analysis that not only saw slave revolt as a righteous struggle for freedom but also endorsed it. In a series of three articles published in at least five Northern newspapers in late 1791, the Connecticut Republican Abraham Bishop laid out perhaps the most passionate public defense of the Haitian revolution in the United States—suggesting that if a heroic account of the Haitian revolution was not common, it was at least "thinkable."[52] "We believe, that Freedom is the natural right of all rational beings," the first article began, "and we know that the Blacks have never voluntarily resigned that freedom." Even though blacks had a "natural right" to freedom—a formulation clearly indebted to a theory of natural rights as innate to all individuals—it was necessary for Bishop to add that they had never "voluntarily resigned" that right. It is telling that Bishop felt the need to make the point at all. According to the Declaration of Independence, a text Bishop cited, were not a person's rights "unalienable"? A different revolutionary slogan, which Bishop invoked three times in a single paragraph, was more ambiguous on the matter. *"Liberty or Death"* had become the rebellious slaves' mantra, Bishop marveled. Their determined resistance gave evidence that Haitians—"sealing with their blood, *the rights of men"*—deserved their freedom.

"He [God] is teaching them, as he taught you," wrote Bishop, "that freedom from the tyranny of men is to be had *only* at the price of blood. By this lesson, he instructs them, as he did you in the *value* of freedom."[53] Even Bishop, with his radical endorsement of the Haitian revolution, suggested that freedom had to be achieved through active resistance—"*only* at the price of blood."

Free African Americans commemorated the Haitian revolution with much the same language. For James T. Holly, perhaps the best-known proponent of African American emigration to Haiti, the revolution proved "the capacity of the Negro race for self-government." Holly believed in the "natural equality" of *all* people, in the "God-given liberty" of blacks. But Holly's proof lay not in a text or a declaration. Rather, it lay in Haitians' actions, in their resistance. Hence, in an 1857 speech, he celebrated Toussaint Louverture in familiar language.

> He made that bold resolution and unalterable determination, which, in ancient times, would have entitled him to be deified among the gods; that resolution was to reduce the fair Edenlike Isle of Hispaniola to a desolate waste like Sahara and suffer every black to be immolated in a manly defense of his liberty, rather than the infernal and accursed system of Negro slavery should again be established on that soil.

Louverture here became a latter-day Cato, a Haitian Patrick Henry. "He considered it far better that his sable countrymen should be dead freemen than living slaves." Even for people who endorsed a natural right of *all* people to freedom, it was the call of liberty or death that ultimately proved slaves' virtue, their worthiness to be free. More than virtue, resistance gave slaves new life and renewed masculinity. In the Haitian revolution, Holly argued, "a nation of abject and chattel slaves arise in the terrific might of their resuscitated manhood and regenerate, redeem and disenthrall themselves."[54]

As proof of African slaves' capacity to resist—as proof of their true *manhood*—Haiti thus became a rallying cry for radical abolitionists throughout the antebellum period. Henry Highland Garnet hoped American slaves would follow Louverture's example. "Brethren, the time has come when you must act for yourselves," Garnet declared in a famous 1843 speech. "Let it no longer be a debatable question whether it is better to choose *liberty or death* . . . Brethren, arise, arise! Strike for your liberties . . . *Rather die [in] freedom than live to be slaves.*" Garnet's rousing conclusion was: "Let your motto be resistance! *resistance!* resistance!"[55]

JOSEPH CINQUEZ
The brave Congolese Chief, who prefers death to Slavery, and who now lies in Jail in Irons at New Haven Conn. awaiting his trial for daring for freedom.

SPEECH TO HIS COMRADE SLAVES AFTER MURDERING THE CAPTAIN &C. AND GETTING POSSESSION OF THE VESSEL AND CARGO

Brothers we have done that which we purposed, our hands are now clean for we have Striven to regain the precious heritage we recieved from our fathers We have only to persevere. Where the Sun rises there is our home, our brothers, our fathers. Do not seek to defeat my orders, if so I shall sacrifice any one who would endanger the rest, when at home we will kill the Old Man, the young one shall be saved he is kind and gave you bread we must not kill those who give us water. Brothers I am resolved that it is better to die than be a white man's slave and I will not complain if by dying I save you. Let us be careful what we eat that we may not be sick The deed is done and I need say no more.

45. *"Joseph Cinquez, the brave Congolese Chief, who prefers death to slavery, and who now lives in jail . . ." lithograph (Boston: Joseph A. Arnold), c. 1839. Probably drawn by James or Isaac Sheffield.*

This exaltation of resistance as proof of virtue also prevailed in response to the famous *Amistad* slave revolt of 1839. Abolitionists celebrated the revolt—and its leader, Sengbe Pieh, known in the United States as Joseph Cinqué—because of the slaves' determination to risk death and fight for their freedom. One abolitionist broadside (figure 45) called Cinqué a "brave Congolese Chief, who prefers death to Slavery," and reproduced his alleged speech to his fellow slaves after they gained possession of the *Amistad*. "Brothers," said Cinqué, cast here as an African George Washington, "I am resolved that it is better to die than be a white man's slave."[56]

Even as slave owners shuddered at such rhetoric, they shared the basic principle that freedom had to be earned through resistance. When Southern slave owners admitted the fact of slave resistance, they, too, expressed admiration. Alfred Hunt has shown that depictions of Toussaint Louverture in Southern newspapers often "paid tribute to his military prowess and, in spite of his color, referred to him with the same propriety as northern newspapers did." Even the rabid fire-eater Edmund Ruffin—no abolitionist he—saw fit to call Louverture "the only truly great man yet known of the negro race."[57] Clearly Ruffin had a different view of race and slavery than did Holly or Garnet, which only makes their mutual admiration of Louverture all the more startling. The same was true of Gabriel's planned rebellion a few years after the Haitian revolution. One report circulating in the South explicitly linked the rebellious slaves to the nation's Founding Fathers. According to a lawyer involved with the trials, one male slave spoke out "in a manly tone of voice" before his execution. "I have nothing more to offer than what General Washington would have had to offer, had he been taken by the British and put to trial by them," this slave allegedly declared. "I have adventured my life in endeavouring to obtain the liberty of my countrymen, and am a willing sacrifice in their cause: and I beg, as a favour, that I may be immediately led to execution."[58] Not only was this rebellious slave portrayed as "manly," in opposition to the feminized abjectness of unworthy slaves, the report explicitly connected him to the nation's founding act of Revolutionary resistance—and to Washington. Having risked his life fighting for freedom, this virtuous slave willingly met, and even asked for, death. Like Quashi, he was too worthy to remain enslaved.

One prominent white seems to have agreed, seeing Gabriel's conspiracy as an act of resistance against tyranny. In contrast to those who denied slaves' resistance, James Monroe, then governor of Virginia, once called the rebels not fanatical or deluded, but "bold adventurers . . . willing to hazard their lives on the experiment." Monroe's analysis echoed that of the character in the *Slaves in Barbary* drama, who said courage might be good for a sailor, but not for a slave. "It is hardly to be presumed," wrote Monroe to Jefferson, that "a rebel who avows it was his intention to assassinate his master &.ᶜ if pardoned will ever become a useful servant." For Monroe the act of rebellion made individuals unfit for slavery. Monroe further underscored this view in his angry orders to the Virginia militia called out to suppress Gabriel's Rebellion. "The Chief Magistrate laments that *citizens*, called into service for the defence of their country, should dishonor that *title*," wrote Monroe of whites caught drunk and asleep while on duty. "They ought to shew themselves worthy of the exalted condition of *freemen* in every situation in which they are placed, especially in the character of *soldiers*." The same logic was at work in both instances: some men resisted slavery and showed themselves unfit for slavery, while others ineptly defended their lives and property, raising doubts about whether they were "worthy of the exalted condition of *freemen*." But the view of the rebellious slaves as "bold adventurers" seems to have been limited to Monroe's private correspondence. In public he, too, denied that slaves were true agents in the rebellion. "It seemed strange that the slaves should embark in this novel and unexampled enterprise of their own accord," Monroe declared to the Virginia General Assembly. "It was natural to suspect they were prompted to it by others who were invisible, but whose agency might be powerful."[59]

In 1816, in the wake of a plotted rebellion in Camden, South Carolina, the slave owner Henry W. DeSaussure also saw rebellious slaves not as mad or deluded, but as heroes resisting tyranny. "They met death with the heroism of Spartans, & displayed a Spirit worthy of a better Cause," he wrote. DeSaussure focused on their manner of meeting death, which clearly made them unfit for slavery. Their "tone, & temper," he wrote, "was of a cast not suited, to their condition." His view of these slaves as rebels led DeSaussure to conclude that an adherence to "the principles of liberty, & a contempt of death in pursuit of it . . . is the most dangerous state of mind for slaves."[60] When able to admit that slaves were rebelling, even Southern slave owners such as Monroe and DeSaussure interpreted rebellion in the terms of the nation's Revolutionary ideology of slavery and freedom, virtue and resistance. They concluded that a willingness to risk death and resist slavery made people unfit for the condition. Slavery, according to this logic, resulted not from circumstance or misfortune and only partly from race. Above all, it resulted from the "temper" (as DeSaussure put it) of slaves, a formulation that smuggled consent into the equation, offering grounds for the legitimacy of slavery in a republican nation.

NOT ALL AMERICANS AGREED. Alternative views of freedom and slavery always existed in the early republic—antislavery and abolitionist interpretations of freedom, most prominently. Grounding themselves in the universalism of the Declaration of Independence, some abolitionists argued that slavery was simply incompatible with American freedom, no matter what the circumstances. Years of persuasion never convinced a largely hostile public, however; the force of arms was ultimately necessary to make that view hegemonic, and even then many former slaves found their "freedom" deceptively shallow. Meanwhile, other views of American freedom continued to flourish—in particular, the belief that freedom results not from a universal grant, but from resistance and struggle: a view of freedom and slavery that was remarkably prevalent. So prevalent, in fact, that no less committed an abolitionist than Frederick Douglass implicitly subscribed to this reasoning.

"You have seen how a man was made a slave," observes Douglass at the mid-point of his autobiographical *Narrative.* Now, he continues, summarizing its second half, "you shall see how a slave was made a man." How does the transformation occur? How is Douglass converted into "a man"? Staring at the ships sailing along Chesapeake Bay, Douglass determines to win his freedom or to die trying. "I will run away. I will not stand it. Get caught, or get clear, I'll try it." Linking himself to the American Revolution by echoing both Addison's *Cato* and Nathan Hale, Douglass vows: "I have only one life to lose. I had as well be killed running as die standing." Thus settled on a determined act of resistance, which replicates the nation's founding act, Douglass begins the process by which a slave becomes "a man."[61]

"I resolved to fight," remembers Douglass. In fighting Edward Covey, the farmer to whom Douglass had been hired out, Douglass risks his life resisting slavery; his freedom becomes inevitable. It is the familiar plotline: resistance leads to freedom. The genius of Douglass's narrative is to show the personal, internal operation of that ideology. "This battle with Mr. Covey was the turning-point in my career as a slave," observes Douglass in retrospect. "It rekindled the few expiring embers of freedom, and revived within me a sense of my own manhood." Willing to face death, Douglass proves his inner virtue; he is no longer a slave in spirit. "The gratification afforded by the triumph [over Covey] was a full compensation for whatever else might follow, even death itself." Douglass's resistance gains its resonance from the nationalist ideology of freedom and slavery, virtue and resistance. Connecting himself to the nation's Founding Fathers, Douglass proudly observes: "He can only understand the deep satisfaction which I experienced, who has himself repelled by force the bloody arm of slavery."[62]

Through this act of violent resistance, Douglass is quite literally born again. By risking physical death, Douglass not only gains his masculinity; he gains social and even spiritual life. "I felt as I never felt before," Douglass recalls. "It was a glorious resurrection, from the tomb of slavery, bold defiance took its place; and I now resolved that, however long I might remain a slave in form, the day had passed forever when I could be a slave in fact. I did not hesitate to let it be known of me, that the white man who expected to succeed in whipping, must also succeed in killing me."[63] It is hard to imagine a better expression of the American exaltation of individual resistance as the path to freedom. In his resistance, in his willingness to die rather than remain a slave, Douglass proves his virtue and gains his freedom.

So powerful was this message, Douglass repeated it in his tale "The Heroic Slave." After escaping, the hero Madison Washington is recaptured and sent aboard a slave ship to New Orleans. As the ship sails down the Atlantic into the Caribbean, Washington leads a revolt. Not only does he fight, he articulates his act of heroic resistance—rebutting those who deny slaves' will to be free, and claiming his legacy in the tradition of the Founding Fathers.

> You call me a black murderer. I am not a murderer. God is my witness that LIBERTY, not malice, is the motive for this night's work . . . We have struck for our freedom, and if a true man's heart be in you, you will honor us for the deed. We have done that which you applaud your fathers for doing, and if we are murderers, so were they.

The first mate to whom Washington addresses these words, overcome by the truth of the message, comments: "I forgot his blackness in the dignity of his manner, and the eloquence of his speech."[64]

For Douglass, slave rebellion descended directly from the founders' legacy, and even went beyond it. "In coming to a fixed determination to run away," writes Douglass in his *Narrative*, "we did more than Patrick Henry, when he resolved upon liberty or death. With us it was a doubtful liberty at most, and almost certain death if we failed." This determination to resist distinguished heroes from cowards—it made resisting slaves braver, even, than the Founding Fathers themselves. "For my part," Douglass mused, "I should prefer death to hopeless bondage." What was more, Douglass added, had he and his fellow runaways not attempted this escape, "we had as well fold our arms, sit down, and acknowledge ourselves fit only to be slaves."[65]

Recall that Douglass had learned to read, to reason, and indeed to imagine himself as an autonomous individual from the *Columbian Orator:* "Every opportunity I got, I used to read this book." The results are obvious and impressive. Immersed in the outlook promoted by civic texts like the *Columbian Orator*—firmly adhering to an understanding of individuals as morally autonomous, capable of remaking their world—Douglass advanced their unflinching vision of a world shaped by individual choices. According to Douglass, a refusal to risk their lives would have made him and his friends "fit only to be slaves." Did this same logic apply to other slaves? Were all slaves who did not resist, no matter what their situation—no matter the circumstances that distinguished urban slavery in Baltimore or aboard a ship from rural slavery in the Carolina lowlands or the Alabama black belt—"fit only to be slaves"?

The Extended Legacy of Civic Texts

John C. Calhoun—exemplar of the Southern order so committed to slavery—had an answer to that question. But his answer did not contradict the nation's Revolutionary ideology. Just the contrary. In an 1848 speech denouncing the Wilmot Proviso, which would have barred slavery from land acquired in the Mexican War, Calhoun invoked the familiar fitness-for-slavery argument to urge resistance to Northern tyranny. "I turn now to my friends of the South," said Calhoun, "and ask, what are you prepared to do? . . . are you prepared to sink down into a state of acknowledged inferiority; to be stripped of your dignity of equals among equals, and be deprived of your equality of rights in this federal partnership of States?" This echo of Addison's *Cato* might well have been learned from Bingham's *Columbian Orator*. The message was identical: a failure to resist tyranny indicated a lack of virtue; it showed that one deserved slavery. "If so," Calhoun added, "you are wo[e]fully degenerated from your sires, and will *well deserve* to change condition with your slaves." "The South must rise up," urged Calhoun, "and bravely defend herself, or sink down into base and acknowledged inferiority."[66]

But Calhoun did not stop with this appeal to Southern resistance against Northern "tyranny"; he went on to offer his own interpretation of the meaning of American freedom. Looking back to the Declaration of Independence, Calhoun attacked the "hypothetical truism" that "all men are born free and equal" and offered an alternative formulation.

> Instead, then, of all men having the same right to liberty and equality, as is claimed by those who hold that they are all born free and equal, [Calhoun declared from the floor of the U.S. Senate,] liberty is the noble and highest reward bestowed on mental and moral development, combined with favorable circumstances. Instead, then, of liberty and equality being born with man; instead of all men and all classes and descriptions being equally entitled to them, they are high prizes to be won . . . the most difficult to be preserved.

Attacking the abolitionist view that liberty is a natural and inherent right, Calhoun posited a more complicated definition. And it is one that descended directly from the American Revolution as it was defined by civic texts. Locating individual action as the determinant of freedom, Calhoun distinguished between people *worthy* of freedom and those *unworthy* of it. Just as the idea was expressed in the *Columbian Orator,* Murray's *English Reader,* and even Frederick Douglass's *Narrative,* Calhoun believed that liberty can exist only among people who have shown "their fitness either to acquire or maintain liberty."[67]

If it is not surprising to find Calhoun and his peers making such arguments, it *is* surprising to find them advanced by people who had little else in common with Calhoun—and Douglass is not the only one in this category. None other than the abolitionist Wendell Phillips once wrote that "the Slave who does not write his own merit in the catalogue of insurrections hardly deserves freedom . . . no slave proves his manhood, except those who rise and at least try to cut their masters' throat."[68] And consider:

> The man who would not fight . . . to be delivered from the most wretched, abject, and servile slavery, that ever a people was afflicted with since the foundation of the world, to the present day— ought to be kept with all of his children or family, in slavery.

Those were not the words of Calhoun or Thomas Roderick Dew or George Fitzhugh or any other proslavery theorist. They were the words of David Walker, written in his great antislavery tract, *Appeal to the Coloured Citizens of the World* of 1829.[69] Urging his African American countrymen to rise up against slavery, Walker employed America's Revolutionary ideology to advance his case. Imbued with Protestant millennialism, intentionally echoing the Declaration of Independence—steeped, in short, in the language, ideologies, and grammar of the civic texts we've examined—Walker's *Appeal* asserted that an unwillingness to fight made people fit for slavery.

The point here is not that Walker or Phillips or Douglass held the same opinions about slavery and freedom as Calhoun. Rather, it is to marvel at the extraordinary influence of the civic texts that associated resistance with virtue and freedom. This association informed Northern views of slavery right into the Civil War, as testified by the widely disseminated images of former slaves turned into soldiers (figure 46). Such images of armed slaves, out on the battlefield fighting for their freedom, suggested they were, indeed, worthy enough to deserve it.

THE ESCAPED SLAVE.—PHOTOGRAPHED BY T. B. BISHOP.—(SEE PAGE 475.)   THE ESCAPED SLAVE IN THE UNION ARMY.—(SEE PAGE 475.)

46. *"The Escaped Slave"* and *"The Escaped Slave in the Union Army,"*
from photographs by T. B. Bishop. Reprinted from Harper's Weekly,
July 2, 1864. *In the original, "The Escaped Slave" appears above*
"The Escaped Slave in the Union Army."

Precisely the same ideology shaped the Southern rhetoric of secession. And so it seems not strange but appropriate that in 1861 white Southerners formed a new nation—in which their right to hold slaves would be forever guaranteed—because they themselves feared becoming enslaved. For them, as for their Revolutionary forebears, the path to freedom lay through resistance. And it was a path that Southern whites persisted in closing off to their slaves until the very last days of legal slavery. As the Confederate military situation grew increasingly desperate in 1864, some people began to consider the unthinkable: arming slaves to fight for the South's freedom. Not surprisingly, opposition to the idea was stiff, and it stemmed from the basic conceptualization of slavery and freedom. "If slaves will make good soldiers," the *Charleston Mercury* observed, "our whole theory of slavery is wrong."[70]

NO ONE has ever had an undisputed hold on the meaning of American nationalism, or on its liberal tradition. Abolitionists advanced one version. Drawing on the Revolution's rhetoric of liberty and equality and individual rights, they dramatically expanded the scope of the nation's civic and political life. This aspect of America's liberal tradition served as a shining light not, just for the abolitionists, but for the many social movements that would later model themselves on abolitionists. It has inspired women's demands for greater rights, labor movements, and of course the civil rights struggles of the twentieth century. But this was just one version of U.S. nationalism, just one definition of America's liberal tradition—not the only definition, and not even the dominant definition until well after the Civil War. Alongside it lay—and have always lain—different strands *within* America's liberal tradition, darker strands that drew on republican, Protestant, and racial ideas to inflect that liberal tradition and shape American nationalism.

It will not do simply to blame racism as the driving force here, and continue to imagine a heroic liberal tradition that led inevitably toward abolitionism. Racism was part of the story, of course. We have seen how racial ideologies reinforced a view of blacks as unvirtuous, unmanly, and unwilling to resist—an idea that would persist long after the abolition of slavery—making it all the more difficult (though not impossible) for whites to recognize the actions of slaves as resistance to slavery itself.[71] Ideologies of gender exclusion also played a central role, creating a binary opposition between the manly, virtuous action associated with whites and the effeminate degeneracy associated with blacks.[72] This gendered dimension, however, helps make it apparent that these forms of racism and gender exclusion did not pose a necessary contradiction to liberal thought. As numerous historians and feminist scholars have shown, liberal ideology and gender exclusion were hardly incompatible. Quite the contrary, the emergence of liberalism—and the constitution of the autonomous liberal "subject"—may well have been predicated on the exclusion of women from the public, political realm.[73]

What made this account of resistance, virtue, and slavery so powerful—indeed, so difficult even to notice—was that it drew on a liberal conception of the autonomous individual. A nation grounded in the consent of the governed, as we have seen, called for a particular kind of individual: a rational, self-willed, self-controlled decision maker. An autonomous individual. This book has shown how civic texts exalted this ideal of the morally autonomous individual as the ba-sic building block of a new liberal order: through the eulogies of Washington, in biographies like Weems's *Life of Washington,* in schoolbooks like the *Columbian Orator* or Murray's *English Reader,* indeed, in the very figure of Washington him-self, promoting a concept of the individual who shapes his own destiny, the indi-vidual idealized as "the architect of his own fortunes."[74] The individual, in short, who could *choose* to give his consent to the nation.

Over the course of the nineteenth century, as we also saw, this conception of the autonomous individual was extended to slaves in order to internalize disci-pline, to promote social order, and to appease dreaded fears of insurrection. In attributing moral autonomy to slaves, it became possible to blame them for their enslavement: to see in the absence of full-scale slave revolution a sign that slaves had indeed "consented" to their enslavement. This formulation paralleled the liberal account of citizenship so dear to U.S. nationalism. In this liberal account, "citizenship must begin with an act of individual choice," as the historian James Kettner puts it. "Every man had to have the right to decide whether to be a citi-zen or an alien."[75] The valorization of individual autonomy, in short, grounded both citizenship *and* slavery in a tacit consent. This account of slavery and con-sent was so powerful, its implications so hidden, because it grew out of the great liberal fiction that had haunted American nationalism since the days of Jefferson and Madison: the notion that *all* Americans had somehow consented to the na-tion of their own free volition.

And so it is tempting to stop here and to conclude that in this long encounter with slavery, civic texts had elevated not Jefferson's vision of actual, recurring consent, but Madison's doctrine of tacit consent. Just as Madison had suggested of constitutional theory in general, this account of slavery rested on the idea that "assent may be inferred, where no positive dissent appears."[76] In this sense, the "liberal" defense of slavery paralleled, and may well have informed, the attenu-ated definition of consent on which U.S. nationalism had been constructed. For it was precisely the same liberal fiction that allowed Americans to believe that they, too, had on some level "consented" to their nation, even if they had become American by an accident of birth rather than by an act of consent.

The exigency of reconciling slavery within a republican nationalism had, in short, promoted an impoverished meaning of consent based on an idealized image of individual achievement. The conviction that Americans had single-handedly emancipated themselves from political slavery allowed them to shackle others in bonds of chattel slavery. It was this same understanding of consent that would continue to inflect U.S. political discourse long after the institution of slavery itself had collapsed. African Americans emerging from generations of slavery would find themselves entering a jungle whose seeds civic texts had planted. Rights only go to those who are worthy; success results from individual effort alone; wealth results from virtue, poverty from vice; and neither the North nor the federal government nor even former slaveholders owe a debt to former slaves.

Later, as the institution of slavery became a distant memory, the idea that—as Lindley Murray's *English Reader* had put it—"the world seldom turns wholly against a man, unless through his own fault" continued to sanction an individualized, libertarian view of social life, in which contempt rather than pity was the proper response to the poor, the oppressed, the excluded. Nowhere has the belief that humans have the power to make their own history been more powerful than in the United States. It has been a constant theme in its literature, from the narratives of antebellum uplift to the Horatio Alger stories of the Gilded Age to F. Scott Fitzgerald's *The Great Gatsby*. It is the great American Dream. Even after the civic texts we have studied here had long disappeared into archives and attics, Americans of the twentieth and then the twenty-first century would continue to imagine that individuals were responsible, in a moral sense, for whatever successes and failures they met.

But did this belief result from the doctrine of tacit consent? Or did the problem lie with the nature of consent itself? It was Jefferson, after all, who had affirmed the "principle that the earth belongs to the living and not to the dead."[77] It was he who had begun the Declaration of Independence defining history as "the course of human events," stating that people confronted with "a long train of abuses and usurpations" had not just the right, but a "duty" to throw off such government. It was he who was, in the final account, the greatest proponent of the idea that the autonomous individual can and indeed should remake history. There was, as Madison may have sensed, a remarkable hubris in this conception of the individual, and it is certainly worth asking whether this aspect of the liberal project—the creation of morally autonomous individuals for a new, republican order—was in some sense too successful for its own good.

"*Individualism* is a recent expression," Alexis de Tocqueville wrote with some bemusement after visiting the United States. "Our fathers only knew egoism."[78] Was the distinction so clear? Even John Locke—the man to whom modern liberalism looks as its founding father, whose writings in large part had inspired Jefferson's Declaration of Independence—understood the dangers implicit in a liberalism grounded in the triumphant exaltation of the individual:

> He that travels the road now, applauds his own strength and legs
> that have carried him in such a scantling of time, and ascribes all to
> his own vigor; little considering how much he owes to their pains,
> who cleared the woods, drained the bogs, built the bridges, and
> made the way passable; without which he may have toiled much
> with little progress.[79]

It is difficult to refrain from wondering how much it was slavery that led Americans away from Locke's more charitable liberalism, which made room for history and circumstance, toward a liberalism that so exalted the heroic exertions of the unshackled individual. And difficult, therefore, not to wonder about the burdens Americans inherited from their dead fathers that weigh, still, like a nightmare on the brain of the living.

Epilogue

AMERICAN NATIONALISM, THE LIVING, AND THE DEAD

———◆▸•◂◆———

Every age and generation is, and must be (as a matter of right), as free to act for itself in all cases, as the age and generation that preceded it . . . If we think otherwise than this we think either as slaves or as tyrants. As slaves, if we think that any former generation had a right to bind us; as tyrants, if we think that we have authority to bind the generations that are to follow.

—THOMAS PAINE, 1795[1]

IN LATE JANUARY of 1838 a young lawyer rose before the Young Men's Lyceum in Springfield, Illinois, to speak on "the perpetuation of our political institutions." The lawyer's subject was the increasing spirit of lawlessness in the nation, which threatened to break down "the *attachment* of the People" to their government. The nation, he argued, was a great experiment, testing *"the capability of a people to govern themselves."* "How shall we fortify" against the dangers the nation faced? "The answer is simple," he averred:

> Let every American, every lover of liberty, every well wisher to his posterity, swear by the blood of the Revolution, never to violate in the least particular, the laws of the country . . . As the patriots of seventy-six did to the support of the Declaration of Independence,

so to the support of the Constitution and Laws, let every American pledge his life, his property, and his sacred honor;—let every man remember that to violate the law, is to trample on the blood of his father, and to tear the character of his own, and his children's liberty. Let reverence for the laws, be breathed by every American mother, to the lisping babe, that prattles on her lap—let it be taught in schools, in seminaries, and in colleges;—let it be written in Primmers, spelling books, and in Almanacs;—let it be preached from the pulpit, proclaimed from the legislative halls, and enforced in courts of justice. And, in short, let it become the political religion of the nation; and let the old and young, the rich and the poor, the grave and the gay, of all sexes and tongues, and colors and conditions, sacrifice unceasingly upon its altars.

It is hard to imagine a better summary of the subject of this book. In those few sentences, that young lawyer—Abraham Lincoln—identified not just the civic texts that promoted early U.S. nationalism (sermons, primers, spelling books, almanacs), not just the audience they targeted (old and young, rich and poor, all sexes and tongues, colors and conditions), but the process by which they worked (read by parents to lisping babes, taught in schools, seminaries, and colleges) and the result they achieved: a political religion that worshipped the Founding Fathers and the Revolution. Lincoln concluded his speech with a prayer that showed he truly was born again into this political religion: "That we improved to the last; that we remained free to the last; that we revered his name to the last; that, during his long sleep, we permitted no hostile foot to pass over or desecrate his resting place; shall be that which to learn the last trump shall awakening our WASHINGTON."[2]

If Lincoln knew intuitively how civic texts promoted U.S. nationalism in the name of the fathers, that is because he was, as much as any nineteenth-century American, their product. Growing up in rural Illinois, Lincoln's childhood had been characterized, like that of many other Americans, by a relative penury of printed matter. But what he did get his hands on—the Bible, Weems's *Life of Washington,* Caleb Bingham's *Columbian Orator,* and Lindley Murray's *English Reader*—profoundly shaped his worldview.[3] Lincoln's political outlook—most particularly, his deep dedication to the Union, which one might call downright Weemsian—not to speak of his rhetoric, reflected the education he had gained from civic texts. When Lincoln rose to address his audience in Springfield, then, he understood the power of texts to shape minds and to create a nation, and he was fully fluent in the language they spoke.

Within two generations, U.S. nationalism had come full circle. Thomas Jefferson had sought, in the halcyon days of 1789, to ground the nation on the will of "the living": on pure consent. This project was carried forward by civic texts that sought to promote the consent of present and future Americans, and to ensure that the nation was, if not a daily plebiscite, at least a multigenerational project. Over time, however, that "consent" had grown ever more attenuated under the strain of holding a nation together while at the same time making room for slavery. Calling on Americans to give their fealty to the nation in the name of dead fathers, civic texts slowly choked off the revolutionary message that the earth belongs to the living.[4] By 1838, nationalists like Lincoln were calling on Americans to "swear by the blood of the Revolution," urging each individual to worship "the blood of his father." The will and even the consent of the living had been overtaken by the political obligation to obey the fathers. By 1861 the whole project would collapse in on itself, fulfilling the prophecy civic texts had long maintained would result from disunion: a civil war in which brother slew brother. The disparate meanings given to these texts—by Northerners and Southerners, slaves and masters, men and women, white and black—would ultimately fracture the nation along lines of race and region, and no frantic invocation of the fathers, no continuous worship at the shrine of the founders, could stem the tide.

If the Civil War represents the monumental failure of civic texts to unify the nation, and to resolve the problem of slavery within a liberal nationalism, however, it also highlights the success of the nation-making project. Civic texts succeeded in attaching the nation to the affections of enough people that hundreds of thousands were willing to fight and die for its survival. If they did not succeed in finally resolving the problem of slavery and U.S. nationalism, they did succeed in defining the terms of the debate, so that the most politically effective abolitionists were those who argued that the founding documents *really did* oppose slavery. The abolitionists engaged not so much in a second American Revolution as an attempt to redefine the meaning of the first, and they succeeded so well that many Americans continue to this day to believe that the Constitution and the American Revolution must really have been opposed to slavery.

More than any abolitionist, though, it was Lincoln who proved most able to reshape U.S. nationalism to cast it in opposition to slavery. Lincoln's vision of the United States as a world-historical experiment endured for the rest of his life, holding firm, even gaining in strength, through the searing years of civil war. When, some thirty-five years after his Lyceum Address, Lincoln traveled to Gettysburg, Pennsylvania, to give a brief oration, he called that terrible war a test, to determine once and for all whether a nation "conceived in Liberty, and dedicated to the proposition that all men are created equal . . . can long endure." But standing above a cemetery of dead Americans—their "final resting place"—Lincoln looked no more to dead fathers to preserve the nation. No longer did he invoke "the blood of the fathers." He looked now to a new set of dead: "those who here gave their lives that the nation might live." If the earth still did not belong to the living, it now belonged to a new set of dead, and it fell to "us the living . . . to be dedicated here to the unfinished work which they who fought here have thus far so nobly advanced." Lincoln vowed that it would be "from these honored dead we take increased devotion to that cause for which they gave the last full measure of devotion," and called for the nation to undergo "a new birth of freedom."[5]

Lincoln, of course, joined those "honored dead" only two years later, vaulting immediately into the pantheon of American greats: Washington the father now joined by Lincoln the son, who died that the nation might live. Lincoln's apotheosis would bear many similarities to Washington's (figure 47), and his role in American memory would even come to surpass that of the father himself. Having personally suffered for the nation's sins, Lincoln added a human dimension to the founders that (despite Weems's best attempts) had always been lacking in Washington. As the Farewell Address's popularity waned in the wake of the Civil War, the fears that had lent that text its urgency fading now that the problem of national existence had been settled once and for all, the Gettysburg Address would come to replace it in the national canon, with children learning and memorizing it in schools, and patriots reading it aloud on national holidays.

As for the slaves, they would soon be written out of the nation's past. The free blacks and former slaves who fought in the war would be erased, just as an earlier generation had forgotten the participation of slaves and free blacks in the Revolution. The slaves who resisted their enslavement by leaving plantations and forcing themselves onto Union armies, transforming Union policy toward slavery and indeed toward the war, would be erased from history, absent from the history books and popular accounts churned out in the wake of the Civil War, all focused on reunion and reconciliation at the expense of the former slaves.[6] Instead, emancipation would come to be seen as a gift bestowed by whites upon blacks, rather than a prize won through resistance and struggle: a familiar narrative that would justify a new legal framework of segregation and racial oppression.

47. S. J. *Ferris*, Washington & Lincoln (Apotheosis), *1865*.

In 1876, the centenary of the Declaration of Independence, just as the federal government began its retreat from the South, and from the enforcement of civil rights for African Americans, a new monument to Abraham Lincoln would be unveiled in Washington, D.C., depicting Lincoln as the great emancipator (figure 48). Holding the emancipation proclamation in his hand, leaning on a pillar engraved with Washington's face, Lincoln stands over a grateful and kneeling slave who receives his freedom as a gift.[7] It was an image that future historians would spend many years correcting, an image they continue even today to combat.

BY PROMOTING a powerful conception of the morally autonomous individual—a cult of the individual that had even proved able to authorize slavery—and fusing that with an even more powerful call to abide by the will of dead fathers, civic

48. *Emancipation Monument, Lincoln Park,*
Washington, D.C., Thomas Ball, sculptor.

texts engaged in a contradictory enterprise that raised a painful and nagging question: a question that has, in a sense, run through this entire book.

The Constitution had initially justified itself as an expression of "We, the People," and came into being through a set of special conventions called forth by those people.[8] The Constitution, like the People for whom it claimed to speak, would represent the will of the living, and it would continue to do so through subsequent generations. Certainly this is how Washington had understood it. Promoting the benefits of the Constitution to his friends in 1787, he repeated numerous times that "a Constitutional door is opened for future amendments and alterations." As he wrote to LaFayette in 1788, "I had never supposed that perfection could be the result of accommodation and mutual concession." The important thing, for Washington, was that the Constitution could and would be made *more perfect* in the course of time, as each generation modified it to suit its will. "With prudence in temper and a spirit of moderation," Washington wrote, "every essential alteration, may in the process of time, be expected." Though he was always more radical than Washington, Jefferson agreed with this assessment. Even Madison, whose conservative inclinations led him to embrace the notion of tacit assent as an alternative to real consent, believed that a properly republican constitution was "always liable to be altered by the people who formed it."[9] The Constitution, as it was originally conceived by the men who created it, would thus be a living document. It would evolve with the course of time, be adapted by future generations, and continually be reshaped to conform to the will of the living.

Here was the remarkable thing: within the span of a few decades this vision of the Constitution had been dramatically transformed—not by the men who wrote it, but by the civic texts that promoted popular allegiance to it. Within two generations, civic texts had so exalted the Constitution, had turned the Founding Fathers into objects of such veneration, that any thought of amendment was rendered nearly sacrilegious. After the Bill of Rights passed in the wake of the Constitution's approval, only two more amendments would make their way through the political system: the eleventh in 1795, the twelfth in 1804. The Constitution would not see another amendment until the very foundations of the nation had been shaken and nearly destroyed. That thirteenth amendment would introduce the term "slavery" into the Constitution for the first time, even as it officially exorcised the institution from the nation. By that time, however, civic texts had turned the Constitution into a dead document, fit only for veneration—indeed, important enough to sacrifice hundreds of thousands of lives for its preservation—its basic pillars now beyond political debate. U.S. political discourse would be limited to interpretive quibbles about the Constitution's meaning in the minds of dead founders. The dead, in short, would perpetually exert their will over the living.

Which raised the nagging question.

Jefferson, true to his principles, watched this process unfold with regret. "Some men look at constitutions with sanctimonious reverence," he wrote in 1816, "and deem them like the arc of the covenant, too sacred to be touched. They ascribe to the men of the preceding age a wisdom more than human, and suppose what they did to be beyond amendment." Jefferson would have none of this.

> I knew that age well; I belonged to it, and labored with it. It deserved well of its country. It was very like the present, but without

the experience of the present; and forty years of experience in government is worth a century of book-reading; and this they would say themselves, were they to rise from the dead . . . laws and institutions must go hand in hand with the progress of the human mind. As that becomes more developed, more enlightened, as new discoveries are made, new truths disclosed, and manners and opinions change with the change of circumstances, institutions must advance also, and keep pace with the times.

Some twenty-seven years after his initial ruminations on the rights of the living, Jefferson continued to believe that the earth belonged to them. "We might as well require a man to wear still the coat which fitted him when a boy, as civilized society to remain ever under the regimen of their barbarous ancestors."[10] It is hard to avoid wondering what Jefferson would think if he were to "rise from the dead" nearly two hundred years later, and look upon those future generations in which he had so much faith, still meekly living under the regimen of their barbarous ancestors.

Somewhere along the way, Jefferson's vision of a republic grounded in the rights of the living—an ideal shared by so many of his enlightened contemporaries—had been turned on its head. By cementing allegiance to the nation in the name of the fathers, civic texts had betrayed the fathers' vision of a nation grounded in the consent of the living. Civic texts had, on the one hand, promoted a powerful idea of moral autonomy: the individual as author of his or her own existence, a conception of the individual so powerful it even allowed white Americans to justify slavery by a logic of individual choice. At the same time, however, civic texts succeeded in attaching the affections of the people to the nation by exalting the Founding Fathers and the founding documents, turning them into objects of veneration and not reflection, of genuflection and not critical appraisal. The Constitution had been rendered into a mystical, transgenerational compact more suited to the antirepublican conservatism of Edmund Burke than to the republicanism of Thomas Jefferson.

"Each generation is equal in rights to the other," Thomas Paine wrote during the turbulent, exhilarating days of the French revolution. "Every age and generation is, and must be . . . as free to act for itself . . . as the ages and generations that preceded it." We think as slaves, Paine accused, "if we think any former generation had a right to bind us." Here lay the nagging question, the question that has

run through this book, the question that may well lie at the heart of liberal political theory; and here it would remain, a perpetual undercurrent troubling the
many future waves of American triumphalism and superpatriotism: By persuading future generations to live by the will of dead fathers, and to do so *by their own
choice,* had civic texts ultimately turned Americans—this people so proud of its
individual achievements, so prepared to live free or die—into slaves?

A BRIEF NOTE ON CIVIC TEXTS

—▸•◂—

CIVIC TEXTS are a broad category, and it is worth distinguishing between two general types as I have treated them in this book. First are the *popularizing* texts: the large body of texts that circulated in the hundreds of thousands of copies, and in some cases in the millions—schoolbooks, political pamphlets, almanacs, newspaper reporting, and so forth. Much like national monuments, they promoted a set of nationalist icons, created a nationalist canon, and helped popularize certain major figures and major texts. Which brings us to the second type: the *canonical* texts, which were one of the principal objects of the popularizing texts. These consisted of a relatively small number of works, but which became particularly important over the course of the nineteenth century. The three most important were the Declaration of Independence, the Constitution, and Washington's Farewell Address. To this list one could add certain other works that later became quasi-canonical: the newspaper articles that came to be called the Federalist Papers, the Kentucky and Virginia Resolutions, and Webster's *Reply to Hayne*, for instance.

As these diverse examples suggest, these documents did not speak with one voice, and did not lend themselves to any simple or unitary interpretation. On the contrary, their interpretation was often hotly contested by writers of different regions, political affiliations, or ethnic groups.[1] But what is critical to understand is that the very act of trying to interpret these documents, no matter how contradictory those interpretations, ultimately served to exalt them even further. Through their continual appropriation by the popularizing civic texts, and through their institutionalization in school curricula and other sites of civic education, these canonical texts embodied and promoted American nationalism. They were set up—in large part by the popularizing texts—as points of eternal recurrence, to be revived and remembered throughout the ages. Ultimately, however, they would elude attempts at fixing their interpretation, and their meanings would continually evolve throughout the nineteenth century. They were all, at least for a time, living documents.

As an example, consider the Declaration of Independence, which, during the course of the nineteenth century, came to embody a set of nationalist principles. As historian Pauline Maier has shown, it did not achieve canonical status instantly, nor was its meaning fixed during its first fifty years.[2] A whole set of intermediary texts intervened to elevate the Declaration of Independence and make it into American scripture. Newspapers republished the Declaration every year for audiences to read and reread; schoolbooks excerpted or reprinted it for children to learn and memorize; July 4 orations throughout the nation were delivered and then published, often quoting extensively from the Declaration, or attaching it as an appendix; pamphlet editions of the text itself were continually reprinted; and handbooks—with titles like *The American Citizen's Sure Guide: Being a Collection of Most Important State Papers: Such as the Declaration of Independence: Articles of Confederation . . . The Constitution* (1804)—were repeatedly published during the years of the early republic. It was this process of dissemination and popularization that gave the Declaration its canonical status.

None other than Thomas Jefferson recognized the importance of this process when, a few days before his death (on July 4, 1826), he wrote to the committee organizing an upcoming July Fourth celebration: "for ourselves let the annual return of this day for ever refresh our recollections of these rights and an undiminished devotion to them."[3] Jefferson here understood that the Declaration could not achieve canonical status by his pen alone, nor was it assured by the Revolution's success. It would take popular celebrations and popularizing texts to persuade audiences to engage in an "annual return . . . for ever." In such moments, Americans would continually recur to the moment of founding, rereading and reciting the Declaration of Independence, regenerating themselves by their "undiminished devotion" to the founders' principles.[4] What were those principles? That remained to be decided, and in different hands they could be made to promote policies Federalist or Republican, Democrat or Whig; to promote abolitionism on the one hand or secession on the other. The meaning of the Declaration

clearly varied over time. What did not change were Americans' continual attempts to justify their present with reference to a set of canonical documents—
which inevitably committed them to the principles and even the laws of the
founding generation. Thus would civic texts persuade future generations to perpetuate their political principles and maintain their nation.

PUBLICATION TREND OF TWO CANONICAL TEXTS

———+>•<+———

THE FOLLOWING GRAPHS represent the results of bibliographic research con-
ducted on the publication history of Washington's Farewell Address and the
Declaration of Independence from 1796, the year of Washington's Farewell Address, to 1865. The sources used here are the WorldCat/OCLC catalog supplemented by the short-title Evans catalog. The total number of editions of the
Declaration of Independence I compiled is 515, and the total number of editions
of the Farewell Address is 342.

Unfortunately, this remains a relatively crude barometer, for it misses a vast
number of pamphlet editions in which these two texts were reprinted but not included in the title. (For instance, Mason Locke Weems's biography of Washington reprinted the Farewell Address in full, but that was not picked up by my
search.) Nevertheless, these charts give a general idea of the publication trends of
these two documents.

PUBLICATION HISTORY OF THE DECLARATION
OF INDEPENDENCE, 1796–1865

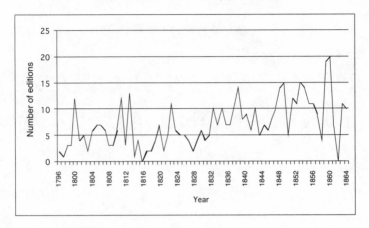

PUBLICATION HISTORY OF WASHINGTON'S
FAREWELL ADDRESS, 1796–1865

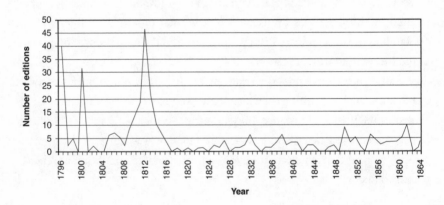

The most intriguing aspect of these graphs is the correlation that results when they are put alongside each other.

PUBLICATION HISTORY OF THE DECLARATION OF INDEPENDENCE AND WASHINGTON'S FAREWELL ADDRESS, 1796–1865

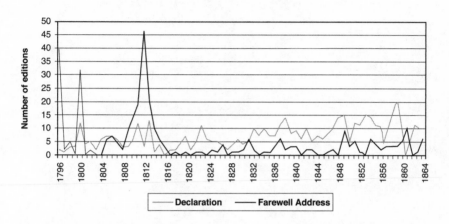

Although any findings from these data remain speculative, it is possible to draw some tentative conclusions. The patterns of publication suggest that these civic texts were being deployed to very specific ends. Note a rise in editions at moments of national crisis: Washington's death in 1799; the War of 1812; nullification in 1832; economic crisis in 1837; threat of national dissolution in 1850; and ultimately secession itself in 1861. The trends in publication suggest that civic texts were deploying these canonical documents in order to promote allegiance and loyalty—and ultimately, consent—to the nation at moments when it seemed perilously close to collapse.

APPENDIX 3

PUBLICATION INFORMATION REGARDING THE *COLUMBIAN ORATOR*

———➤•◄———

PUBLICATION HISTORY OF THE
***COLUMBIAN ORATOR*, 1797–1840**

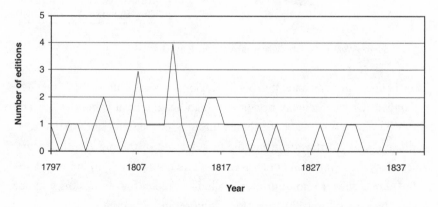

(Source: WorldCat, Nietz Catalog of Early American Schoolbooks)

The figure above reflects the publication trend of *Columbian Orator* editions in the forty years following its initial publication from 1797. We know very little about the actual number of copies printed; since a single edition could vary a great deal in number. Once stereotyping technology became widely used— involving a cast that allowed printers to reprint very popular texts without reset-

ting their type—the number of copies of a single "edition" become's very difficult to establish. Nevertheless, it is noteworthy that the number of editions saw
an important spike during the nationalist crisis of the War of 1812: something
that was also apparent in the publication of editions of the two canonical texts
described in appendix 2.

The publication location of *Columbian Orator* editions centered largely in
New England and its cultural hinterland, upstate New York, although the book
was also published in Philadelphia and Baltimore.

Geographic Distribution of the *Columbian Orator*, 1797–1840

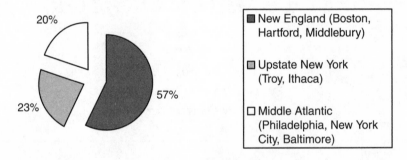

(Source: WorldCat, Nietz Catalog of Early American Schoolbooks)

This figure may overstate the book's regional specialization, however. The
Columbian Orator probably began with high geographical concentration and
slowly became more evenly distributed throughout the states of the Middle Atlantic and Old Northwest during the first decades of the nineteenth century.
After 1828, the *Columbian Orator* seems to have been jointly produced and distributed by a consortium of printers, including at least four in Boston, and one
each in New York, Troy, Philadelphia, Baltimore, and Cincinnati.

LINDLEY MURRAY'S
ENGLISH READER

—➤•◆←—

THE GRAPH BELOW represents the rising sales of Murray's *English Reader*. These numbers represent the number of editions published per year, measured in five-year intervals. Here again, the graph may exaggerate the declining number of editions. Once stereotyped, new editions of these texts were a simple matter to print. In addition, it is likely that each year saw rising numbers of copies per edition. Although we don't know the numbers of copies, the graph offers a rough guide to the astonishing rise in editions of the *English Reader*.

PUBLICATION HISTORY OF THE
***ENGLISH READER*, 1799–1830**

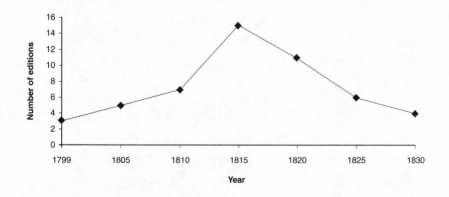

Publication Location of the *English Reader,* 1799–1830

DATE	NUMBER OF EDITIONS	PLACE OF PUBLICATION	
1799	3	London New York (Isaac Collins) York, U.K.	
1805	5	Boston Brattleborough, Vt. Charlestown, Mass. London Newbern, S.C.	
1810	7	Albany Charleston, S.C. Hallowell, Maine Haverhill, Mass. New York (2) York, U.K., and London	
1815	15	Ballston Spa, N.Y. Baltimore Belfast Boston Bridgeport, Conn. Burlington, Vt. Greenfield, Mass.	Hallowell, Maine Lansingburgh, N.Y. New York (2) Newburyport Mass. Philadelphia (2) Pittsburgh
1820	11	Baltimore Bellows Falls, Vt. Bennington, Vt. Boston Concord, N.H.	Exeter, N.H. New York (2) Philadelphia Pittsburgh Utica, N.Y.

(continued)

Date	Number of Editions	Place of Publication
1825	6	Albany Boston Philadelphia (2) Pittsburgh York, U.K., and London
1830	4	Baltimore and Boston Georgetown, D.C. Kingston, Canada Philadelphia

NOTES

PROLOGUE: WHAT THE NATION WAS UP AGAINST

1 John Clement Fitzpatrick, ed., *The Writings of George Washington from the Original Manuscript Sources, 1745–1799,* 39 vols. (Washington, D.C.: U.S. Government Printing Office, 1931), XXXV:218. The title of this prologue pays homage to David Brion Davis, *The Problem of Slavery in the Age of Revolution, 1770–1823* (Ithaca, N.Y.: Cornell University Press, 1975), chapter 1.

2 Certification of David D. Claypoole, February 22, 1826, in Victor Hugo Paltsits, ed., *Washington's Farewell Address, in Facsimile, with Transliterations of All the Drafts of Washington, Madison, & Hamilton, Together with Their Correspondence and Other Supporting Documents* (New York: New York Public Library, 1935), 290–92, quotation at 291. Considering its importance, the Farewell Address has been largely underexamined by historians. As my analysis attests, I am deeply indebted to the invaluable work by the great bibliographer and scholar Victor Hugo Paltsits, which is, alas, out of print. The Farewell Address is usually examined in the context of U.S. foreign policy: Samuel Flagg Bemis, "Washington's Farewell Address: A Foreign Policy of Independence," *American Historical Review* 39 (1934): 250–68; Alexander DeConde, "Washington's Farewell, the French Alliance, and the Election of 1796," *Mississippi Valley Historical Review* 43 (1957): 641–58; Felix Gilbert, *To the Farewell Address; Ideas of Early American Foreign Policy* (Princeton, N.J.: Princeton University Press, 1961). Important exceptions are Joseph Charles, *The Origins of the American Party System; Three Essays* (Williamsburg, Va.: Institute of Early American History and Culture, 1956), and

Robert A. Ferguson, *The American Enlightenment, 1750–1820* (Cambridge, Mass.: Harvard University Press, 1997). See also Edmund Sears Morgan, *The Genius of George Washington* (New York: W. W. Norton, 1980); Garry Wills, *Cincinnatus: George Washington and the Enlightenment* (Garden City, N.Y.: Doubleday, 1984); Albert Furtwangler, *American Silhouettes: Rhetorical Identities of the Founders* (New Haven, Conn.: Yale University Press, 1987), 85–114; Joseph J. Ellis, *Founding Brothers: The Revolutionary Generation* (New York: Knopf, 2000), 120–61; and Matthew Spalding and Patrick J. Garrity, *A Sacred Union of Citizens: George Washington's Farewell Address and the American Character* (Lanham, Md.: Rowman & Littlefield, 1996). On Washington's retirements more broadly, see the penetrating analyses in Morgan, *The Genius of George Washington*; Wills, *Cincinnatus*; and Barry Schwartz, *George Washington: The Making of an American Symbol* (Ithaca, N.Y.: Cornell University Press, 1990). The full text of the Farewell Address is printed in Fitzpatrick, ed., *Writings*, XXXV:214–38.

3 Paltsits, ed., *Washington's Farewell Address*, 9–24; quotation at 15.

4 Fitzpatrick, ed., *Writings*, XXXV:409.

5 Ibid., XXVI:487; the full text of the address is on XXVI:493–96. On the 1783 address, see also Ferguson, *The American Enlightenment*, 38–41.

6 Madison to Washington, June 20, 1792, in Paltsits, ed., *Washington's Farewell Address*, 227, 229; the full text of Madison's draft is on 160–63.

7 John Jay to Richard Peters, March 29, 1811, quoted in Paltsits, ed., *Washington's Farewell Address*, 271. For Washington's draft, see "Washington's First Draft for an Address, Enclosed in his Letter to Hamilton, May 15, 1796," in Paltsits, ed., *Washington's Farewell Address*, 164–73.

8 The Farewell Address thus differed in form as well as ideology from the Declaration of Independence. On which, see Jay Fliegelman, *Declaring Independence: Jefferson, Natural Language and the Culture of Performance* (Stanford, Calif.: Stanford University Press, 1993).

9 These were: *The New World: or, the Morning and Evening Gazette*, printed by Harrison Smith; and *The Philadelphia Gazette & Universal Daily Advertiser*, published by Andrew Brown.

10 This paragraph is based on the bibliography compiled in Paltsits, ed., *Washington's Farewell Address*, 307–60, supplemented by bibliographic work on the WorldCat Web site and Clifford Kenyon Shipton, James E. Mooney, and Roger P. Bristol, *National Index of American Imprints through 1800: The Short-Title Evans*, 2 vols. (Worcester, Mass.: American Antiquarian Society, 1969), II, 961–63.

11 James McHenry to Washington, September 25, 1796; and Bartholomew Dandridge to Washington, September 26, 1799, in Paltsits, ed., *Washington's Farewell Address*, 261, 262. On the response to the address, see ibid., 55–74.

12 The danger most exemplified during Washington's presidency by the Whiskey Rebellion. On which, see Thomas P. Slaughter, *The Whiskey Rebellion: Frontier Epilogue to the American Revolution* (New York: Oxford University Press, 1986), esp. 28–45. On the problem of retaining the West, see esp. D. W. Meinig, *The Shaping of America: A Geographical Perspective on 500 Years of History, Volume 1: Atlantic America, 1492–1800* (New Haven, Conn.: Yale University Press, 1986) and ibid., *Volume 2: Continental America, 1800–1867* (1993). On the West as a consideration at the Constitutional Convention, see Jack N. Rakove, *Original Meanings: Politics and Ideas in the Making of the Constitution* (New York: Knopf, 1996). See also Andrew R. L. Cayton, "'Separate Interests' and the Nation-State: The Washington Administration and the Origins of Regionalism in the Trans-Appalachian West," *Journal of American History* 79 (1992): 39–67.

13 The work on political parties that has most influenced the following analysis is Richard Hofstadter, *The Idea of a Party System: The Rise of Legitimate Opposition in the United States, 1780–1840* (Berkeley: University of California Press, 1969). A more recent analysis of the relationship between nationalism and partisanship that rightly (and unusually) treats the two not as oppositional is David Waldstreicher, *In the Midst of Perpetual Fetes: The Making of American Nationalism, 1776–1820* (Chapel Hill: University of North Carolina Press, 1997).

14 The danger of faction was closely related to the problem of men of ambition. On which, see esp. George B. Forgie, *Patricide in the House Divided: A Psychological Interpretation of Lincoln and His Age* (New York: W. W. Norton, 1979), 55–88, and Douglass Adair, *Fame and the Founding Fathers: Essays* (Indianapolis: Liberty Fund, 1998).

INTRODUCTION: CONSENT, SLAVERY, AND THE PROBLEM OF U.S. NATIONALISM

1 Benjamin Rush, "Address to the People of the United States," in *The American Museum, or, Repository of Ancient and Modern Fugitive Pieces, &c. Prose and Poetical, for January 1787*, I (Philadelphia: Mathew Carey, 1790), 8.

2 George Washington, "General Orders," July 9, 1776, in Fitzpatrick, ed., *Writings*, V:245.

3 "Declaration of Independence," in Julian P. Boyd, et al., eds., *The Papers of Thomas Jefferson*, 30 vols. to date (Princeton, N.J.: Princeton University Press, 1950–), I:429.

4 Linda Colley, *Britons: Forging the Nation, 1707–1837* (New Haven, Conn.: Yale University Press, 1992); T. H. Breen, "Ideology and Nationalism on the Eve of the American

Revolution: Revisions *Once More* in Need of Revising," *Journal of American History* 84 (1997): 13–39; Eliga H. Gould, *The Persistence of Empire: British Political Culture in the Age of the American Revolution* (Chapel Hill: University of North Carolina Press, 2000); David Armitage, *The Ideological Origins of the British Empire* (Cambridge, Eng.: Cambridge University Press, 2000), 170–98; Lois G. Schwoerer, "Law, Liberty, and Jury 'Ideology': English Transatlantic Revolutionary Traditions," in *Revolutionary Currents: Nation Building in the Transatlantic World,* Michael A. Morrison and Melinda S. Zook, eds. (Lanham, Md. : Rowman & Littlefield, 2004).

5 Thomas Paine, *Common Sense,*Thomas P. Slaughter, ed. (Boston: Bedford/St. Martin's, 2001), 113–14.

6 Liberation from the dead hand of patriarchal authority, observes the scholar Jay Fliegelman, was "the quintessential motif" of America's Revolutionary and post-Revolutionary ideology. Jay Fliegelman, *Prodigals and Pilgrims: The American Revolution Against Patriarchal Authority, 1750–1800* (Cambridge, Eng.: Cambridge University Press, 1982), 3. On the Revolution as "rupture," see also Michael Kammen, *Mystic Chords of Memory: The Transformation of Tradition in American Culture* (New York: Knopf, 1991), 3–61.

7 Those versed in the historiography of the early republic will note that I use republicanism here in its broader, eighteenth- and nineteenth-century meaning: A form of government opposed to monarchy, in which "the people" are considered sovereign, and in which government derives its legitimacy from the consent of the governed. Many historians who use the term republicanism today refer to a historiographical debate that sets "republicanism" in opposition to "liberalism." Both these terms meant very different things in the nineteenth century than they do today. The literature on republicanism is too vast to fully cite here. For useful historiographical summaries, with extensive references, see: Robert E. Shalhope, "Republicanism and Early American Historiography," *The William and Mary Quarterly* 3rd Ser., 39 (1982): 334–56; Daniel Rodgers, "Republicanism: The Career of a Concept," *Journal of American History* (1992): 11–38; and, with a more updated bibliography, Alan Gibson, "Ancients, Moderns and Americans: The Republican-Liberalism Debate Revisited," *History of Political Thought* 21 (2000): 261–307. The scholarship on republicanism that has influenced my thinking on the subject is cited in full in François Furstenberg, "Civic Texts, Slavery, and the Formation of American Nationalism" (Ph.D. dissertation, Johns Hopkins University, 2003), 10n8.

8 "Whatever else a nation was," observes Eric Hobsbawm, "the element of citizenship and mass participation or choice was never absent from it." E. J. Hobsbawm, *Nations and*

Nationalism Since 1870: Programme, Myth, Reality, 2d ed. (Cambridge, Eng.: Cambridge University Press, 1990), 19.

9 One might fairly wonder whether it is appropriate to speak of "nationalism" in the post-Revolutionary United States context. It is true that, in contrast to many later Europeans, late eighteenth- and nineteenth-century Americans generally spoke of "Union," rather than "nation." Nevertheless, to speak about nationalism in the post-Revolutionary United States context is appropriate. For Americans of the age, the term *Union* drew not just on legalistic notions of contract and consent, but also on sentimental ideas of marriage and family. Much like nationalism, the term *Union* grounded the polity not just in the rational operation of mutual consent, but on affective sentiments grounded in mutual attraction. From George Washington's "sacred fire of liberty" to Abraham Lincoln's "mystic chords of memory," Americans of the post-Revolutionary period often talked about the Union in quasi-mystical terms not so different from what later generations would call "nationalism."

10 Statistics from Inter-University Consortium for Political and Social Research. Study 00003: Historical Demographic, Economic, and Social Data: U.S., 1790–1970. Anne Arbor: ICPSR. http://fisher.lib.virginia.edu/collections/stats/histcensus/, accessed April 22, 2004. On slavery and the Founding Fathers, see: Robert McColley, *Slavery and Jeffersonian Virginia* (Urbana: University of Illinois Press, 1964); Duncan J. MacLeod, *Slavery, Race, and the American Revolution* (New York: Cambridge University Press, 1974); John Chester Miller, *The Wolf by the Ears: Thomas Jefferson and Slavery* (New York: Free Press, 1977); Drew R. McCoy, *The Last of the Fathers: James Madison and the Republican Legacy* (Cambridge and New York: Cambridge University Press, 1989), 217–322; William W. Freehling, *The Reintegration of American History: Slavery and the Civil War* (New York: Oxford University Press, 1994), 12–33; Paul Finkelman, *Slavery and the Founders: Race and Liberty in the Age of Jefferson* (Armonk, N.Y.: M.E. Sharpe, 1996); Peter S. Onuf, *Jefferson's Empire: The Language of American Nationhood* (Charlottesville: University Press of Virginia, 2000); Garry Wills, *"Negro President": Jefferson and the Slave Power* (Boston: Houghton Mifflin, 2003); and David Waldstreicher, *Runaway America: Benjamin Franklin, Slavery, and the American Revolution* (New York: Hill and Wang, 2004). On slavery in the colonial period, see esp. Philip D. Morgan, *Slave Counterpoint: Black Culture in the Eighteenth-Century Chesapeake and Lowcountry* (Chapel Hill: University of North Carolina Press, 1998); Ira Berlin, *Many Thousands Gone: The First Two Centuries of Slavery in North America* (Cambridge, Mass.: Belknap Press, 1998). On slavery and southwestern expansion, see Adam Rothman, *Slave Country: American*

Expansion and the Origins of the Deep South (Cambridge, Mass.: Harvard University Press, 2005).

11 *The Complete Poetical Works of James Thomson,* quoted in Colley, *Britons: Forging the Nation, 1707–1837,* 11; John Adams quoted in David A. Hollinger and Charles Capper, *The American Intellectual Tradition: A Sourcebook,* 2nd ed., 2 vols. (New York: Oxford University Press, 1993), I:119; Bernard Bailyn, *The Ideological Origins of the American Revolution* (Cambridge, Mass.: Belknap Press, 1967), 232.

12 Harold Coffin Syrett and Jacob Ernest Cooke, eds., *The Papers of Alexander Hamilton,* 27 vols. (New York: Columbia University Press, 1961), I:47, quoted in Richard C. Sinopoli, *The Foundations of American Citizenship: Liberalism, the Constitution, and Civic Virtue* (New York: Oxford University Press, 1992), 95. The idea was common to Anglo-American political discourse. "If the laws," Richard Price wrote, are "not [made] by COMMON CONSENT, a government by them does not differ from Slavery." Price, *Observations* (1776), pp. 4–7, quoted in Barry Alan Shain, *The Myth of American Individualism: The Protestant Origins of American Political Thought* (Princeton, N.J.: Princeton University Press, 1994), 297. On the relationship between slavery and consent in early republican political discourse, see esp.: Jack P. Greene, *All Men Are Created Equal: Some Reflections on the Character of the American Revolution* (Oxford: Clarendon Press, 1976); Shain, *The Myth of American Individualism,* 299–319; François Furstenberg, "Beyond Freedom and Slavery: Virtue, Autonomy, and Resistance in Early American Political Discourse," *The Journal of American History* 89 (2003): 1295–1330.

13 I should here acknowledge three brilliant works that have been particularly influential in shaping my ideas of slavery and early American nationalism: Winthrop D. Jordan, *White over Black: American Attitudes Toward the Negro, 1550–1812* (Chapel Hill: University of North Carolina Press, 1968); Edmund Morgan, *American Slavery, American Freedom: The Ordeal of Colonial Virginia* (New York: W.W. Norton, 1975); and David Brion Davis, *The Problem of Slavery in the Age of Revolution.* Many other historians have poked holes into traditional accounts of slavery in the early republic, of course. In addition to the works cited above in note 10, see esp. Nathan Irvin Huggins, "The Deforming Mirror of Truth," in *Black Odyssey: The African-American Ordeal in Slavery* (New York: Vintage Books, 1990). Other intellectual debts will be made obvious in the text and in the notes that follow.

14 On the relationship between republicanism and existence in historical time, see esp. J.G.A. Pocock, *The Machiavellian Moment: Florentine Political Thought and the Atlantic Republican Tradition* (Princeton, N.J.: Princeton University Press, 1975).

15 Jefferson to Madison, September 6, 1789, in Boyd et al., eds., *Papers,* XV:392. On this exchange between Jefferson and Madison, see esp. Adrienne Koch, *Jefferson and*

Madison: The Great Collaboration (New York: Knopf, 1950), 62–96; "Editorial Note," in Boyd et al., eds., *Papers,* XV:384-91; McCoy, *Last of the Fathers,* 53–59; and Herbert E. Sloan, *Principle and Interest: Thomas Jefferson and the Problem of Debt* (New York: Oxford University Press, 1995), 50–85.

16 Thomas Jefferson to James Madison, September 6, 1789, in Boyd et al., eds., *Papers,* XV:392, 394, 396. In fact, as Herb Sloan has shrewdly observed, Jefferson did not actually say the earth blongs to the living—something he is often taken to have said—but rather that the earth belongs "in usufruct," or in trust, to the living. The distinction is an important one, as Sloan shows, though for the purposes of this discussion we can safely bracket the problem of usufruct. See Sloan, *Principle and Interest,* 50–85.

17 On Madison's conservatism with regard to the notion of living generations, see esp. McCoy, *Last of the Fathers.* See also Madison's "Federalist 49."

18 Madison to Jefferson, February 4, 1790, in Boyd et al., eds., *Papers,* VXI:147, 149.

19 On the "problem" of consent, I have found the following particularly useful: Hanna Fenichel Pitkin, "Obligation and Consent—I," *The American Political Science Review* 59, no. 4 (1965): 990–99; Hanna Pitkin, "Obligation and Consent—II," *The American Political Science Review* 60, no. 1 (1966): 39–52; David Brion Davis, *The Problem of Slavery in Western Culture* (Ithaca, N.Y.: Cornell University Press, 1966); James H. Kettner, *The Development of American Citizenship, 1608–1870* (Chapel Hill: University of North Carolina Press, 1978); John Dunn, "Consent in the Political Theory of John Locke," in *Political Obligation in Its Historical Context* (Cambridge, Eng.: Cambridge University Press, 1980); Carole Pateman, *The Problem of Political Obligation: A Critique of Liberal Theory* (Berkeley: University of California Press, 1985); Carole Pateman, *The Disorder of Women: Democracy, Feminism and Political Obligation* (Oxford: Policy Press, 1989); Charles Taylor, *Sources of the Self: The Making of the Modern Identity* (Cambridge, Mass.: Harvard University Press, 1989); Quentin Skinner, *Liberty Before Liberalism* (Cambridge, Eng.: Cambridge University Press, 1998).

20 Recent historiography on print culture and politics in the early republic that has influenced this study includes: Michael Warner, *The Letters of the Republic: Publication and the Public Sphere in Eighteenth-Century America* (Cambridge, Mass.: Harvard University Press, 1990); Fliegelman, *Declaring Independence;* Shirley Samuels, *Romances of the Republic: Women, the Family, and Violence in the Literature of the Early American Nation* (New York: Oxford University Press, 1996); Christopher Looby, *Voicing America: Language, Literary Form, and the Origins of the United States* (Chicago: University of Chicago Press, 1996); Ferguson, *The American Enlightenment;* Waldstreicher, *Perpetual Fetes;* Pauline Maier, *American Scripture: Making the Declaration of Indepen-*

dence (New York: Knopf, 1997); Scott E. Casper, *Constructing American Lives: Biography & Culture in Nineteenth-Century America* (Chapel Hill: University of North Carolina Press, 1999); Saul Cornell, *The Other Founders: Anti-Federalism and the Dissenting Tradition in America, 1788–1828* (Chapel Hill: University of North Carolina Press, 1999); and Joyce Oldham Appleby, *Inheriting the Revolution: The First Generation of Americans* (Cambridge, Mass.: Belknap Press, 2000). On the relationship between print and nationalism generally, see esp. Ernest Gellner, *Nations and Nationalism* (Ithaca, N.Y.: Cornell University Press, 1983); Benedict Anderson, *Imagined Communities: Reflections on the Origin and Spread of Nationalism,* rev. and extended ed. (New York: Verso, 1991); Homi K. Bhabha, "DissemiNation: Time, Narrative, and the Margins of the Modern Nation," in *Nation and Narration,* Homi K. Bhabha, ed. (New York: Routledge, 1990). Also Karl Wolfgang Deutsch, *Nationalism and Social Communication: An Inquiry into the Foundations of Nationality* (Cambridge, Mass.: MIT Press, 1953). On their relationship in the context of early American politics and culture, see: Karen Halttunen, *Confidence Men and Painted Women: A Study of Middle-Class Culture in America, 1830–1870* (New Haven, Conn.: Yale University Press, 1982); Jean Baker, "From Belief into Culture: Republicanism in the History and Historiography of the United States," *American Quarterly* 37 (1985): 532–50; Steven Watts, *The Republic Reborn: War and the Making of Liberal America, 1790–1820* (Baltimore, Md.: Johns Hopkins University Press, 1987); Jill Lepore, *A Is for American: Letters and Other Characters in the Newly United States* (New York: Knopf, 2002); and Robert A. Ferguson, *Reading the Early Republic* (Cambridge, Mass.: Harvard University Press, 2004). Histories of reading and of the book that have most influenced this study include: William Leonard Joyce, *Printing and Society in Early America* (Worcester, Mass.: American Antiquarian Society, 1983); Cathy N. Davidson, *Revolution and the Word: The Rise of the Novel in America* (New York: Oxford University Press, 1986); Michael Denning, *Mechanic Accents: Dime Novels and Working-Class Culture in America* (New York: Verso, 1987); Richard D. Brown, *Knowledge Is Power: The Diffusion of Information in Early America, 1700–1865* (New York: Oxford University Press, 1989); William J. Gilmore, *Reading Becomes a Necessity of Life: Material and Cultural Life in Rural New England, 1780–1835* (Knoxville: University of Tennessee Press, 1989); David D. Hall, "Books and Reading in Eighteenth-Century America," in *Of Consuming Interests: The Style of Life in the Eighteenth Century,* Cary Carson, Ronald Hoffman, and Peter J. Albert, eds. (Charlottesville, Va.: Published for the United States Capitol Historical Society by the University Press of Virginia, 1994), David D. Hall, *Cultures of Print: Essays in the History of the Book* (Amherst: University of Massachusetts Press, 1996), David D. Hall, *Worlds of Wonder, Days of Judgment: Popular Reli-*

gious Belief in Early New England (New York: Knopf, 1989); Ronald J. Zboray, *A Fictive People: Antebellum Economic Development and the American Reading Public* (New York: Oxford University Press, 1993); Hugh Amory and David D. Hall, *The Colonial Book in the Atlantic World*, Vol. 1: *A History of the Book in America* (Cambridge, Eng.: Cambridge University Press, 2000). I have also benefited enormously from conversations with Jim Green of the Library Company of Philadelphia, who has been extremely generous in sharing his vast knowledge in this area.

21 Bernard Bailyn, *The Peopling of British North America: An Introduction* (New York: Knopf, 1986), 112.

22 U.S. nationalism has been approached from a variety of angles. Older studies tended to approach it in terms of intellectual history: Paul C. Nagel, *One Nation Indivisible: The Union in American Thought, 1776–1861* (New York: Oxford University, 1964); Fred Somkin, *Unquiet Eagle; Memory and Desire in the Idea of American Freedom, 1815–1860* (Ithaca, N.Y.: Cornell University Press, 1967); Paul C. Nagel, *This Sacred Trust: American Nationality, 1798–1898* (New York: Oxford University Press, 1971); and Michael G. Kammen, *People of Paradox: An Inquiry Concerning the Origins of American Civilization* (New York: Knopf, 1972). A comparative examination drawing on this literature is Liah Greenfeld, *Nationalism: Five Roads to Modernity* (Cambridge, Mass.: Harvard University Press, 1992). Some excellent psychological interpretations to U.S. nationalism were also produced in the 1970s, the two best of which are: Forgie, *Patricide in the House Divided;* and Michael Paul Rogin, *Fathers and Children: Andrew Jackson and the Subjugation of the American Indian* (New York: Knopf, 1975). Studies of U.S. nationalism emphasizing its aspect as a "civil religion" include: Robert N. Bellah, "Civil Religion in America," *Daedalus* 96 (1967): 1–21; Jurgen Gebhardt, *Americanism: Revolutionary Order and Societal Self-Interpretation in the American Republic*, trans. Ruth Hein (Baton Rouge: Louisiana State University Press, 1993); Catherine L. Albanese, *Sons of the Fathers: The Civil Religion of the American Revolution* (Philadelphia: Temple University Press, 1976); Sacvan Bercovitch, *The American Jeremiad* (Madison: University of Wisconsin Press, 1978). A related study by an historical geographer is Wilbur Zelinsky, *Nation into State: The Shifting Symbolic Foundations of American Nationalism* (Chapel Hill: University of North Carolina Press, 1988). The religious elements of U.S. nationalism are explored in: Ernest Lee Tuveson, *Redeemer Nation: The Idea of America's Millennial Role* (Chicago: University of Chicago Press, 1968); Nathan O. Hatch, *The Sacred Cause of Liberty: Republican Thought and the Millennium in Revolutionary New England* (New Haven, Conn.: Yale University Press, 1977); Ruth H. Bloch, *Visionary Republic: Millennial Themes in American Thought, 1756–1800* (Cambridge, Eng.: Cambridge University Press, 1985);

J.C.D. Clark, *The Language of Liberty, 1660–1832: Political Discourse and Social Dynamics in the Anglo-American World* (Cambridge, Eng.: Cambridge University Press, 1994); Anders Stephanson, *Manifest Destiny: American Expansion and the Empire of Right* (New York: Hill & Wang, 1995). Studies stressing British imperial contexts include: John M. Murrin, "A Roof without Walls: The Dilemma of American National Identity," in *Beyond Confederation: Origins of the Constitution and American National Identity*, Richard R. Beeman, Stephen Botein, and Edward Carlos Carter, eds. (Chapel Hill: University of North Carolina Press, 1987); Jack P. Greene, *Pursuits of Happiness: The Social Development of Early Modern British Colonies and the Formation of American Culture* (Chapel Hill: University of North Carolina Press, 1988), 170–206; T. H. Breen, "An Empire of Goods: The Anglicization of Colonial America, 1690–1776," *Journal of British Studies* 25 (1986): 467–99; Breen, "Ideology and Nationalism on the Eve of the American Revolution"; John M. Murrin, "1776: The Countercyclical Revolution," in *Revolutionary Currents*, Morrison and Zook, eds., 65–90. Two recent studies focusing on the founders for insight into early American nationalism are: Ellis, *Founding Brothers*; Onuf, *Jefferson's Empire*. Important recent studies have focused on nationalism in the context of popular celebrations. The best work in this vein is: Simon P. Newman, *Parades and Politics of the Street: Festive Culture in the Early American Republic* (Philadelphia: University of Pennsylvania Press, 1997); Mary P. Ryan, *Civic Wars: Democracy and Public Life in the American City During the Nineteenth Century* (Berkeley: University of California Press, 1997); Len Travers, *Celebrating the Fourth: Independence Day and the Rites of Nationalism in the Early Republic* (Amherst: University of Massachusetts Press, 1997); Waldstreicher, *Perpetual Fetes;* and Albrecht Koschnik, "The Democratic Societies of Philadelphia and the Limits of the American Public Sphere, circa 1793–1795," *The William and Mary Quarterly* 3rd ser., 58 (2001): 615–36. On the formation of U.S. nationalism in a broader, transatlantic context, see: Matthew Rainbow Hale, "Neither Britons nor Frenchmen: The French Revolution and American National Identity" (Ph.D. dissertation, Brandeis University, 2002).

CHAPTER 1: THE APOTHEOSIS OF GEORGE WASHINGTON

1 William Kauffman Scarborough, ed., *The Diary of Edmund Ruffin*, 3 vols. (Baton Rouge: Louisiana State University Press, 1972), entry for October 31, 1858, 242–43.

2 Samuel Tomb, *An oration on the auspicious birth, sublime virtues, and triumphant death of General George Washington; pronounced Feb. 22, 1800; in Newbury Second parish* (Newburyport, Mass.: Edmund M. Blunt, 1800), 9.

3   Annapolis resident: Thomas Mason to Elizabeth Mason, Annapolis, Maryland, December 17, 1799, Mason Papers, Manuscripts Department, Maryland Historical Society Library; Boston resident: John Warren to John Collins Warren, Boston, Massachusetts, December 26, 1799, Warren Papers, Massachusetts Historical Society; Anna Eliot Ticknor, ed., *Life, letters, and journals of George Ticknor*, 2 vols. (Boston: J. R. Osgood and Company, 1876), I:21. Several scholars have examined the response to Washington's death for clues on early U.S. political culture. See James H. Smylie, "The President as Prophet, Priest, King: Reflections on the Death of George Washington and Types of American Leadership," in *Civil Religion in America: Manifest Destiny and Historical Judgement* (Carlisle, Penn.: Dickinson College, 1973); Fliegelman, *Prodigals and Pilgrims*, chapter 7; Schwartz, *George Washington*, 91–103; and Edwin S. Gaustad, *Neither King nor Prelate: Religion and the New Nation, 1776–1826* (Grand Rapids, Mich.: Wm. B. Eerdmans, 1993), 71–84. On the Washington mythology more generally, the best works are Marcus Cunliffe, *George Washington, Man and Monument* (Boston: Little, Brown, 1958); Wills, *Cincinnatus*; Paul K. Longmore, *The Invention of George Washington* (Berkeley: University of California Press, 1988); and Schwartz, *George Washington*. Studies of the visual imagery of Washington include Mark Edward Thistlethwaite, *The Image of George Washington: Studies in Mid-Nineteenth-Century American History Painting* (New York: Garland, 1979); Patricia A. Anderson, *Promoted to Glory: The Apotheosis of George Washington* (Northampton, Mass.: Smith College Museum of Art, 1980); Margaret Brown Klapthor and Howard Alexander Morrison, *G. Washington: A Figure Upon the Stage* (Washington, D.C.: Smithsonian Institution Press, 1982); Wendy Wick, *George Washington, An American Icon: The Eighteenth-Century Graphic Portraits* (Washington, D.C.: The Barra Foundation, 1982); and Barbara J. Mitnick, ed., *George Washington: American Symbol* (New York: Hudson Hills Press, 1999). Studies of his literary representation include William Alfred Bryan, *George Washington in American Literature, 1775–1865* (New York: Columbia University Press, 1952); Robert P. Hay, "George Washington: American Moses," *American Quarterly* 21, Winter 1969 (1969): 780–91; and Lawrence Jacob Friedman, *Inventors of the Promised Land* (New York: Knopf, 1975). A fine study of the Washington monument is Kirk Savage, "The Self-Made Monument: George Washington and the Fight to Erect a National Monument," *Winterthur Portfolio* 22 (1987): 225–42. See also Robert F. Dalzell and Lee Baldwin Dalzell, *George Washington's Mount Vernon: At Home in Revolutionary America* (New York: Oxford University Press, 1998); Waldstreicher, *Perpetual Fetes*, 117–26; Scott E. Casper, "First First Family: Seventy Years with Edward Savage's *The*

Washington Family," Imprint 24, no. 2 (1999): 2–15; and William M. S. Rasmussen and Robert S. Tilton, *George Washington—the Man Behind the Myths* (Charlottesville: University Press of Virginia, 1999), esp. 261–73.

4 Georgetown visitor: "John Davis, *Travels of four years and a half in the United States of America: During 1798, 1799, 1800, 1801, and 1802* (London: R. Edwards, 1803), 145; Massachusetts farmer: *Farm Diary,* entry for February 22, 1800, David S. Greenhough Papers, Massachusetts Historical Society. For a brief description of events in Lexington, Kentucky, see J. Moore to Reverend Samuel Keene, Jr., April 1, 1800, Vertical Files, Episcopal Diocese of Maryland; for Detroit, see William Henry to Elizabeth Henry, February 10, 1800, Henry Mss. Vol. 2, p. 85, Historical Society of Pennsylvania.

5 See, for example, the Baltimore *Federal Gazette and Daily Advertiser,* front page, December 31, 1799.

6 On the politicization of material objects during the Revolution, see esp. T. H. Breen, "'Baubles of Britain': The American and Consumer Revolutions of the Eighteenth Century," *Past and Present* 119 (1988): 73–104; and T. H. Breen, *The Marketplace of Revolution: How Consumer Politics Shaped American Independence* (New York: Oxford University Press, 2004). For a small sampling of these Washington objects, see Anderson, *Promoted to Glory.*

7 John M. Mason, *A funeral oration: Delivered in the Brick Presbyterian church in the city of New-York, on the 22d day of February, 1800, being the day recommended by Congress to the citizens of the United States, publicly to testify their grief for the death of Gen. Washington: By appointment of a number of the clergy of New-York, and published at their request* (New York: G. F. Hopkins, 1800), 5; Abigail Adams to Mary Cranch, December 22, 1799, in Mitchell, ed., *New Letters of Abigail Adams, 1788–1801* (California: Reprint Services Corp., 1991), 223; Mrs. Carey to Mathew Carey, December 20, 1799, Selections from the Letters of Mrs. Mathew Carey, 1796–1815 (Box 84-B), Historical Society of Pennsylvania; Adams to Cranch, December 30, 1799, in Mitchell, ed., *New Letters of Abigail Adams,* 225; Jean Simon Chaudron, *Funeral oration on Brother George Washington* (Philadelphia: J. Ormrod, 1800), 3. On parlors in early U.S. political life, see Catherine Allgor, *Parlor Politics: In Which the Ladies of Washington Help Build a City and a Government* (Charlottesville: University Press of Virginia, 2000); Susan Branson, *These Fiery Frenchified Dames: Women and Political Culture in Early National Philadelphia* (Philadelphia: University of Pennsylvania Press, 2001).

8 Some estimates run even higher. For various estimates, see Joseph Charles, "Hamilton and Washington: The Origins of the American Party System," *William and Mary*

Quarterly 3rd ser. (1955): 217–67, 264; Howard Mumford Jones, *O Strange New World: American Culture: The Formative Years* (New York: Viking Press, 1964), 263; Emily Ellsworth Ford Skeel, ed., *Mason Locke Weems, His Works and Ways,* 3 vols. (New York: Privately printed, 1929), I:1. For contemporary commentary on the eulogies, see Charles Ewing to Samuel Hazard, April 5, 1800, Hazard Family Papers (Folder: Charles Ewing, 1799–1803), Historical Society of Pennsylvania; and *Monthly Magazine and American Review,* Feb. 1800, 103, 105. See also Fliegelman, *Prodigals and Pilgrims,* 221.

9 *Washington's political legacies. To which is annexed, an appendix, containing an account of his illness, death, and the national tributes of respect paid to his memory, with a biographical sketch, of his life and character. His will, and Dr. Tappan's discourse, before the University of Cambridge* (New York: Printed for George Forman, 1800), 142–43. Also quoted in *The Washingtoniana: Containing a Biographical Sketch of the late General George Washington, with various Outlines of his Character . . .* (Baltimore: Samuel Sower, 1800), 104; and in the *American Mercury* (Hartford), December 26, 1799.

10 The general political situation in the 1790s is well summed up in many places. Classic accounts are Stanley M. Elkins and Eric L. McKitrick, *The Age of Federalism* (New York: Oxford University Press, 1993); Linda K. Kerber, *Federalists in Dissent: Imagery and Ideology in Jeffersonian America* (Ithaca, N.Y.: Cornell University Press, 1970); and Richard Buel, *Securing the Revolution: Ideology in American Politics, 1789–1815* (Ithaca, N.Y.: Cornell University Press, 1972). See also Hofstadter, *The Idea of a Party System,* chapters 2–4. More recent accounts of the political struggles of the 1790s include Waldstreicher, *Perpetual Fetes,* chapter 3; Travers, *Celebrating the Fourth;* Newman, *Parades and Politics of the Street,* and Ellis, *Founding Brothers.*

11 Abigail Adams to her sister, May 10, 1798, in Mitchell, ed., *New Letters of Abigail Adams,* 172. On the "Revolution of 1800" as a civil war, see Michael A. Bellesiles, " 'The Soil Will Be Soaked with Blood: Taking the Revolution of 1800 Seriously," in *The Revolution of 1800: Democracy, Race, and the New Republic,* James Horn, Jan Lewis, and Peter S. Onuf, eds. (Charlottesville: University of Virginia Press, 2002), 59–86; and John Ferling, *Adams vs. Jefferson: The Tumultuous Election of 1800* (New York: Oxford University Press, 2004), 181–82, 188–89.

12 On the impact of refugees from Saint Domingue, see esp. Ashli White, " 'A Flood of Impure Lava': Saint Dominguan Refugees in the United States, 1791–1820" (Ph.D. dissertation, Columbia University, 2003). On refugees in Louisiana, see Paul Lachance, "Repercussions of the Haitian Revolution in Louisiana," in *The Impact of the Haitian Revolution in the Atlantic World,* David P. Geggus, ed. (Columbia: University of South Carolina Press, 2001), 209–30. On Gabriel's conspiracy, see esp.

Douglas R. Egerton, *Gabriel's Rebellion: The Virginia Slave Conspiracies of 1800 and 1802* (Chapel Hill: University of North Carolina Press, 1993); and James Sidbury, *Ploughshares into Swords: Race, Rebellion, and Identity in Gabriel's Virginia, 1730–1810* (New York: Cambridge University Press, 1997). On the connection between Gabriel's conspiracy and the political context of the 1800s, see Douglas R. Egerton, "Gabriel's Conspiracy and the Election of 1800," in *Rebels, Reformers, and Revolutionaries: Collected Essays and Second Thoughts* (New York: Routledge, 2002), 39–56, esp. 50–51 and 53–54.

13 Quoted in the *Federal Gazette and Baltimore Daily Advertiser,* December 28, 1799. See also Aaron Bancroft, *An eulogy on the character of the late Gen. George Washington* (Worcester, Mass.: Isaiah Thomas, jun., 1800), 14.

14 The famous phrase was first pronounced in the Congressional resolutions authored by Lee, but spoken by John Marshall, and reprinted in newspapers throughout the nation as well as in collections of Washington's writings and eulogies. See, most accessibly, *Washingtoniana* [Sower ed.], 110. On pamphlet editions of Lee's eulogy, see Shipton, Mooney, and Bristol, *The Short-Title Evans.* I found newspaper reprints of Lee's eulogy in the *Federal Gazette and Baltimore Daily Advertiser,* January 10, 1800; *American Mercury* (Hartford), January 16, 1800; *Gazette of the United States, and Philadelphia Daily Advertiser,* January 7, 1800; *Constitutional Diary and Philadelphia Evening Advertiser,* January 9, 1800; *Independent Gazetteer,* vol. I, no. 4, Worcester, Mass., January 28, 1800. This is only a small fraction of the newspapers that reprinted this most famous of all eulogies. In addition, Lee's eulogy was included in every collection of Washington eulogies that I encountered. I have found Lee's eulogy excerpted in the following schoolbooks: Albert Picket, *The juvenile mentor: Being the second part of the Juvenile spelling-book: containing progressive reading lessons in prose and verse, adapted to the comprehension of youth: calculated to improve them in reading and speaking, with elegance and propriety, and to imbue their minds with sentiments of virtue, morality, and religion* (New York: Smith & Forman, 1809), 185–88; Abner Alden, *The Speaker being the fourth part of a Columbian exercise: the whole comprising an easy and systemical method of teaching and learning the English language* (Boston: Printed by Buckingham & Titcomb for Thomas & Andrews, 1810), 130–34; Ignatius Thomson, *The patriot's monitor, for Vermont designed to impress and perpetuate the first principles of the revolution on the minds of youth; together with some pieces important and interesting* (Randolph, Vt.: Sereno Wright, 1810), 68–69; and William Holmes McGuffey, *McGuffey's sixth eclectic reader,* rev. ed. (Cincinnati: Van Antwerp, Bragg & Co., 1879), 444–45. It was printed in many, many other schoolbooks. One last point of interest about this eulogy is that it seems to have been praised nearly uni-

versally. One telling indication of the extent of its approbation is that admiration of Lee's eulogy may be one of the only issues on which the Republican *American Aurora* and the Federalist *Gazette of the United States, and Philadelphia Daily Advertiser* ever agreed. The *Aurora* called Lee's eulogy an "admirable production," while on the same day, the *Gazette* informed its readers that "The graceful attitudes and gesticulation, the manly tones, and fine declamation of the Orator, commanded the profoundest attention, from an auditory of four thousand persons" (*American Aurora,* December 27, 1799; *Gazette of the United States, and Philadelphia Daily Advertiser,* December 27, 1799). The only negative word I found came from the crotchety *Monthly Magazine,* which, while it had general praise for the eulogy as a whole, faulted it for oversimplification and exaggerating the "national grief." (*Monthly Magazine and American Review,* February 1800, 123.)

15 Reinhart Koselleck has argued that a modern historical consciousness began to emerge in the wake of the Enlightenment and French revolution. This new historical consciousness was characterized by a wholly new understanding of the future: a future that could be characterized by novelty. Reinhart Koselleck, *Futures Past: On the Semantics of Historical Time* (Cambridge, Mass.: MIT Press, 1985). See also M. H. Abrams, *Natural Supernaturalism: Tradition and Revolution in Romantic Literature* (New York: W. W. Norton, 1973), esp. chapter 1. On American historical consciousness, see Dorothy Ross, *The Origins of American Social Science* (Cambridge, Eng.: Cambridge University Press, 1991), 3–21; Pocock, *The Machiavellian Moment,* 423–505; Dorothy Ross, "The Liberal Tradition Revisited and the Republican Tradition Addressed," in *New Directions in American Intellectual History,* John Higham and Paul Conkin, eds. (Baltimore, Md.: Johns Hopkins University Press, 1979); Drew R. McCoy, *The Elusive Republic: Political Economy in Jeffersonian America* (New York: W. W. Norton, 1982); Bloch, *Visionary Republic;* Bercovitch, *American Jeremiad;* Tuveson, *Redeemer Nation;* Somkin, *Unquiet Eagle,* 55–90; Perry Miller, *The New England Mind: The Seventeenth Century* (Cambridge, Mass.: Harvard University Press, 1983), 463–91; Dorothy Ross, "Historical Consciousness in Nineteenth-Century America," *American Historical Review* 89 (1984): 909–28; Lester H. Cohen, *The Revolutionary Histories: Contemporary Narratives of the American Revolution* (Ithaca, N.Y.: Cornell University Press, 1980); and Anthony Kemp, *The Estrangement of the Past: A Study in the Origins of Modern Historical Consciousness* (New York: Oxford University Press, 1991).

16 George Bancroft, *History of the United States of America, from the Discovery of the Continent,* 6 vols. (Port Washington, N.Y.: Kennikat Press, 1967), VI:90; Henry Lee, "Funeral Oration on The Death of General Washington. Delivered at the Request of

Congress, Dec. 26, 1799," in *Eulogies and orations on the life and death of General George Washington* (Boston: Manning & Loring, 1800), 9–10;

17 Josiah Dunham, *A funeral oration on George Washington* (Boston: Manning & Loring, 1800), 13; *Federal Gazette and Baltimore Daily Advertiser*, December 17, 1799; *The Washingtoniana: Containing a Sketch of the Life and Death of the Late Gen. George Washington with a Collection of Elegant Eulogies, Orations, Poems, &c. Sacred to his Memory* (Lancaster, Penn.: William Hamilton, 1802), 317.

18 "Explanation of the Plate," printed on the back of the broadside, Historical Society of Pennsylvania.

19 George Richards, *The Accepted or the Multitude of his Brethren: An Historical Discourse, in Two Parts, Gratefully Commemorating, the Unparalleled Services, and Preeminent Virtues of General George Washington* (Portsmouth, N.H.: 1800), 77.

20 See also Waldstreicher, *Perpetual Fetes*, 42–51.

21 Uzal Ogden, *Two discourses, occasioned by the death of General George Washington, at Mount-Vernon, December 14, 1799* (Newark, N.J.: Matthias Day, 1800), 28; oration by the Rev. Dr. Linn, delivered in New York City, printed in the New York *Weekly Museum*, December 28, 1799.

22 *Washington's political legacies. To which is annexed an appendix, containing an account of his illness, death, and the national tributes of respect paid to his memory, with a biographical outline of his life and character* (Boston: Printed for John Russell and John West, 1800), v; *The Times: and District of Columbia Daily Advertiser* (Alexandria), December 20, 1799; *Federal Gazette and Baltimore Daily Advertiser*, December, 27, 1799. For similar statements, see also Lee, "Funeral Oration," 10; and Fisher Ames, "An Oration on the Sublime Virtues of General George Washington," in *Eulogies and orations*, 108.

23 "A Proclamation by Benjamin Ogle, Governor of Maryland," in *Washingtoniana* [Sower ed.], 185; *The Times; and District of Columbia Daily Advertiser* (Alexandria), December 20, 1799. See also the discourse by the Reverend Mr. Muir, in *The Times; and District of Columbia Daily Advertiser* (Alexandria), February 25, 1800.

24 "Washington our model" quoted in *Washingtoniana* [Sower ed.], 264, and in *The Times; and District of Columbia Daily Advertiser* (Alexandria), February 25, 1800; Adams's message was reprinted in every newspaper I have examined from the period; it may be found most accessibly in *Washingtoniana* [Sower ed.], 115; Joseph Story, *An eulogy on General George Washington; written at the request of the inhabitants of Marblehead, and delivered before them on the second day of January, A. D. 1800* (Salem, Mass.: Joshua Cushing, 1800), 4, 15; "his example shall live": from Samuel Stanhope Smith, *An oration upon the death of General George Washington,*

delivered at the State-House at Trenton, on the 14th of January, 1800 (Trenton, N.J.: G. Craft, 1800), 45.

25 Quoted in Charles, "Hamilton and Washington," 266.

26 Quoted in the *Federal Gazette and Baltimore Daily Advertiser,* January 4, 1800.

27 M. L. Weems, *Hymen's Recruiting Sergeant,* in *Three Discourses,* Emily Ellsworth Ford Skeel, ed. (New York: Random House, 1929), 22, 26. On this new family model, see especially Fliegelman, *Prodigals and Pilgrims.*

28 On this point, see esp. Linda K. Kerber, *Women of the Republic: Intellect and Ideology in Revolutionary America* (Chapel Hill: University of North Carolina Press, 1980).

29 *The Times; and District of Columbia Daily Advertiser,* February 25, 1800; *Weekly Museum* (New York), February 21, 1800; Alden, *The Speaker being the fourth part of a Columbian exercise: the whole comprising an easy and systemical method of teaching and learning the English language,* 217.

30 Mason, *Funeral oration,* 16; Rufus Wilmot Griswold, *The Republican Court; or American Society in the Days of Washington* (New York: D. Appleton and Company, 1856), 176; *Weekly Museum* (New York), December 13, 1800.

31 Boston *Mercury,* January 7, 1800; Bancroft, *An eulogy,* 17 (my emphasis). A Philadelphia newspaper similarly averred that "his fame lives in everlasting duration in every page of our history." *Philadelphia Gazette and Universal Daily Advertiser,* December 27, 1800. On history as "text" see esp. Kemp, *The Estrangement of the Past;* Hayden White, "The Context in the Text: Method and Ideology in Intellectual History," in *The Content of the Form: Narrative Discourse and Historical Representation* (Baltimore: Johns Hopkins University Press, 1987), 185–213; and Fredric Jameson, "The Ideology of the Text," in *The Ideology of Theory: Essays, 1971–1986. Vol. 1: Situations of Theory* (Minneapolis: University of Minnesota, 1989), 17–71.

32 Roger Chartier, "Reading Matter and 'Popular' Reading: From the Renaissance to the Seventeenth Century," in *A History of Reading in the West,* Guglielmo Cavallo and Roger Chartier, eds. (Amherst: University of Massachusetts Press, 1999), 276. A classic account of reader interpretation is Stanley Eugene Fish, *Is There a Text in This Class? The Authority of Interpretive Communities* (Cambridge, Mass.: Harvard University Press, 1980), 303–21, which is where I draw the notion of "interpretive community."

33 Richards, *The Accepted,* 32.

34 *Washington's political legacies* [Forman ed.], 279.

35 Rollo G. Silver, *The American printer, 1787–1825* (Charlottesville: Published for the Bibliographical Society of the University of Virginia by the University Press of Vir-

ginia, 1967), 159–60. On editions of the Farewell Address after 1796, see Shipton, Mooney, and Bristol, *The Short-Title Evans,* II:961–63.

36 Levi Frisbie, *An eulogy on the illustrious character of the late General George Washington, commander in chief of all the armies of the United States of America . . . Delivered at Ipswich, on the 7th day of January, 1800* (Newburyport, Mass.: Printed by Edmund M. Blunt, 1800).

37 Bancroft, *An eulogy,* 49; David Ramsay, "An Oration on the Death of Lieutenant-General George Washington . . ." in *Eulogies and orations,* 88; Timothy Bigelow, *An eulogy on the life, character and services of Brother George Washington, deceased* (Boston: I. Thomas and E. T. Andrews, 1800), 14; Isaac Story, *An eulogy in the glorious virtues of the illustrious Gen. George Washington* (Worcester, Mass.: Isaiah Thomas, jun., 1800), 23. See also Henry Holcombe, *A sermon occasioned by the death of Lieutenant-General George Washington, late President of the United States of America; who was born February 11th, 1732, in Virginia, and died, December 14th, 1799, on Mount Vernon, his favorite seat in his native country* (Savannah, Ga.: Seymour & Woolhopter, 1800), 14–15; and John Prince, *Part of a discourse delivered on the 29th of December, upon the close of the year 1799, recommending the improvement of time* (Salem, Mass.: Thomas C. Cushing, 1800), 23.

38 Joseph Tuckerman, *A funeral oration. Occasioned by the death of General George Washington* (Boston: Manning & Loring, 1800), 17–18; Richards, *The Accepted* (he was referring here to Washington's 1783 address); *Washingtoniana: A collection of papers relative to the death and character of General George Washington, with a correct copy of his last will and testament: To which are added his legacy to the people of America, &c &c &c* ([Petersburg, Va.]: From the Blandford Press and sold by Ross & Douglass, Petersburgh, and by all the booksellers in Virginia, 1800), vii; Earl of Buchan to Martha Washington, January 28, 1800, in Joseph E. Fields, ed., *Worthy Partner: The Papers of Martha Washington* (Westport, Conn.: Greenwood Press, 1994), 346–47.

39 Joseph Story, *An eulogy on General George Washington; written at the request of the inhabitants of Marblehead, and delivered before them on the second day of January, A. D. 1800* (Salem, Mass.: Joshua Cushing, 1800), 12; Ramsay, "An Oration," in *Eulogies and orations,* 92; William Jackson, *Monuments of Washington's patriotism: Containing a facsimile of his publick accounts kept during the Revolutionary War; and some of the most interesting documents connected with his military command and civil administration; embracing, among others, the Farewell Address to the people of the United States* (Washington: P. Force, 1838); and *Monuments of Washington's patriotism,* 3d

ed. (Washington: By the trustees of Washington's Manual Labour School and Male Orphan Asylum, 1841).

40 H. Hastings Weld, *Pictorial life of George Washington: embracing anecdotes, illustrative of his character. And embellished with engravings. For the young people of the nation he founded* (Philadelphia: Lindsay and Blakiston, 1845), iii–iv. On *virtù*, see esp. Pocock, *Machiavellian Moment.*

41 Merrill D. Peterson, ed., *Writings* (New York: The Library of America, 1984), 480; John Quincy Adams quoted in Spalding and Garrity, *A Sacred Union of Citizens,* 3; *The constitution of the state of Massachusetts. And that of the United States. The Declaration of Independence. With President Washington's Farewell address* (Boston: Printed for the state, by Manning & Loring, 1805).

42 Mathew Carey, *The olive branch: or, Faults on both sides, Federal and Democratic. A serious appeal on the necessity of mutual forgiveness & harmony to save our common country from ruin* (Philadelphia: Published by M. Carey, 1814), 1, 26. On this work, see Watts, *The Republic Reborn,* 304; and Edward C. Carter, "Mathew Carey and 'The Olive Branch,' 1814–1818," *Pennsylvania Magazine of History and Biography* 89 (1965): 399–415.

43 Richard Rush, *Occasional productions, political, diplomatic, and miscellaneous. Including, among others, a glance at the court and government of Louis Philippe and the French revolution of 1848, while the author resided as envoy extraordinary and minister plenipotentiary from the United States at Paris, by the late Richard Rush* (Philadelphia: J. B. Lippincott & Co., 1860), 137.

44 Fliegelman, *Prodigals and Pilgrims,* 30–31; Fliegelman, *Declaring Independence.*

45 William Cunningham, *An eulogy delivered at Lunenburg, on Saturday the 22d of February 1800. The day recommended by Congress to commemorate the unequalled virtues and preeminent service of Gen. George Washington: First president of the United States of America, and commander in chief of the American forces during the Revolutionary War* (Worcester, Mass.: Isaiah Thomas, jun., 1800), 15; *The Federal Gazette and Baltimore Daily Advertiser,* December 19, 1799; Abiel Holmes, *The Counsel of Washington, Recommended in a Discourse, Delivered at Cambridge, February 22, 1800* (Boston: Samuel Hall, 1800), 20–21.

46 On this conservative, "Humean" strain in Madison's thought, see esp. McCoy, *Last of the Fathers,* 39–83.

47 On this tendency during the sectional crisis of the 1850s, see David Morris Potter, "The Historian's Use of Nationalism and Vice Versa," in *The South and the Sectional Conflict* (Baton Rouge: Louisiana State University Press, 1968), 34–83; on its use to-

day, see virtually any statement of the Republican Party from September 2001 onward.

48 Quoted in Charles, "Hamilton and Washington," 266. On Washington's use by Federalists, see Charles, "Hamilton and Washington," 263–67; DeConde, "Washington's Farewell, the French Alliance, and the Election of 1796," 645–47; Buel, *Securing the Revolution,* 114, 142–43. Federalists delivered the vast majority of the printed eulogies, hoping to help the party's chances in the elections of 1800. Barry Schwartz categorized his sample of fifty-five eulogies drawn from the *Early American Imprints* series by regional, political, and partisan affiliation. Of the eulogists whose regional background he could identify, twenty-two were born in New England, thirteen in the Middle Atlantic states, and two in the South. Of the twenty whose political preferences he could identify, nineteen were Federalists. "The lopsided regional and political representation," Schwartz argues, "reflects in part the distribution of printing presses, which in 1800 were concentrated in Federalist New England." In addition, Schwartz might have added that Washington's Federalist persuasion probably accounted for a part of this political distribution. Although my sample was much bigger, I do not believe it differs dramatically from Schwartz's findings in geographical or political representation. See Schwartz, *George Washington,* 223–24, n. 16 and 17. Schwartz goes on to observe, however, that "most Republicans adored Washington as much as the Federalists did, and their eulogies, which were more likely to be delivered outside New England and therefore less likely to be published, probably gave the same account of his virtues."

49 On the relationship between partisanship and early U.S. nationalism, the best analysis is Waldstreicher, *Perpetual Fetes,* esp. 177–245.

50 As historian Joseph Ellis rightly remarks, "Taking on Washington was the fastest way to commit political suicide in the revolutionary era." Ellis, *Founding Brothers,* 126.

51 "When Washington died on December 14, 1799, he was anything but a noncontroversial figure," notes Daniel Boorstin, and adds: "What is most remarkable is not that Washington eventually became a demigod, Father of his Country, but that the transfiguration happened so quickly." See Daniel J. Boorstin, *The Americans: The National Experience* (New York: Random House, 1965), 339.

52 St. George Tucker to James Monroe, December 22, 1799, *Papers of James Monroe* [Microform] (Washington, D.C.: Library of Congress), series 1, reel 2.

53 *American Mercury,* December 26, 1799; ibid. January 2, 1800; Boston *Patriot,* April 1, 1812. Even the account printed in the Philadelphia *Aurora* differed in few respects from accounts in Federalist newspapers. Although the *Aurora* did report the existence of a second parade—separate from the official (and presumably Federalist) one—it,

too, stressed the unity of sentiment exhibited by Washington's death. "Yesterday presented a scene of public mourning, of solemnity and respect, which this city has never before on any occasion witnessed in an equal degree." December 17, 1799.

54 Alexander Graydon, *Memoirs of a Life, Chiefly Passed in Pennsylvania, within the Last Sixty Years, with Occasional Remarks upon the General Occurrences, Character and Spirit of that Eventful Period* (Harrisburgh [*sic*]: John Wyeth, 1811), 360, 366.

55 "Joint Activities of the Democratic, Tammany, Mechanic and Other Societies of New York City," from *The Herald* (New York), July 7, 1794, quoted in Philip Sheldon Foner, *The Democratic-Republican Societies, 1790–1800: A Documentary Sourcebook of Constitutions, Declarations, Addresses, Resolutions, and Toasts* (Westport, Conn.: Greenwood Press, 1976), 221.

56 On American ideology as a "hermeneutic system," see Sacvan Bercovitch, "The Ritual of Consensus," in *The Rites of Assent: Transformations in the Symbolic Construction of America* (New York: Routledge, 1993), 29–67. For a discussion of ideology understood as a battle on the level of the symbol, see Terry Eagleton, *Ideology: An Introduction* (New York: Verso, 1991), esp. 193–224.

57 "pledge of adhesion"quoted in Maier, *American Scripture,* 186; James Madison quoted in Michael G. Kammen, *A Machine That Would Go of Itself: The Constitution in American Culture* (New York: Knopf, 1986), xiii; Guizot quoted in Gilbert Chinard, *George Washington as the French Knew Him* (Princeton, N.J.: Princeton University Press, 1940), 151.

58 On religion and the Seven Years War, see esp. Hatch, *Sacred Cause of Liberty;* and Bloch, *Visionary Republic.*

59 Quoted in I. M. Green, *Print and Protestantism in Early Modern England* (Oxford: Oxford University Press, 2000), 43.

60 Guglielmo Cavallo and Roger Chartier, eds., *A History of Reading in the West* (Amherst: University of Massachusetts Press, 1999), 32.

61 "Bind it in your Bible": Cunningham, *An eulogy delivered at Lunenburg,* 15; Philadelphia publisher proposal: *Philadelphia, 11 August, 1782. Sir, Various inducements have led me to print a neat and correct edition of the Bible, containing the Old and New Testaments, which, I expect, will be ready for sale by the beginning of October* [Philadelphia: Printed by Robert Aitken, 1782], 1. On psalms, almanacs, and Bibles as the most commonly owned books, see James N. Green, "Benjamin Franklin as Publisher and Bookseller," in J. A. Leo Lemay, *Reappraising Benjamin Franklin* (Newark: University of Delaware Press, 1993), 101.

62 Chartier, "Reading Matter and 'Popular' Reading," 275; "sanction of divinity" from Story, *An eulogy on General George Washington,* 13; Thaddeus Mason Harris, *A dis-*

course, delivered at Dorchester (Charlestown, Mass.: Samuel Etheridge, 1800), 13; Boston *Mercury,* January 10, 1800; Newark report is from a newspaper, as quoted in Alexander Macwhorter, *A Funeral Sermon, preached in Newark, December 17, 1799, A Day of Public Mourning, Observed by the Town, for the Universally Lamented, General Washington* . . . (Newark, N.J.: Jacob Halsey, 1800), iii.

63 Jedidiah Morse, *A prayer and sermon, delivered at Charlestown, December 31, 1799, on the death of George Washington* . . . *with an additional sketch of his life* (London: J. Bateson, 1800), 30; James Kemp, *A sermon, delivered in Christ church, Cambridge, in Maryland; on the twenty-second of February, 1800, being the day of mourning appointed by Congress, for the death of General George Washington, late president of the United States* (Easton, Md.: James Cowan, 1800), 6, 9. For further analyses of Washington as Moses, see Schwartz, *George Washington,* 28–30; Wills, *Cincinnatus,* 31–35; and Hay, "George Washington: American Moses." Hay provides some evidence suggesting that Wills's conclusion—that Mosaic comparisons faded rapidly after 1800 "toward almost entire disappearance"—may be overdrawn.

64 George Richards Minot, *An eulogy on George Washington, late commander in chief of the armies of the United States of America* . . . *Delivered before the inhabitants of the town of Boston, at the request of their committee* (Boston: From the printing office of Manning & Loring, 1800), 12–13. Minot's eulogy was excerpted in Picket, *Juvenile Mentor,* 188–91. See also the wonderful examples in *Sacred dirges, hymns, and anthems, commemorative of the death of General George Washington, the guardian of his country, and the friend of man* (Boston: I. Thomas and E. T. Andrews No 45 Newberry-Street Pref., 1800).

65 Timothy Alden, *A sermon, delivered at the South Church in Portsmouth, on the V January, M,DCCC: occasioned by the sudden and universally lamented death of George Washington, Commander of the American armies, and late President of the United States* (Portsmouth, N.H.: Printed at the United States' Oracle-office by Charles Pierce, 1800), 21. See also Thomas [Treat] Paine, *An eulogy on the life of General George Washington* (Newburyport, Mass.: Edmund M. Blunt, 1800), 20. For more on this issue, see Fliegelman, *Prodigals and Pilgrims;* Schwartz, *George Washington;* Wills, *Cincinnatus;* and Gebhardt, *Americanism,* 153–55.

66 Peter Thacher, *A sermon, occasioned by the death of General George Washington: and preached Feb. 22, 1800, by their direction, before His Honor Moses Gill, esq., commander in chief, the honorable Council, the honorable Senate and House of representatives of the commonwealth of Massachusetts* (Boston: Printed by Young & Minns, 1800), 7; George Richards, ed., *Hymns and Odes on the Death of George Washington* (Portsmouth, N.H.: Charles Pierce, 1868), title page; John Brooks, *An eulogy, on Gen-*

eral Washington; delivered before the inhabitants of the town of Medford, agreeably to their vote, and at the request of their committee, on the 13th of January, 1800 (Cornhill, Boston: Printed by Samuel Hall, 1800), 5; Isaac Stockton Keith, *National affliction and national consolation! A sermon on the death of General George Washington, late Commander in Chief of the armies; and formerly President of the United States of America . . . Delivered on the twelfth of January, one thousand eight hundred, in the Independent, or Congregational church, in Charleston, South-Carolina* (Charleston, S.C.: Printed by W. P. Young, 1800), 5; Jonathan Mitchell Sewall, *Eulogy on the late General Washington; pronounced at St. John's church, in Portsmouth, New Hampshire, on Tuesday, 31st December, 1799. At the request of the inhabitants* (Portsmouth, N.H.: William Treadwell, 1800), 23.

67 John Foster, *A discourse delivered December 29, 1799: occasioned by the melancholy death of George Washington, lieutenant general and commander in chief of the armies of the United States of America, who departed this life, December 14, 1799* (Boston: Samuel Hall, 1800), 12; Richards, *The Accepted*, 26; Sewall, *Eulogy on the late General Washington*, 25; *Washingtoniana* [Sower ed.], 110; Rush, *Occasional productions*, 137; "Joint Activities of the Democratic, Tammany, Mechanic and Other Societies," quoted in Foner, *The Democratic-Republican societies*, 221.

68 2 Corinthians 3:3, 3:6 King James Version. In this passage the New Testament is made to supercede the Old Testament, because unlike the Ten Commandments, the words of Christ are "not of the letter, but of the spirit."

69 Elizabeth Carroll Reilly and David D. Hall, "Modalities of Reading," in *The Colonial Book in the Atlantic World. A History of the Book in America*; v. 1. Hugh Amory and David D. Hall, eds. (Cambridge, Eng.: Cambridge University Press, 2000), 408. I owe a great deal in this and the previous paragraphs to the seminar I attended on religious publishing at the American Antiquarian Society in 2005, and in particular to the comments of Peter Stallybrass.

70 Mark A. Noll, *America's God: From Jonathan Edwards to Abraham Lincoln* (New York: Oxford University Press, 2002), 163.

71 *The Self-Interpreting Bible: Containing the Sacred Text of the Old and New Testaments. By the Late Reverend John Brown* (New-York: T. Allen, 1792).

72 *Washington's political legacies* [Forman ed.], 282.

73 *The Times; and District of Columbia Daily Advertiser* (Alexandria), February 27, 1800.

74 Avrahm Yarmolinsky, *Picturesque United States of America, 1811, 1812, 1813, being a memoir on Paul Svinin, Russian diplomatic officer, artist, and author, containing copious excerpts from his account of his travels in America, with fifty-two reproductions of water colors in his own sketch-book* (New York: W. E. Rudge, 1930), 34.

75 P. H. Snow, *The American Reader* (Hartford, 1840), quoted in Ruth Miller Elson, *Guardians of Tradition: American Schoolbooks of the Nineteenth Century* (Lincoln: University of Nebraska Press, 1964), 199.

76 Anderson, *Imagined Communities*, esp. chapters 1–2. David A. Bell, *The Cult of the Nation in France: Inventing Nationalism, 1680–1800* (Cambridge, Mass.: Harvard University Press, 2001), emphasizes the compatibility of nationalism and religion in France—something historians have long noticed about the United States.

77 "That same attitude which led Americans to regard the Washington portrait as a sacred object," observes sociologist Barry Schwartz, "goes a long way to helping us understand its widespread dissemination." (Schwartz, *George Washington*, 36.) On civil religion, see esp. Albanese, *Sons of the Fathers;* Bercovitch, *American Jeremiad;* and Bellah, "Civil Religion in America." Mark Noll refers to this as the "American Synthesis." See Noll, *America's God*.

78 This analysis has been particularly influenced by Charles Taylor, *Sources of the Self: The Making of the Modern Identity* (Cambridge, Mass.: Harvard University Press, 1989).

79 Noll, *America's God*, 193; "religious populism": Nathan O. Hatch, *The Democratization of American Christianity* (New Haven, Conn.: Yale University Press, 1989), 5. On evangelism and moral autonomy, see also Daniel Walker Howe, "Protestantism, Voluntarism, and Personal Identity in Antebellum America," in *New Directions in American Religious History,* Harry S. Stout and D. G. Hart, eds. (New York: Oxford University Press, 1997), 206–35; and Leo P. Hirrel, *Children of Wrath: New School Calvinism and Antebellum Reform* (Lexington: University Press of Kentucky, 1998).

80 "Our Ark of Covenant": Caleb Cushing referring to the Constitution in 1834 (Chief Justice Taft would make the same remark in 1922), as quoted in Kammen, *A Machine That Would Go of Itself,* xii; "the constitution God has given us" is from Prince, *Part of a discourse,* 23.

81 Abigail Adams to Mary Smith Cranch, February 22, 1800, in Mitchell, ed., *New Letters of Abigail Adams,* 235.

82 Slavoj Žižek, "The King Is a Thing," *New Formations* 13 (1991): 19–37.

83 *Federal Gazette and Baltimore Daily Advertiser,* December 27, 1800; Harris, *A discourse,* 9–10. For more on the problem of ambition in the republic, see Adair, *Fame and the Founding Fathers,* and Forgie, *Patricide in the House Divided,* 55–88. On the power of Washington's resignations, readers familiar with their work will notice my debt to Wills, *Cincinnatus,* and to Morgan, *The Genius of George Washington*.

84 Ogden, *Two discourses,* 17; Cunningham, *An eulogy delivered at Lunenburg,* 11; King George III quoted in Wills, *Cincinnatus,* 13. On that comment, see also Smylie, "The President as Prophet," 99; and M. L. Weems, *A history, of the life and death, virtues,*

and exploits of General George Washington; dedicated to Mrs. Washington; and containing a great many curious and valuable anecdotes, tending to throw much light on the private as well as public life and character, of that very extraordinary man: The whole happily calculated to furnish a feast of true Washingtonian entertainment and improvement, both to ourselves and our children. (George-Town, D.C.: Printed for the Reverend M. L. Weems, by Green & English, 1800), 2.

85 Sewall, Eulogy on the late General Washington, 13.

86 On Trumbull's portrait, see esp. Wills, Cincinnatus, 14, 61; on the staging of Washington's resignation, see Schwartz, George Washington, 139–43.

87 Willliam B. Fowle, The Companion to Spelling Books (Boston, 1843), quoted in Elson, Guardians of Tradition, 201.

88 "To the Speakers of the House of Delegates," January 28, 1802, in Stanislaus Murray Hamilton, ed., The writings of James Monroe, including a collection of his public and private papers and correspondence now for the first time printed, 7 vols. (New York: G. P. Putnam's Sons, 1898), III:333; Mason, Funeral oration, 17; Smith, An oration upon the death of General George Washington, 21. I am particularly indebted in this section to the analyses of Schwartz, George Washington, esp. 137–148, and Wills, Cincinnatus, 1–25.

89 Lee, "Funeral Oration," 12.

90 On gratitude, see the insightful analysis in Fliegelman, Prodigals and Pilgrims, 93–106, 214–19. See also Somkin, Unquiet Eagle, esp. 137–48.

91 "What constitutes the legitimacy of a political society is precisely its recognition as legitimate by its subjects . . . It is the recognition of legitimacy which creates the legitimacy of the sovereign." John Dunn, "Consent in the Political Theory of John Locke," in Political Obligation in Its Historical Context (Cambridge, Eng.: Cambridge University Press, 1980).

92 Smith, An oration upon the death of General George Washington, 4; Boston Mercury, January 7, 1800; Monthly Magazine, March 1800, 224; Mason, Funeral oration, 23. See also Seth Williston, The agency of God, in raising up important characters, and rendering them useful (Geneva, N.Y.: Eaton Walker, 1800), 23

93 Joseph Allen, An oration on the character of the late Gen. George Washington (Brookfield, Mass.: E. Merriam & Co., 1800), 4; Bigelow, An eulogy on the life, 7. For more references to gratitude by eulogists, see: Francis Kinloch, Eulogy on George Washington, reprint, New York, 1867 ed. (Georgetown, S.C.: John Burd, 1867), 5; Ogden, Two discourses, 40; Minot, An eulogy on George Washington, 19–20; Lee, "Funeral Oration," 16.

94 See Giorgio Agamben, Homo Sacer: Sovereign Power and Bare Life (Stanford, Calif.: Stanford University Press, 1998).

CHAPTER 2: WASHINGTON'S FAMILY

1 Frederick Douglass, *Narrative of the Life of Frederick Douglass, an American Slave* (Boston: The Anti-Slavery Office, 1845), 4.

2 Philip Morgan, " 'To Get Quit of Negroes': George Washington and Slavery," *Journal of American Studies* 39 (December, 2005), 405. On Washington's relationship to slavery, see James Thomas Flexner, *George Washington: Anguish and Farewell (1793–1799)* (Boston: Little, Brown, 1972), 112–25, 423–48; Fritz Hirschfeld, *George Washington and Slavery: A Documentary Portrayal* (Columbia: University of Missouri Press, 1997); Kenneth Morgan, "George Washington and the Problem of Slavery," *Journal of American Studies* 34 (2000): 279–301; Philip J. Schwarz, ed., *Slavery at the Home of George Washington* (Mount Vernon, Va.: Mount Vernon Ladies' Association, 2001); Dorothy Twohig, " 'That Species of Property': Washington's Role in the Controversy over Slavery," in *George Washington Reconsidered,* Don Higginbotham, ed. (Charlottesville: University Press of Virginia, 2001), 114–36; and Henry Wiencek, *An Imperfect God: George Washington, His Slaves, and the Creation of America* (New York: Farrar, Straus and Giroux, 2003). In addition, Joseph Ellis's recent biography of Washington takes his relationship to slavery as an important feature of his life, rather than as an irritating distraction. Joseph J. Ellis, *His Excellency: George Washington* (New York: Alfred A. Knopf, 2004).

3 The details of Washington's death have been painstakingly reconstructed in Douglas Southall Freeman, John Alexander Carroll, and Mary Wells Ashworth, *George Washington, a Biography,* 7 vols. (New York: Scribner, 1948), VII:617–25, and Flexner, *Washington: Anguish and Farewell,* 456–62. To the observation that blacks outnumbered whites in the room as Washington died, I am indebted to Morgan, " 'To Get Quit of Negroes': George Washington and Slavery," 403. The story of Washington burning one will comes from the account left by his personal secretary, Tobias Lear, which has been widely used in reconstructing Washington's last hours. Lear's account can be found in Worthington Chauncey Ford, ed., *The Writings of George Washington,* 14 vols. (New York: G. P. Putnam's Sons, 1889), XIV:245–55, and in Dorothy Twohig, ed., *The Papers of George Washington: Retirement Series,* 4 vols. (Charlottesville: University Press of Virginia, 1998), IV:542–55. See also John Clement Fitzpatrick, ed., *The Last Will and Testament of George Washington and Schedule of his Property, to which is Appended the Last Will and Testament of Martha Washington* (Mount Vernon, Va.: The Mount Vernon Ladies' Association of the Union, 1939), v, and Eugene Ernst Prussing, *The Estate of George Washington* (Boston: Little, Brown and Company, 1927), 24–83.

4 Twohig, ed., *Papers, Retirement Series,* IV:538–39.

5 Fitzpatrick, ed., *Last Will and Testament,* 2.

6 On Martha Washington's views on slavery, see esp. Wiencek, *An Imperfect God.*

7 George Washington Parke Custis, *Recollections and Private Memoirs of Washington* (New York: Derby & Jackson, 1860), 158.

8 Adams quoted in Hirschfeld, *George Washington and Slavery,* 214.

9 In this section, I have found the following work particularly insightful: Russ Castronovo, *Fathering the Nation: American Genealogies of Slavery and Freedom* (Berkeley: University of California Press, 1995). The fine scholarship on Washington's image unfortunately pays little attention to his relationship to slavery. On Washington's image, see esp. Cunliffe, *George Washington, Man and Monument;* Wills, *Cincinnatus;* Longmore, *The Invention of George Washington;* and Schwartz, *George Washington.* As suggested by my notes in the previous chapter, the work on the political significance of fatherhood that has most influence my analysis is Fliegelman, *Prodigals and Pilgrims.* An important recent analysis is Matthew Backes, "The Father and the Middle Class: Paternal Authority, Filial Independence, and the Transformation of American Culture, 1800–1850" (Ph.D. dissertation, Columbia University, 2005). On the political importance of the family metaphor in Revolutionary and post-Revolutionary France, see Lynn Avery Hunt, *The Family Romance of the French Revolution* (Berkeley: University of California Press, 1992).

10 Reprinted everywhere. May be found most accessibly in *Washingtoniana* [Sower 1802], 159.

11 *Washington's political legacies* [Forman ed.], 9; Prince, *Part of a discourse,* 19; Dunham, *Funeral Oration,* 9. The references to Washington's fatherhood of the nation were truly ubiquitous. If the numerous examples given in text have not yet proven tiresome, the particularly assiduous reader might look to Smith, *An Oration,* 3; Dunham, *A Funeral Oration,* 9; Prince, *Part of a discourse,* 19; Kemp, *A sermon, delivered in Christ church,* 4 and 11; Tuckerman, *Funeral oration,* 8 and 18; David Tappan, *A Discourse . . .* (n.p.: Samuel Ethridge, 1800), 9; *Washingtoniana* [Sower ed.], 159; New York *Weekly Museum,* February 22, 1800; *Federal Gazette and Baltimore Daily Advertiser,* January 2, 1800; *The Times; and District of Columbia Daily Advertiser* (Alexandria), December 20, 1800; William Pitt Beers, *An oration, on the death of General Washington; pronounced before the citizens of Albany, on Thursday, January 9th, 1800* (Albany, N.Y.: Charles R. and George Webster, 1800), 6; Cunningham, *An eulogy delivered at Lunenburg,* 14; *Monthly Magazine,* February 1800, 125; and many, many more.

12 Gouverneur Morris, *An oration, upon the death of General Washington* (New-York: John Furman, 1800), 3.

13 *Monthly Magazine and American Review,* February 1800, 121.

14 Lee, "Funeral Oration," 17; Rasmussen and Tilton, *George Washington*, xi. Garry Wills makes this point about the often-omitted but important second half of Lee's quotation: Wills, *Cincinnatus*, 240.

15 M. L. Weems, *The Life of Washington*, Marcus Cunliffe, ed. (Cambridge, Mass.: Belknap Press, 1962), 2–4. On the connection between public and private in early national political discourse, I have found the following most useful: Kerber, *Women of the Republic: Intellect and Ideology in Revolutionary America*; Fliegelman, *Prodigals and Pilgrims*; Fliegelman, *Declaring Independence*; and Casper, *Constructing American Lives*. For a broader conceptual frame, see the essays collected in Carole Pateman, *The Disorder of Women: Democracy, Feminism and Political Obligation* (Oxford: Polity Press, 1989).

16 Casper, "First First Family," 5, and Ellen G. Miles, *American Paintings of the Eighteenth Century* (Washington: National Gallery of Art, 1995), 146–60 (quotation at 154). On Savage's portrait, see also Hugh Honour, *The Image of the Black in Western Art. Volume 4: From the American Revolution to World War I. Part I: Slaves and Liberators* (Cambridge, Mass.: Harvard University Press, 1989), 46–48; and Thistlethwaite, *The Image of George Washington*, 131–32.

17 "In the General" quoted in Miles, *American Paintings of the Eighteenth Century*, 154. On the center of the vista behind as the real center of the painting, see Casper, "First First Family," 4. On geographic expansion and millennial progress, see esp. Tuveson, *Redeemer Nation*; Pocock, *Machiavellian Moment*; Hatch, *The Sacred Cause of Liberty*; McCoy, *The Elusive Republic*; Bloch, *Visionary Republic*; Michael Lienesch, *New Order of the Ages: Time, the Constitution, and the Making of Modern American Political Thought* (Princeton, N.J.: Princeton University Press, 1988). On conceptions of the future and their political implications, see esp. Koselleck, *Futures Past*.

18 This anonymity is certainly understandable, since Savage only added the slave to the painting as an afterthought, while he was in London. Not having any of Washington's slaves at hand, he "borrowed" the valet of Thomas Pinckney, then the U.S. ambassador to Great Britain, and later replaced that figure with another, painted over the original. See Miles, *American Paintings of the Eighteenth Century*, 152.

19 Many thanks to Tom DeWesselow for his insight and help decoding this image.

20 Jordan, *White over Black*, 115. On fears in the colonial period, see 110–22; on fears in the early national period, see 375–402.

21 Davis, *The Problem of Slavery in the Age of Revolution*, 283.

22 *Notes on the State of Virginia*, in Peterson, ed., *Writings*, 264, 288, 289; Jefferson to St. George Tucker, August 28, 1787, *Papers of Thomas Jefferson*, Julian P. Boyd, L. H. Butterfield, Charles T. Cullen, and John Catanzariti, eds., 30 vols. to date (Princeton, N.J.: Princeton University Press, 2002), XXIX:519. See also Onuf, *Jefferson's Empire*,

147–58; and Ferguson, *Reading the Early Republic*, 204–5. Interestingly, Jefferson's bitter political enemy, James Calender, who first publicized Jefferson's relationship with Sally Hemings, charged that if every white man had done as Jefferson had done, "The country would no longer be habitable, till after a civil war, and a series of massacres. We all know with absolute certainty that the contest would end in the utter extirpation both of blacks and mulattoes. We know that the continent has as many white people, as could eat the whole race at a breakfast." Quoted in Jordan, *White over Black*, 469.

23 On American responses to the Haitian revolution, see Jordan, *White over Black*, esp. 375–86; Donald R. Hickey, "America's Response to the Slave Revolt in Haiti, 1791–1806," *Journal of the Early Republic* 2 (1982): 361–79; Alfred N. Hunt, *Haiti's Influence on Antebellum America: Slumbering Volcano in the Caribbean* (Baton Rouge: Louisiana State University Press, 1988); David Brion Davis, *Revolutions: Reflections on American Equality and Foreign Liberations* (Cambridge, Mass.: Harvard University Press, 1990), 49–54; Marie-Jeanne Rossignol, *The Nationalist Ferment: The Origins of U.S. Foreign Policy, 1789–1812*, trans. Lillian A. Parrott (Columbus: Ohio State University Press, 2004), 119–40; Michael Zuckerman, "The Power of Blackness: Thomas Jefferson and the Revolution in Saint-Domingue," in *Almost Chosen People: Oblique Biographies in the American Grain* (Berkeley: University of California Press, 1993), 175–218; Tim Matthewson, "Jefferson and Haiti," *Journal of Southern History* 61 (1995): 209–48; Chris Dixon, *African America and Haiti: Emigration and Black Nationalism in the Nineteenth Century* (Westport, Conn.: Greenwood Press, 2000); Lachance, "Repercussions of the Haitian Revolution in Louisiana," esp. 210–13; Douglas R. Egerton, "The Tricolor in Black and White: The French Revolution in Jefferson's Virginia," in *Rebels, Reformers, and Revolutionaries: Collected Essays and Second Thoughts* (New York: Routledge, 2002), 163–74; Wills, *Negro President*, 35–46; and White, "Flood of Impure Lava." On its impact in the broader Atlantic world, see Michel-Rolph Trouillot, *Silencing the Past: Power and the Production of History* (Boston: Beacon Press, 1995); and David P. Geggus, ed., *The Impact of the Haitian Revolution in the Atlantic World* (Columbia: University of South Carolina Press, 2001); and Laurent Dubois, *A Colony of Citizens: Revolution & Slave Emancipation in the French Caribbean, 1787–1804* (Chapel Hill: Published for the Omohundro Institute of Early American History and Culture by the University of North Carolina Press, 2004).

24 Jordan, *White over Black*, 391, 385; Genet to Minister of Foreign Affairs, October 7, 1793, in Frederick Jackson Turner, ed., *Annual Report of the American Historical Association for the Year 1903*, 2 vols., *Vol. II: Seventh Report of the Historical Manuscripts Commission. Correspondence of the French Ministers to the United States, 1791–1797*

(Washington: Government Printing Office, 1904), 245–46; James Monroe to John Cowper, March 17, 1802, quoted in Egerton, "The Tricolor in Black and White," 171; St. George Tucker, *A Dissertation on Slavery: With a Proposal for the Gradual Abolition of it, in the State of Virginia* (Philadelphia: Mathew Carey, 1796), 105; Thomas Jefferson to Aaron Burr, February 11, 1799 and Jefferson to Madison, February 12, 1799, both in Boyd et al., eds., *Papers*, 31:22, 31:29–30. "Slaves were the nightmare presence behind a white quest for independence," observes the literary scholar Robert Ferguson. Ferguson, *Reading the Early Republic*, 206. These fears seem to have existed in North as well as in the South. "Most northerners somehow felt that they too had a stake in quaranting Haiti," Jordan observes. Jordan, *White over Black*, 385. On the trope of the Jeremiad, see esp. Bercovitch, *American Jeremiad*.

25 On the links between Gabriel's plot, international politics, and French republicans, see Egerton, *Gabriel's Rebellion*. For its larger significance in Virginia political culture, see Sidbury, *Ploughshares into Swords;* and on U.S. political culture, see the contributions by Michael A. Bellisles, James Sidbury, Laurent Dubois, and Douglas R. Egerton, in Horn, Lewis, and Onuf, eds., *The Revolution of 1800.*

26 Alexis de Tocqueville, *De la démocratie en Amérique*, 2 vols. (Paris: Gallimard, 1961), I:523; my translation. Also: "Hitherto wherever the whites have been the most powerful, they have held the blacks in degradation or in slavery; wherever the Negroes have been strongest, they have destroyed the whites: this has been the only balance that has ever taken place between the two races." (Ibid., 502).

27 Fanny Kemble, *Journal of a Residence on a Georgian Plantation in 1838–1839* (New York: Harper & Brothers, 1863), 295–96. For more travelers' observations of Southerners' fear of slave insurrection, see Clement Eaton, *The Freedom-of-Thought Struggle in the Old South*, rev. and enl. ed. (New York: Harper & Row, 1964), 111–12.

28 Nat Turner, *The Confessions of Nat Turner and Related Documents*, Kenneth S. Greenberg, ed. (Boston: Bedford Books, 1996), 40.

29 Quoted in Alison Goodyear Freehling, *Drift toward Dissolution: The Virginia Slavery Debate of 1831–1832* (Baton Rouge: Louisiana State University Press, 1982), 6. For abundant evidence that fears of insurrection lay just beneath the surface of the Virginia debates of 1831–32, see pp. 129, 135, 137, and 142. "A *Domestic* Institution," notes the historian William Freehling, "was peculiarly vulnerable, physically and psychologically, to a pair of trusted household servants." Freehling, *The Reintegration of American History*, 57.

30 Eaton, *Freedom-of-Thought Struggle*, 96–97, 116. See also Davis, *Slavery in the Age of Revolutions*, 326–42.

31 Richards, *The Accepted*, 66–68. It may be worth noting the irony of this oration

being delivered in the same town to which Martha Washington's slave Ona Judge had fled some years earlier, and in which she probably still lived. One wonders if she herself heard the speech. For more on Judge, see Wiencek, *An Imperfect God*, 321–34.

32 Smith, *An oration upon the death of General George Washington*, 35. For an argument that locates Samuel Stanhope Smith as part of a Northern coterie of proslavery clergymen, see Larry E. Tise, *Proslavery: A history of the Defense of Slavery in America, 1701–1840* (Athens: University of Georgia Press, 1987), esp. 232–34.

33 "The relatively small number of servile rebellions in the United States," observes John Ashworth, "does not seem to have afforded the masters much peace of mind." But, as Ashworth rightly notes, "To say that many of the slaveholders' actions were prompted by black resistance is by no means to claim that the slaveholders themselves identified these prompts correctly." See John Ashworth, *Slavery, Capitalism, and Politics in the Antebellum Republic* (Cambridge, Eng.: Cambridge University Press, 1995), 4, 9.

34 *Monthly Magazine and American Review*, (February, 1800), 84.

35 John Corry, *The life of George Washington, late president and commander in chief of the armies of the United States of America* (Philadelphia: Joseph Charless, 1801), 203.

36 For the publication of Washington's will, see Shipton, Mooney, and Bristol, *The Short-Title Evans*, II:961–63. The will was published in the Boston *Mercury* on February 11 and again on the 14th; in the *American Mercury* of Hartford on February 20; in the New York *Weekly Museum* on February 8 and again on the 15th.

37 Richards, *The Accepted*, 26.

38 Thomas Morrell, *A sermon on the death of Gen. Geo. Washington* (Baltimore, Md.: Warner & Hannah, 1800), 25.

39 Bigelow, *An eulogy on the life*, 16.

40 Bancroft, *An eulogy*, 16; New York *Weekly Museum*, January 18, 1800; Thomas Thacher, *An eulogy on George Washington, first president of the United States, and late commander in chief of the American army . . . Delivered at Dedham, February 22, 1800, at the request of the inhabitants of said town* (Dedham, Mass.: H. Mann, 1800), 17.

41 I have found Allen's speech in the Baltimore *Federal Gazette*, January 3, 1800, and the *Philadelphia Gazette and Universal Daily Advertiser*, December 27, 1799.

42 It is interesting to note that Allen believed Washington performed the so-called emancipation "secretly and almost unknown." Very few of Washington's actions were performed "secretly," and this act, in particular, was clearly designed with a large audience in mind.

43 John Barent Johnson, *Eulogy on General George Washington* (Albany, N.Y.: L. An-

drews, 1800), 15; Sewall, *Eulogy on the Late General Washington*, 19–20; Foster, *A discourse delivered*, 10–11.

44 Tucker, *A Dissertation on Slavery*, 13, 67; see also 46–47; Max Farrand, ed., *The records of the Federal convention of 1787*, 3 vols. (New Haven, Conn.: Yale University Press, 1911), II:370. (August 22, 1787); Henry Laurens quoted in Gregory D. Massey, "The Limits of Antislavery Thought in the Revolutionary Lower South: John Laurens and Henry Laurens," *Journal of Southern History* 36 (1997): 495–530, quotation at 507; Mercer quoted in Douglas R. Egerton, " 'Its Origin Is Not a Little Curious': A New Look at the American Colonization Society," *Journal of the Early Republic* 5 (1985): 436–80.

45 Peterson, ed., *Writings*, 22; Rush, *Occasional productions*, 126. For James Madison's similar view, see McCoy, *Last of the Fathers*, 235, 237. See also Davis, *The Problem of Slavery in the Age of Revolution*, 273.

46 Henry quoted in J. Franklin Jameson, *The American Revolution Considered as a Social Movement* (Princeton, N.J.: Princeton University Press 1927; rpt. 1967), 23; Thomas Jefferson to Edward Coles, August 25, 1814, and Thomas Jefferson to James Heaton, May 20, 1826, all in Peterson, ed., *Writings*, 592, 1345, and 1516. On Jefferson's faith in "time," see Paul Finkelman, "Jefferson and Slavery: 'Treason Against the Hopes of the World,' " in *Jeffersonian Legacies*, ed. Peter S. Onuf (Charlottesville: University Press of Virginia, 1993), 181–221, esp. 207–210; and Davis, *The Problem of Slavery in the Age of Revolution*, 169–84. On Jefferson and slavery more generally, see McColley, *Slavery and Jeffersonian Virginia*; Jordan, *White over Black*, 429–81; Miller, *Wolf by the Ears*; Finkelman, *Slavery and the Founders*, 129–96; and Onuf, *Jefferson's Empire*, 147–88.

47 Madison quoted in McCoy, *Last of the Fathers*, 265; George Washington to John Francis Mercer, September 9, 1786, in W. W. Abbot and Dorothy Twohig, eds., *The Papers of George Washington: Confederation Series*, 6 vols. (Charlottesville: University Press of Virginia, 1992), IV, 243; John Bernard, *Retrospections of America, 1797–1811*, Mrs. Bernard Bayle, ed. (New York: Benjamin Blom, 1969), 91. Joseph Ellis takes Washington's private endorsement of seeing "some plan adopted . . . [to end slavery] by slow, sure, & imperceptable degrees" as definitive evidence of Washington's antislavery views—an assumption that is problematical at best. See Ellis, *Founding Brothers*, 113.

48 Mitnick, "Parallel Visions: The Literary and Visual Image of George Washington," 63–64. This was only one of several midcentury versions of Savage's painting that omitted the slave. See Casper, "First First Family," 6–7.

49 See Freehling, *Reintegration of American History*, esp. 35–36, 256–60.

50 On the deathbed scene in literature, see Philippe Ariès, *Western Attitudes Toward Death: From the Middle Ages to the Present* (Baltimore, Md.: Johns Hopkins University Press, 1974), esp. 7–14.

51 Sewall, *Eulogy on the late General Washington,* 16; Morse, *A prayer and sermon,* 34, also quoted in the New York *Weekly Museum,* January 11, 1800; Bigelow, *An eulogy on the life,* 16; South Carolina *Gazette,* January 15, 1800. Many thanks to Mike Johnson for passing along this last citation.

52 Jedidiah Morse, *The American geography, or, A view of the present situation of the United States of America: illustrated with two sheet maps . . . to which is added a concise abridgment of the geography of the British, Spanish, French, and Dutch dominions in America, and the West Indies, of Europe, Asia, and Africa* (Elizabeth Town, N.J.: Shepard Kollock for the author, 1789). This sketch appears to have provided the basis for many accounts of Washington's life, including Weems's.

53 Thacher, *An eulogy on George Washington,* 16.

54 Richards, *The Accepted,* 65–66.

55 William Spohn Baker, *Character portraits of Washington as delineated by historians, orators and divines* (Philadelphia: R. M. Lindsay, 1887), 150–51.

56 Freehling, *The Reintegration of American History,* 257–58; see also 35–36. Winthrop Jordan argues that slaveowners' insistence that slaves were content with their condition was something new to the nineteenth century. See Jordan, *White over Black,* 394–95.

57 On paternalist ideology, see esp. Eugene D. Genovese, *Roll, Jordan, Roll: The World the Slaves Made* (New York: Vintage Books, 1972); James Oakes, *The Ruling Race: A History of American Slaveholders* (New York: Knopf, 1982); and Jeffrey Robert Young, *Domesticating Slavery: The Master Class in Georgia and South Carolina, 1670–1837* (Chapel Hill: University of North Carolina Press, 1999).

58 Rush, *Occasional productions,* 74.

59 For an analysis of Confederate nationalism that corresponds largely with the one suggested here, see Drew Gilpin Faust, *The Creation of Confederate Nationalism: Ideology and Identity in the Civil War South* (Baton Rouge: Louisiana State University Press, 1988).

60 Abraham Lincoln, "Second Inaugural Address," in Roy P. Basler, ed., *Collected Works of Abraham Lincoln,* 9 vols. (New Brunswick, N.J.: Rutgers University Press, 1953), VIII:333.

61 The words are those of Ronald Walters, characterizing (and critiquing) a trend in much historiography. Ronald Walters, "The Boundaries of Abolitionism," in *Antislavery Reconsidered: New Perspectives on the Abolitionists,* ed. Lewis Perry (Baton

Rouge: Louisiana State University Press, 1979), 6. "If the Revolution had antislavery implications (as I believe it did)," Walters adds, "they had to be worked out painfully, haltingly, and unevenly over a half century."

62 By the same token, casting the Constitution as an antislavery document served as a powerful tool to oppose slavery. This is what Frederick Douglass realized in the early 1850s when, after a long period of hesitation, he broke with the Garrisonians to argue that the Constitution—far from being a proslavery document as the Garrisonians held—was in fact antislavery. Why did he change his mind? In part, it was because an antislavery interpretation of the Constitution could be among "the most effective measures for the abolition of slavery." At stake in the question: "Whether abolitionists shall be restricted in their instrumentalities to pen and tongue, or whether they may wield against slavery the press, and the living speaker, and all the powers of the Constitution and Government." Clearly, reinterpreting the Constitution to suit antislavery ends was a more effective strategy than to oppose the document. Frederick Douglass, "Is the United States Constitution For or Against Slavery?" in *The Life and Writings of Frederick Douglass,* ed. Philip Sheldon Foner, 5 vols., (New York: International Publishers, 1975), V:192, 191–92. See also David W. Blight, *Frederick Douglass' Civil War: Keeping Faith in Jubilee* (Baton Rouge: Louisiana State University Press, 1989), 31–35.

63 Davis, *The Problem of Slavery in the Age of Revolution,* 257. On the expansion of slavery in the early republic, see esp. Rothman, *Slave Country.*

64 These questions have, of course, been addressed by numerous feminist historians and theorists, and it is this scholarship more than any other that has helped me think through the problem of consent in liberal theory. The works I have found particularly useful are Pateman, *The Disorder of Women;* Pateman, *The Problem of Political Obligation: A Critique of Liberal Theory* (Berkeley: University of California Press, 1985); Carole Pateman, *The Sexual Contract* (Stanford, Calif.: Stanford University Press, 1988); and Martha Craven Nussbaum, *Sex and Social Justice* (New York: Oxford University Press, 1999). Also Joan Wallach Scott, *Only Paradoxes to Offer: French Feminists and the Rights of Man* (Cambridge, Mass.: Harvard University Press, 1996).

65 On active versus passive citizenship in different contexts, see William H. Sewell Jr., "Le Citoyen / la Citoyenne: Activity, Passivity, and the Revolutionary Concept of Citizenship," in *The French Revolution and the Creation of Modern Political Culture, vol. II: The Political Culture of the French Revolution,* ed. Colin Lucas (Oxford: Oxford University Press, 1988), 105–23; and Dubois, *Colony of Citizens.*

CHAPTER 3: MASON LOCKE WEEMS

1 Mason Locke Weems [hereafter "MLW"] to Mathew Carey [hereafter "MC"], n.d. [probably sometime in late 1810s, early 1820s]. Edward Carey Gardiner Collection (#227A), Historical Society of Pennsylvania, Mathew Carey Correspondence, Carey Section, Box 91, No. 707.

2 MLW to MC, November 24, 1799, and December 31, 1799, in Skeel, ed., *Mason Locke Weems, His Works and Ways* [hereafter "*MLW*"], II:124.

3 Oliver Goldsmith, *An History of the Earth, and Animated Nature*, 2 vols. (Philadelphia: Mathew Carey, 1795); William Guthrie, *A New System of Modern Geography: or, A geographical, historical, and commercial grammar; and present state of the several nations of the world*, 2 vols. (Philadelphia: Mathew Carey, 1794).

4 MLW to MC, December 31, 1794, in Skeel, ed., *MLW*, II:2.

5 MLW to MC, January 12 or 13, 1800, in Skeel, ed., *MLW*, II:126.

6 The only full-length studies of Weems are Lawrence C. Wroth, *Parson Weems; A Biographical and Critical Study* (Baltimore, Md.: The Eichelberger Book Company, 1911); Harold Kellock, *Parson Weems of the Cherry-Tree* (New York: The Century Co., 1928); and Lewis Gaston Leary, *The Book-Peddling Parson: An Account of the Life and Works of Mason Locke Weems, Patriot, Pitchman, Author, and Purveyor of Morality to the Citizenry of the Early United States of America* (Chapel Hill, N.C.: Algonquin Books, 1984). Weems has been featured in enough works as a minor character to make it possible to piece together many details of his life. Discussions of Weems and his career on which I have drawn include Evert Augustus Duyckinck and George Long Duyckinck, *Cyclopadia of American literature*, 2 vols. (Philadelphia, New York, and London: T. E. Zell, 1875), II:501–9; William Alfred Bryan, "The Genesis of Weems' 'Life of Washington,'" *Americana* 36 (1942): 147–65; Bryan, *George Washington in American literature*, 89–96; Marcus Cunliffe, "Introduction," in *The Life of Washington*, ix–lxii; Cunliffe, "Parson Weems and George Washington's Cherry Tree," *Bulletin of the John Rylands Library* 45, no. 1962–63 (1962–63): 58–96; Boorstin, *The Americans: The National Experience*, 340–45; James Gilreath, "Mason Weems, Mathew Carey and the Southern Booktrade, 1794–1810," *Publishing History* 10, no. 1981 (1981): 27–49; Wills, *Cincinnatus*, 35–53; Watts, *The Republic Reborn*, 141–51; Zboray, *A Fictive People*, 37–54; Hall, "Books and Reading in Eighteenth-Century America"; James N. Green, "'The Cowl knows best what will suit in Virginia': Parson Weems on Southern Readers," *Printing History* 17 (1995): 26–34; Peter S. Onuf, "Introduction," in *The Life of Washington, by Mason Locke Weems* (Armonk, N.Y.: M. E. Sharpe, 1996); and Casper, *Constructing American Lives*, 68–76. With the exception of Wroth, Kellock, and the Duyckincks (who seem to have relied on many

firsthand accounts), all of these works have relied on Skeel, ed., *MLW,* an indispensable three-volume work that contains a nearly comprehensive bibliography and an essential collection of Weems's correspondence. Though the correspondence is occasionally fallible and is not entirely complete, I have found Skeel to be reliable. Skeel's brief introduction of Weems's life can be found in Skeel, ed., *MLW,* II:xi–xxiv. The appendices in volume 3 contain detailed information on Weems's life and family. For the sheer poetry of the descriptions—though I do not think they are reliable—it is worth reading William Gilmore Simms, "Weems, The Biographer and Historian," in *Views and Reviews in American Literature, History, and Fiction,* 2 vols. (New York: Wiley & Putnam, 1845), 2:123–41, and Van Wyck Brooks, *The World of Washington Irving* (n.p.: E. P. Dutton & Co., 1944), 1–4. The enduring resonance of Weems's life and stories can be glimpsed in the published sermon on Weems given by Jerry Wallace, *A Parson at Large, Being an Account of Mason Locke Weems, George Washington's Quaint Biographer, and His Relation to the American Episcopate* (Springfield, Ill. n.p., 1934). For background on Weems's family history, I drew mostly on Wroth, *Parson Weems,* 11–18; Douglas Andes Weems, *History of the Weems Family* (Annapolis, Md.: Weems System of Navigation, 1945); Cunliffe, "Introduction," in *The Life of Washington,* ix–xiii; and Skeel, ed., *MLW,* III:365–79.

7   Noll, *America's God,* 205 and passim.

8   Skeel finds no evidence of Weems's participation in the Revolution, and gives little credence to the rumors that he served aboard a British ship. However, the intensity with which she defends Weems against any "discredit" that might attach to him for having served on a British ship casts some doubt on her own judgment in this matter. See Skeel, ed., *MLW,* III:383–87. A few hints in Weems's writings suggest he may have had at least some experience on a warship. See, for example, M. L. Weems, *The Philanthropist, or, A good twenty-five cents worth of political love powder, for honest Adamites and Jeffersonians: with the following recommendation by George Washington* (Alexandria, Va.: John & James D. Westcott, 1799), 22.

9   Davis, *Travels of four years and a half,* 307.

10 According to legend, when he was about fourteen years old, Mason often left his house in the evening after tea and stayed away until well into the night. As one narrator relates the story: "The family began to be afraid that he was getting into corrupt habits, and, notwithstanding his assurance that he would do nothing that would render him unworthy of their esteem and friendship, they felt uneasy . . . Accordingly one night a plan was laid by which he was tracked. After pursuing his trail for some distance into the pines, they came to an old hut, in which was young Weems, surrounded by the bareheaded, barefooted, and half-clad children of the

neighborhood, whom he had been in the habit of thus gathering around him at night, in order to give them instruction." Quoted in William Meade, *Old Churches, Ministers and Families of Virginia*, 2 vols. (Philadelphia: J. B. Lippincott & Co., 1861), II:234. See also Wroth, *Parson Weems*, 14–15, and Skeel, ed., *MLW*, III:378.

11 For more details, see Wroth, *Parson Weems*, 19–26; Skeel, ed., *MLW*, III:390–99; and Wallace, *A Parson at Large*, 20–26, 29.

12 Several Church officials testified to Weems's diligence, including a friend who commented in his diary that Weems was "chiefly remarkable for his zeal and industry." Quotations from Wroth, *Parson Weems*, 33; and Skeel, ed., *MLW*, III:419. See (Rev.) William Duke, Journals, 1775–1788, Subject File, Archives of the Episcopal Diocese of Maryland.

13 Rev. Ethan Allen, D.D., *Clergy in Maryland of the Protestant Episcopal Church Since the Independence of 1783* (Baltimore, Md.: James S. Waters, 1860), 16; Wroth, *Parson Weems*, 24, 26; Skeel, ed., *MLW*, 410–11.

14 On evidence of Weems's rise in the Church during this period, see (and note his co-authorship of) *A Journal of the Proceedings of the Superintending Committee of the Protestant Episcopal Church for the Western Shore of Maryland, instituted at Baltimore, the 29th of May 1788* [filed under "Superintending Committee—Western Shore: Proceedings, 1788–89,"], Duke MSS, Archives of the Episcopal Diocese of Maryland. In the report, Weems is identified as superintendent of the parishes of Anne Arundel County. See also the *Notices and Journals, and Remains of Journals . . . Of the Protestant Episcopal Church in the Diocese of Maryland, in the Years 1783, 1784, 1785, 1786, 1787, 1788 . . .* [publishing info is unclear]; the *Journal of the Proceedings of the Protestant Episcopal Church . . . 1789* (Baltimore, Md.: William Goddard, 1789); and the *Journal of the Proceedings of a Convention . . .* [for the years 1790–93].

15 Reverend Thomas John Claggett to Reverend William West, August 23, 1788 [?], Archives of the Episcopal Diocese of Maryland. This letter is also quoted in George B. Utley, *The Life and Times of Thomas John Claggett* (Chicago: R. R. Donnelley & Sons, 1913), 51–52, and in Skeel, ed., *MLW*, III:411–12.

16 Mr. Higinbotham to William West, November 22, 1788 [copied in Rev. William West to Bishop White, January 19, 1789], Archives of the Episcopal Diocese of Maryland. For more evidence of Weems's bookselling during this period, see also Rev. William West to Bishop White, January 19, 1789, and Rev. Higinbotham to Rev. William West, February 16, 1789, both in the Archives of the Episcopal Diocese of Maryland. Skeel dates the earliest of Weems's bookselling to 1791.

17 See excerpts from Duke's diary in Skeel, ed., *MLW*, III:419–23. On the peddlers in a larger context, see David Jaffee, "Peddlers of Progress and the Transformation of the

Rural North, 1760–1860," *Journal of American History* 78 (Sept. 1991): 511–35. On itinerancy in a religious context, see Timothy D. Hall, *Contested Boundaries: Itinerancy and the Reshaping of the Colonial American Religious World* (Durham, N.C.: Duke University Press, 1994).

18 Quoted in Skeel, ed., *MLW*, III:421.

19 See the "Journal of a Convention of the Protestant Episcopal Church in Maryland, Held in the City of Annapolis, from Thursday, May 31st to Saturday, June 2nd 1792," MSS, filed under "Maryland Convention, 1792–1806," Subject File, Archives of the Episcopal Diocese of Maryland. See also Wroth, *Parson Weems*, 36. The Russel sermons were published as: Robert Russel, *Sermons on different important subjects* (Baltimore, Md.: Samuel and John Adams . . . for M. L. Weems, 1791).

20 See MLW to George Washington, received July 6, 1792, Gratz American Prose Collection, Case 6 Box 13, Historical Society of Pennsylvania. Weems entered a market awash with Blair's *Sermons:* between 1790 and 1800, at least nine editions were published in the United States, and thirteen in the United Kingdom. The U.S. editions included Hodge, Allen, and Campbell, New York, 1790; Spotwood and Carey, Philadelphia, 1791; T. Allen, New York, 1792; I. Thomas and E. T. Andrews, Boston, 1792; Robert Campbell, Philadelphia, 1794 and 1795; John M'Donald, Albany, 1796 and 1797. Weems was to have great difficulty selling these *Sermons*.

21 One letter finds Weems in New York in 1794. Another records his increasing involvement in bookselling—but still of a religious nature: "Mr Weems informs me he intends to publish a Volume of Sermons under the Title of *the American Prot^{es}. Episcopal Preacher*—the Plan which he will have an Opportunity to present to you in person, is, I think, a good one—& cannot but wish him Success." Rev. Abraham Beach to Bishop Claggett, February 20, 1794, Archives of the Episcopal Diocese of Maryland. Also quoted in Skeel, ed., *MLW*, III:413–14, and in Wroth, *Parson Weems*, 39. I have not located any book by this title.

22 On this contact, see Washington's diary entry for March 3, 1787, in Donald Dean Jackson and Dorothy Twohig, eds., *The Diaries of George Washington*, 6 vols. (Charlottesville: University Press of Virginia, 1976), V:112. On that occasion Dr. Craik married one of Frances Ewell's sisters. Writing to George Washington in 1792, Weems twice reminded him, "I was once introduced to your Excellency by Doctor Craik . . . Doctor Craik had introduced me to your Excellency some years ago at M Vernon." See MLW to George Washington [received July 6, 1792], Gratz American Prose Collection, Case 6 Box 13, Historical Society of Pennsylvania.

23 MLW to George Washington, 1795, George Washington Papers at the Library of

Congress, 1741–1799: Series 4. General Correspondence, 1697–1799. On Weems's claim to be the rector of Mt. Vernon, see Wroth, *Parson Weems,* 41–42; M. L. Weems, *The life of George Washington with curious anecdotes, equally honourable to himself and exemplary to his young countrymen,* 9th ed. (Philadelphia: Mathew Carey, 1809), title page. This text will hereafter be cited as *Life* (1809 ed.); page numbers have been drawn from the Cunliffe edition, the most accessible, cited above in note 15, page 274.

24 MLW to MC, November 17, 1800, in Skeel, ed., *MLW,* II:152.

25 In his first known letter to Carey, Weems closed: "Wishing that we may always print & reprint such Books as may do good in Society I remain . . ." MLW to MC, December 31, 1794, in Skeel, ed., *MLW,* II:2.

26 Printed in *The immortal mentor, or, Man's unerring guide to a healthy, wealthy & happy life: in three parts* (Philadelphia: Printed for the Rev. Mason L. Weems, by Francis and Robert Bailey, no. 116, High-Street, 1796); Franklin's essay is printed on 107–25. This book received a glowing endorsement from Washington, which Weems had printed facing the title page, and is reprinted in George Washington to MLW, July 3, 1799, in Twohig, ed., *Papers, Retirement Series,* 4:173. On this theme in Weems's writings, see esp. Watts, *The Republic Reborn,* 141–51.

27 M. L. Weems, *God's revenge against gambling* (Philadelphia: Printed for the author, 1822), 20–21 and passim. On the relationship between gambling and an emerging capitalist ethos, see Ann Fabian, *Card Sharps, Dream Books, and Bucket Shops: Gambling in 19th-Century America* (Ithaca, N.Y.: Cornell University Press, 1990). What Weems preached publicly, he also advised privately. In 1818, Weems urged Carey to give his son—then apprenticed to Carey's firm—a stern lecture: "Remind him of . . . the importance of laying now a grand foundation for character, self approbation & Wealth." MLW to MC, n.d., after May 6, 1817, in Skeel, ed., *MLW,* III:194.

28 Weems, *A history, of the life and death, virtues, and exploits,* 28–29; Skeel, ed., *Three Discourses,* 166; Max Weber, *The Protestant Ethic and the Spirit of Capitalism;* trans. Talcott Parsons (London: Routledge, 1992), 51.

29 Credit is specifically due in this sentence—and more generally throughout the manuscript—to the excellent suggestions (and prose) of Fred Bode.

30 Skeel, ed., *Three Discourses,* 132.

31 Many thanks to Jim Green for making this observation to me. On the Methodist publishing industry, see James Penn Pilkington and Walter N. Vernon, *The Methodist Publishing House: A History* (Nashville, Tenn.: Abingdon Press, 1968); Candy Gunther Brown, *The Word in the World: Evangelical Writing, Publishing, and Reading in*

America, 1789–1880 (Chapel Hill: University of North Carolina Press, 2004); and David Paul Nord, *Faith in Reading: Religious Publishing and the Birth of Mass Media in America* (New York: Oxford University Press, 2004).

32 "The evangelist's ability" and "Doctors of Divinity": Frank Lambert, "Subscribing for Profits and Piety: The Friendship of Benjamin Franklin and George Whitefield," *William and Mary Quarterly* 3rd ser., 50 (1993): 529–54; quotations at 537–38; "Bishops and Lords": MLW to MC, September 1, 1799, in Skeel, ed., *MLW*, II:107; "Bench of Bishops" quoted in Skeel, "Mason Locke Weems: A Postscript," 245; Meade, *Old Churches, Ministers and Families*, II:234–35. On Weems's preaching, see Davis, *Travels of four years and a half*, 228–29. Davis's description of Weems's preaching is quoted at some length in William Stevens Perry, *The History of the American Episcopal Church, 1587–1883*, 2 vols. (Boston: J. R. Osgood, 1885), 631; and in Duyckinck and Duyckinck, *Cyclopedia of American literature*, 504–5. Davis also notes that Weems continued to preach to African Americans. For instances of sermons merged with bookselling, see MLW to MC, September 2, 1801, in Skeel, ed., *MLW*, II:198; January 15, 1802, in *MLW*, II:226; February 19, 1802, in *MLW*, II:229; July 22, 1802, in *MLW*, II:245; October 2 and 12, 1802, in *MLW*, II:249; and July 20, 1803, in *MLW*, II:267.

33 Benson Lossing, *Our Countrymen; or Brief Memories of Eminent Americans* (Philadelphia: Lippincott, Grambo & Co., 1855), 112.

34 On Mathew Carey—a distressingly understudied figure—see: *Mathew Carey Autobiography*, reprint ed. (New York: Research Classics, 1942); Earl Lockridge Bradsher, *Mathew Carey, Editor, Author and Publisher; A Study in American Literary Development* (New York: Columbia University Press, 1912); Edward C. Carter, "The Political Activities of Mathew Carey, Nationalist, 1760–1814" (Ph.D. dissertation, Bryn Mawr College, 1962); Carter, "Mathew Carey and 'The Olive Branch,' 1814–1818"; John William Tebbel, *A History of Book Publishing in the United States, Vol. 1: The Creation of an Industry, 1630–1865* (New York: R. R. Bowker Co., 1972), 106–14; Richard E. Amacher, "Mathew Carey," in *American Writers Before 1800: A Biographical and Critical Dictionary*, ed. James A. Levernier and Douglas R. Wilmes (Westport, Conn.: Greenwood Press, 1983), 272–75; James N. Green, *Mathew Carey, Publisher and Patriot* (Philadelphia: The Library Company of Philadelphia, 1985); and James N. Green, "Mathew Carey," in *American National Biography*, John A. Garraty and Mark C. Carnes, eds., 24 vols. (New York: Oxford University Press, 1999), IV:381–83.

35 Fitzpatrick, ed., *Writings*, XXX:7–8. For more on *The American Museum*, see Frank Luther Mott, *A History of American Magazines, 1741–1850*, 5 vols. (Cambridge, Mass.: Harvard University Press, 1938), 100–103.

36 "Your book no longer sells": Emily Ellsworth Ford Skeel, "Mason Locke Weems: A Post-

script," in *The New Colophon: A Book-Collectors' Miscellany* (New York: Duschnes Crawford, 1950), 244; "comic marriage": Wills, *Cincinnatus,* 45.

37 MLW to MC, March 24, 1801, in Skeel, ed., *MLW,* II:186; MLW to MC, June 19, 1807, in Skeel, ed., *MLW,* II:364–5. "For my own part," Weems once wrote, "I am not asham^d to acknowledge myself a firm *Believer* and, let me add, an ardent Admirer also of the Christian System. A Religion wh. teaches so Rational and Sublime a Devotion—'*Thou shalt love the Lord Thy God with all thy heart.*' A Religion which breathes such Angelic Charity—'*Thou shalt love thy Neighbor as thyself, and shalt do unto him as thou woudst he shou^d do unto thee.*' A Religion which confirms those best and noblest hopes of Nature—'*The Immortality of the Soul and a Glorious Futurity to the Virtuous,*' Such a religion is surely the most worthy of God, and most worthy of human acceptation; and I confess I have no idea of a religion better calculated to draw men off from Vice, to animate them to every thing Great and Good; and thus to refine, to sublime and to make Happy the whole Human Race." MLW to MC, October 12, 1802, in Skeel, ed., *MLW,* II:249–50. This use of the figure "Great and Good"—a characteristic so often ascribed to Washington—offers a telling hint of Weems's fusion of religion and nationalism.

38 Recorded as Evans numbers 36694, 36696, 36697, and 36698.

39 Weems, *The Philanthropist,* 2. The Brown essay was published as: William Laurence Brown, *An essay on the natural equality of men, on the rights that result from it and on the duties which it imposes* (Philadelphia: Printed for John Ormrod by William W. Woodward, 1793); it was also published the same year in Edinburgh by T. Duncan. John Ormrod, incidentally, was the person in charge of getting subscribers for Marshall's Washington biography in the North.

40 MLW to MC, September 17, 1799, in Skeel, ed., *MLW,* II:121. For the full text of Washington's endorsement letter, see Twohig, ed., *The Papers of George Washington: Retirement Series,* IV:273.

41 Weems, *The Philanthropist,* 4, 25, 26, 28.

42 MLW to MC, September 28, 1801, in Skeel, ed., *MLW,* II:202. The spelling of *sooth* is from the original text.

43 MLW to MC, December 3, 1801, in Skeel, ed., *MLW,* II:209.

44 MLW to MC, November 30, 1801, in Skeel, ed., *MLW,* II:208. Weems published Sidney's *Discourses* in 1805: Algernon Sidney, *Discourses concerning government: to which is added, a short account of the author's life and a copious index,* 2 vols. (Philadelphia: Printed and published by C. P. Wayne for M. L. Weems, 1805). On the influence of Sidney's *Discourses* in the American colonies, see Caroline Robbins, "Algernon Sidney's Discourses Concerning Government: Textbook of Revolution,"

William and Mary Quarterly 3rd ser., 4 (1947): 267–96, esp. 269–73. Thomas Jefferson was also a great admirer of Sidney's *Discourses*. When Weems asked Jefferson his opinion about the prospect of publishing Sidney's *Discourses*, Jefferson responded enthusiastically. If Weems was hoping for an endorsement from Jefferson, he could not have wished for better: "It is probably the best elementary book of the principles of government, as founded in natural right which has ever been published in any language," wrote Jefferson, "and it is much to be desired in such a government as ours that it should be put into the hands of our youth as soon as their minds are sufficiently matured for that branch of study . . . Should you proceed to the publication, be so good as to consider me a subscriber." (Thomas Jefferson to MLW, December 13, 1804, in Skeel, ed., *MLW,* II:307.) Jefferson's admiration for Sidney continued throughout his life. In 1825, Jefferson cited Sidney's work as one of the two best sources "as to the general principles of liberty and the rights of man, in nature and in society," and made it—along with Washington's Farewell Address— required reading for students at the University of Virginia. See "Minutes of the Board of Visitors," March 4, 1825, in Peterson, ed., *Writings,* 480.

45 Mason Locke Weems, *The True Patriot: or, An Oration, on the Beauties and Beatitudes of a Republic; and the Abominations and Desolations of Despotism* (Philadelphia: Printed for the author, by William W. Woodward, 1802), 13.

46 Weems, *The True Patriot,* 55, 56. This section was a jumble of quotations and paraphrases from Washington. The first three lines of what is identified by Weems as "Washington's Prayer for his Country" is from Washington's First Inaugural Address. The quoted words clearly echo the following from Washington's Farewell Address: "it is of infinite moment, that you should properly estimate the immense value of your national Union to your collective and individual happiness." See "Farewell Address," in Fitzpatrick, ed., *Writings,* XXXV:219.

47 MLW to MC, February 19, 1802, in Skeel, ed., *MLW,* II:229; *The Maryland & Virginia almanac; or Washington ephemeris: for the year of our Lord 1798; . . . Likewise, The way of wealth, Advice to young tradesmen and several useful tables* (George-Town [D.C.]: Printed by Green, English, & Co. for the Reverend Mason L. Weems, 1797), in "Preface" [no pagination]; *Weems's Washington Almanack* (Philadelphia: John Adams, 1803), n.p.; the quoted advertisement appeared in the *City Gazette,* March 6, 1804, in Skeel, ed., *MLW,* I:185.

48 *Weems's Washington Almanack,* [no pagination]; *City Gazette,* March 6, 1804, quoted in Skeel, ed., *MLW,* I:185; MLW to MC, July 25, 1803, in Skeel, ed., *MLW,* II:268.

49 See, for instance, Lance Banning, "Jeffersonian Ideology Revisited: Liberal and Classical Ideas in the New American Republic," *William and Mary Quarterly* 3rd ser., 43

(1986): 3–19, and Joyce Appleby, "Republicanism in Old and New Contexts," *William and Mary Quarterly* 3rd ser., 43 (1986): 20–43.

50 Weems, *A history of the life and death, virtues, and exploits,* "Dedication"; MLW to MC, February 2, 1800, in Skeel, ed., *MLW,* II:128.

51 Weems, *A history of the life and death, virtues, and exploits,* 77, 79; Weems, *The Life of Washington* (1809 ed.), 219; "First Inaugural Address," in Basler, ed., *Collected Works,* IV:268.

52 Weems, *A history, of the life and death, virtues, and exploits,* 79–80.

53 Ibid., 80.

54 MLW to MC, July 12, 1815, in Skeel, ed., *MLW,* III:128; *Life* (1809 ed.), 9, 6–23, 24, 213.

55 On the authenticity of the cherry tree story—a fruitless question to pursue, in my view—see Arthur H. Merritt, "Did Parson Weems Really Invent the Cherry-Tree Story?" *New-York Historical Society Quarterly* 40 (July 1956), 252–63.

56 William Holmes McGuffey, *McGuffey's new high school reader: for advanced classes, embracing about two hundred classic exercises* (Cincinnati and New York: Wilson, Hinkle and Co., 1857), 123–24. This anecdote, too, was often reprinted in nineteenth-century didactic literature. See, for instance, Weld, *Pictorial life of George Washington;* and Elson, *Guardians of Tradition,* 200–201. On the evangelization of the public sphere, see esp. Noll, *America's God.*

57 *Life* (1809 ed.), 17. It is interesting to note that by dwelling on the relationship between Washington and his father, Weems presents a striking contrast to the theme of bad fathers and orphaned children Lynn Hunt found running through French revolutionary literature. On which, see Hunt, *The Family Romance of the French Revolution.*

58 *Life* (1809 ed.), 25, 210; *Life* (1800 ed.), 5.

59 Quoted in Casper, *Constructing American Lives,* 69. Weems's 1809 edition was subtler on this matter.

60 Weems's book was not the only one to be dedicated to the youth of America. David Ramsay's history of Washington published in 1807 was also dedicated to the "Youth of the United States"—though another edition was (ironically?) dedicated to "Emporors, Kings and others." Likewise, after the 1809 edition, John Corry dedicated his biography of Washington to "the Youth of America." See W. S. Baker, ed., *Biblioteca Washingtoniana: A Descriptive List of the Biographies and Biographical Sketches of George Washington* (Philadelphia: Robert M. Lindsay, 1889 [1967]).

61 Weems, *Life* (1800 ed.), 1; [Mason Locke Weems,] *The Life and Memorable Actions of George Washington, General and Commander of the Armies of America, A New Edition Corrected* (Fredericktown [Md.]: M. Bartgis, 1801), 5; Baker, ed., *Biblioteca Washingtoniana;* Weems, *Life* (1800 ed.), 13.

62 MLW to MC, August 25, 1800, in Skeel, ed., *MLW,* II:141; MLW to MC, n.d. [late January] 1809, in Skeel, ed., *MLW,* II:387. These suggested revisions may have been proposed with an eye to recovering the copyright from Carey.

63 Duyckinck and Duyckinck, *Cyclopadia of American literature,* I:502.

64 Elson, *Guardians of Tradition,* 202–4.

65 On this image, see Wills, *Cincinnatus,* 39–41, and Casper, *Constructing American Lives.* Many thanks to David Steinberg for pointing out to me the slavery reference in Wood's painting.

66 Morrison Heady, *The farmer boy, and how he became commander-in-chief,* William Makepeace Thayer, ed. (Boston: Walker, Wise, and Company, 1864), 4, viii, 40–41. On this text, see also Castronovo, *Fathering the Nation,* 47–51. On the sales figures of Thayer's books, see James Grant Wilson and John Fiske, *Appleton's cyclopædia of American biography,* 6 vols. (New York: D. Appleton and Company, 1889), VI:74.

67 Heady, *The farmer boy,* 41–44.

68 Ibid., 44–45.

69 Webster's *New American Speller* translates "ad captandum" as "captivating."

70 Wallace, *A Parson at Large,* 18.

71 MLW to MC, January 12 or 13, 1800, in Skeel, ed., *MLW,* II:126; February 2, 1800, in *MLW,* II:127; July 12, 1800, in *MLW,* II:132; August 25, 1800, in *MLW,* II:141; November 26, 1800, in *MLW,* II:152. For other instances of Weems's use of martial language in reference to his books, see also MLW to MC, November 26, 1800, and March 24, 1801.

72 MLW to MC, n.d. [late January] 1809, in Skeel, ed., *MLW,* II:387; Friedman, *Inventors of the Promised Land,* 46.

73 Boorstin, *The Americans: The National Experience,* 340. Calling Weems "a literary Friar Tuck," Cathy Davidson accurately gauges Weems's creative process. "As he traveled around the country selling books, he also constantly sounded out booksellers and individual readers as to their literary preferences and then shaped his own impressionistic biographies accordingly, thereby anticipating the contemporary movie or television practice of polling the prospective audience and then creating the desired product." See Davidson, *Revolution and the Word,* 24. More recently, Scott Casper noted that "Weems's biographies sold prodigiously because he knew his audience better than any other biographer in the early republic." Casper, *Constructing American Lives,* 70.

74 MLW to MC, January 22, 1797, in Skeel, ed., *MLW,* II:72; MLW to MC, January 20, 1797, in Skeel, ed., *MLW,* II:70.

75 The $60,000 figure is from Tebbel, *History of Book Publishing*, 109. On Weems devoting himself to the sale of expensive books, see also MLW to MC, November 8, 1800: "Let me once more tell you that a fortune may be made by directing me to give my *whole attention* to subscription & distribution of Large & Valuable Works." Skeel, ed., *MLW*, II:150–51. The profit margin issue was clarified to me by Jim Green of the Library Company, to whom I owe many thanks for helping me sharpen this chapter, and for educating me on the early republican print industry more generally.

76 MLW to MC, October 30, 1796, in Skeel, ed., *MLW*, II:91; MLW to MC, January 22, 1797, in Skeel, ed., *MLW*, II:72; MLW to MC, February 1801, in Skeel, ed., *MLW*, II:167; MLW to MC, February 20, 1809, in Skeel, ed., *MLW*, II:391–92; MLW to MC, March 25, 1809, in Skeel, ed., *MLW*, II:397; MLW to MC, January 20, 1802, in Skeel, ed., *MLW*, II:227. On pricing books, see also MLW to MC, June 15, 1796, in Skeel, ed., *MLW*, II:17; and MLW to MC, November 19, 1798, in Skeel, ed., *MLW*, II:109. Cathy Davidson argues that low-priced books would not become profitable for several more decades—an assertion that seems belied (though perhaps uniquely so) by Weems's experiences. See Davidson, *Revolution and the Word*, 24. On the issue of pricing Bibles, see Scott Mandelbrote, "The English Bible and Its Readers in the Eighteenth Century," in *Books and Their Readers in Eighteenth-Century England: New Essays*, Isabel Rivers, ed. (London: Continuum, 2001), esp. 50–51.

77 MLW to MC, August 22, 1800, in Skeel, ed., *MLW*, II:140. Bracketed text in original.

78 MLW to MC, March 25, 1799, in Skeel, ed., *MLW*, II:116.

79 MLW to MC, January 20, 1797, in Skeel, ed., *MLW*, II:70; May 12, 1796, in *MLW*, II:10. The books requested are possibly the following editions: Charles Rollins, *The Ancient History of the Egyptians, Carthaginians, Assyrians, Babylonians, Medes and Persians, Grecians and Macedonians* (London: Printed for Allen and West, 1795); Thomas Hutchinson, *The History of Massachusetts, From the Settlement Thereof in 1628 Until the Year 1750* (Salem, Mass.: Thomas C. Cushing, 1795); and David Ramsay, *The History of the American Revolution*, 2 vols. (London: J. Stockdale, 1793). I have not been able to identify any edition of Smith's *History*, which suggests that Carey never followed Weems's advice to print the work.

80 MLW to MC, January 22, 1797, in Skeel, ed., *MLW*, II:72.

81 Almanacs, apparently, sold particularly well in the South. Referring to North Carolina, South Carolina, and Georgia, Weems once wrote that "They sell their Kalendars, as they do everything else here, as Men who think very little about God or Devil. I beg to tell you once more that Almanacks sell very high in this Country." MLW to MC, May 29, 1804, in Skeel, ed., *MLW*, II:298.

82 MLW to MC, January 20, 1797, in Skeel, ed., *MLW,* II:70; MLW to MC, March 22, 1797, in Skeel, ed., *MLW,* II:79; MLW to MC, October 30, 1796, in Skeel, ed., *MLW,* II:91; MLW to MC, March 10, 1798, in Skeel, ed., *MLW,* II:98; MLW to MC, September 28, 1801, in Skeel, ed., *MLW,* II:201; Weems, *Life* (1801 ed.), title page; Weems, *Life* (1809 ed.), 11–12.

83 MLW to MC, March 10, 1798, in Skeel, ed., *MLW,* II:98; MLW to MC, October 12, 1797, in Skeel, ed., *MLW,* II:44; MLW to MC, February 24, 1798, in Skeel, ed., *MLW,* II:96; MLW to MC, November 14, 1797, in Skeel, ed., *MLW,* II:92. For other examples of Weems using his fiddle expression, see March 10, 1798 and March 15, 1811. The books requested were perhaps the following editions: Philip Doddridge, *The Rise and Progress of Religion in the Soul . . .* (Philadelphia: Robert Campbell, 1794); Robert Russel, *Sermons on Different Important Subjects* (Baltimore, Md.: Samuel and John Adams for M. L. Weems, 1791), later published by Mathew Carey in 1795; George Whitefield, *Fifteen Sermons Preached on Various Important Subjects* (Philadelphia: Mathew Carey, 1794); Madame La Comtesse de Genlis, *Sacred Dramas: Written in French,* trans. Thomas Holcroft (Fredericksburg: Printed by L. A. Mullin for the Reverend Mason Locke Weems, 1797); and Henry Hunter, *Sacred Biography; or, The History of the Patriarchs . . .* (Boston: Manning & Loring, 1795). Offering one more piece of evidence that links Weems to later religious nineteenth-century religious publishing, it should be noted that Doddridge was the first book stereotyped by the American Tract Society, in 1828. See Karl Eric Valois, "To Revolutionize the World: The American Tract Society and the Regeneration of the Republic, 1825–1877" (Ph.D. dissertation, University of Connecticut, 1994), 117.

84 Meade, *Old Churches, Ministers and Families,* II:235; MLW to MC, September 1, 1799, in Skeel, ed., *MLW,* II:107. Meade continued: "He carried this spurious charity into his sermons. In my own pulpit at the old chapel, in my absence, it being my Sunday in Winchester, he extolled Tom Paine and one or more noted infidels in America, and said if their ghosts could return to the earth they would be shocked to hear the falsehoods which were told of them. I was present the following day, when my mother charged him with what she had heard of his sermon, and well remember that even he was confused and speechless." The edition of Paine Weems sold was most likely: Thomas Paine, *The Age Of Reason. Part the Second: Being an investigation of True and Fabulous Theology* (Philadelphia: Printed for the Booksellers [James Carey], 1796); the Watson edition was: Richard Watson, *An Apology for the Bible, In a Series of Letters Addressed to Thomas Paine, Author of the Book Entitled, The Age of Reason, Part the Second, Being an Investigation of True and Fabulous Theology*

(Philadelphia: James Carey, 1796). On religious divides in eighteenth-century Virginia, see esp. Isaac, *Transformation*.

85 MLW to MC, October 21, 1799, in Skeel, ed., *MLW*, II:123; MLW to MC, June 24, 1799, in Skeel, ed., *MLW*, II:120. The phrase translates roughly as "captivating to Americans' popular tastes."

86 Cunliffe, "Introduction," xvii. This story, along with a story about George's father planting cabbage plants in his name, were reprinted in McGuffey's *Eclectic Reader* series, thus canonizing them as central parables of a national mythos. See William Holmes McGuffey, *McGuffey's New Fourth Eclectic Reader: Instructive Lessons for the Young* (Cincinnati [and other places]: Wilson, Hinkle & Co. [and others], 1866), 69–74. The cherry tree story was later reprinted in other didactic literature, including *The Life of George Washington, Written for the American Sunday-School Union, and Revised by the Committee of Publication*, new ed. (Philadelphia: American Sunday School Union, 1842), and Jonathan Cross, *The Pilgrim Boy: With Lessons from His History: A Narrative of Facts* (New York: American Tract Society, 1857).

87 MLW to MC, October 12, 1796, in Skeel, ed., *MLW*, I:44.

88 Previous three quotations all from *Life* (1809 ed.), 18.

89 Ibid., 140, 161.

90 Fox quoted in Warner, *The Letters of the Republic: Publication and the Public Sphere in Eighteenth-Century America*, 2. On elite fears of novel reading, see Davidson, *Revolution and the Word*, chapter 3. On mediated reading in the eighteenth century, see also David D. Hall and Elizabeth Carroll Reilly, "Practices of Reading—Introduction," in Amory and Hall, eds., *History of the Book in America*, 379–80.

91 MLW to MC, July 12, 1800, in Skeel, ed., *MLW*, II:132, and October 17, 1800, in ibid., II:146; MLW to MC, August 8, 1800, ibid., II:135; MLW to MC, September 10, 1803, in ibid., II:274; MLW to MC, January 31, 1807, in ibid., II:358. For evidence of Weems selling books at court dates and horse races, see, inter alia, MLW to CPW, September 15, 1800; October 17, 1800; August 12, 1803; August 17, 1803; August 27, 1803; September 24, 1803; January 31, 1807; and more.

92 William Gilmore Simms, for one, had a sense of having seen Weems as a child: "I know not whether I can assert a personal knowledge of the venerable biographer. I am not sure that the vague impressions which I have of his air, gesture and physique, do not originate in the revelations of others. I will not be positive, but I certainly have some faint notion that mine eyes have been gratified, at a very early period in my life, with glimpses of his person." Simms, "Weems, The Biographer and Historian," 126–27. Consider, also, Van Wyck Brooks's description: "With his ruddy visage

and the lock that flowed over his clerical coat, one saw him bumping along in his Jersey wagon, a portable bookcase behind and a fiddle beside him. A little ink-horn hung from one of his lapels, and he carried a quill pen stuck in his hat; and he stopped now and then at a pond or a stream to wash his shirt and take a bath, suspending his linen to dry on the frame of the wagon." I do not know where Brooks found this detail; perhaps it is a feat of pure imagination, perhaps a description handed down to him orally. Many people, for instance, associate Weems with a fiddle, though I did not find any reference to it in his correspondence. Nevertheless, these descriptions of Weems suggest not only his ubiquity, but also paint him as a quasi-mythical figure in his own right. See Brooks, *The World of Washington Irving*, 1; and also Meade, *Old Churches, Ministers and Families*, II:235.

93 See Skeel, "Mason Locke Weems: A Postscript," 244. Carey also cultivated endorsements from local and national elites to help peddle his *American Museum* in the late 1780s and early 1790s. See Chester T. Hallenbeck, "Book-Trade Publicity Before 1800," *Papers of the Bibliographic Society of America* 32 (1938): 47–56.

94 MLW to George Washington, received July 6, 1792, Gratz American Prose Collection, Case 6 Box 13, Historical Society of Pennsylvania.

95 MLW to MC, July 19, 1812, in Skeel, ed., *MLW*, III:75; MLW to MC, December [18?], 1815, in ibid., III:143; MLW to CPW, December 10, 1802, in ibid., II:255; quoted in Skeel, "Mason Locke Weems; A Postscript," 245.

96 MLW to MC, January 12 or 13, 1800, in Skeel, ed., *MLW*, II:126–27; MLW to MC, n.d. (sometime in 1810), in ibid., III:26. The very act of traveling the country getting subscriptions for forthcoming books carried traces of older social hierarchies. As James Green has noted, the subscription method of selling books, which dated back to seventeenth-century England, "was an extension of the ancient system of aristocratic patronage of literature into the public sphere of print." James Green, "The Publishing History of Equiano's *Interesting Narrative*," *Slavery and Abolition* 16 (December 1995): 364.

97 MLW to MC, October 22, 1800, in Skeel, ed., *MLW*, II:148. I was unable to establish the nature of the conversation between Weems and Bushrod. On the use of the term "scribbling" to refer to his biography, see MLW to MC, n.d., received March 13, 1818, in ibid., III:230, and August 10, 1819, in ibid., III:250. Marshall's biography would be published as: John Marshall, *The Life of George Washington, commander in chief of the American forces, during the war which established the independence of his country, and first president of the United States*, 5 vols. (Philadelphia: Printed and published by C. P. Wayne, 1804–1807). On Marshall's biography, see Albert Jeremiah Beveridge,

The Life of John Marshall, 4 vols. (Boston: Houghton Mifflin, 1916), III:223–273; Daniel R. Gilbert, "John Marshall and the Development of a National History," in *The Colonial Legacy, vol. IV: Early Nationalist Historians,* Lawrence H. Leder, ed. (New York: Harper & Row, 1973); and the detailed editorial note in Charles E. Hobson, ed., *The Papers of John Marshall,* vol. IV (Chapel Hill: University of North Carolina Press in association with the Institute of Early American History and Culture, 1990), 219–226, along with the correspondence therein.

98 CPW to [Bushrod Washington?], December 20, 1801, "Negotiation for purchase of copy right," Historical Society of Pennsylvania, Dreer Collection, Box #58, Wayne-Weems Hills Papers, Folder: C. P. Wayne Letters (copies) 1801–03 to Washington & Marshall; and Beveridge, *Life of John Marshall,* III:225–26. They settled on $100,000. On the Ramsay figure, see Fredrika Teute, "Marshall's Life of George Washington: A Book Publishing Episode in the Early Republic" (Paper presented at the Institute of Early American History and Culture, in possession of James Green of the Library Company of Philadelphia).

99 Wayne "has met with such disappointments in this affair of Washington," Weems wrote to Carey in 1807, "gave so much for it—got so few sub^s. in comparison of what he expected . . . that I don't think he will do much more at the printing business." MLW to MC, May 24, 1807, in Skeel, ed., *MLW,* II:362.

100 Teute, "Marshall's Life of George Washington."

101 MLW to CPW, December 8, 1802, in Skeel, ed., *MLW,* II:254; MLW to CPW, December 10, 1802, in ibid., II:255; also quoted in Beveridge, *The Life of John Marshall,* III:232. On the importance of rural readers to the development of American literary culture, see William Charvat, *Literary Publishing in America, 1790–1850* (Philadelphia: University of Pennsylvania Press, 1959).

102 Jefferson quoted in Beveridge, *The Life of John Marshall,* III:229; MLW to CPW, December 14, 1802, in Skeel, ed., *MLW,* II:256; also quoted in Beveridge, *The Life of John Marshall,* III:232. On Jefferson/Barlow, see Teute, "Marshall's Life of George Washington," 16.

103 Bushrod Washington to CPW, March 1, 1803, in C. P. Wayne, Correspondence on *Life of Washington* by John Marshall, Historical Society of Pennsylvania, Dreer Collection, vol. 177, folder: Bushrod Washington, 1803; MLW to CPW, December 17, 1802, in Skeel, ed., *MLW,* II:257; MLW to CPW, April 18, 1803, in ibid., II:266; MLW to CPW, April 8, 1803, in ibid., II:264.

104 CPW to [Marshall?], February 17, 1803, Historical Society of Pennsylvania, Dreer Collection, Box #58, Wayne-Weems Hills Papers, Folder: C. P. Wayne Letters (copies)

1801–03 to Washington & Marshall; MLW to CPW, April 18, 1803, in Skeel, ed., *MLW,* II:265–66.

105 MLW to MC, May 24, 1807, in Skeel, ed., *MLW,* II:362; MLW to Thomas Jefferson, February 1, 1809, in Skeel, ed., *MLW,* II:389.

106 MLW to MC, September 16, 1800, in Skeel, ed., *MLW,* II:143.

107 MLW to MC, May 24, 1807, in Skeel, ed., *MLW,* II:362.

108 Beveridge, *The Life of John Marshall,* III:231–32, n1 and 2.

109 MLW to MC, March 25, 1809, in Skeel, ed., *MLW,* II:396; MLW to MC, October 12, 1821, in Skeel, ed., *MLW,* III:321.

110 Charles Francis Adams, Jr., to his father, November 30, 1862, in Worthington Chauncey Ford, ed., *A Cycle of Adams Letters, 1861–1865,* 2 vols. (Boston and New York: Houghton Mifflin Company, 1920), II:200.

CHAPTER 4: CIVIC TEXTS FOR SLAVE AND FREE

1 Douglass, *Narrative,* 33. I have drawn the page numbers of Frederick Douglass's auto-biographies from their original publications, which are now accessible online at the University of North Carolina's "Documenting the American South" project: http://docsouth.unc.edu.

2 Douglass, *Narrative,* 33.

3 The term "social death," of course, is drawn from the brilliant analysis of slavery in Orlando Patterson, *Slavery and Social Death: a Comparative Study* (Cambridge, Mass.: Harvard University Press, 1982).

4 Frederick Douglass, *My bondage and my freedom* (New York: Miller, Orton & Mulligan, 1855), 157; Douglass, *Narrative,* 39; Douglass, *My bondage and my freedom,* 158–59.

5 Douglass, *Narrative,* 40.

6 James T. Kloppenberg, "The Virtues of Liberalism: Christianity, Republicanism, and Ethics in Early American Political Discourse," *Journal of American History* 74 (1987): 9–33; quotation at 23.

7 Friedrich Nietzsche, *On the Genalogy of Morals* and *Ecce Homo,* trans., Walter Kaufmann (New York: Vintage Books, 1967), 57. On the development of the "modern self," I have been particularly influenced by Taylor, *Sources of the Self;* also Michel Foucault, *Surveiller et punir: naissance de la prison* (Paris: Gallimard, 1975); Agamben, *Homo sacer;* Michel Foucault, *Les mots et les choses; une archéologie des sciences humaines* (Paris: Gallimard, 1966). My account of autonomy is not a strict one by philosophical standards, and should not be confused with Kantian conceptions. For a much more rigorous and detailed philosophical study of the "invention" of autonomy, see J. B.

Schneewind, *The Invention of Autonomy: A History of Modern Moral Philosophy* (New York: Cambridge University Press, 1998). For an excellent related study, see Jean-Christophe Agnew, *Worlds Apart: The Market and the Theater in Anglo-American Thought, 1550–1750* (Cambridge, Eng.: Cambridge University Press, 1986). I clarify my understanding of the relationship between autonomy and the major American political traditions in Furstenberg, "Beyond Freedom and Slavery," 1298–1300.

8 Davis, *The Problem of Slavery in the Age of Revolution,* 264, 263. On the relationship of new conceptions of subjectivity to antislavery, see Thomas L. Haskell, "Capitalism and the Origins of the Humanitarian Sensibility, Part 1," *American Historical Review* 90 (1985): 339–61; Haskell, "Capitalism and the Origins of the Humanitarian Sensibility, Part 2," *American Historical Review* 90 (1985): 547–66; Haskell, "Convention and Hegemonic Interest in the Debate Over Slavery: A Reply to Davis and Ashworth," *American Historical Review* 92 (1987): 829–78.

9 The classic account of this is Eric Foner, *Free Soil, Free Labor, Free Men: The Ideology of the Republican Party before the Civil War* (New York: Oxford University Press, 1970).

10 MLW to MC, February 23, 1809, in Skeel, ed., *MLW,* II:393; MLW to Thomas Jefferson, February 1, 1809, in Skeel, ed., *MLW,* II:389.

11 Elson, *Guardians of Tradition,* vii. See also Anne M. Boylan, *Sunday School: The Formation of an American Institution, 1790–1880* (New Haven, Conn.: Yale University Press, 1988), 53.

12 Shipton, Mooney, and Bristol, *The Short-Title Evans,* II: 556–59. Charles F. Heartman counted 213 editions printed before 1800, and 244 between 1800 and 1830. Charles F. Heartman, *The New-England Primer Issued Prior to 1830; A Bibliographical Check-List for the More Easy Attaining the True Knowledge of This Book* (New York: R. R. Bowker Company, 1934). See also Paul Leicester Ford, *The New-England primer; A history of its origin and development; with a reprint of the unique copy of the earliest known edition and many fac-simile illustrations and reproductions* (New York: Printed for Dodd Mead and Co., 1897). A figure of 6 to 8 million comes from Heartman, *The New-England Primer,* xxii. The figure of 6 million is endorsed in: Patricia Crain, *The story of A: The Alphabetization of America from* The New England Primer *to* The Scarlet Letter (Stanford, Calif.: Stanford University Press, 2000), 15. John Nietz, however, puts the figure at 3 million: See John Alfred Nietz, *Old Textbooks: Spelling, Grammer, Reading, Arithmetic, Geography, American History, Civil Government, Physiology, Penmanship, Art, Music, as Taught in The Common Schools from Colonial Days to 1900* (Pittsburgh: University of Pittsburgh Press, 1961), 50.

13 [Benjamin Harris,] *The Protestant tutor. Instructing children to spel [sic] and read English and grounding them in the true Protestant religion and discovering the errors and*

deceits of the papists (London: Printed for Ben. Harris under the Piazza of the Royal Exchange in Cornhill, 1679); *The Protestant Tutor for Children . . . To which is Added Verses made by Mr. John Rogers a Martyr in Queen Maries Reign . . .* (Boston in New-England: Samuel Green, 1685 and 1689); *The New-England primer enlarged. For the more easy attaining the true reading of English. To which is added, the Assembly of divines catechism* (Boston: S. Kneeland, & T. Green, 1727). On Harris and his shop and the *New-England Primer,* see Nietz, *Old Textbooks,* 47–50. Nietz states that a newspaper advertised a second and enlarged edition of the *New England Primer* in 1690. On Franklin's edition: *The New-England primer enlarged. For the more easy attaining the true reading of English. To which is added, the Assembly's catechism* (Philadelphia: Printed and sold by B. Franklin, and D. Hall, in Market-street, 1764); and Heartman, *The New-England Primer.*

14 Ford, *The New-England primer,* 92.

15 Ibid., 2.

16 Michael Walzer, *The Revolution of the Saints: A Study in the Origins of Radical Politics* (London: Weidenfeld & Nicolson, 1965), 312.

17 Taylor, *Sources of the Self,* 256, 195, and passim. See also Perry Miller, *New England Mind: The Seventeenth Century,* 365–491.

18 Hatch, *The Democratization of American Christianity,* 41; Sidney Earl Mead, *The Lively Experiment: The Shaping of Christianity in America* (New York: Harper & Row, 1963), 113; see 65–66, 90–102, 113–21. See also Gordon S. Wood, "Religion and the American Revolution," in *New Directions in American Religious History,* Harry S. Stout and D. G. Hart, eds. (New York: Oxford University Press, 1997), 173–205, esp. 194–95. "To be religious in America [during the nineteenth century] was not only to make choices, but to choose among astonishing varieties of religion created in America." Jon Butler, *Awash in a Sea of Faith,* quoted in Howe, "Protestantism, Voluntarism, and Personal Identity in Antebellum America," 207.

19 Ford, *The New-England primer,* 89. The *New-England Primer* shown here (figure 38) misdates Roger's execution, putting it in 1554.

20 Compare *Beauties of the New-England Primer* (New York: Samuel Wood & Sons, 1822) to Ford, *The New-England primer.* See also Fliegelman, *Prodigals and Pilgrims,* 129.

21 Nietz, *Old Textbooks,* 54, and the table on pp. 52–53, itself gleaned from Roscoe R. Robinson, *Two Centuries of Change in the Content of School Readers* (Nashville, Tenn.: George Peabody College for Teachers, 1930).

22 The 200,000 figure is from David Blight's introduction in Caleb Bingham, *The Columbian Orator: Containing a Variety of Original and Selected Pieces Together with*

Rules, Which Are Calculated to Improve Youth and Others, in the Ornamental and Useful art of Eloquence, ed. David W. Blight (New York: New York University Press, 1998), xvii, itself drawn from an unpublished paper to which I do not have access; and from Granville Ganter, "The Active Virtue of the *Columbian Orator,*" *New England Quarterly* 70, no. 3 (1997): 463–76. Blight estimates the number of editions of the *Columbian Orator* at twenty-three, so he may understate this figure of 200,000. Ganter (463, n3) also suggests the figure might be understated. On Lincoln, see Michael P. Johnson, ed., *Abraham Lincoln, Slavery, and the Civil War: Selected Writings and Speeches* (Boston: Bedford/St. Martin's, 2001), 4, and Blight, "Introduction" in Bingham, *Columbian Orator,* xviii; on Emerson and Stowe, see Ganter, "The Active Virtue of the *Columbian Orator,*" 464.

23 Page numbers have been taken from the Blight edition of the *Columbian Orator,* cited above. The text is also accessible via the Internet, at the 19th-Century Schoolbooks project at the University of Pittsburgh. See http://digital.library.pitt.edu/ nietz/. On the relationship between oratory and republicanism, see esp. Kenneth Cmiel, *Democratic Eloquence: The Fight over Popular Speech in Nineteenth-Century America* (New York: W. Morrow, 1990), and Carolyn Eastman, "A Nation of Speechifiers: Oratory, Print, and the Making of a Gendered American Public" (Ph.D. dissertation, Johns Hopkins University, 2001). On the importance of virtue in the *Columbian Orator,* see Ganter, "The Active Virtue of the *Columbian Orator.*"

24 Charles Rollin, in John Locke, *Some Thoughts Concerning Education, To which are added New Thoughts Concerning Education* (Dublin: R. Reilly, 1738), 14; Charles Rollin, *De la maniere d'enseigner et d'etudier les belles lettres . . . Troisième Edition, revue & corrigée* (Paris: Jacques Estienne, 1730); Rollin, *New Thoughts,* iv, bound with: Locke, *Some Thoughts Concerning Education.* See also Lawrence Arthur Cremin, *American Education, the National Experience, 1783–1876* (New York: Harper and Row, 1980), 148; and Ganter, "The Active Virtue of the *Columbian Orator,*" 471. For more on the use of exemplary figures in schoolbooks, see Elson, *Guardians of Tradition,* 186–208. The copy of Rollin, *De la maniere,* in the Library Company of Philadelphia bears the inscription: "R^d Rush's / Presented to him by his father." All quotations from this book are my translation. On Rollin assigned at Dartmouth, see Ganter, "The Active Virtue of the *Columbian Orator,*" 470–71. On Rollin's influence more generally, see David Lundberg and Henry F. May, "The Enlightened Reader in America," *American Quarterly* 28 (Summer, 1976), esp. 265–71, 278–79; and Fliegelman, *Prodigals and Pilgrims,* 42–44.

25 Fliegelman, *Prodigals and Pilgrims,* 12.

26 Locke, *Some Thoughts Concerning Education,* 5; Fliegelman, *Prodigals and Pilgrims,* 13.

27 Locke, *Some Thoughts Concerning Education*, 8. On the importance of this phrase, see esp. Uday Singh Mehta, *The Anxiety of Freedom: Imagination and Individuality in Locke's Political Thought* (Ithaca, N.Y.: Cornell University Press, 1992).

28 Locke, *Some Thoughts Concerning Education*, 27–28.

29 Ibid., 32, 38, 45. On the problem of physical discipline in antebellum U.S. literature, see esp. Richard H. Brodhead, *Cultures of Letters: Scenes of Reading and Writing in Nineteenth-Century America* (Chicago: University of Chicago Press, 1993), 13–47.

30 Locke, *Some Thoughts Concerning Education*, 44. On this theme, see the very insightful discussion in Fliegelman, *Declaring Independence*.

31 Walzer, *Revolution of the Saints*, 302. Walzer is referring generally to Puritans here, but it is hardly a distortion to apply his statement to Locke and to modern political practice.

32 Here my interpretation departs from the excellent article by Ganter, "The Active Virtue of the *Columbian Orator*."

33 Bingham, *Columbian Orator*, 43–44.

34 Ibid., 114, 134.

35 Ibid., 167.

36 Brodhead, *Cultures of Letters*, 47. See also Reilly and Hall, "Modalities of Reading," 407.

37 Bingham, *Columbian Orator*, 171.

38 Schneewind, *Invention of Autonomy*, 47.

39 Bingham, *Columbian Orator*, 200.

40 Lincoln on Murray's reader is quoted in the excellent study by Charles Monaghan, *The Murrays of Murray Hill* (Brooklyn, N.Y.: Urban History Press, 1998); the two subsequent quotations are from ibid., 4, 137. The Murray publication numbers are from ibid., 95, 130–34. According to Jennifer Monaghan, only two books can claim to have surpassed the total sales of Webster's *Speller* in the United States: the Bible and McGuffey's readers. Consider Webster's sales by way of contrast. Although the publishers claimed that 70 million copies were sold by 1950, Monaghan estimates that 8.85 million copies of the speller were sold by 1832. Total sales of the speller from 1783 to 1843 she estimates at 12.7 million, stressing, however, that her guesses are conservative. E. Jennifer Monaghan, *A Common Heritage: Noah Webster's Blue-Back Speller* (Hamden, Conn.: Archon Books, 1983). On Murray as the most widely read schoolbook, see also Nietz, *Old Textbooks*, 13. Murray's readers, along with the Bible, appear to have composed the backbone of Quaker publisher George Collins's business once he established himself in New York—he was the only authorized

American printer. Collins printed no fewer than sixteen editions of Murray's various schoolbooks, and in all likelihood printed far more. See Monaghan, *Murrays of Murray Hill*, 193–97. In 1804 Collins also published Joseph Lancaster, *Improvements in Education*, a thirty-nine-page pamphlet.

41 Elizabeth Frank, ed., *Memoirs of the Life and Writings of Lindley Murray: In a Series of Letters, Written by Himself* (York, Eng.: Longman, Rees, Orme, Brown, and Green, 1826), 95; Lindley Murray, *The English Reader: Or, Pieces in Prose And Poetry. Selected From the Best Writers. Designed to Assist Young Persons to Read With Propriety and Effect; to Improve Their Language and Sentiments; and to Inculcate Some of the Most Important Principles of Piety and Virtue. With a Few Preliminary Observations on the Principles of Good Reading* (New York: Isaac Collins and Son, 1802), 1. The book was so popular that a French version was published in New York and Philadelphia in 1812 with the same aims of teaching virtue and morality through the instruction of language—although the actual selection of works was very different. Curiously, however—since the French Bibliothèque Nationale has no copies of this work in its collection—it appears not to have been published in France. Perhaps it was intended for the instruction of French as a foreign language, or for the French-speaking expatriate communities living in those two North American cities. Murray's *Reader* is also listed as one of the few assigned books in the annual reports of the free school society from 1814 to 1825. See the *Ninth Annual Report of the Trustees of the Free School Society of New-York*; the *Tenth Annual Report of the Trustees of the Free School Society of New-York*; and so on, dated 1814 to 1825. The ninth through the eighteenth annual reports can be found in a bound volume of pamphlets filed under: Trustees, Printed Annual Reports, Circulars, and Other Printed Matter, 1814–1841, Public School Society of the City of New-York, The New-York Historical Society.

42 Murray, *English Reader* (1802 ed.), 1, 12, 13, 14.

43 Lindley Murray, *The English reader, or Pieces in prose and poetry: selected from the best writers: designed to assist young persons to read with propriety and effect, to improve their language and sentiments, and to inculcate some of the most important principles of piety and virtue: with a few preliminary observations on the principles of good reading* (Utica, N.Y.: Hastings & Tracy, 1827), 29; *Nineteenth Annual Report of the Trustees of the Free School Society of New-York* . . . (New York: Samuel Wood and Sons, 1824), 6–7. See also Michael B. Katz, "From Voluntarism to Bureaucracy in American Education," *Sociology of Education* 44 (1971): 297–332.

44 Murray, *English Reader* (1802 ed.), 3, 21; Murray, *English Reader* (1827 ed.), 79. This selection also appeared in: Rufus Adams, *The Young Gentleman and Lady's Ex-*

planatory Monitor (Zanesville, Ohio: 1815), quoted in Elson, *Guardians of Tradition*, 214.

45 Isaac Kramnick, "Children's Literature and Bourgeois Ideology: Observations on Culture and Industrial Capitalism in the Later Eighteenth Century," in *Studies in Eighteenth-Century Culture* 12, Harry C. Payne, ed. (Madison: University of Wisconsin Press, for the American Society for Eighteenth-Century Studies), 11–44, esp. 23, 27, 36; quotation at 23. See also Elson, *Guardians of Tradition*, 212–28.

46 Kramnick, "Children's Literature and Bourgeois Ideology," 23. On the significance of orphans in the cultural production of the French revolution, see Hunt, *The Family Romance of the French Revolution*.

47 Noah Webster, *An American selection of lessons in reading and speaking. Calculated to improve the minds and refine the taste of youth. And also to instruct them in the geography, history, and politics of the United States. To which are prefixed, rules in elocution, and directions for expressing the principal passions of the mind. Being the third part of A grammatical institute of the English language* (Boston: Isaiah Thomas and Ebenezer T. Andrews, 1799), 32–34.

48 Caleb Alexander, *The young gentlemen and ladies instructor: being a selection of new pieces; designed as a reading book for the use of schools and academies . . .* (Boston: Printed [by Samuel Etheridge] for E. Larkin, and W. P. & L. Blake, 1797), 12–14.

49 Elson, *Guardians of Tradition*, 213; Abner Alden, *The Reader: Containing I. The art of delivery, articulation . . . a selection of lessons in the various kinds of prose: II. Poetick numbers . . . a selection of lessons in the various kinds of verse: being the third part of a Columbian exercise* (Boston: I. Thomas and E. T. Andrews, 1802), 21; Elson, *Guardians of Tradition*, 213; Nathaniel Heaton, *The Columbian preceptor: Containing a Variety of New Pieces in Prose, Poetry, and Dialogues; with Rules for Reading. Selected from the Most Approved Authors. For the Use of Schools in the United States*, 2nd ed. (Wrentham, Mass.: D. Heaton for the Author, 1801), 9.

50 John William Ward, *Andrew Jackson: Symbol for an Age* (New York: Oxford University Press, 1955), 171, 176; schoolbooks quoted in ibid., 166, 175.

51 On refinement, see esp. Richard L. Bushman, *The Refinement of America: Persons, Houses, Cities* (New York: Vintage Books, 1992); on the association between industry and virtue, see esp. Gordon S. Wood, *The Radicalism of the American Revolution* (New York: Knopf, 1992), 170–71, 276–86; Judith N. Shklar, *American Citizenship: The Quest for Inclusion* (Cambridge, Mass.: Harvard University Press, 1991), 63–101; and Eric Foner, "The Idea of Free Labor in Nineteenth-Century America," in *Free Soil, Free Labor, Free Men* (1995 edition), xiii–xiv, xxiii–xxiv. Joyce Appleby sees the

texts like the popular autobiographies she examined as testaments to the liberal, capitalist ethos of antebellum America. What she may underestimate is the extent to which these kinds of texts were not just reflecting, but actively promoting, this ethos. See Appleby, *Inheriting the Revolution.*

52 The literature on this subject is too vast to cite here. See, however, Amy Dru Stanley, *From Bondage to Contract: Wage Labor, Marriage, and the Market in the Age of Slave Emancipation* (Cambridge, Eng.: Cambridge University Press, 1998), and the literature she cites on ix–xiii and 5, n12.

53 Weber, *The Protestant Ethic,* 62.

54 Edgar Wallace Knight, *A Documentary History of Education in the South before 1860,* 5 vols. (Chapel Hill: University of North Carolina Press, 1949), V:474–77; Robert L. Hall, "Black and White Christians in Florida, 1822–1861," in *Masters and Slaves in the House of the Lord: Race and Religion in the American South, 1740–1870,* John B. Boles, ed. (Lexington: University Press of Kentucky, 1988), 257. See also the fine study by Janet Duitsman Cornelius, *"When I Can Read My Title Clear": Literacy, Slavery, and Religion in the Antebellum South* (Columbia: University of South Carolina Press, 1991); Horace Mann Bond, *Negro Education in Alabama: A Study in Cotton and Steel* (New York: Octagon Books, 1969), 14–15; and Dana Nelson Salvino, "The Word in Black and White: Ideologies of Race and Literacy in Antebellum America," in *Reading in America: Literature and Social History,* Cathy N. Davidson, ed. (Baltimore, Md.: Johns Hopkins University Press, 1989), 197. Virginia law quotation is from Knight, *A Documentary History of Education in the South before 1860.* See also June Purcell Guild, *Black Laws of Virginia: A Summary of the Legislative Acts of Virginia concerning Negroes from Earliest Times to the Present* (New York: Negro Universities Press, 1969), and Paul Finkelman, *Statutes on Slavery: The Pamphlet Literature,* 2 vols., (New York: Garland, 1988). For a comprehensive bibliography on reading, rumor, and the relationship between literacy and social stability, see Michael P. Johnson, "Denmark Vesey and His Co-conspirators," *William and Mary Quarterly* 3rd ser., 58 (2001): 915–76.

55 Quoted in Richard D. Brown, *The Strength of a People: The Idea of an Informed Citizenry in America, 1650–1870* (Chapel Hill: University of North Carolina Press, 1996), 27.

56 Douglass, *Narrative,* 37.

57 Seabrook, *Southern Presbyterian Review,* and the Southerner (Judge John Belton O'Neall, South Carolina Baptist), all quoted in Cornelius, *"When I Can Read My Title Clear,"* 41, 139, 57; Edward R. Laurens, *A letter to the Hon. Whitemarsh B. Seabrook, of St. John's Colleton . . . in Explanation and Defence of An Act to Amend the*

Law in Relation to Slaves and Free Persons of Color (Charleston, S.C.: Observer Office Press, 1835), 23–24.

58 W. E. B. DuBois estimated that a majority of free blacks could read and write at the time of emancipation, and that about 5 percent of slaves could. See W. E. B. DuBois, *Black Reconstruction in America* (New York: Atheneum, 1992), 638. Thomas L. Webber, author of the only full-length monograph on slave education that I know of, supports that conclusion. See Thomas L. Webber, *Deep Like the Rivers: Education in the Slave Quarter Community, 1831–1865* (New York: W. W. Norton, 1978), 13. Eugene Genovese quotes the DuBois figure, adding, "it is entirely plausible and may even be too low." See Genovese, *Roll, Jordan, Roll,* 563. Carter Woodson estimated slave literacy at 10 percent of slaves. See C. G. Woodson, *The Education of the Negro prior to 1861* (Salem, N.H.: Ayer, 1991), chapter 1. Janet Cornelius agrees with this estimate. See Cornelius, *"When I Can Read My Title Clear,"* 7–10. See also Eric Foner, *Reconstruction: America's Unfinished Revolution, 1863–1877* (New York: Harper & Row, 1988), 96.

59 Cornelius, *"When I Can Read My Title Clear,"* 6.

60 "Far from being the appendage to proslavery that it would afterward become," argues historian Larry Tise, "the movement to give slaves the essence of Christian knowledge seems clearly to have been an outgrowth of benevolence as it bubbled up through the placid surface of pre-abolitionist southern culture." Tise, *Proslavery,* 298.

61 The best work I have found on Charles Colcock Jones is Erskine Clarke, *Wrestlin' Jacob: A Portrait of Religion in the Old South* (Atlanta, Ga.: John Knox Press, 1979). See also Robert Manson Myers, ed., *The Children of Pride: A True Story of Georgia and the Civil War* (New Haven, Conn.: Yale University Press, 1972).

62 Charles Colcock Jones, *The religious instruction of the Negroes. A sermon, delivered before associations of planters in Liberty and M'Intosh counties, Georgia* (Princeton, N.J.: D'Hart & Connolly, 1832), 6–7, 26, 25.

63 *Fifth Annual Report of the Association for the Religious Instruction of the Negroes in Liberty County, Georgia. January 1840* (Charleston, S.C.: Observer Office Press, 1840), 14; Pinckney quoted in Jones, *Religious Instruction, (*1832 ed.), 35, nA; "Sermon Addressed to Masters and Mistresses," in T. T. Castleman, *Plain Sermons for Servants* (Philadelphia: King & Baird, 1851), 17–18, 16; Charles Colcock Jones, *The religious instruction of the Negroes in the United States* (Savannah, Ga.: Thomas Purse, 1842), 208–9.

64 B. McBride in *Southern Agriculturalist* III (May, 1830), 238; Roswell King, "On the Management of the Butler Estate, and the Cultivation of the Sugar Cane," *Southern Agriculturalist* I (1828), 527; *Proceedings of the meeting in Charleston, S. C., May 13–15, 1845, on the religious instruction of the Negroes, together with the report of the committee, and the address to the public. Pub. by order of the meeting* (Charleston, S.C.:

B. Jenkins, 1845), 9; "Sermon Addressed to Masters and Mistresses," in Castleman, *Plain Sermons for Servants*, 17–18. On the Charleston meeting, see also Donald G. Mathews, *Slavery and Methodism: A Chapter in American Morality, 1780–1845* (Princeton, N.J.: Princeton University Press, 1965), 83; Blake Touchstone, "Planters and Slave Religion in the Deep South," in *Masters and Slaves in the House of the Lord: Race and Religion in the American South, 1740–1870*, John B. Boles, ed. (Lexington: University Press of Kentucky, 1988), 101; and Clarke, *Wrestlin' Jacob*, 100–107.

65 Pinckney, *Address to the Agricultural Society . . .* (1829), quoted in Jones, *Religious Instruction* (1832 ed.), 37, nE; Jones, *The religious instruction* (1842 ed.), 215.

66 C. F. Sturgis, "Melville Letters; or, The Duties of Masters to their Servants," in *Duties of Masters to Servants: Three Premium Essays* (Freeport, N.Y.: Books for Libraries Press, 1971), 26–128, quotation at 133; *Fifth Annual Report of the Association for the Religious Instruction of the Negroes*, 13.

67 Jones, *The religious instruction* (1842 ed.), 244; Watts quoted in Kramnick, "Children's Literature and Bourgeois Ideology," 21; Jones, *The religious instruction* (1842 ed.), 266. On Lancaster's endorsement of Watts, see Joseph Lancaster, *Improvements in education, as it respects the industrious classes of the community . . . From the Third London Edition, with Additions, to which is prefaced a Sketch of the New-York Free School* (New York: Collins and Perkins, 1807); on Weems's sales of Watts, see Skeel, ed., *MLW*, II:404; on Jones's endorsement, see Jones, *The religious instruction* (1842 ed.), 265–66. On Watts's influence more generally, see Gilmore, *Reading Becomes a Necessity of Life*, 262; and Fliegelman, *Prodigals and Pilgrims*, 19–21. On slave songs, see esp. Shane White and Graham White, *The Sounds of Slavery: Discovering African American History through Songs, Sermons, and Speech* (Boston: Beacon Press, 2005).

68 T. T. Castleman, "The Christian's Life a Life of Prayer," in Castleman, *Plain Sermons for Servants*, 32; Randy J. Sparks, "Religion in Amite County, Mississippi, 1800–1861," in Boles, ed., *Masters and Slaves in the House of the Lord*, 58–80, quotation at 64; Thomas Bacon [abridged by Bishop Meade], "Duties of Servants to Masters and Fellow-Servants," in Castleman, *Plain Sermons for Servants*, 368. On the use of Episcopalian catechisms by Methodist clergymen, see Mathews, *Slavery and Methodism*, 77.

69 "Servants Should Obey Their Masters," in Castleman, *Plain Sermons for Servants*, 45; "Duties of Servants to God," in Castleman, *Plain Sermons for Servants*, 363; Bacon, "Duties of Servants to Masters and Fellow-Servants," in Castleman, *Plain Sermons for Servants*, 368; Castleman, *Plain Sermons for Servants*, 371.

70 Jones, *The religious instruction* (1842 ed.), 242. This quotation, unlike the others in this paragraph, was directed to masters and not to slaves.

71 Baptist Association quoted in Sparks, "Religion in Amite County," 64; John F. Hoff, *A Manual of Religious Instruction, Specially Intended for the Oral Teaching of Colored Persons, but adapted to general use in Families and Schools* (Philadelphia: King & Baird, 1852). Bishop Whittingham's "Prayer for Servants" urged the same. "Give us grace, O LORD, to be sober, diligent, and honest, in the business of our stations, and to behave ourselves with respect and submission to those whom thou has set over us." Bishop William R. Whittingham, Prayers for Servants, n.d., MSS, Episcopal Diocese of Maryland.

72 "Servants Should Obey Their Masters," in Castleman, *Plain Sermons for Servants,* 44–45.

73 "Servants Should Obey Their Masters," in Castleman, *Plain Sermons for Servants,* 40, 37, 38. For this theme in Northern didactic literature, see, for instance, "Little Dog Trusty," in William Biglow, *The youth's library: A Selection of Lessons in Reading. Intended as a Sequel to "The Child's Library."* (Salem, Mass.: Joshua Cushing, 1803); *American Popular Lessons, Chiefly Selected From the Writings of Mrs. Barbauld, Miss Edgeworth, and other approved writers . . .* (New York: R. Lockwood, 1830); Hannah More, *Stories for the Young; or, Cheap Repository Tracts: Entertaining, Moral, and Religious. A New Revised Edition. Vol. V* (New York: American Tract Society, 1845).

74 "Servants Should Obey Their Masters," in Castleman, *Plain Sermons for Servants,* 39–40; Methodist catechism quoted in Mathews, *Slavery and Methodism,* 78 and 78, n38.

75 Ibid., 78.

76 Charles E. Ambler, "The Gain of a Lost Soul," in Castleman, *Plain Sermons for Servants,* 394; Asbury quoted in Davis, *The Problem of Slavery in the Age of Revolution;* Cornelius, *"When I Can Read My Title Clear,"* 28; Boles, ed., *Masters and Slaves in the House of the Lord,* 9. See also Mathews, *Slavery and Methodism.*

77 John W. Blassingame, *The Slave Community: Plantation Life in the Antebellum South,* rev. and enl. ed. (New York: Oxford University Press, 1979), 130–31; ex-slave quoted in Cremin, *American Education,* 223.

78 Blassingame, *The Slave Community,* 145; Albert J. Raboteau, *Slave Religion: The "Invisible Institution" in the Antebellum South* (New York: Oxford University Press, 1978), 311.

79 Raboteau, *Slave Religion,* 287–88.

80 On which, see esp. Raboteau, *Slave Religion,* 290–318. A slightly different view is elaborated in Genovese, *Roll, Jordan, Roll.*

81 Raboteau, *Slave Religion,* 318; Blassingame, *The Slave Community,* 147–48.

82 "The civil law does not forbid us to give them the Gospel *orally.* We can therefore employ or permit men to visit our plantations for the purpose of instructing them; or

we can undertake to instruct them ourselves." Jones, *The religious instruction,* (1832 ed.), 7–8, 18.

83 Hoff, *A Manual of Religious Instruction;* Jones, *The religious instruction* (1842 ed.), 159.

84 Castleman, *Plain Sermons for Servants,* 7; Nelson, "The Advantages of Hearing God's Word"; Nelson, "What the Scriptures Teach Us"; and Castleman, "The Christian's Life a Life of Prayer," all in Castleman, *Plain Sermons for Servants,* 239, 228, 24.

85 Alexander Glennie, *Sermons preached on plantations to congregations of negroes* (Charleston, S.C.: A. E. Miller, 1844), iii; *Proceedings of the meeting in Charleston,* 20; A. T. Holmes, "The Duties of Christian Masters," in *Duties of Masters to Servants,* 149; Bingham, *Columbian Orator,* 167.

86 Holland Nimmons McTyeire, "Master and Servant," in *Duties of Masters to Servants,* 1–46; quotation at 26; King, "On the Management of the Butler Estate," 525; Jones, *The religious instruction* (1842 ed.), 241; King, "On the Management of the Butler Estate," 524.

87 Jones, *The religious instruction* (1832 ed.), 26. On prison reform, see David J. Rothman, *The Discovery of the Asylum: Social Order and Disorder in the New Republic,* rev. ed. (Boston: Little, Brown, 1990); Walters, *American Reformers, 1815–1860,* esp. 196–97; Fliegelman, *Declaring Independence,* 138 and passim; and, of course, Foucault, *Surveiller et punir,* on which all of these authors draw.

88 Bingham, *Columbian Orator,* 171; Sermon Preached to the Negroes, August 20, 1797, in Shelf: Reverend Bend, Sermons 1792, Episcopal Diocese of Maryland; "Duties of Servants to Masters and Fellow-Servants. By The Reverend. Thomas Bacon— Abridged By Bishop Meade," in Castleman, *Plain Sermons for Servants,* 368; Methodists quoted in Mathews, *Slavery and Methodism,* 79.

89 Castleman, "God's Eye Always On Us"; "Sermon 1. Addressed To Masters And Mistresses, On The Subject Of The Religious Instruction Of Their Slaves; Extracted From The Sermons Of The Rev. Thomas Bacon, By The Right Rev. Bishop Meade," both in Castleman, *Plain Sermons for Servants,* 319–20, 16. Episcopalian Bishop William Whittingham's morning prayer intended for "servants" began the slaves' day with: "Oh, make us to remember this through all this day, that we may neither say, nor do, anything for wch we may be afraid to answer in the dreadful day when thou shalt judge the world." Bishop William R. Whittingham, Prayers for Servants, n.d., MSS, Episcopal Diocese of Maryland.

90 Quoted in Frederick A. Bode, "The Formation of Evangelical Communities in Middle Georgia: Twiggs County, 1820–1861," *Journal of Southern History* 60 (1994): 711–48, quotation at 733. Many thanks to Fred Bode for sharing his research with me, as well as his excellent comments on this chapter.

91 *Proceedings of the meeting in Charleston,* 9; Sturgis, "Melville Letters," in *Duties of Masters to Servants,* 93; Holmes, "The Duties of Christian Masters"; McTyeire, "Master and Servant"; and Holmes, "The Duties of Christian Masters," all in *Duties of Masters to Servants,* 147, 26–27, 132.

CHAPTER 5: SLAVERY AND THE AMERICAN INDIVIDUAL

1 Karl Marx, "The Eighteenth Brumaire of Louis Bonaparte," in Robert C. Tucker, ed. *The Marx-Engels Reader,* 2d ed., (New York: Norton, 1978), 595. This chapter, in a slightly different version, was published as: François Furstenberg, "Beyond Freedom and Slavery: Virtue, Autonomy, and Resistance in Early American Political Discourse," *Journal of American History* 89 (2003): 1295–1330. I am grateful to the *Journal of American History* for permission to reprint it here.

2 Bingham, *Columbian Orator,* 209–10. This same dialogue was also printed in Heaton, *Columbian preceptor,* 39–42.

3 Bingham, *Columbian Orator,* 211.

4 Douglass, *My bondage and my freedom,* 158.

5 Douglass, "The Heroic Slave," in Foner, ed., *The Life and Writings of Frederick Douglass,* V:473–505, quotations on 474–75. For more on Douglass's tale, and the real insurrection on which the story was based, see William L. Andrews, "The Novelization of Voice in Early African American Narrative," *PMLA: Publications of the Modern Language Association of America* 105 (1990): 23–34; Castronoro, *Fathering the Nation,* esp. 210–26; and Maggie Montesinos Sale, *The Slumbering Volcano: American Slave Ship Revolts and the Production of Rebellious Masculinity* (Durham, N.C.: Duke University Press, 1997), 173–97, 120–45. I have greatly benefitted from the analyses of Castronovo and Sale.

6 Boyd et al., eds., *Papers,* XVI:149.

7 David M. Potter, *The Impending Crisis, 1848–1861,* edited and compiled by Don E. Fehrenbacher (New York: Harper & Row, 1976), 145.

8 William Lloyd Garrison, *The Liberator,* January 1, 1831, in John Grafton ed., *The Declaration of Independence and Other Great Documents in American History, 1775–1865* (Mineola, N.Y.: Dover Publications, 2000), 70.

9 Huggins, "The Deforming Mirror of Truth," xii.

10 For recent examples by eminent historians, see Wood, *The Radicalism of the American Revolution,* 186–87; Appleby, *Inheriting the Revolution,* esp. 241–44; and Ellis, *Founding Brothers,* 4, 17, 89, 103.

11 For studies that locate liberalism in the variegated ideological landscape of American political culture, see esp. Dorothy Ross, "Liberalism," in *Encyclopedia of American Po-*

litical History: Studies of the Principal Movements and Ideas, Jack P. Greene, ed. (New York: Scribner, 1984), II:750–62; Shklar, *American Citizenship;* Rogers M. Smith, *Civic Ideals: Conflicting Visions of Citizenship in U.S. History* (New Haven, Conn.: Yale University Press, 1997); Kloppenberg, "Virtues of Liberalism;" Eric Foner, *The Story of American Freedom* (New York: W. W. Norton, 1998); and Stanley, *From Bondage to Contract.* For depictions of liberalism as shaped in tandem with other sometimes opposing ideologies, see James T. Kloppenberg, *Uncertain Victory: Social Democracy and Progressivism in European and American Thought, 1870–1920* (New York: Oxford University Press, 1986); Ross, *Origins;* and Gary Gerstle, "The Protean Character of American Liberalism," *American Historical Review* 99 (1994): 1043–73.

12 The most strenuous argument along these lines is Greenfeld, *Nationalism: Five Roads to Modernity.*

13 On the expansion of slavery in the post-Revolutionary period, see esp. Rothman, *Slave Country.* On the persistence of racism, see, inter alia, Alexander Saxton, *The Rise and Fall of the White Republic: Class Politics and Mass Culture in Nineteenth-Century America* (London and New York: Verso, 1990); Roediger, *The Wages of Whiteness;* Theodore Allen, *The Invention of the White Race,* 2 vols. (New York: Verso, 1994 and 1997); Noel Ignatiev, *How the Irish Became White* (New York: Routledge, 1995); and Matthew Frye Jacobson, *Whiteness of a Different Color: European Immigrants and the Alchemy of Race* (Cambridge, Mass.: Harvard University Press, 1998).

14 Smith, *Civic Ideals,* 470, 18. See also Rogers M. Smith, "Beyond Tocqueville, Myrdal, and Hartz: The Multiple Traditions in America," *American Political Science Review* 87 (1993): 549–66, 556; Jacqueline Stevens, "Beyond Tocqueville, Please!" *American Political Science Review* 89 (1995): 987–95; Rogers M. Smith, "Beyond Tocqueville, Please!: Response," *American Political Science Review* 90 (1995): 990–95; Ira Katznelson, "Review of Rogers M. Smith, Civic Ideals," *Political Theory* 27 (1999): 565–70; and Carol Horton, "Liberal Equality and the Civic Subject: Identity and Citizenship in Reconstruction America," in *The Liberal Tradition in American Politics: Reassessing the Legacy of American Liberalism,* David F. Ericson and Louisa Bertch Green, eds. (New York: Routledge, 1999). See also Mark Hulliung, "Republicanism, Liberalism, Illiberalism: An American Debate in French Translation," *Tocqueville Review/La Revue Tocqueville* 21 (2000): 109–32; and Rogers M. Smith, "Beyond the Liberal-Republican Debate: A Response to Mark Hulliung," *Tocqueville Review/La Revue Tocqueville* 21 (2000): 133–40.

15 Louis Hartz, *The Liberal Tradition in America: An Interpretation of American Political Thought Since the Revolution* (New York: Harcourt Brace, 1955), 8. This assumption about the South is common in much of even the best intellectual history on the antebel-

lum period. In his sweeping account, Michael O'Brien has recently sought to pull South-
ern intellectual life back into the broader intellectual currents of American—and indeed
Atlantic—history. See Michael O'Brien, *Conjectures of Order: Intellectual Life and the
American South, 1810–1860* (Chapel Hill: University of North Carolina Press, 2004).

16 I draw the term "counterrevolution" from Sinha, *Counterrevolution of Slavery;* the
historian of proslavery is Tise, *Proslavery,* 37. Emphasis added. See also ibid., 33, 36,
39, 262. Tise's work is excellent and important. I cite him here to emphasize my differences with the strongest, rather than the weakest, historiography. For a discussion
that locates both pro- and antislavery thought in a broad liberal universe, see also
David F. Ericson, *The Debate over Slavery: Antislavery and Proslavery Liberalism in
Antebellum America* (New York: New York University Press, 2000), 16–36, 93–153.

17 On the rhetorical connections between liberty and slavery in U.S. political discourse,
see Donald L. Robinson, *Slavery in the Structure of American Politics, 1765–1820* (New
York: Harcourt Brace Jovanovich, 1970); Morgan, *American Slavery, American Freedom,*
376–87; F. Nwabueze Okoye, "Chattel Slavery as the Nightmare of the American Revolution," *William and Mary Quarterly* 3rd ser., 37 (1980): 3–28; Richard L. Bushman,
King and People in Provincial Massachusetts (Chapel Hill: University of North Carolina Press, 1985), 197–98; Greene, *Pursuits of Happiness;* Roediger, *The Wages of
Whiteness;* Shklar, *American Citizenship;* Toni Morrison, *Playing in the Dark: Whiteness and the Literary Imagination* (Cambridge, Mass.: Harvard University Press,
1992), 37; Kenneth S. Greenberg, *Honor and Slavery: Lies, Duels, Noses, Masks, Dress-
ing as a Woman, Gifts, Strangers, Humanitarianism, Death, Slave Rebellions, the
Proslavery Argument, Baseball, Hunting, and Gambling in the Old South* (Princeton,
N.J.: Princeton University Press, 1996); Foner, *The Story of American Freedom;* and
Onuf, *Jefferson's Empire.* On a later period, see Anders Stephanson, "Liberty or Death:
The Cold War as U.S. Ideology," in *Reviewing the Cold War: Approaches, Interpreta-
tions, and Theory,* Odd Arne Westad, ed. (London: F. Cass, 2000), 81–100. On Protes-
tant theories of resistance in the Revolutionary period, see Hatch, *The Sacred Cause
of Liberty;* James H. Moorehead, "Between Progress and Apocalypse: A Reassessment
of Millennialism in American Religious Thought, 1800–1880," *Journal of American
History* 71 (1980): 524–42; Bloch, *Visionary Republic;* and Clark, *The Language of
Liberty;.* On early Protestant resistance theory, see Robert M. Kingdon, "Calvinism
and Resistance Theory," in *The Cambridge History of Political Thought, 1450–1700,*
J. H. Burns and Mark Goldie, eds. (Cambridge, Eng.: Cambridge University Press,
1991), 193–218.

18 Massachusetts resident Daniel Leonard quoted in Bushman, *King and People,* 202;
Patrick Henry quoted in William Wirt, *Sketches of the life and character of Patrick*

Henry (Philadelphia: James Webster, 1817), 120; Stephen Hopkins, *Rights of the Colonies Examined* (1764), in Bernard Bailyn, *Pamphlets of the American Revolution, 1750–1776* (Cambridge, Mass.: Belknap Press, 1965), 516; William Tennent quoted in Kenneth S. Greenberg, *Masters and Statesmen: The Political Culture of American Slavery* (Baltimore, Md.: Johns Hopkins University Press, 1985), 88; "General Orders," July 2, 1776, in Philander D. Chase et al., eds., *The Papers of George Washington: Revolutionary War Series,* 11 vols. (Charlottesville: University Press of Virginia, 1985–), V:180; Thomas P. Slaughter, ed., *Common Sense and Related Writings* (Boston: Bedford/St. Martin's, 2001), 86.

19 Shklar, *American Citizenship,* 22–23; Galloway quoted in Okoye, "Chattel Slavery as the Nightmare of the American Revolution," 12; George Washington to Bryan Fairfax, August 24, 1774, in W. W. Abbot, Dorothy Twohig, and Philander D. Chase, eds., *The Papers of George Washington: Colonial Series,* 10 vols. (Charlottesville: University Press of Virginia, 1983), X:155; [Richard Wells], *The Middle Line* (1775), quoted in Okoye, "Chattel Slavery," 13–14; George Washington to George William Fairfax, June 10, 1774, Abbot, Twohig, and Chase, eds., *Papers: Colonial Series,* X:97; Washington to Bryan Fairfax, July 20, 1774, Abbot, Twohig, and Chase, eds., *Papers: Colonial Series,* X:131.

20 Quoted in Bushman, *King and People,* 209.

21 Davis, *The Problem of Slavery in the Age of Revolution,* 293.

22 "George Washington to Meschech Weare, et al., June 8, 1783, Circular Letter of Farewell to Army," in Fitzpatrick, ed., *Writings,* XXVI:484–85. On this theme, see also Pauline Maier, *From Resistance to Revolution: Colonial Radicals and the Development of American Opposition to Britain, 1765–1776* (New York: Knopf, 1972), 31, 42–43, 62; and Greenberg, *Honor and Slavery,* 88. "Free and honorable gentlemen," observes Greenberg, "unlike the slaves they governed, were not afraid to die." On abject as "other," see Judith Butler, *Gender Trouble: Feminism and the Subversion of Identity* (New York: Routledge, 1990), 169–70.

23 Wirt, *Sketches of the life and character,* 123. Since Wirt reconstructed the speech much later, the accuracy of its most felicitous phrase is questionable. Whether or not Wirt's reconstruction was accurate, however, is hardly the point: its enormous diffusion easily projected it into the ranks of the nation's more popular civic texts. On Wirt's reconstruction, see Looby, *Voicing America,* 270–78.

24 William H. McGuffey, *McGuffey's New Sixth Eclectic Reader: Exercises in Rhetorical Reading, With Introductory Rules and Examples* (Cincinnati and New York: Sargent, Wilson & Hinkle; Clark & Maynard, 1857), 118–21. The circulation figures are from the introduction to Elliott J. Gorn, ed., *The McGuffey Readers: Selections from the*

1879 Edition (Boston: Bedford Books, 1998), 2. Henry's speech was reprinted in many other schoolbooks, e.g., E. B. Williston, *Eloquence of the United States* (Middletown, Conn.: E. & H. Clark, 1827), 60–63.

25 Weems, *Life* (1809 ed.), 59, 62, 68, 69; Weems, *A history, of the life and death, virtues, and exploits*, 10.

26 Daniel Webster, "An Address Delivered at the Laying of the Corner-Stone of the Bunker Hill Monument, June 17th, 1825," in *A Memorial of The American Patriots Who Fell at The Battle of Bunker Hill, June 17, 1775; With an Account of The Dedication of the Memorial Tablets on Winthrop Square, Charlestown, June 17, 1889, and an Appendix Containing Illustrative Papers* (Boston: Printed by order of the City Council, 1889), 197–217; quotation at 206–7.

27 Monroe: "To the Speakers of the House of Delegates, and of the Senate," December 7, 1801, in Hamilton, ed., *Writings*, III:305; Washington chorus from anonymous ode performed at Boston, February 22, 1800, quoted in Elson, *Guardians of Tradition*, 200; the evolution of the letter W in New England is noted in George Livermore, *The Origin, History and Character of the New England Primer* (New York: C. F. Heartman, 1915), 27; and also in John W. Francis, *Old New York; or, Reminiscences of the past sixty years. Being an enlarged and revised edition of the anniversary discourse delivered before the New York historical society, (November 17, 1857)* (New York: C. Roe, 1858), 343.

28 *New York Journal*, July 8, 1795, quoted in Foner, *Democratic-Republican Societies*, 224, 231.

29 Josiah Quincy, *An oration delivered before the Washington Benevolent Society of Massachusetts on the thirtieth day of April, 1813: being the anniversary of the first inauguration of President Washington* (Boston: William S. and Henry Spear, 1813), 12.

30 Mathew Carey, *The school of wisdom, or, American monitor: containing a copious collection of sublime and elegant extracts, from the most eminent writers, on morals, religion, & government* (Philadelphia: Printed for the editor, 1803), 100–101, 165.

31 See also Greene, *All Men are Created Equal*, 30–31; the association of "obnoxious" with slavery is explained in Skinner, *Liberty Before Liberalism*.

32 Haskell, "Capitalism and the Origins of Humanitarian Sensibility, Part I," 342; Haskell, "Convention and Hegemonic Interest," 829; Haskell, "Capitalism and the Origins of Humanitarian Sensibility, Part II," 553, 556–7, 560.

33 Haskell, "Capitalism and the Origins of Humanitarian Sensibility, Part II," 557. My quotation of Haskell in this sentence should not suggest that his argument agrees with the one I am making here.

34 Bingham, *Columbian Orator*, 232–33. I have found the same excerpt from *Cato* in

Biglow, *The youth's library,* 208–11; and J. Hamilton More, *The Young Gentleman and Lady's Monitor, and English Teacher's Assistant; Being a Collection of Select Pieces From our Best Modern Writers . . .* (Wilmington, Del.: Peter Brynberg, 1803), 343–45. On the influence of Addison's *Cato* during this period, see Frederic M. Litto, "Addison's Cato in the Colonies," *William and Mary Quarterly* 3rd ser., 23 (1966): 431–49; H. Trevor Colbourn, *The Lamp of Experience: Whig History and the Intellectual Origins of the American Revolution* (Indianapolis, Ind.: Liberty Fund, 1998), 28–29; and Furtwangler, *American Silhouettes,* 72–84. On the relationship between honor and slavery, see Patterson, *Slavery and Social Death,* and Greenberg, *Honor and Slavery.* On the connection between Addison's *Cato* and Patrick Henry's famous speech, see Litto, "Addison's Cato in the Colonies," 445, and Furtwangler, *American Silhouettes,* 75–76.

35 Bingham, *Columbian Orator,* 238. This trope of the noble Indian who will die before submitting to slavery seems to have been fairly common in schoolbooks of the day. See also "Lesson XIII," in William Johnston, *A New Introduction to Enfield's Speaker; or A Collection of Easy Lessons, Arranged on an Improved Plan. Designed For the Use of Schools* (London: T. Plummer, 1800), 49–50.

36 Bingham, *Columbian Orator,* 204. For yet another example of this theme, see also the "Speech of the Caledonian General," Bingham, *Columbian Orator,* 162–65.

37 The term "bashaw" would likely have been familiar to many of Bingham's audience, thanks to Noah Webster's famous "blue-backed" speller, which included the term, and even helped define it in a sentence: "A bashaw is a title of honor among the Turks; a governor." Noah Webster, *The Elementary Spelling Book; Being An Improvement on the American Spelling Book* (Cazenovia, N.Y.: S. H. Henry, 1838), 72.

38 Bingham, *Columbian Orator,* 89, 100. Notice, also, that these slaves are not only white Europeans, but from Venice, the exemplary republic. Barbary slavery was a prominent feature of political discourse, because here was an instance where white Europeans actually *were* made slaves. If the fear that white Americans might be rendered into chattel slaves appeared exaggerated to some people—all Europeans, of course—the case of Barbary slavery was an instance where white Americans were in fact enslaved. That it thus blurred the distinction between metaphorical and chattel slavery may explain its prominence in early American political discourse.

39 Bingham, *Columbian Orator,* 100–101.

40 Mukhtar Ali Isani, "Far from 'Gambia's Golden Shore': The Black in the Late Eighteenth-Century American Imaginative Literature," *William and Mary Quarterly* 3rd ser., 36 (1979): 353–72; *The Columbian Reading Book, or Historical Preceptor: A Collection of Authentic Histories, Anecdotes, Characters, &c. &c. Calculated to Incite in*

Young Minds a Love of Virtue, From Its Intrinsic Beauty, and a Hatred of Vice, from its Disgusting Deformity (Philadelphia: Printed for M. Carey, 1802), 91–93; Thomas Branagan, *A preliminary essay on the oppression of the exiled sons of Africa . . . To which is added, A Desultory Letter Written to Napoleon Bonaparte, anno domini 1801* (Philadelphia: John W. Scott, 1804), 112; Abigail Mott, *Biographical sketches and interesting anecdotes of persons of colour* (New-York: M. Day, 1826), 162–65. Mott's book, which was subsidized by a fund established by Lindley Murray's will, was reprinted in York, England, in 1828, and in New York in 1837, 1838, 1839, 1850, 1854, 1875, 1877, and 1882. The publication history of Mott's book is briefly summarized in James N. Green, "The Publishing History of Equiano's *Interesting Narrative,*" *Slavery and Abolition* 16 (1995), 372, 375 n23.

41 *The Columbian Reading Book,* 92–93. For a related story, see Alexander, *The young gentlemen and ladies instructor,* 61–62.

42 Quoted in James H. Kettner, *The Development of American Citizenship, 1608–1870* (Chapel Hill: University of North Carolina Press, 1978), 216.

43 *The American jest book: containing a choice selection of jests, anecdotes, bon mots, stories, &c,* (Harrisburg, Penn.: John Wyeth for Mathew Carey, 1797). Various antecedents of this book circulated in eighteenth-century England in over thirty editions. For instance: *Coffee-house jests: being a merry companion, containing witty jests . . . with several short delightful histories, novels and other curious fancies* (London: Thos. Norris, 1724); *The Entertaining companion, or, The merry jester: being a choice collection of the most entertaining jests, witty sayings, smart repartees, remarkable stories, comical tales, &c . . .* (London: C. Sympson, 1745); *Jemmy Buck's Witty jester, or, The merry mortals companion . . .* (London: J. Cooke, 1760). This book was also published in at least nine editions in America between 1789 and 1814. I have been unable to examine these editions to see if they contain this story about escaped slaves.

44 Davis, *The Problem of Slavery in the Age of Revolution,* 257; also 259, 282. See also Maier, *From Resistance to Revolution;* and Shain, *The Myth of American Individualism,* 293–94.

45 Davis, *The Problem of Slavery in the Age of Revolution,* 304.

46 Žižek, "The King Is a Thing." Compelling parallels also exist with the theory of ideology in Fredric Jameson, *The Political Unconscious: Narrative as a Socially Symbolic Act* (Ithaca, N.Y.: Cornell University Press, 1981), esp. 48, 81–83.

47 On slave resistance, see Raymond A. Bauer and Alice H. Bauer, "Day to Day Resistance to Slavery," in *Rebellions, Resistance, and Runaways within the Slave South,* Paul Finkelman, ed. (New York: Garland Publishing, 1989); Kenneth M. Stampp, *The Pe-*

culiar Institution: Slavery in the Ante-bellum South (New York: Knopf, 1956), 86–132; Genovese, *Roll, Jordan, Roll*, 597–660; Blassingame, *The Slave Community*, 192–222; and John Hope Franklin and Loren Schweninger, *Runaway Slaves: Rebels on the Plantation* (New York: Oxford University Press, 1999). On white responses to slave resistance, see esp. Jordan, *White over Black*, 375–402; Trouillot, *Silencing the Past*, 70–107; and Greenberg, *Honor and Slavery*, 98–107. The analysis in the following section has been especially influenced by Greenberg's excellent analysis. A suggestive article raising many of the same issues I am raising here is Walter Johnson, "On Agency," *Journal of Social History* 37 (2003): 113–24. Another work with similar themes, unfortunately read too late by me to have a material impact here, is the remarkable study by Laurent Dubois, *A Colony of Citizens*, esp. 171–221 and 374–401.

48 Franklin and Schweninger, *Runaway Slaves*, 250–51, 274–79; White, "A Flood of Impure Lava," 210; anonymous author quoted in Hunt, *Haiti's Influence on Antebellum America*, 142. On U.S. responses to the Haitian revolution, see the works cited in chapter 2, n23. The notion that blacks had chosen slavery over death offers a particularly cruel irony, since many enslaved Africans did kill themselves rather than remain in bondage—acts that certain West African traditions (unlike Christianity) actually encouraged. See Piersen, "White Cannibals, Black Martyrs: Fear, Depression, and Religious Faith as Causes of Suicide Among New Slaves," *Journal of Negro History* 62 (1977): 147–59. On suicide and political sovereignty, see Agamben, *Homo Sacer*, 136–37.

49 "Drapetomania" is from Samuel Cartwright, 1851, *De Bow's Review*, as quoted in Franklin and Schweninger, *Runaway Slaves*, 274; Jefferson quoted in Matthewson, "Jefferson and Haiti," 217; *Pennsylvania Gazette* quoted in White, "A Flood of Impure Lava," 222; descriptions of Nat Turner all quoted in Henry Irving Tragle, *The Southampton Slave Revolt of 1831: A Compilation of Source Material* (Amherst: University of Massachusetts Press, 1971), 40, 42, 37, 43, 53.

50 Egerton, *Gabriel's Rebellion*, 111 and 219, n50.

51 Quoted in Tragle, *The Southampton Slave Revolt*, 133, 135, 136.

52 Contra Trouillot, *Silencing the Past*.

53 Tim Matthewson, "Abraham Bishop, 'The Rights of Black Men,' and the American Reaction to the Haitian Revolution," *Journal of Negro History* 67 (1982): 148–54; quotations at 150, 153, 152.

54 James T. Holly, *A Vindication of the Capacity of the Negro Race for Self-Government and Civilized Progress as Demonstrated by the Historical Events of the Haytian Revolution* (1857), in Philip Sheldon Foner and Robert J. Branham, *Lift Every Voice:*

African American Oratory, 1787–1900 (Tuscaloosa: University of Alabama Press, 1998), 291, 289, 299, 291.

55 Henry Highland Garnet, "An Address to the Slaves of the United States of America," in Carter G. Woodson, ed., *Negro Orators and Their Orations* (New York: Russell & Russell, 1969), 154, 156–57. See also Hunt, *Haiti's Influence on Antebellum America,* 149, 156; Dixon, *African America and Haiti,* 61; and David Brion Davis, "Impact of the French and Haitian Revolutions," in *The Impact of the Haitian Revolution in the Atlantic World,* David P. Geggus, ed. (Columbia: University of South Carolina Press, 2001), 8.

56 On the *Amistad* revolt, see especially Sale, *The Slumbering Volcano,* 58–119. For other depictions of Cinqué, see Honour, *The Image of the Black in Western Art,* 158–61.

57 Hunt, *Haiti's Influence on Antebellum America,* 85, 89. Louverture was portrayed as a hero throughout the Atlantic world. See Seymour Drescher, "The Limits of Example," in Geggus, ed., *The Impact of the Haitian Revolution in the Atlantic World,* 12; and Robin Blackburn, "The Force of Example," ibid., 17. For a glowing biography that circulated in the United States, see "Toussaint L'Ouverture," in Mott, *Biographical sketches and interesting anecdotes,* 65–73. The valorization of Haitian slaves made it possible for some people to believe that "French Negroes"—not American slaves—were the cause of American slave resistance, providing yet another strategy for denying slave resistance. See White, "Flood of Impure Lava," chapter 5.

58 Robert Sutcliff, *Travels in some parts of North America in the years 1804, 1805 & 1806* (Philadelphia: B. & T. Kite, 1812), 30. On this episode, see also Ferguson, *Reading the Early Republic,* 198–217.

59 James Monroe to John Drayton, October 21, 1800, in Hamilton, ed., *Writings,* III:217; Monroe to Thomas Jefferson, September 15, 1800, in Hamilton, ed., *Writings,* III:209; "General Orders," September 25, 1800, in Hamilton, ed., *Writings,* III:210; "To the Speakers of the General Assembly," December 5, 1800, in Hamilton, ed., *Writings,* III:240–41. See also Sidbury, *Ploughshares into Swords,* 133. John Randolph believed the rebelling slaves displayed a proud "sense of their rights, [and] a contempt of danger." John Randolph to Joseph Nicholson, September 26, 1800, quoted in Egerton, *Gabriel's Rebellion,* 102.

60 Henry W. DeSaussure to Timothy Ford, July 9, 1816, in David Waldstreicher, ed., *The Struggle Against Slavery: A History in Documents* (New York: Oxford University Press, 2001), 116. Many thanks to David Waldstreicher for providing me with a copy of this document.

61 Douglass, *Narrative,* 65. See also Albert E. Stone, "Identity and Art in Frederick

Douglass's *Narrative,*" *College Language Association Journal* 17 (1973), 208–10. Douglass echoed Addison's *Cato*: "What a pity it is," said he, "that we can die but once to save our country." See Litto, "Addison's Cato in the Colonies," 446.

62 Douglass, *Narrative,* 71, 72–73.

63 Ibid., 73. On escape as a religious rebirth, see also Raboteau, *Slave Religion,* 304–5.

64 Douglass, "The Heroic Slave," 503.

65 Douglass, *Narrative,* 85–86, 87.

66 Clyde Norman Wilson and Shirley Bright Cox, eds., *The Papers of John C. Calhoun,* 27 vols. (Columbia: Published by the University of South Carolina Press for the South Caroliniana Society, 1999), XXV:531–32, 532.

67 Ibid., 534, 537.

68 Quoted in Ronald G. Walters, *The Antislavery Appeal: American Abolitionism after 1830* (Baltimore, Md.: Johns Hopkins University Press, 1976), 28.

69 Peter P. Hinks, ed., *David Walker's Appeal to the Coloured Citizens of the World* (University Park: Pennsylvania State University Press, 2000), 14–15, see also 16, 28, 31; and Sale, *The Slumbering Volcano,* 53–54.

70 Quoted in James M. McPherson, *Battle Cry of Freedom: The Civil War Era* (New York: Oxford University Press, 1988), 835. See also William W. Freehling, *Prelude to Civil War: The Nullification Controversy in South Carolina, 1816–1836* (New York: Harper & Row, 1966), 3, 234–35, 248–49; Greenberg, *Masters and Statesmen,* 141; and Faust, *The Creation of Confederate Nationalism.*

71 See Waldstreicher, *Perpetual Fetes,* 232. On the persistence of this form of racism, see esp. Daryl Michael Scott, *Contempt and Pity: Social Policy and the Image of the Damaged Black Psyche, 1880–1996* (Chapel Hill: University of North Carolina Press, 1997).

72 On feminized understandings of virtue, see esp. Hanna Fenichel Pitkin, *Fortune Is a Woman: Gender and Politics in the Thought of Niccolò Machiavelli* (Berkeley: University of California Press, 1984); and Ruth H. Bloch, "The Gendered Meanings of Virtue in Revolutionary America," *Signs: Journal of Women in Culture and Society* 13 (1987): 37–58.

73 My overall thinking on matters of consent and its blindness has been greatly shaped by this feminist literature, especially the work of Carole Pateman. See Pateman, *The Problem of Political Obligation;* Pateman, *The Sexual Contract;* and Pateman, *The Disorder of Women,* esp. 33–57, 118–40. I have also benefited from the work of French historians on the relationship among individuality, agency, and active citizenship: Scott, *Only Paradoxes to Offer,* 1–56, 163–64, 168–69; Sewell Jr., "Le Citoyen/la Citoyenne"; and Hunt, *The Family Romance of the French Revolution.* For a fascinating analysis of the problems of consent see Scutt, "The Standard of Con-

sent in Rape," *New Zealand Law Journal* (1976). On the relationship between liberalism and feminism, see also Nussbaum, *Sex and Social Justice*, esp. 55–80.

74 Andrew Stevenson describing the life of Andrew Jackson after his death in 1845, quoted in Ward, *Andrew Jackson*, 166.

75 Kettner, *The Development of American Citizenship*, 208; see, more generally, 173–209.

76 James Madison to Thomas Jefferson, February 4, 1790, in Boyd et al., eds., *Papers*, XVI:149.

77 Thomas Jefferson to James Madison, September 6, 1789, in Boyd et al., eds., *Papers*.

78 Alexis de Tocqueville, *De la Démocratie en Amérique*, 2 vols. (Paris: Gallimard, 1961), II:143.

79 John Locke, "The Reasonableness of Christianity, as Delivered in the Scriptures," in *The Works of John Locke*, 10 vols. (London: Thomas Davison, 1823), VII:145, as quoted in Sinopoli, *The Foundations of American Citizenship*, 32.

EPILOGUE: AMERICAN NATIONALISM, THE LIVING, AND THE DEAD

1 "Dissertation on First Principles of Government," in Philip Sheldon Foner, ed., *The Complete Writings of Thomas Paine*, 2 vols. (New York: The Citadel Press, 1945), 576, 575, quoted in Pierre Nora, "La Génération," in Pierre Nora, ed., *Les Lieux de Mémoire*, 3 vols. (Paris: Quarto Gallimard, 1997), 2:2977. Following Nora, I have reversed the order of the quotations here; I believe the changed order is faithful to the meaning of the text, however. On the relationship between Paine's theory of generations and Jefferson's, see also Koch, *Jefferson and Madison*, 82–88; and Sloan, *Principle and Interest*, 239–43.

2 "Address Befor the Young Men's Lyceum of Springfield, Illinois," January 27, 1838, in Basler, ed., *Collected Works*, I:108, 112, 115.

3 Johnson, ed., *Abraham Lincoln, Slavery, and the Civil War*, 3–4; for Lincoln's appreciation of Murray's reader, see Monaghan, *The Murrays of Murray Hill*.

4 On which, see esp. Sacvan Bercovitch, *The Rites of Assent*. For a slightly different view, see Castronovo, *Fathering the Nation*.

5 "Address Delivered at the Dedication of the Cemetary at Gettysburg," in Basler, ed., *Works*, VII:23. My debt here to Garry Wills will be obvious to those who have read his fine book, *Lincoln at Gettysburg: The Words that Remade America* (New York: Simon & Schuster, 1992).

6 On the memory of the Civil War being used to justify a new regime of segregation and racial oppression, see esp. David W. Blight, *Race and Reunion: The Civil War in American Memory* (Cambridge, Mass.: Belknap Press, 2001).

7 On the use of monuments in this process, see esp. Kirk Savage, *Standing Soldiers,*

Kneeling Slaves: Race, War, and Monument in Nineteenth-Century America (Princeton, N.J.: Princeton University Press, 1997). Many thanks to Fred Bode for making the connection with this monument for me.

8 On which, see esp. Gordon S. Wood, *The Creation of the American Republic, 1776–1787* (Chapel Hill, N.C.: University of North Carolina Press, 1969).

9 George Washington to David Humphreys, October 10, 1787, and George Washington to LaFayette, April 28, 1788, both in Fitzpatrick, ed., *Writings,* 29:287, 29:478; Madison quoted in McCoy, *Last of the Fathers,* 68. See also Koch, *Jefferson and Madison,* 57–59, 74–75.

10 Thomas Jefferson to Samuel Kercheval, July 12, 1816, in Peterson, ed., *Writings,* 1401.

APPENDIX 1: A BRIEF NOTE ON CIVIC TEXTS

1 On attempts by proponents of nullification to appropriate the Virginia and Kentucky Resolutions, see Freehling, *Prelude to Civil War,* 207–10 and McCoy, *Last of the Fathers,* 139–51. This episode is particularly interesting, since Madison found himself arguing over the meaning of texts which he himself had helped author! What Madison did not understand is that their meaning actually evolved through their appropriation—through the use later Americans made of the founding texts.

2 Maier, *American Scripture.*

3 Peterson, ed., *Writings,* 1517.

4 On this theme, see esp. Kemp, *The Estrangement of the Past.*

ACKNOWLEDGMENTS

PERHAPS MY SKEPTICISM about the notion of individual authorship—indeed, of heroic, autonomous agency—can explain this lengthy expression of gratitude to the institutions, scholars, friends, and family who have made this book possible. As with my civic texts, all should in some sense be considered coauthors of this book.

For supporting me financially, I am grateful to the Jacob Javits program of the U.S. Department of Education, the Columbia University Department of History, the Johns Hopkins University Department of History, the Mellon Fund at the University of Cambridge, the Université de Montréal, and to the Library Company of Philadelphia and the New-York Historical Society. Many librarians helped enormously, especially Connie King and Phil Lapsansky at the Library Company, the Special Collections staff at Johns Hopkins, and the wonderful librarians at Mount Vernon. I was very sorry to learn of the passing of the late F. Garner Ranney of the Episcopal Diocese of Maryland, whose friendliness and charm were matched only by his knowledge; the remarkable archive he built stands as a fine memorial.

Though I have tried to make specific intellectual debts known in my notes, it is impossible there to acknowledge the many obligations I have accumulated in the form of detailed readings and feedback on individual chapters, as well as in more diffuse ways: over food and drink, in conversations, challenges, and criticism. I cannot thank all the people who helped. I'll try anyway. At Columbia: Matt Backes, Chris Bilodeau, Doug Goldstein, Andy McStay, and Ashli White.

Eric Foner supervised the essay that remains the nugget of this book, and I remain grateful. Johns Hopkins provided the ideal environment for my graduate work. I especially want to thank David Bell, Jane Dailey, Toby Ditz (the influence of her marvelous seminar is evident throughout this book), Jack Greene, Rick Keyser, Matt Lauzon, Guy Lazure, Phil Morgan, Anthony Pagden, Neil Safier, Paul Tonks, Ron Walters, Craig Yirush, and Giovanni Zanalda.

A year at Cambridge provided a wonderfully conducive environment to revise this work. I am particularly grateful to Tony Badger, Tom DeWesselow, John Dunn, Bill Dusinberre, Tim Guinane, Simon Hall, John Thompson, Elana Wilson, Betty Wood, and especially Andy Merrills. Colleagues in Montreal have been similarly stimulating: Susan Dalton, James Delbourgo, Ollivier Hubert, Bruno Ramirez, Greg Robinson, and most especially Cynthia Milton. Julie de Chantal provided indispensable help with the images for this book. Others accumulated and contributed along the way, especially Jim Green, Brooke Hunter, Marty Rojas, Tom Slaughter, and Mike Zuckerman. A seminar at the American Antiquarian Society run by Peter Stallybrass and Michael Warner proved unusually helpful; I am grateful to the co-conveners and the other participants.

Most of all, I am grateful to the people who read the entire manuscript in its different incarnations: Ben Anderson, Giovanni Arrighi, Fred Bode, Jim Kloppenberg, Michael O'Brien, and especially David Waldstreicher, who supported this project from its very inception. All of these people have, through their own scholarship as well as their comments on mine, improved this book in important ways. None of them, of course, is responsible for its many flaws.

I was fortunate as an undergraduate to take classes with Richard Bushman, Anders Stephanson, and the late, great James P. Shenton, all of whom left an enduring stamp on my intellectual development. All remained involved in my later work, reading sections of this book and offering advice along the way. I regret terribly that Jim is no longer here to receive my appreciation—over a fine meal, of course.

It was nothing less than a stroke of providential fortune to be able to publish this work under the auspices of the Penguin History of American Life. I am most grateful to Jill Lepore for her interest in and enthusiasm for this work, as well as for her critical interventions; I hope the final product bears out whatever promise she saw in it. Thanks, also, to Tim Seldes for his interest and advice. At The Penguin Press, I am grateful to Janie Fleming and especially to Scott Moyers for his insight, intelligence, and skill. He is the editor I had always hoped to have, but was always told no longer exists; I'm glad to have learned that is not true.

My greatest debts by far are to Michael Johnson and Dorothy Ross, who served as advisers to the dissertation on which this book is based, who have no doubt read versions of this work more times than they could care to remember. Their ideas have shaped this book in so many ways it is impossible fully to acknowledge everything it owes to them. I can, however, recognize the extent to which they have and continue to serve as models: intellectual, professional, and personal.

Finally, I owe much to my family, who have supported me in other ways, especially to the Furstenbergs and to my grandmother Edith; to the Codaccionis and, more recently, the Patels; to my late grandfather Félix-Paul Codaccioni, a great historian and model of intellectual breadth and passion; to Max; to my brother Philippe for his interest and support (and his photographic skills); and most of all to my parents, to whom this work is gratefully dedicated. I hardly need to acknowledge Vaishali Patel here, nor could I even hope to.

INDEX

Page numbers in *italics* refer to picture captions.

Illustration credits:

1. The Lilly Library, Indiana University, Bloomington, Indiana
2. The Library Company of Philadelphia
3. The Gilder–Lehrman Institute of American History
4. The Lafayette College Art Collection, Easton, Pennsylvania
5. The Library Company of Philadelphia
6. Department of Special Collections, University of Virginia Library
7. The National Museum of American History, Smithsonian Institution
8. The Historical Society of Pennsylvania
9. The Historical Society of Pennsylvania
10. The Library of Congress (LC-USZ62-20834)
12. The Historical Society of Pennsylvania, Baker Collection
13. The Mount Vernon Ladies' Association
14. The Historical Society of Pennsylvania
15. The American Antiquarian Society
16. The Library Company of Philadelphia
17. The Library Company of Philadelphia
18. Architect of the Capitol
19. Photograph by Philippe Furstenberg
20. Courtesy of the National Gallery of Art, Washington, Andrew W. Mellon Collection, image © 2005 Board of Trustees

21. The Boston Public Library/Rare Books Department

22. Reprinted from *Harper's New Monthly Magazine,* July 1856. The Library of Congress (LC-USZ62-12960)

23. Harry T. Peters, "America on Stone" Lithography Collection, National Museum of American History, Behring Center, Smithsonian Institution

24. The Historical Society of Pennsylvania

25. The Library Company of Philadelphia

26. The Historical Society of Pennsylvania

27. The Mount Vernon Ladies' Association

28. The Historical Society of Pennsylvania

29. Courtesy the Museum of the Confederacy, Richmond, Virginia. Photography by Katherine Wetzel

30. The Historical Society of Pennsylvania

31. The Library Company of Philadelphia

32. The Library Company of Philadelphia

33. The National Portrait Gallery, Smithsonian Institution

34. The Historical Society of Pennsylvania

35. The Library of Congress (LC-USZ62-4036)

36. The Amon Carter Museum, Fort Worth, Texas (1970.43)

37. The Historical Society of Pennsylvania

38. The American Antiquarian Society

39. Yale Collection of American Literature, Beinecke Rare Book and Manuscript Library

40. The Division of Rare and Manuscript Collections, Cornell University

41. Howard–Tilton Library, Tulane University, New Orleans

42. The Lilly Library, Indiana University, Bloomington, Indiana

43. Brown University Library

44. The Lilly Library, Indiana University, Bloomington, Indiana

45. The Library of Congress (LC-USZ62-12960)

46. The Lilly Library, Indiana University, Bloomington, Indiana

47. The Library of Congress (LC-USZ62-119445)

48. Photograph by Philippe Furstenberg